Maranatha

Maranatha

WOMEN'S FUNERARY RITUALS
AND CHRISTIAN ORIGINS

KATHLEEN E. CORLEY

Foreword by

JOHN DOMINIC CROSSAN

Fortress Press
Minneapolis

MARANATHA
Women's Funerary Rituals and Christian Origins

Kathleen Corley is Oshkosh Northwestern Distinguished Professor and Professor of New Testament at the University of Wisconsin at Oshkosh.

Cover design: Laurie Ingram
Book design: Hillspring Books, Inc.

Library of Congress Cataloging-in-Publication Data
 Maranatha : women's funerary rituals and Christian origins / Kathleen E. Corley; foreword by John Dominic Crossan.
       p. cm.
  Includes bibliographical references (p. 203) and index.
  ISBN 978-0-8006-6236-3 (alk. paper)
1. Women in Christianity—History—Early church, ca. 30-600.
2. Funeral rites and ceremonies, Early Christian. 3. Dinners and dining—Religious aspects—Christianity—History. 4. Lord's Supper—History—Early church, ca., 30-600. 5. Christianity—Origin. I. Title.
  BR195.W6C665 2010
                                                    270.1082—dc22
2009043285

FOR JOHN

CONTENTS

FOREWORD

I have always thought that exegetical scholarship and historical reconstruction have failed rather dismally in research on the traditions concerning the passion and resurrection of Jesus.

In terms of the passion tradition, there was a fairly good consensus that Matthew and Luke used Mark as the primary—and probably even as the exclusive—source for their versions. There was no such consensus on whether John's version was or was not independent of the Synoptics. Those for whom John is also dependent must explain why and how Mark alone has transmitted—or created—that story. Or, better, why there ever was such a story. If it came from oral tradition, where is the independent evidence? If it came from a preexisting written tradition, there is no consensus on the content of that pre-Markan source. My own proposal of a non-Markan tradition (the so-called

Cross Gospel), later conflated into the *Gospel of Peter*, did achieve a rather massive consensus—of disdain and rejection. But that proposal was at least a positive suggestion within a heavily negative arena.

In terms of the resurrection tradition, scholarly research seemed to me once again magnificently negative. We saw with great detail and accuracy the differences between Paul's account in 1 Corinthians 15 and the stories in the terminal chapters of the Gospels. We also noted fully the differences between those four versions themselves. We recognized their irreconcilable divergences concerning apparitions of Jesus in terms of time, place, to whom, and with what content. We noted the conflicts between Galilee and Jerusalem and between Luke 24 and Acts 1. But, once again, the major successes were negative. What was still needed was even the hint of a positive proposal regarding the tradition history of the passion–vindication or execution–resurrection traditions in the midst of all those negatives.

That was the background of my own thinking between 1994 and 1995. The constitutive problem for me was still this: in the terms I used in *Who Killed Jesus?* how and why did "the prophetic passion" (which correlated Jesus' death with scriptural texts read as prophecies) become "the narrative passion"? That is, how and why did exegesis give way to story? For example, for me the *Epistle of Barnabas* was independent of the canonical Gospels and showed how someone could have discussed the passion–vindication tradition without ever moving from exegesis to story. For example, I could not imagine *Epistle of Barnabas* 7:6-11 being derived from the story about the mockery of Jesus, but I could easily imagine the reverse situation. Be that right or wrong, I had concluded by late 1995 that the development from passion-exegesis to passion-story required some special explanation and should not be taken as an inevitable development. In an address to the Jesus Seminar in October of that year, I argued that "we must take with utter seriousness the *non-inevitability* of that transition from prophetic to narrative passion, from exegetical scholarship to popular narrative." I had no idea why or how that transition might have happened, and my only explanation was that it "took a single act of creative genius."

In January of 1996, Kathleen Corley sent me a copy of her manuscript titled *Gender and Jesus: History and Lament in Gospel Tradition*. I read it through and was extremely impressed with her research on female lament tradition. It was clearly a finished volume ready for publication and was already contracted with Oxford University Press. I had seen an earlier correlation between female lament and resurrection tradition in Marianne Sawicki's 1994 book *Seeing the Lord*, but it had not struck me forcibly until I read Kathleen's research. In the massive cross-cultural matrix with which Kathleen was working, lament often contained an account of the dead person's life and/or death. This struck me as a new, positive, and powerful contribution to the whole discussion of the passion–resurrection tradition.

At the same time, I was working on the final chapters of *The Birth of Christianity* (published in 1999). In that book, of course, I was still dealing with the same constitutive problem that had occupied me in a whole series of hopefully correct but certainly prior decisions and conclusions from my own earlier research. Within that problematic— and without at all limiting its value to that situation—what struck me immediately from Kathleen's work was this: what if my rather feeble suggestion of "a single act of creative genius" that moved from passion-exegesis to passion-story had in fact been the female lament tradition itself? I was so impressed by Kathleen's research in quantity and quality that I checked out for myself every single item on female lament in her bibliography. I could find almost nothing she had missed.

Because I was quite confident that her book would be out well ahead of mine, as it was clearly finished and mine was still months from completion, I quoted directly from her book by name and referenced it as "forthcoming" in my manuscript's bibliography. (I presumed that by the time my final page proofs were ready, I could insert more precise and exact references to her by-then published book.) As it happened, however, Kathleen's book was never published, and my citations in *The Birth of Christianity* were left referring to a "forthcoming" book that never came forth. Let it be quite clear, however, that I was, as I said in *The Birth of Christianity*, deeply indebted to her work in that earlier book and wish to emphasize that in this foreword.

What that earlier, unpublished volume proposed, and what is even more central to this present published one, is made clear in its subtitle. How should funerary rituals, eucharistic meals, and mortuary laments be given their rightful role in Christian origins, their full and female, creative and constitutive contribution to the origins of Christianity?

This book argues that women have their own rituals and rites that are central to their spiritual and religious lives and are often quite different from what men are doing—or from what men see when they research such engendered activities! For example: funerary ritual and lament are one of those women's rituals in antiquity, and they persist. Funerary meals give participants the sense of *the presence of* the dead person, of *communion with* the dead person, and of *memorialization of* the dead person. That experience is what led to the Eucharist with its sense of memorial and presence.

But it is precisely here that the book's powerful thesis points to a tragic irony. The central rite of the church—the Eucharist—which is credited to a man (Jesus) in early church tradition (pre-Pauline material, the Gospels) and officiated over in the Roman Catholic tradition by an all-male priesthood—goes back to a memorial meal for the dead held *by women* for Jesus. But if women's lament gets the men to Jesus' resurrection, and their funerary meal gets them to the Eucharist, how do we end up with not a single woman explicitly mentioned in 1 Corinthians 15 and not a single woman eventually imagined at the last supper? Furthermore, has focusing on what the men were doing led contemporary male scholars—including myself—to miss where the real action was? Was it what the women were doing that got it all going? And since that ancient exclusion has had permanent and present consequences, can we at least recognize it and remedy it at last?

Maranatha is both that recognition and that remedy.

John Dominic Crossan

PREFACE

Behind every book is a story. The origins of this study on women, meals, and Christian origins go back to the original research I did for the book that became *Women and the Historical Jesus*. I presented what became chapter 5 of that book to the Jesus Seminar in the mid-1990s, and it was published early on in the *Forum* of the Jesus Seminar. At that time, I completed a sixty-three-page chapter on the funerary rituals, meals, and lamentation of women in antiquity and a chapter devoted to my thesis that the origins of the passion narrative could be found in the context of women's lamentation for the dead, for which I used cross-cultural documentation of women's laments. I also had a chapter on meals stories and the Gospels, and a chapter on the resurrection narratives interpreted in the context of women's funerary rituals and lament. That larger book draft, which was under contract for publication at the time with Oxford University Press, was never published. At the time Dom Crossan received it, he was fully under the impression that my book would come out before his book, *The Birth of Christianity.* He therefore cited my forthcoming book at that time. I would like to take this opportunity to thank Dom Crossan for contributing his foreword, which puts the process of what happened to this research in its larger perspective and shows the significance of funerary rituals, lament, and meals for women's experience in antiquity and for reconstructing Christian origins. I would also like to acknowledge that my interactions with Dom about this material led to additional insight into the creative process between men and women in the primitive church that led to the development of the idea of the raising and appearing of Jesus, church liturgy, practice, and Gospel tradition.

Because I still hoped to publish this research eventually, due to its importance, I continued to update and refine my larger chapter on women, lament, and funerary meals. During the first year of grieving over the death of my husband in 2005, I came back to this research in the context of giving three presentations on meals, mourning, and Christian origins with Hal Taussig in the Jesus Seminar on the Road program. Through those presentations, I realized that I indeed had something additional to contribute to the discussion on Christian origins by refocusing my attention on the original area of my first research on women and meals. I therefore owe my kind and gracious colleague Hal Taussig a great debt, as it is only through our joint presentations and conversations during that year of grief that I came to see how this material could still be used to make an additional insight about the role of women in Christian origins by focusing on funerary meals and Greco-Roman associations. I also wish to acknowledge the critique and contributions of the Greco-Roman Meals Seminar of the Society of Biblical Literature, headed by Dennis Smith and Hal Taussig, who read my chapter on funerary rituals, lament, and meals in the fall of 2006 and gave me additional ideas and bibliographic sources, for which I am grateful. It should also be noted at the outset that the first to recognize the importance of the lament context for the shaping of Gospel traditions, including the passion narrative, was Marianne Sawicki, who published her work in her book *Seeing the Lord.* She presented this material first in the context of a Society of Biblical

Literature session on the anointing story, which I attended. I hope I have given her adequate credit in this book for first realizing the significance of the funerary context as a potential location of the creation and shaping of Gospel traditions, including the passion narrative.

Finally, I would like to thank the scholars who read and critiqued my tentative thesis for this book and gave me help in the areas of Q research, *Didache* research, and research on meals and associations, Richard Ascough, John Kloppenborg, Clayton Jefford, and of course Hal Taussig. Conversations with my good friend and colleague Richard Pervo over these many years have also always been supportive and stimulating. Amy-Jill Levine has also tirelessly responded to both my research and my numerous emails. I would also like to thank Alan Segal, Jennifer Glancy, John Kloppenborg, Hal Taussig, Carolyn Osiek, Ross Kraemer, Sterling Bjorndahl, Amy-Jill Levine, Richard Pervo, Glenna Jackson, Alan Segal, Gale Yee, and Joanna Dewey for reading through early drafts of my manuscript. As always, I continue to be enriched by conversations with my friend of twenty-five years, Diana Bailey, who forces me to focus on the ways in which women contributed to the growth of early Christian worship and liturgy. Thanks go to my good friend Abby Frucht for being right.

Also, I would like to acknowledge my debt to the well-known psychiatrist and scholar of psychoanalysis and creativity John Gedo. Our correspondence of nearly twelve years, and my reading of his books on creativity, *Portraits of the Artist and the Emotional World*, greatly contributed to the formation of this thesis. I would like to publicly thank him for carefully responding by hand to each of my letters over these many years during many trying and turbulent times in my life. His words have given me not only comfort but great insight into myself and my own creative process. My debt to him cannot be overstated. I would not have progressed in my career, or finished this book, without his support and long correspondence. The process of research is ultimately the result of many conversations among scholars and friends, and I owe a tremendous debt to all those who helped me shape the thesis and focus of this book.

I should also say at the outset that my own experience of deep and overwhelming grief over the unexpected death of my husband in July 2005 has greatly altered some of my conclusions and has given me new insight into women's expression of grief in funerary rituals, lament, and meals both in antiquity and in cross-cultural studies by cultural anthropologists. Ultimately it is my own experience of great grief that has given me further insight into the significance of this body of research for reconstructing the contribution of women to the shaping of primitive Christian tradition, practice, and worship. I, of course, dedicate this book to my much loved and now deceased husband, John C. Harris.

INTRODUCTION

Ancient meals have become the center of study for Christian origins. This book looks at women and their roles in funerary meals and rituals as the best context for solving many vexing problems of Christian origins. We will see that the creative work of ordinary women and ordinary people fueled the origins of the Christian community. For it is funerary meals that create community, both continuity with the living and the deceased—in this case, the dead Jesus. Jesus became the special dead whose presence was celebrated in memorial meals served and organized by women. We will also see that women's ritual laments give us the oral core of what became the passion narrative as well as the belief that Jesus was "raised and appeared" within the Christian community.

Chapter 1 reviews the place of women in meals and New Testament texts, including the four Gospels and Paul. The New Testament betrays controversy over the place and roles of women in meal situations and public banquets. This is because women's roles were undergoing flux and change from 300 BCE to 200 CE, and their position and posture at meals was being negotiated: separate from men or together with men, seated or reclining. The behavior of women at banquets can be used to chart an ongoing social innovation for women's roles generally, from the late Hellenistic era until the mid-third century CE. As one of the most conservative aspects of a culture, change in meal etiquette can be used to chart social progress for women during these centuries.

A further avenue of cutting edge research that can be used to reconstruct the practices of the earliest Christian groups is the correspondence between early Christian communities and Greco-Roman associations. Much leadership and community terminology of Christian groups can be shown to reflect the organizational language of early Christian groups, which would have been perceived as local associations by their Greco-Roman neighbors. Further, associations, like earliest Christian groups, were class- and gender-inclusive and provided for the funeral and funerary meals of their members. Funerary meals are thus the best social and ritual location to chart the creative influence of women in shaping New Testament traditions about the passion, Gospel meal stories, and the beginnings of resurrection beliefs.

Women can be shown to be the central participants in ancient funerals and funerary meals, the collection of rituals referred to as the "cult of the dead" in Greek, Roman, and Jewish practice. Women lamented the dead, composing elaborate narratives about the life and cause of death of the deceased, prepared and served funerary meals, and made offerings to the dead at tombs. Funerary rites were regularly held on the third day after death, the ninth day after death, the thirtieth day after death, and then annually throughout the ancient Mediterranean world. The emphasis in these rites was on communing with and propitiating the spirit of the deceased, who was thought to be present in the memorial meals and whose presence was invoked by the lament of the women. At such times, stories of the deceased were told, laments and songs were sung, and toasts were made to the dearly departed. Not surprisingly, women also feature prominently in the lamenting of heroes and heroines and in the various mystery religions. Due to their common association with the cult of the dead and funeral rites proper, women are also featured prominently in noble death scenes, such as those of Socrates, Hercules, and Moses. This evidence is fleshed out in chapter 2.

Chapter 3 brings us to the New Testament texts proper and the earliest source for Christian ritual and practice, the *Didache*. This chapter charts a trajectory from the meal practices of the Jesus movement around Jesus to the eventual recitations of the Lord's Supper in Mark and Paul that have the "words of institution." The Jesus movement itself did not practice meals of Jesus' presence, but celebrated inclusivity and class equality at their meals. Men and women, free and slave, gathered for these meals of the kingdom of God, instituted by Jesus during his lifetime. Both the Q community and the Thomas community continued these celebratory meals of the kingdom of God (*basileia*). Jesus himself rejected excessive attention to the dead at funerals by declaring, "Let the dead bury their own dead!" and by saying, "Become passersby," which meant bypassing graveyards and tombs and ignoring the epitaphs of the dead.

In contrast to the Jesus movement which did not practice meals that celebrated Jesus' presence, the *Didache* contains two separate meal rituals that do celebrate the presence of Jesus. The earliest proclaims, "Maranatha"—"Our Lord, come!" (to the meal: Did. 10:6). The second is called a eucharist but does not contain the words of institution. Finally, this chapter overviews the early oral tradition behind the two recitations of the last supper accounts in Mark and Paul, which have Jesus (a man) instituting this memorial meal for the dead Jesus, not women.

Chapter 4 gives attention to the Gospel miracle stories in which the themes of funerals, women and meals intersect, including the miraculous feedings in Matthew, the story of the Syro-Phoenician woman, and the anointing story in all four Gospels. The chapter ends with further attention to the last supper narratives in Mark and Paul. The miracle stories suggest the practices of oral storytelling about Jesus, miracles, funerals, and meals by women, whereas the last supper narratives attribute the storytelling to a man, namely, Jesus.

Chapter 5 addresses the likely origin of the passion story and the idea that Jesus was "raised and appeared on the third day" in the context of women's ritual funerary laments. Cross–cultural evidence is amassed to locate oral traditions behind the Passion accounts in the Gospels. Scriptural proofs and scribal activity are not enough to explain the development of the narrative core of the Passion account. Further, this chapter makes the bold suggestion that the announcement that "he was raised and appeared" "on the third day" (1 Cor 15) has its roots in women's grassroots practice of funerary rituals, meals, and lament, rather than in the experiences of a list of elite leaders and male apostles.

The entire book thus makes an argument for the nonsupernatural origins of early Christian communities, Gospel traditions, and the idea of a "raised and appeared" Lord. The cults of the dead involved common human religious experiences that do not require divine intervention of any sort. In the cult of the dead, participants only imagine they are communicating with the dead, but having a sense of the presence of the dead is a quite normal experience and part of the grief process. This was a grassroots movement among ordinary people, the lower classes and women, not a movement spearheaded by an all–male elite leadership as the Gospels suggest.

WOMEN AND EARLY CHRISTIAN MEALS AND ASSOCIATIONS

Meals and commensality have become the main focus in the study of the origins of the Christian community. Like other ancient clubs and religions, Christians met regularly for meals. In the earliest times, these were complete meals with the standard pattern of the formal meal, the *deipnon*, followed by the drinking portion of the banquet, the *symposion*. The drinking portion—though regularly the occasion for heavy drinking, frivolity, entertainment, games, dramas, and sexual goings on—was in many religious and philosophical groups the occasion for philosophical discourse, liturgy, and worship. This is no doubt the case with Christian groups, though as 1 Corinthians attests, Christian banquets could also get out of hand and need to be reined in. Rules for clubs often included fines for misbehavior at community gatherings due to the erotic and frivolous nature of the symposium itself, going back to ancient Greek times. Literary and pictorial representations of the banquet attest to the erotic and meretricious overtones that any such gathering might entail. Due to the reputation of the banquet as a location for sexual and entertainment purposes, the legitimacy of the presence of women was disputed and negotiated from 200 BCE to 300 CE. Women, if present, were often assumed to be prostitutes of some sort, as respectable women in ancient times were excluded from such banquets, especially in the Greek East. However, social customs were undergoing change from 200 BCE to 300 CE, and respectable women began to attend formal banquets, with or without their husbands, and even took the reclining position rather than the ancient seated posture depicted in most funerary representations of the banquet scene. Still, if present and reclining, such women could be assumed to have a sexual connection to the men they reclined with, and for this reason, in many cases, women reclined separately, on separate couches or in separate banquet rooms. Women were often present for family meals and gatherings, such as weddings and funerals, as well as religious festivities, but their presence and position was a matter of great debate and negotiation—seated or reclining, separate, or next to men and husbands on the banquet couch. Evidence now suggests that as early as 300 BCE respectable married women could be expected to recline with their husbands for banquets, though literature still attests to the backlash against this practice, which was seen as threatening to the ideals of women's proper roles in the public and private spheres.[1]

The New Testament itself shows differing opinions on the place and role of women in meals scenes. Mark shows little concern for the presence of women in the meal scenes in his Gospel. Women appear as members of the group of disciples, and a female triumvirate, Mary, Mary, and Salome, mirrors the male triumvirate of Peter, James, and John. Women appear at meals as table servants and do "table service" for the community, especially Jesus. In Mark's version of the anointing of Jesus at a meal by an unnamed women, the disciples do not object to her presence because of its impropriety but because of the high cost of her ointment, which could better be used and sold to give help to the poor. Likewise, Jesus does not reject the Syro-Phoenician woman, who requests "crumbs" under the table, because she fits a stereotype of a "promiscuous" woman but because she is a Gentile. Jesus was known for eating and drinking with "tax collectors and sinners," which included women, but Mark does not emphasize the presence of women at these meals. As "table servants," the women exemplify Markan discipleship. Thus, in Mark, the male disciples are encouraged to take on the role of lower-class women and slaves.

Mark is no liberal, however, as it is unlikely that Mark depicts women as "leaders," as many have suggested. Further, women are never depicted as openly reclining or eating with men in Mark's Gospel. Women are rarely portrayed as speaking in public, the hemorrhaging woman being the one exception. All other scenes with women are set in private homes, such as the scene with Peter's mother-in-law, the story with the Syro-Phoenician woman, and the anointing story. When Jesus eats and drinks with "tax collectors and sinners," it is in a private home. And although we can assume women were present for such scenes, Mark does not comment on it. The only woman clearly depicted as a meretricious "courtesan" is the stepdaughter of Herod, who dances like a prostitute for Herod's birthday party and requests the head of John the Baptist as a birthday boon. All other women around Jesus are in contrast to her. They are present for meals, but respectable.

Luke also shows ample presence of women in his literary portrayals of meals, both in the Gospel and in the book of Acts, which portrays the early Hellenistic mission. Like Mark, Luke has Jesus accept "tax collectors and sinners," but in Luke this category clearly includes women. This can be seen in the Lukan version of the anointing story, where Jesus is anointed by a "woman known in the city as a sinner," whom Luke probably intended to be a prostitute of some kind. Still, this woman "sinner" does not join Jesus at the table, nor are women explicitly shown as reclining with men for meals. Nor is the anointing woman called a *pornē*. If Q had this term for this tradition, Luke omits it. As part of a larger omission, Luke also omits entirely the story of Herod's birthday banquet and dancing courtesan and the story of the Syro-Phoenician woman. He probably keeps the tradition that Jesus dined with "tax collectors and sinners" because of its antiquity—it is in his sources, both Mark and Q.

Luke is also careful to protect the reputation of the women most often around Jesus, lest their reputations be besmirched. Even respectably married women follow Jesus and do so out of gratitude for their healings. These women are the major philanthropists of the groups and support Jesus and his disciples financially. They are respectable patronesses. In a special Lukan passage, Mary and Martha join Jesus for a meal, but it is the private and old-fashioned Mary, who sits silently at Jesus' feet, who is set apart for Jesus' praise, not the active, vocal Martha who is doing *diakonia*, what the men in ministry are described as doing in Acts. Luke thus portrays a conservative meal posture for Mary and preserves a private role for the women in his community.

It is Matthew who varies from this pattern, which is surprising, since Matthew's Gospel is usually set apart as the most conservative and therefore "Jewish" of the Gospels—Judaism often being cast as more patriarchal during this historical period. Only Matthew adds women and children to his miraculous feeding narratives, which become eucharistic family feasts where all attend. The feast parable depicts the messianic feast as a wedding, which women family members would have attended. In his version of Herod's birthday party, Matthew casts blame on Herod, not the women, for the death of John the Baptist. The story of the Canaanite woman is rendered more naturally outdoors, and she is favored for her "great faith." Only in Matthew are the women at the end of the Gospel story examples of true discipleship. The women do not flee the tomb, but report what they have seen, unlike the scene in Mark.

Furthermore, only Matthew is unafraid of connecting women in his narratives with meretricious women. Jesus' group is joined by "tax collectors and courtesans"—clearly women of ill repute. Plus, he puts women with bad reputations right up front in his genealogy. Like Mary, who was accused of adultery, Jesus' lineage included women who were known for bad sexual behavior. Matthew's portrayal of women is more class inclusive and shows less concern for traditional Greco-Roman ideals of women's proper behavior at meals.[2]

In John, there are six major meals where Jesus is present, several of which feature both respectable and unrespectable women prominently. In the first meal, the wedding at Cana, Jesus miraculously provides wine at the request of his mother. This is a messianic meal, being a wedding, and women, especially Jesus' mother, are present. John makes no comment on the presence of women for this meal, and their respectability is assumed. The second scene in which food figures is the story of the Samaritan woman, who offers Jesus water while his disciples go to buy him some food. Mealtime is the setting. The water Jesus provides, however, is superior to the woman's, as it is "living water" that brings "eternal life." The woman, though functioning as an evangelist who brings her community to belief in Jesus, is a woman of ill repute, having had several husbands and is living with one who is not her husband. John makes no comment on this but uses her as a type of evangelist. In the final meal scene that features women, Jesus is served at a family meal with Mary, Martha, and the risen Lazarus. Martha serves the meal, and Mary anoints Jesus with ointment. The propriety of the women is in no way questioned in this scene, even though the banquet scene is fraught with erotic overtones. As in Mark, it is the cost of the ointment that is objectionable, not the propriety of Mary's action.[3] Thus, John seems comfortable with women in his meal scenes, though in no place does he depict women reclining with men for meals.

Community meals figure also in the Pauline churches. There are two major passages showing that Paul's churches met regularly for meals, the incident at Antioch recorded in Gal 2:11-14 and the material from 1 Cor 11:20-22, 33-34a. The earliest description of a meal is described in the letter to the Galatians. The traditions practiced there seem to predate Paul. Paul's description suggests that similar meals were being held at Jerusalem. The problem Paul is dealing with is Jewish dietary restrictions. Apparently, the group at Antioch was holding meals where both Jews and Gentiles were present, but Peter had stopped eating in these corporate meals after some emissaries from Jerusalem approached him and told him not to join the Gentiles for meals. The concern was for the foodstuffs being eaten, not the people themselves. There were various foods that Jews were not to eat, including pork, shellfish, and meat, that had not been butchered according to Levitical requirements. Paul does not want to have "works of the law," namely, Sabbath observance, dietary restrictions, and circumcision, serve as boundary markers in the community but wants all, Jews and Gentiles alike, to come to the table freely.[4] These restrictions may have had some effect upon women in the community, although they were not circumcised. Jewish Christian women would have been essential in preparing kosher food for the community and would have had relevant roles in preparing for Sabbath and lighting Sabbath candles.

The second section of Paul that deals with meal practice in the early Pauline churches is found in 1 Corinthians 8 and 10. These chapters deal with the issue of idol meat being consumed in the community and the controversy over this practice. The terminology Paul uses reflects again Jewish sensibilities. He speaks of *eidōlothyton*, "meat sacrificed to idols." A Gentile would be unlikely to have concern for idol meat in this way. Paul is concerned about "the weak," who now refuse this practice and the "strong," who still eat the meat. The most common interpretation is that the "weak" were lower-class members of the community who were unaccustomed to eating meat except on feast days, and the "strong," upper-class members who could afford to eat meat regularly.[5] The controversy is probably over the meals of the community and the appropriateness of meat being served. Paul wants the "strong" to abstain out of conscience for the "weak."[6] A similar problem seems to have occurred at Rome. In Rom 14:1—15:13, Paul addresses a situation that seems similar to that of 1 Corinthians 8. The issue is more clearly that of Jewish dietary laws and the table fellowship of the Roman community. Some have chosen vegetarianism. Paul again encourages those who are "strong": "it is good not to eat meat or drink wine or do anything that makes your brother or sister stumble" (Rom 14:21).[7] Again, women would have played a role in preparing these meals for the community, so the admonitions of Paul speak directly to their concerns and activities.

In 1 Corinthians, Paul indicates that meals were a common part of community gatherings. He writes, "when you come together as a church" (1 Cor 11:17-18) and "when you come together to eat" (1 Cor 11:20-21, 33), both of which seem to be synonymous for community gatherings. We can assume that the Corinthian church met regularly together for meals and probably worshiped at table.[8] This gathering is called "the Lord's Supper," and Paul says that this tradition, in which a memorial meal is given that reflects the last meal of Jesus, "the Lord," has been passed on to him (1 Cor 11:23-25). This suggests that this meal is done in all the communities of which he is aware. This meal is clearly also a full banquet and shares elements with the meals described in Galatia, Antioch, and possibly Jerusalem.[9] These meals were probably held in homes of prominent members of the church (patrons). Such a house would have to have been large enough to have a substantial dining room or rooms, or a courtyard that could hold many people. As Paul describes these meals, they are full-course meals with a *deipnon*, the dinner course, followed by the *symposion*, which would have been for Christians a time of worship and reading of Scriptures rather than the entertainments of more frivolous events.[10] However, Paul complains that equality is not being practiced—some eat their fill while others go away hungry. This seems to have been a sort of "potluck," but those who brought lots of food were not sharing it.[11] The worship of the community was also at the table. Women were obviously present for these times of worship according to 1 Corinthians. Paul mentions women prophets in 1 Corinthians 11 and allows them to use this "highest gift," though he prefers that they be properly clothed by wearing a veil while prophesying. Some concern for women's presence is also found in 1 Cor 14:35-38, where Paul wants women to be silent and ask their husbands questions at home. This probably reflects the common practice of separate seating for women and men. Paul would rather not have women and men shouting back and forth during what seems to be an already disorderly meeting. The New Testament itself thus reflects that early Christians met together for meals and that the presence of women was assumed, though being negotiated as it was throughout the Hellenistic world in which women's roles at table were undergoing flux and change.

Voluntary Associations: Cultic and Community Contexts

Cutting edge research has now identified the organization of the Greco-Roman voluntary associations as the best analogue for understanding the organization of early Christian groups. Although Meeks and others have made objections to this comparison,[12] recent studies have affirmed the comparison of early Christian communities and Greco-Roman voluntary associations.[13] Voluntary associations included various groups that met for professional and religious reasons, although even in professional associations there was always a cult aspect of some kind, as meetings were held in the honor of a patron god or deity. Shopkeepers, weavers, coppersmiths, bakers, purple sellers, and the like gathered together for primarily social purposes, as did members of various mystery cults and other religious sects. Groups provided for conviviality, in the celebration of monthly feasts, as well as providing for the burial and burial feasts for members. Members paid dues to support the activities of the group. Although one could be a member of more than one group, finances for those who joined such groups, usually the lower classes, often precluded membership in more than one association at a time. Further, group identity and cohesion made members somewhat exclusive in their preference of their own associative organization.

There are many reasons why voluntary associations are now used as the primary analogue for understanding early Christian group formation. First, the group terminology for leadership and organizational roles is similarly diverse, and the title *ekklēsia* is found for associations as well as for early Christian groups. This is not the only designation for an association, however, as groups could use a number of various names. Names might come from their common association, such as *Aigyptioi, Salaminioi, Molpoi, Porphyobaphon*, or from their patron deity, such as *Dionysiastai, Herakleistai*, or *Asklepiastoi. Thiasos* is a common name for an association in Macedonia; in Latin *collegium* is found. We also find the use of *synētheia*, as well as *symposia*. Often, adherents named their own associations. *Mystai* is the most common, found six different times in Macedonia, four used for groups worshiping Dionysius. Other terms found are *Maenads* for a group of women worshipers of Dionysius, *Consacrani, Synthiasitai, Theskeutai*, and *Suetheis*. This diversity of group designations suggests that there was no single designation for an individual voluntary association. This brings us to the use of *ekklēsia*.

The use of *ekklēsia* is widely attested within the New Testament as a designation of Christian groups. It is found in Acts, Matthew (Matt. 16:18; 18:17), and Paul (Rom 16:16; 1 Cor 7:17; 11:16; 16:19; 2 Cor 8:1; 11:28; Gal 1:22 in the plural; 1 Cor 10:32; 15:9; Gal 1:13; Phil 3:6 for the singular universal church; Rom 16:1, 5; 1 Cor 1:2; 11:18; Phil 4:15; 1 Thess 1:1 for the local community). Scholars often use the LXX to explain this usage, in that *ekklēsia* is used over one hundred times to translate the Hebrew *qhl*, "assembly." This underscores the Jewish background of early Christian groups. However, those same scholars do not explain why early Christian groups did not choose the more common Jewish term *synagogē*. Actually, *synagogē* occurs more frequently in the LXX as a translation of *qhl*. Thus, *synagogē* would have been the more likely choice if Christian groups were invoking their Jewish background by their choice of self-designation.

However, *ekklēsia* is found as a designation for voluntary associations. It is not found frequently, but it is one of the many self designations of associations derived from civic terminology. Thus, Ascough is no doubt correct when he claims that for urban-based Christian communities the term *ekklēsia* would have been understood as the designation of a voluntary association, particularly by Greco-Roman outsiders.[14]

Other terminology is common to Christian communities and associations. In Paul, the common name for members of a community is *adelphoi*. This occurs often as a fictive kinship term for Pauline communities. It is noteworthy that this fictive kinship term also occurs in associations for members. Ascough cites examples from mid-first-century Rough Cilicia, third-century-BCE Manshiyeh, and for members of a Serapeum at Memphis. In Latin inscriptions, Ascough also cites the use of the term *fratres*.[15] Further, leadership language is also common between voluntary associations and Christian communities, particularly in the use of *episkopos* and *diakonos*. These are the titles for leaders that Paul uses in Phil 1:1. The letter itself makes no clear identification of the actual duties of those so titled. Again, scholars usually cite the LXX as the background for these terms. The verb *episkopein* is a common LXX translation for *bqr* and *pqr*. The noun *episkopos* occurs in the LXX as a term for "overseer" or "inspector." Or they invoke the use of *mbqr* in the Damascus Document of the Dead Sea Scrolls, which means "shepherding of the flock and returning the lost" (CD 13.7-9). Again, these scholars are invoking Jewish sources to explain New Testament usage. However, the Philippians would not have found such backgrounds in their predominantly non-Jewish environment, as the Philippian church was predominantly Gentile. Rather, it is the classical use of *episkopos* that is far more likely to be the source of the Christian use of the term. In general, *episkopos* meant "overseer" and was used for supervisory officers in the state, in societies, and in other Greco-Roman groups. The title usually designated one with financial responsibility. Again, it is found for financial officers in associations. Ascough cites inscriptions from Thera, Bostra, Kanata, Mykonos, Thrace, and Delos. Though the use of the title is clear, Ascough says the function of these officers is ambiguous.[16] These various officials could have had different functions in different groups.

Again, with the case of the title *diakonos*, scholars have attempted to find a Jewish background for its occurrence in the New Testament. These attempts have failed in light of the common usage of *diakonos* in guilds and associations for those who assist in the cult of the group.[17] Ascough cites numerous inscriptions using this term for sacred officers in various club organizations. It is also found in private associations, where both men and women can hold the title. This usage in the associations is the more obvious choice for the background of the term in Christian communities than any kind of Jewish usage, for which evidence is at best negligible. The Philippians would have been far more likely to have adopted the language found in the many voluntary associations in their surrounding city community and the larger Greco-Roman world. Even though these titles are not used across the board, there is enough evidence that they did occur in voluntary associations to account for their usage in Philippians, in that there is generally no clear consistency in official titles for voluntary associations to begin with.[18] Again, the nature of these offices and what such officials' functions were remains unclear.[19] Other titles found in the associations do not occur in the New Testament, such as "priest/priestess" or "president" and "treasurer." Ascough says it is unclear that there is an interest in avoiding such titles (Matt 23:6-12) or that perhaps such titles only come into use at a later date for Christians (1 Pet 2:9).

Christian communities also mirror the associations in other ways. One clear example is the social makeup of these groups and their maintenance of both a hierarchical leadership structure and an egalitarian membership base. Both had patrons and leaders based on hierarchical models, and both had membership that came from a wide social stratification and network, including men and women, slaves and free. Further, both Christian groups like Corinth and voluntary associations had similar problems with wealthier members taking one another to court over matters best settled within the individual community (1 Cor 6 1-11).[20] It is also the case, however, that associations could be gender exclusive, particularly professional guilds, which were often made up of members from trades that were numbered by members of a particular sex.[21] Textile work, for example, was dominated by women; other professions, such as metal work, by men. Religious groups were more likely to have membership of both men and women. The crux of this debate is clear. Many scholars prefer to find "Jewish" backgrounds (read inspired) for Christian usage, but the evidence is much better explained on the basis of Hellenistic sources, a point well made in the past by Jonathan Z. Smith.[22]

It is also the case that members of Christian groups were not exclusive in their membership, as is the case with those who joined other associations. It was possible to be a member of more than one group. "Membership in one association did not preclude membership in another."[23] Ascough cites many instances where association members had dual memberships. This occurred to the point that officials saw it as a problem and enacted laws to preclude membership in more than one guild. Enforcement of these laws, however, did not occur.[24] Meeks and others usually argue that membership in Christian and Jewish groups precluded allegiance to any other group, thus differentiating them from Greco-Roman associations.[25] However, there was no true monolithic Christianity or Judaism during these early centuries, but rather great diversity among Christian and Jewish groups. Again, separating Jews and Christians from their "pagan" environment is the interest of those scholars making such claims. Rather, the New Testament evidence itself suggests that Christians did indeed participate in other cultic associations, and this was particularly a problem at Corinth. In 1 Cor 8–10 Paul deals with the "strong," who are attending temple sacrifices and banquets (1 Cor 8:10—10:14). Paul does not disallow the practice but seems to affirm it. Someone like Erastus in Corinth, being the city treasurer, would most certainly have attended other civic functions. Thus, it seems that Christian groups did not require exclusive participation.[26] Jews also could affiliate with guilds of their individual professions. Jews were shippers and merchants and artisans, and no doubt went to groups and clubs associated with these lines of work.[27] In fact, Philo affirms this practice by opposing the participation of Jews in clubs and guilds in Alexandria:

> There exist in the city associations (*thiasoi*) with numerous members, and there is nothing healthy in their fellowship (*koinōnia*), which is based on unmixed wine, drunkenness, feasts, and the unbridled conduct which results from these.[28]

Obviously, Philo is opposing the practice of actual Jews in Alexandria who attended such functions. Harland notes the connection of Jews with associations in numerous locales, including Miletus, Smyrna, Sardis, Ephesus, Alexandria, and Hierapolis.[29] Thus, Jews as well as Christians participated in these so-called pagan groups. Although primary allegiance was probably due to the costs incurred by membership, Jews and Christians did participate in the civic life of the city, including religious and professional clubs.[30]

Meeks also argues that Jewish and Christian groups differed from Greco-Roman associations by having a moral focus. Clubs and guilds, he argues, did not.[31] However, there is evidence for the moral interest and regulations for certain Greco-Roman clubs. Moral regulations came from dreams from the gods and include, even rules against adultery on the part of members. The club imposed penalties for infractions.[32] Women, of course, faced harsher penalties for marital infractions.[33] Inscriptions also show an interest in the purity and impurity of club members, both for men after sexual intercourse and for women following menstruation or abortion or miscarriage. Contact with a corpse also required purification before participation in the cultic activities of the group.[34] The cult of Mithras also had moral codes, which were required for elevation in the higher ranks of the group.[35] Although not all associations had such an interest in morality, it is not true that Jewish and Christian groups' interest in morality separated them from other Greco-Roman groups. The immorality of Greco-Roman groups is exaggerated and is part and parcel to common slander of groups involved in communal meals, which often included both men and women.[36]

Another way certain scholars differentiate Jewish and Christian groups from their so-called pagan environment is to point out the supposed absence of cultic activities in Jewish and Christian groups. This again can be disclaimed. Christian gatherings did include some rituals, such as baptism and the eucharist. Both have a cultic function.[37] Further, the language of mystery and purification does occur in some New Testament texts (Rom 16:25; 1 Cor 2:1; 4:1; 15:51; Phil 2:17; 4:12). And, of course, prayers, hymns, teachings, and communal meals were all a part of Jewish and Christian gatherings.[38]

For our purposes, the most important way in which Christian and Jewish groups were similar to voluntary associations was in their provision of burials of members and a burial feast. Such activities were provided for out of the dues the members paid. Going without a proper burial was horrifying in antiquity, and many poorer members of society joined such groups precisely to make sure their burials would be properly attended to. Although the purpose of all associations was primarily social, the provision of proper burials and burial services was a large part of what made membership in such groups so attractive. Both the burial proper and reception with members present were part of the funerary activities of the group. Associations also set up epitaphs for deceased members to commemorate their lives. Again, Christians also provided these services for their members.[39]

Ensuring such burials would have been of more importance to poorer members of these clubs, who would have had fewer means to ensure their proper burial rites. Regulations of some associations gave extensive attention to issues relating to the proper burial of members precisely for this purpose.[40] Wreaths were often stipulated to be provided for graves on death anniversaries as well.[41] Associations of all sorts provided for the upkeep of members' graves, including Jews, silversmiths, physicians, and hemp workers in Ephesus alone.[42] Christians, too, gathered on death anniversaries of members, and these gatherings were closely related to the funerary function of Christian groups.[43] Thus, according to Harland, "These funerary functions were an integral part of the varied social and religious purposes of associations that helped to provide members with a sense of belonging and community."[44]

Thus, we can see that the intersection of meals, associations, and funerary activities in the Greco-Roman world provides the best context for understanding Christian origins. Such groups were often inclusive of men and women, provided for communal meals, which included men and women, and provided funerary rituals and banquets for the deceased of the community. These funerary rituals are what created community, by solidifying the relationship between the living members of the community and by connecting them with the deceased of the community. There is connection, there is presence, both of the living and the dead. We will see that it is women who were the primary actors in these funerary rituals and meals, which were so important to the communal lives of the earliest Christian groups, and therefore it was the women who generated the central elements that created the Christian community: memorial meals for the dead Jesus, the passion narrative, which memorialized Jesus' death in narrative form, and the notion that the dead Jesus was "raised and appeared" in the midst of the community in their memorial meals and rituals through the lament of ancient Christian women.

Funerary Meals as the Context for Women's Participation
in the Process of Christian Origins

Women's participation in funerary feasts for the dead goes back very early, to at least 200 BCE.[45] At Greek funerary feasts, food would be offered at the tomb for the deceased, including milk, honey, water, wine, celery, and dried fruits. The living would probably not have eaten the food at this point, for fear of passing "under the influence of the spirit world."[46] The ritual meal shared by the living took place at the deceased's home immediately following the funeral, the *perideipnon*, on the third day after death.[47] Mourners said eulogies, sang laments, and remembered stories about the life of the dead person, who was thought to be present for this meal. The purpose of the meal was for the family and friends to form a "united group in the aftermath of their loss."[48] Further offerings were made at the tomb on the third, ninth, and thirtieth days following death, and after one year. The emphasis was on propitiating the spirit of the deceased. Later writers mention a meal known as the *kathedra*, which friends and relatives shared, marking the end of the mourning period.[49] Romans also practiced an elaborate ritual series of meals and celebrations surrounding the time of mourning, and art and iconography attest to this practice of the *Totenmahl*—the "meal of the dead."[50] The living honored the dead by dining with them, thus confronting the transitory nature of life. Funeral banquets were held first on the day of burial, then on the ninth day after the funeral. The major foodstuffs appear to have been bread and fish. Some writers recommend modest gifts for the dead, but neglecting these rites would cause disaster and the release of malicious spirits of the dead. Other festivals for the dead were held by Romans—there was an annual festival set aside for honoring ancestors, on their birthday (*dies natalis*) and on a special festival day (*parentalia*), which was between February 13–21. On these days marriages were prohibited and the hearth was not lit. Another festival that was known for commemorating the dead was the *dies rosationis* or *rosalia*, in May or June, when family members brought roses to the graves of their loved ones.[51] Christians continued these traditional funerary practices, "probably because they did not view giving honors to their dead relations as having anything to do with a pagan god, religion or idols."[52] Church officials, however, objected to these practices and encouraged mourners to observe mourning rites by giving alms to the church or giving eucharistic offerings rather than by sharing food at the tomb.[53] Paintings of banquet scenes found on the walls of Christian catacombs or carvings on Christian sarcophagi give ample attestation to the continuation of these Christian family funerary feasts, and we can assume that such celebrations were practiced in earlier centuries. Though these representations are often thought to be pictures of Christian *agapē* feasts, or the eucharist, they are probably scenes of funerary banquets, with offerings of bread and fish. Inscriptions give additional evidence for the continuation of the funerary feasts among Christians, which describe the laying out of food and drink, reciting of eulogies and stories of the deceased, which went long into the night.[54] The spirit of these banquets was optimistic and fun, with pictures of family members holding up their glasses for refills of wine.[55] Christians thus honored their "ordinary" dead but also extended such practices to include the honoring of dead clergy, and eventually martyrs.[56] The bawdiness of these repasts became a problem for church officials, who began to instruct Christians to have calm and charitable funeral banquets.[57] There was definitely a move to squelch Christians' riotous banquets at cemeteries.[58] By the time of Augustine, it was expected that funerals for the ordinary dead would come to an end, and that family members would "voluntarily replace the feasts with almsgiving to the poor and commemorate their 'dear ones' inside the church, rather than at the tomb." Augustine clearly wanted to get the funerary banqueting out of the cemeteries and into the quiet solitude of the church.[59] That this was a concern as late as the time of Augustine in the fifth century shows the long history of Christians feasting at the tombs of their dead. Jensen suggests that even the eucharist "never really ceased to be a certain kind of funeral meal—a meal at which the once dead host is now living and present." These practices were not easily eradicated.[60]

We will see upon further exploration of the evidence that women figured most prominently at these all-too-common funerary feasts and rituals, and had the major liturgical roles in the lamentation of the dead loved one, which contributed the telling of the tale of the death of the loved one. Women were also the ones who enacted the majority of funerary rituals all over the Mediterranean world. These funerary rituals were often held in corporate groups and associations, and Christians were no different from their pagan neighbors in their celebrations of mourning throughout the year and on special holidays on which the dead were honored and remembered. The context of the Christian associations, with their provision of funerary rituals for members of the group, is thus the best location for finding the source of early Christian traditions such as the eucharist, the passion story, and the idea of the "raised and appeared" Jesus, who was thought to be present for these celebrations, as the "ordinary" dead were thought to be present at theirs.[61]

CHAPTER 2

WOMEN'S FUNERARY RITUALS, MEALS, AND LAMENT IN ANTIQUITY

Following Jesus' death, his followers repeated his sayings among themselves, created and re-created stories of his miracles and interactions with Jewish authorities, and retold the story of his crucifixion. For most of this century, scholars of the New Testament have used the literary theories of redaction, form, and source criticism in order to find the earliest materials in the written Gospels that can tell us about Jesus' life, words, and mission. Redaction criticism identifies and separates out interpretive materials created by the Gospel writers as editors; source criticism identifies earlier written sources behind the Gospels, such as Mark and Q; and form criticism isolates early materials that circulated within particular liturgical or didactic contexts. This section reconstructs another viable liturgical context for the creation and passing on of Gospel traditions about Jesus following his death, one

which in fact was central to women's religious lives: funerals and subsequent funerary rites, which were undertaken throughout the year on
behalf of relatives and other members of the community, commonly
called the "cult of the dead."

This major center for women's religious activity, which focused
on cultic activities surrounding the care of the family dead, has been
neglected in scholarly study. It would be inaccurate to label this complex of religious activities as merely "family" or "private," as both kin
and non-kin participated in ancient funerals, and many funerals were
decidedly public affairs for which the entire town would turn out.[1]
Furthermore, such rites cannot be merely dismissed as "superstitious,"
"popular," "vulgar," or reflecting a "lower form" of belief. Rather,
these rites were central to the practice of ancient religion by all classes
throughout the Mediterranean.[2] The cult of the dead is to be distinguished from both tomb cults, in which ancient tombs of the dead were
reused, and hero cults, in which ongoing rites were held at monuments
to various well-known city heroes or the mythologized special dead
but where there was usually no actual tomb and a cenotaph or monument instead.[3] The complex of activities related to the cult of the dead
included participation in funeral rites, especially ritual lamentation,
tomb visitation at regular intervals throughout the year, the making
of various offerings and sacrifices to the dead at the tombs, as well as
the celebration of funerary feasts, both at the tomb and at home after
the funeral proper. These sorts of rites were connected to the common
cultural care for family ancestors and even ancestor veneration, a concern still prevalent in many modern cultural contexts.[4] We will see that
women's roles in ritual lamentation from family cult of the dead were
mirrored in other cultic contexts as well, most notably in the liturgical
lamentation of gods and dead heroes and heroines.

In many cultures, women play an important role in the customs
surrounding the care for the dead. Women often wash and prepare
the corpse for burial, lead the community and family in bereavement
for the dead, and prepare festive meals for the enjoyment of both the
living and the departed. The connection of women to death is often a
source of fear of women in many cultures, not only because a corpse
is often considered a source of pollution, but because women's role in
funeral proceedings potentially gives them control over two of the
most important rites of passage in a culture: birth and death.[5] It is

not surprising that over the centuries women's control over funerals and mourning rituals has often been challenged and sometimes overwhelmed. In spite of this, there has been a tenacity of certain burial rituals involving women, particularly the tradition of formal lamentation, still practiced by women in rural Greece and elsewhere, which have remained largely unchanged for thousands of years.[6] Burial customs remain among the most stable aspects of culture throughout the Mediterranean world.[7] There is ample evidence that even pre-Constantinian Christians continued a tradition of the cult of the dead, gathering in family and communal tombs.[8] Evidence for the cult of the dead and ritual lamentation from antiquity therefore provides an additional context for the development of liturgical traditions in ancient Judaism and early Christianities.[9] The role of women in the cult of the dead and other occasions of ritual lamentation will also provide a needed background for understanding the development of various Gospel traditions found in Q, early miracle and meal scenes, and the passion narrative.

Women, Death, and Burial in Ancient Greece

In ancient Greece, women indeed played a central role in the burial and lamentation of the dead. Death brought with it ritual pollution, but care for the dead was a family responsibility.[10] Women in a family customarily washed and anointed the dead (the laying out of the body, or *prothesis*).[11] A coin could be placed in the mouth of the deceased (for the ferryman, Charon).[12] In Homer, the duration of the *prothesis* is indefinite, but in classical Athens it lasted only twenty-four hours.[13] Ritual laments were conducted during this time primarily by women. The grief expressed during the *prothesis* was thought to confirm that the person was really dead and not merely sleeping.[14] In literature, ritual lament of the *prothesis* is sometimes described concurrently with the burial proper.[15] A formal funeral procession followed the *prothesis* (or wake) to the gravesite (the *ekphora*) three days after death.[16]

Women mourners also figured prominently in this procession.[17] Men are described as performing various tasks, such as washing, anointing, and lamenting the dead, but this is often in battlefield situations, where the womenfolk would not ordinarily be present.[18] It also seems that attitudes about the respectability of masculine grief underwent change in ancient Greece, so that men's grief as depicted in Homer eventually became unacceptable.[19] In vase-representations, women are certainly in the majority of those participating in mourning processions and leading dirges. Women are depicted as putting both hands to their heads and tearing their hair, whereas men are shown holding one hand to the head but not tearing the hair.[20] Men, however, are depicted on vase-representations as joining women in funerary dances,[21] and a few vases depict reduced characters, which are intended to be children in traditional mourning postures.[22] Funeral processions were often very public affairs, took place during the daylight hours, and made various stops along the way to the burial grounds.[23] Women joining in these processions could be family members, friends of the family, or household slaves or professional mourners hired just for the occasion. Musicians could also be hired for funerals. Flute players are the most commonly depicted. Women could be flute players, but male flute players are often depicted in funerary contexts.[24] Many of these hired professionals would be slaves hired from the marketplace. Once at the tomb, rites at the gravesite that women performed included continued lamentation and calling to the dead, which was accompanied by various offerings (often food) and libations. These rituals, especially the cries and wailings, were thought to raise the spirit of the dead from the grave.[25] At the gravesite, the body would be cremated, although inhumation was probably also done, especially among the poor.[26] Following burial rites for the recently deceased, the funeral party would then visit the graves of other family members buried nearby, making additional lamentations and probably offerings.[27] Gravesite rites did not presume later notions of an afterlife or "resurrection" for the deceased but rather functioned to establish a sense of connection or continuity with the dead.[28] The deceased were remembered, their presence felt; they were praised as well as mourned.[29]

Mourners also regularly held funerary meals. In Geometric times, funeral participants ate at the gravesite portions of the sacrifice made on behalf of the deceased. In the past, scholars assumed that the departed joined in partaking of the offered food and libations. Scholars now widely question this assumption.[30] Eventually, a ritual funerary meal, the *perideipnon*, was held in the house of the deceased, probably immediately following the funeral.[31] Funerary sacrifices, mourning, and banquets at the gravesite were repeated at intervals on the third and ninth days following the burial.[32] On the thirtieth day, the participants celebrated the end of mourning by a communal feast including the relatives of the deceased, and the death was then commemorated annually.[33] Later writers refer to a communal meal of relatives as seated (rather than reclining)—the *kathedra*, which demonstrated the end of mourning and was celebrated at monthly intervals.[34] Although funeral feasts were family celebrations,[35] it may be that women did not attend them once they were moved into the home, due to the strong influence of the all-male symposium tradition.[36] Since the Kean lawcode requires that men and women leave the cemetery separately,[37] this may imply an expected cultural interest in the separation of the sexes for the funerary meal; perhaps the women held a meal seated separately from the men.[38] Still, women are portrayed on funerary monuments either standing or seated, but not reclining. Only the men are portrayed as reclining.[39] These portrayals, however, may be idealizations of the "good life."[40] The later association of these feasts with the all-male symposium or "drinking party" no doubt contributed their characterization as opportunities for revelry, drunkenness, and sexual sport.[41] Even the funeral proper would have been one of the few opportunities for young men and women to mingle in a social situation.[42] Since death, association with corpses, and walking in cemeteries brought impurity and pollution, following a wake (*prothesis*) guests would ritually wash themselves with water provided at the door of the home of the deceased. Following the funeral proper, family members would take baths, and their house would be cleaned and purified.[43]

However, there were ancient attempts to curb the prominence of women in Greek funerals, particularly their role as mourners. In a relatively short time, and in spite of the conservative nature of burial customs, legislation restricting various funeral practices was enacted in a number of places in the Greek world from the seventh to the third centuries BCE.[44] Although restrictions varied from place to place, the restrictions placed on women had amazing uniformity. Certain scholars would even argue that women were the special targets of this legislation.[45] At Athens, the legislation restricted women participants to immediate kinswomen or women over sixty years old, limited the number of offerings brought to the gravesite, and required that women march behind men in the funeral processions. The procession was to proceed quickly to the gravesite and be completed before sunrise. Notably absent are any such restrictions to the number of male mourners. Excessive signs of grief, such as laceration of the flesh, were banned, as were excessive displays of wealth. Mourners were not to visit tombs of nonrelatives, except at the time of their burial, and mourners were prohibited from mourning anyone except the person being buried.[46] In other places, similar restrictions were enacted. At Delphi, the funeral procession itself was to be done in silence, and the bier was not to be put down at various stopping points, effectively prohibiting mourning along the way. Set laments and mourning at the grave on customary days following the funeral and on the anniversary of death were also prohibited.[47] Alexiou suggests that these restrictions on women were related to the shift of emphasis in inheritance laws from clan to family, in that women played a role in the determination of inheritance by means of their funeral participation.[48] Following Plutarch's discussion of the Solonian legislation, which implies the use of funerals to encourage rivalries between clans, Alexiou comments, "In the inflammatory atmosphere of blood feud between the families of Megakles and Kylon that was raging in Solon's time, what more effective way could there be to stir up feelings of revenge than the incessant lamentation at the tomb by large numbers of women for 'those long dead'?"[49] Women's lamentation could thus function as a form of political protest,[50] and their paying their respects to family ancestors could serve as a display of family solidarity rather than religious piety.[51]

At the same time that women's public mourning was restricted, a new masculine genre was created, the funeral oration (*epitaphios logos*), which declared that men who died on behalf of the state were not to be mourned, but praised.[52] Women's mourning, which was associated with the pain of the loss and continued connection with the loved one, became negatively coded, whereas male praise of the dead became positively coded. Women's mourning was considered "uncontrolled" and "unmanly," whereas male grief was characterized by restraint and praise for the dead. However, this was no doubt a stereotype of women's rituals. Not only are women mourners on ancient Greek vases portrayed as formal and dignified[53] but cross-cultural studies show ritual lamentation to be orderly[54] and even unemotional. Hired mourners have the ability to wail on cue; it is a performance.[55] By means of both negative cultural stereotyping and by means of legislation, public funerals came under the firm control of men and the state.[56] Subsequently, women mourners could be called upon to restrain their grief, or are even summarily dismissed from death and mourning scenes.[57] However, in spite of these legislative restrictions, women continued to participate in funerals and mourning, and continued to regularly visit and take food offerings to the dead. Some funeral proceedings, however, may have been moved indoors. Later representations of funeral proceedings are lighted by torches, suggesting that mourners eventually held processions before dawn.[58] Holst-Warhaft demonstrates the continued connection of women to laments in subsequent Greek literature. In that context, especially tragedy, women's laments could still function as calls for revenge and violence, create a sense of continuity with the dead, and serve to protest the various inequities and sufferings of women.[59] That does not mean that these protests changed the social situation in which women found themselves all that much, but it does explain in part the continued need for their control. The powerful potential of funerals for complaint and protest through the mourning of women and kin is no doubt one reason why criminals and traitors were usually denied burial rites and mourning, and were either dumped into mass graves or simply left to rot unburied outside the city walls. In spite of legislation banning tomb visitation at unspecified times, women continued to visit tombs of nonrelatives with other women and to mourn and take offerings to their dead.[60]

Women, Death, and Burial in Ancient Rome

We can also find the connection of women to burial, funerals, and mourning in Roman burial customs. Although Greek customs influenced the West, it is also the case that the connection of women to funerals and mourning has Etruscan antecedents.[61] As in Greek culture, death brought pollution, but providing a proper burial for the deceased was essential.[62] Friends and family usually gathered at the deathbed, and the nearest relative gave the dying his or her last kiss, ostensibly to catch the soul as it left the body with the last breath.[63] Catching this last breath was very important to the bereaved, and Cicero reports that mothers even spent the night outside prisons hoping to give their sons this final kiss before their executions.[64] Upon death the eyes and mouth were closed by a close relative, often a woman or mother,[65] a coin was placed in the mouth to pay the fare for Charon's ferry (a Greek custom), the corpse was washed and anointed,[66] and a wreath was placed around the head.[67] Women kin or other relatives usually performed these tasks, but at times domestic servants or an undertaker performed them as well. Perfumes could also later be placed in tombs or sprinkled on the ashes of the remains.[68] Women began mourning immediately at the time of death (the *conclamatio mortis*), calling out to the dead. This established a sense of continued contact with the deceased. Some thought that the wailing and crying would awaken the person if he or she was not really dead.[69] A male slave—the *Pollinctor*, a slave of the *Libertinarius*—often then made funeral arrangements.[70] Women, however, still featured prominently as mourners at the wake held in the home and in processions for public funerals. They are found in this role in artistic representations of wakes and funeral processions, beating their breasts or stretching out their arms toward the deceased. The tearing of hair is also a posture of grief in Roman art.[71] The mourning of women throughout the funeral proceedings continued the *conclamatio*, which immediately followed the death.[72] Mourners expressed grief both by laments (Gr. *thrēnos*, Lat. *nenia*) and by gestures (Gr. *kopetos*, Lat. *planctus*).[73] The kinswomen of the dead lamented, as well as women and men hired to mourn along with mothers, daughters, and sisters.[74] Again, flute players also often featured in funerals. Musicians could be either men or women but were usually slaves.[75] The laments musicians sang at wakes focused on grief and sorrow but were also used as opportunities to sing the praises of the deceased.[76] At more formal funerals, such as state funerals, prominent men delivered funeral orations (the *laudatio funebris*). However, rather than being a collective praise for war dead as in ancient Greece, in Rome individuals were eulogized, both men and women.[77] Bodies were generally cremated and the ashes kept in urns in the tomb. Urns were made of various materials (depending on the wealth of the family). Inhumation was practiced concurrently, particularly among the poor.[78] Eventually, the entire Roman Empire took up the practice of inhumation.[79] The poor could not afford their own tombs, and they often buried their dead in common graves or public cemeteries.[80] Others joined guilds or burial societies, which assured the poorer classes proper burials.[81] Following the funeral, homes were purified.[82]

Romans also visited the graves of their family members and held funerary feasts at the tomb on the day of the funeral,[83] on the ninth day after the funeral, and at the end of the mourning period, as well as at various times throughout the year. Roman funeral feasts could also be held in a home[84] or even outside in the cemetery like a picnic, on folding chairs or simply seated in a circle on the ground.[85] The deceased were thought to be present for these meals, and the mourners set food out for them, even pouring food into the burial site if the meal was being held at the gravesite.[86] Some tombs even had kitchens.[87] Until the end of the mourning period, participants would mourn, praise, and remember the deceased at gravesite meals; on subsequent visits, the deceased would be remembered, their presence assumed, and praises and fond stories of the person would be recounted.[88]

Since the Roman period, women began to attend more meals with men, including formerly all-male banquets like symposia. Women also attended Roman funerary meals, although it is more likely they would have been seated separately from the men, as they were at weddings.[89] Funerary monuments do show women seated next to their husband's banquet couch,[90] although these scenes probably have little to do with actual funerary banquets but are rather stereotypical scenes of an ideal life.[91] Roman catacomb art, on the other hand, shows men reclining for meals with men, and women with women.[92] Not surprisingly, funerary banquets, as all ancient banquets, were stereotyped as occasions for drunkenness and sexual license.[93] This is no doubt due to the presence of both men and women for the various funerary celebrations, which in antiquity was a social mixture fraught with sexual danger, especially for young virgin girls.[94] Still, these funerary rites and meals were a stable fixture of ancient society and could be enjoyed in some fashion by rich and poor alike.[95] Of these funeral meals and the cult of the dead generally, Franz Cumont writes:

No religious ceremony was more universally performed in the most diverse regions of the Empire than this cult of the dead. At every hour of every day families met in some tomb to celebrate there an anniversary by eating the funeral meal.[96]

The pervasive nature of these customs renders inaccurate the designation of the cult of the dead as merely a "popular" or "superstitious" aspect of the religion of the masses. Although certain ancient writers expressed concern about these customs, as a religious *practice*, we may assume the cult of the dead for all classes.[97]

As in ancient Greece, legislators attempted to limit what they considered Roman excesses in funerary rituals, both emotional and financial. Cicero, in about 70 BCE, writes that the Solonic restrictions on funerals were written into Roman law, hence similar funeral restrictions are found in the *Twelve Tables*.[98] They introduced restrictions on expenditure, as well as limitations on women's expressions of grief. Cicero also mentions other later regulations, such as the size of the crowd or the attendance of nonfamily members. Funeral orations were allowed only at public funerals, and only appointed orators could deliver them.[99] Although these regulations surely reflect an interest in curbing expenditure,[100] the interest in controlling the potential power of funeral proceedings is also evident. It is the case, however, that the expensive individual monuments so characteristic of the Late Republic eventually gave way to a fashion of simpler family plots and group burials with standardized accessories. The burial practices of the poor eventually mimicked the simplified funerary conventions of the rich.[101] This simplification of Roman burial practices was part of the larger effort to consolidate the power of the state through newer art and imagery, which created a homogeneous culture of "uniformity and prosperity" in the imperial age.[102] As in Greek areas, it is questionable how successful such efforts were in controlling the behavior of women at Roman wakes and funerals. Lucian continues to parody women mourners in the second century CE, arguing that surely the deceased received no benefit from such behavior.[103] In the role of the departed, he comments:

What good do you think I get from your wailing, and this beating of the breasts to the music of the flute and the extravagant conduct

of the women in lamenting? (*hē tōn gunaikon peri thrēnōn ametria*) Or
from the wreathed stone above my grave? Or what, pray, is the use
of your pouring out the pure wine? You don't think, do you, that
it will drip down to where we are and get all the way through to
Hades?[104]

Thus, it seems reasonable to conclude that the funerary rites connected
to the cult of the dead continued as a central part of Roman religious
and family life in spite of legislation enacted to restrict it.

Funeral rites were often denied to criminals and traitors. However,
as has already been mentioned, family members and close associates of
the condemned could go to great effort to secure the remains of their
loved ones, either by purchasing them or even stealing them.[105] Per-
functory rites were performed whenever feasible.[106] The vast majority of the condemned, however, were no doubt consigned to mass
graves or cremations. The denial of burial and funeral rites was part
of the punishment meted out to the condemned.[107] Those executed
for treason, particularly by means of crucifixion, were more likely
to be denied basic burials and funeral rites.[108] Some officials might
show clemency by granting bodies to the family of the deceased,[109] but
this was probably exceptional.[110] It should be remembered that there
is some evidence that women as well as men, particularly slavewomen
and women of the lower classes, could be arrested and even executed
by means of impalement, crucifixion, or beheading. Further, women
and children were simply slaughtered in times of political upheaval
and war. Even if some ancient descriptions of women's death are exaggerated, the execution of women was quite imaginable.[111] The family tomb excavated at Giv'at ha-Mivtar from first-century Palestine,
which contains the only evidence for crucifixion in antiquity, illustrates that other members of the family besides the crucified man,
Yohannan, met with death by violence. Also found in this tomb are a
strong fifty-to-sixty-year-old woman who died by a blow to the head,
a twenty-four-to-twenty-six-year-old woman who burned to death, a
three-to-four-year-old child who died from an arrow wound, and several children who died of starvation.[112] Violence, warfare, and political
unrest during ancient times could affect all ages and members of a family, not just the men. This family succeeded in providing at least final
burial in an ossuary for one who had been crucified in the provinces,

presumably for anti-Roman activities.[113] The denial of funeral rites, however, was a great tragedy among the Romans, since the shades or ghosts of those not properly lamented and buried were condemned to wander without a final resting place.[114]

Women's Ritual Lamentation of Greco-Roman Gods and Heroes

We can find a related role for women in ritual lamentation in cults surrounding various Greco-Roman "heroes" as well as in certain mystery religions. Although both men and women participated in these rites, women often led the other participants in the cultic lamentation for the dead god or hero. Hero (and heroine) cults were cults of the special dead, those idealized and mythologized as a class of individuals somewhere in between human beings and gods. Throughout the Hellenistic world, a special gravesite, a *heroon*, was set apart from other burials. A special monument and sanctuary were built and sacrifices and offerings were brought to the site.[115] The special dead was thought to remain at the site of this cultic center, present and available for invocation, prayers, and requests.[116] Many graves of heroes were in fact not real gravesites at all. When excavated, archaeologists have found no remains.[117] Still, as in the case of tombs, ritual uncleanliness could be connected with sanctuaries of heroes, and purification rites could be required after contact with them.[118] Cultic feasting at either the cultic center or a sacred house[119] in the supposed company of the hero or heroine was common. The hero is thus often depicted as reclining for a banquet surrounded by admirers.[120] Women and family associates were likely present for these meals, especially if the woman held some cult position.[121] The inscription called "A Decree of Orgeones" (third-century BCE Athens) describes the details of the distribution of sacrificial meat for feasts of their cultic association, which meets in honor of the hero Echelos and unnamed "heroines." Absent members receive no portion.[122] Free matrons, daughters, and slavewomen are clearly apportioned a part of the sacrifice, although they receive half of what the male members receive. Thus, they are probably present for the meal.[123] Well-dressed and veiled women also appear in banquet representations of feasting heroes. Again, such scenes are probably stereotypical of an ideal life rather than scenes of actual cultic or funerary feasts.[124] Finally, dogs, either lying under the table gnawing on a bone or piece of meat, or tied by a leash to the banquet table or couch, are commonly depicted in funerary banquet reliefs featuring heroes.[125]

Women also practiced ritual lamentation in the context of cultic festivals dedicated to heroes and heroines.[126] Such lamentation further indicates the similarity of hero-cult rituals to funerary practices from the cult of the dead. For example, women in Kroton, Elis, and Thessaly mourned Achilles.[127] In Corinth, Medea's children were mourned at an annual festival,[128] and the Megarians sent their young boys and girls to Corinth to lament the early death of a Megarian princess who died soon after marrying into the Corinthian royal house.[129] Two choirs, one of boys and one of girls, probably sang this lament antiphonally.[130] Although the limited nature of our sources makes it difficult to know the social class of the women who sang such dirges, ritual lamentation in hero cults would have been public performances in ceremonies that were both religious as well as social.[131]

Ritual lamentation was also a regular part of various mystery religions, which focused on the death and renewed presence of a particular god.[132] Public mourning for the death of a god was prominent in three particularly popular and widespread cults, those of Adonis (Greece), Isis/Osiris (Egypt), and Tammuz (Mesopotamia), as well as in the Dionysiac, Orphic, and Eleusinian traditions.[133] The most ancient of these deities is the youthful shepherd god Tammuz, or Dumuzi, whose cult spread from Mesopotamia to Syria and Palestine and then to Greece, where he was known as Adonis.[134] In various versions of the story, the death of Tammuz is mourned by his mother, Dattur, his sister Geshtinanna, and his wife Inanna (or Ishtar). Subsequently, ancient laments to Tammuz focus on the inspiring love for the god and the grief and anguish of his loss, expressed in sung laments to the music of pipes. In many texts, Inanna's loss as a young widow predominates; in others the sister and mother predominate; in others all three play a role.[135] Ancient Israelite women even participated in the worship of Tammuz. The prophet Ezekiel is shown women weeping for Tammuz in the temple precincts (Ezek 8:14).[136] The cry of lament for Tammuz may have been *hui Adon*, "alas Lord."[137] Myths about Ishtar and Tammuz survived in Syria and Palestine into Christian times,[138] and the lament for Tammuz persisted in Harran into the Middle Ages.[139]

The yearly festival of weeping for Tammuz spread to Greece, where the young dead god was known as Adonis, probably derived from the Semitic title *Adon*, "Lord."[140] In its Greek form, the death of the young god Adonis (killed while hunting) was mourned at a yearly festival called the *Adonia*, which was celebrated exclusively by women.[141] The earliest reference to the lament for Adonis comes from two fragments usually attributed to Sappho (seventh to sixth centuries BCE) in which young women are called upon to beat their breasts and cry out *o ton Adonin*, "Oh Adonis!"[142] In *Lysistrata* (fifth century BCE), Aristophanes describes women making wooden images of Adonis, which they place on rooftops for mock burial, accompanied by dancing and lamentation, crying *aiai Adonin*, "Woe, woe, Adonis!"[143] In the third century BCE in Alexandria, Theocritus describes two women characters named Gorgo and Praxinoa in his *Idyll* as jostling their way through crowded streets to the queen's palace, where they join in an *Adonia* festival. There they hear a young woman who has won her right to sing in a competition singing a lament for Adonis. On the second day of the festival, the women carry the god to the sea and lament him with funeral dirges while baring their breasts and loosening their hair. After such excitement, Gorgo is no doubt ready to get home in time to fix her husband's supper.[144] The worship of Adonis was very popular and survived until the fourth century CE.[145] Later Christian leaders may have capitalized on the identification of Christ with the dead god Adonis among their women constituents.[146]

A third important religion that included ritual lamentation in the context of a reenactment of the death of a god was the Egyptian Isis religion. Isis was paired with Osiris in Egyptian mythology. Upon the death of her husband, Isis (along with her sister Nephthys) was said to search for his dismembered body, which was then reconstructed in the Underworld. Isis was a popular deity, and her cult spread throughout many parts of the Roman Empire, even to Rome. From most ancient times, ritual lamentation was a part of the cultus of this religion. This festival of the passion of Osiris was called the *Isia*. Three liturgical texts involving ritual lamentation of the death of Osiris survive from the Ptolemaic period, now called "The Songs of Isis and Nephthys,"

"The Lamentation of Isis and Nephthys," and "The Hour Watches." Instructions are given for choosing the women who are to sing the parts of Isis and Nephthys. The women must be virgin and completely hairless, but are allowed to wear wigs. The entire service includes recitations, duets by Isis and Nephthys, and solos by Isis.[147] In "The Songs of Isis and Nephthys," Isis and Nephthys lament:

> We lament the Lord,
> for love of thee is not lacking with us.
> O thou Male, lord of passion,
> King of Lower Egypt, lord of eternity
> Ascend to life, O prince of eternity.[148]

Women all over Egypt, and eventually throughout the Greek world, Asia Minor, and in Rome, reenacted and led the role of Isis as mourner.[149] As late as the fourth century CE, the calendar of Philocalus lists the dates of October 29 through November 1 as the time for the festival *Isia*. Little is known about the celebrations as practiced at Rome, except that it involved a reenactment of the lamentation of Isis, her search for Osiris, and her joyous discovery of him.[150] There is little question that women participated in the public performance of the ritual reenactment of Isis's lament for her husband.[151] There are many references to this rite in ancient literature.[152] Furthermore, there is ample evidence that women also attended cultic meals in honor of Isis or Osiris that were held in either temples, dining halls, or homes, although it is unclear whether women sat or reclined for these meals.[153]

Stereotypes of Women's Rituals: Noble Death Scenes

Given the role of women in ritual lamentation of gods and heroes, we would expect to find women portrayed in mourning roles in literary scenes involving the deaths of heroes and other notable individuals. Concern with women's religious rituals of grief and the marginalization of women's customs in antiquity evolved into social stereotypes, which furthered the marginalization process on an ideological level. These images reflect ideals of behavior during the Hellenistic period. One way to control human behavior is through criticism. Labeling and setting up categories of ideal and proscribed behaviors are powerful forms of social control. In antiquity, preferred gender roles were reinforced through catalogues of virtues (how men and women were supposed to behave) and vices (how men and women often behaved, but were not supposed to). Stereotypical gendered categories of ideal behavior appear in epitaphs and pervade Greek, Roman, Jewish, and Christian literature of the Hellenistic period.[154] Such ideal categories include cultural stereotypes about male and female grief. Laments (Gr. *threnos*, Lat. *nenia*) and expressions of grief (Gr. *lypē*, Lat. *luctus*) are associated with femininity, moderation of grief with masculinity. Plutarch writes in his *Letter to Apollonius*:

> Yes, mourning is truly feminine, weak and ignoble, since women are more given to it than men, and barbarians more than Greeks, and inferior men more than better men.[155]

According to Plutarch, if at all, grief and emotion (*pathos*) should be expressed in moderation, particularly by men.[156] However, Plutarch also praises his wife in *Consolation to His Wife* for her moderate behavior following the death of their daughter, Timoxena. He is pleased that she did not allow behavior he considers excessive at their daughter's funeral, which was conducted in silence (*siopē*) with only close family members present.[157] Conversely, in his discussion of Solon's funerary legislation, Plutarch remarks that women breaking the new restrictions would be punished by a board of censors of women for unmanly (*anandros*) and effeminate (*gynaikōdēs*) behavior.[158] Cicero expresses similar sentiments. Such displays of grief lead to "womanish superstition" (*superstitio muliebris*).[159] Ideal masculine behavior is stoic and controlled, as in that of the noble philosopher Pythagoras, who was said to show neither gaiety (*chara*) nor grief (*lypē*).[160] Thus, concurrent with a variety of actual burial customs and mourning practices, a particular demeanor is recommended in Hellenistic literature, one that is culturally coded as masculine rather than feminine. Such views of ancient women's experience reflect the nature of the extant literary sources, which were written by upper-class men and therefore probably do not reflect widely held views. These stereotypes influence literary portrayals of deaths, particularly deaths of notable men and women, known in Latin as *exitus illustrium virorum*.[161]

Generally, in most "noble death" stories, women play a minor, supporting role, gathering around the hero or martyr to cry, weep, and wail. The man, usually the martyr or hero, then gets annoyed, tells them to be quiet, or asks them to leave. The classic case is that of the death of Socrates, from which many later scenes are no doubt derived. Socrates's wife is not even present for the death scene; she has been taken weeping from the room much earlier.[162] His children are presented to him, the other women of the family gather around him, he says his good-byes, and then the women are dismissed from the scene.[163] Thus, only the male disciples of Socrates (and a servant) are present for the death scene proper. Some of the men start to weep (*dakryō*), and Socrates tells them to stop. Eventually they all break down weeping (*apoklaiō*). Socrates, annoyed with them, says:

> "What conduct is this, you strange men! I sent the women away chiefly for this reason, that they might not behave in this absurd way; for I have heard that it is best to die in silence. Keep quiet and be brave." Then we were ashamed and controlled our tears.[164]

Many death scenes follow this basic model in ancient literature. Family, friends, or disciples gather; the women weep, are told to be quiet, and are then asked to leave or are escorted from the scene. The hero is circled by his close male friends, or attendants, but not mothers, wives, or daughters. If the men start to carry on, they too are told to stop weeping—and be *men*.[165] A certain amount of restrained grief, however, is a sign that the onlooking friends and family honor the dead and dying. Grief, when restrained, is a sign of true friendship and discipleship. In order to show true courage (*andreia*), men must exhibit characteristics culturally defined as feminine and then overcome them.[166] However, too much grief is "womanish" and "irrational."[167] There is one scene in which a woman's death is "noble." In the scene of the death of Iphegenia in Euripides, *Iphegenia at Aulis,* her death is also noble because it is voluntary and on behalf of the state.[168]

In scenes of the death of Hercules, generally only men or his mother are featured prominently. The scene in Seneca's *Hercules Oetaeus* is a good example. Hercules' mother leads the crowd in mourning; she beats her breasts (while stripped naked to the waist), filling the air with "womanish bewailings" (*voce feminea*). Hercules tells her to stop weeping. When she is quiet at last, the narrator declares her "well nigh equal to her son." Still, when the funeral pyre is lit, Hercules declares: "Now you are parent true of Hercules; thus it is proper that you should stand, my mother, beside the pyre, and thus it is proper that Hercules be mourned." The crowd, however, is speechless. After his death, Hercules appears to his mother.[169] The story of the death of Hercules in Diodorus of Sicily, however, does not feature Hercules' mother. Hercules' companions build the pyre. One friend, Iolaüs, after doing what Hercules asks, withdraws from the pyre (*apobainō*) to watch. Another, Philoctetes, lights the fire. Afterward, Iolaüs and his friends come to retrieve Hercules' remains, but no bones can be found.[170] Lucian, a Greek rhetorician and satirist writing in the second century CE, parodies a combination of both the death of Socrates and that of Hercules in *The Passing of Peregrinus*:

> The Cynics stood about the pyre, not weeping to be sure, but silently evincing a certain amount of grief as they gazed into the fire. . . .
> I said, "Let us go away, you simpletons. It is not an agreeable spectacle to look at an old man who has been roasted, getting our nostrils filled with a villainous reek. Or are you waiting for a painter to come and picture you as the companions of Socrates in prison are portrayed beside him?"[171]

Thus, in the majority of death scenes, only male disciples or friends are present for the death, the women often having been dismissed. The men show some grief and then cease weeping, usually after being reprimanded by the teacher/hero. The exception is certain stories of the death of Hercules, where his mother is often present.

Hellenized Death Scenes in Jewish Literature

Hellenistic Jewish literature reflects similar stereotypical ideals. The Alexandrian *Sentences of Pseudo-Phocylides,* written roughly between 30 BCE and 40 CE, recommends, "Be moderate in your grief; for moderation is the best."[172] Similarly, the *Wisdom of Ben Sira,* written in Jerusalem around 180 BCE, recommends mourning for a day or two, but more than that does the dead no good.[173] Josephus's first-century-CE description of Herod's funeral instructions, which include the slaughter of one person in every household in the country to ensure protracted grief throughout the land, is no doubt meant to portray Herod as crass.[174] Further, Josephus's death of Moses follows the noble death model. The crowd weeps, the women weep and beat their breasts, Moses tells them to be quiet, steps away from them so they are only weeping in the distance, and then Eleazar and Joshua escort him up the mountain, where he disappears.[175] Although not a death scene, 2 Esdras 9:26—10:54 portrays Zion as a weeping woman. She so annoys the prophet that she is transformed into a vision of a resplendent city to shut her up.[176] The most interesting development in Jewish martyrological literature, however, is the martyrdom of the woman and her seven sons in 2 and 4 Maccabees.[177] Here, it is a woman who dies a truly noble death and encourages each of her children to do so as well.[178] There are very few similar stories featuring women. Susanna is a model of a suffering righteous person, surrounded by weeping family and friends at her trial, but she does not die.[179] But the mother of seven sons in 2 and 4 Maccabees dies a "noble death."[180] Most interesting in the account in 4 Maccabees, however, are the two speeches in chapter 16. In the first speech, the narrator describes what the mother would have said if she were weak. She would have wept and mourned for the death of her children (4 Macc 16:5-11). The narrator goes on that she of course did not give this speech, but rather gave the speech in 4 Macc 16:16-23. Barbara Miller has identified elements in the first speech that coincide with women's ancient and modern formal laments.[181] This is an example of a scribal appropriation of a woman's lament. The lament still contains essential elements common to other Greek and Hebrew laments, and the formal address and reproach to the dead remains (4 Macc 16:6-11).[182] The mother's second speech, which the narrator assures the audience she really spoke, encourages the sons to die on behalf of their people. Elements of this speech coincide more with the masculine eulogy in praise of men who die on behalf of the state.[183] For this speech, the mother is called "manly"; she is a "soldier of God" who is "more powerful than a man" (anēr) (4 Macc 16:14 RSV).

These Jewish stories follow a set pattern, so that the person suffering is portrayed as "righteous," as well as "noble." George Nickelsburg has established this genre of the suffering righteous one. This story pattern or "Wisdom Tale" can be found in Genesis 37–42, Esther, Wisdom of Solomon, Daniel, and Susanna, as well as in 2 and 4 Maccabees.[184] The Psalms also imply the presence of family and friends as onlookers for a death, if only from a distance.[185] As in Greek and Roman literary scenes, the presence of family and friends is expected, and expressed grief is a prerequisite for the scene. Generally, women are expected to weep, whereas men should restrain their grief in the face of death. If a woman does not mourn, but shows restraint, she can be described as a "man."

Stereotypes of Women's Rituals: Tomb Visitation and Magic

As well as being stereotyped as overly emotional, women's tomb visitation and lamentation also came to have necromantic overtones more so than men's, even though men too are described as participating in funerals, magical practices, and conjuring the dead at tombs. Necromancy is the invocation of spirits of the dead for the purposes of fortune-telling. First, there is a strong tradition in Greek and Roman literature featuring laments that links the lamentation of women (and sometimes men) to the conjuring up of the dead, especially in the context of visits to the tomb. The shade or spirit of the dead, called by the Greeks *daimōn*, or *eidōlon*, or collectively as *lemures* or *manes* by the Romans, were thought to remain near the place of burial, where they could be visited as well as fed. The tomb was therefore the most likely place for an appearance of a departed spirit, the tomb being their "house," as it were.[186] The shades of the dead were considered powerful, able to inflict illness or distress if neglected or bring good fortune or aid in healing if propitiated.[187] Magical texts were therefore often folded neatly and placed in graves, requesting help in various circumstances as well as curses or revenge.[188] For example, in one magical spell from Egypt, a widow tucks her ritual spell into the bindings of a mummy and invokes the spirit of the dead to bring her vengeance in a judicial matter. This Coptic spell dates from the seventh century and comes from Christian Egypt. The late date demonstrates the persistence of these graveside customs:

> The mummy [on] which this [papyrus for] vengeance is placed must appeal night and day [to the lord (?)], from its [bed] to the ground in which it is buried with the other mummies lying around this grave, all of them calling out, together, what is in this papyrus, until god hears and [brings] judgment on our behalf, quickly! Amen.[189]

The spirits of those who had died untimely or violent deaths (those murdered or executed) were considered especially powerful, and many magical texts include a piece of such a corpse in the list of ingredients. To have possession of the body was to have control over the power of the dead person's spirit.[190] The spirits of those untimely or violently killed were condemned to wander the earth, and it was these spirits that were thought particularly open to invocation by workers of necromancy.[191] This potential traffic in corpses in part explains the constant curse formulas found in funerary inscriptions, which lay curses on any who would disturb the resting place of the deceased.[192] Cynics, Epicureans, and Stoic philosophers considered such beliefs superstitious, and were fond of quoting Theodore the Atheist's words to Lysimachus, who was threatening him with death without burial: "What matters it if I rot on the earth or under it?"[193] Socrates, of course, was also notable for his lack of concern for his own burial. When asked how he would like to be buried, he replied, "However you please, if you can catch me."[194] Other philosophers, especially Cynics, expressed a similar lack of concern for the disposal of their remains.[195] Still, for many ancient people, such beliefs and religious practices connected to gravesites were no doubt simply a part of everyday religious life. What is often labeled "magic" is frequently indistinguishable from other practices labeled and thus legitimized as "religion." Magical texts from antiquity attest to the pervasive interest of many ancient people in rituals that would provide healing, help in childbirth, ensure faithfulness in marriage, help in the courts or in their businesses and financial security, as well as provide protection from evil people or demonic powers.[196] Workers of this kind of religious ritual in antiquity could be either male or female, and there are plenty of ritual spells in which the ritualist is a man, not a woman.

However, literary portrayals negatively define women working such rituals as witches, and even juxtapose them over against male necromancers or magicians. Male ritualists can be labeled wonder-workers or prophets, and are given positive appeal. A good example of this is found in Apuleius's *Metamorphoses*, written in Roman Africa in the early to mid-second century CE. The character Thelyphron is hired to watch the remains of a man the night before the funeral lest his corpse be mutilated by witches. He hesitates:

> I greatly fear the blind and inevitable hits of witchcraft, for they say that not even the graves of the dead are safe, but the bones and slices of such are slain to be digged up from tombs and pyres to afflict and torment such as live: and the old witches [*cantatrices anus*] as soon as they hear of the death of any person do forthwith go and uncover the hearse and spoil the corpse before it ever be buried.[197]

What will these old hags do? They are planning to take bites out of the corpses' faces to use in their magical arts (*artis magicae supplementa*).[198] The next morning, as the body is being carried through the streets, the widow is accused of poisoning him. An Egyptian prophet "of the first rank" (*Aegyptius propheta primarius*) steps forth to settle the matter by raising the man from the dead by means of herbs and incantations.[199] The raised man declares that he was indeed murdered by his wife. Notice that the man involved in such ritual arts is a "prophet" but the women are "witches," even though both are practicing what would be called "magic" or "necromancy." There are similar stories linking women to the raising of the dead by means of religious rituals at gravesites and tombs. Lucan, writing in Rome around 50 CE, writes of women who frequent funerals and graveyards in order to steal pieces of corpses, especially from those left unburied. Even the vultures are scared away by these women, who take the place of carrion birds by their scooping out eyeballs from the dead or gnawing at fingers or noses in the grisliest manner. One poor corpse is stolen, raised, and used by a woman to speak oracles about the future.[200]

Since lamentation was done by the gravesite, women associated dirges with the raising of the dead at tombs by women, and thereby with necromancy and magical arts. Since the chief mourner was considered to be in direct communication with the dead, the role of the mourner is thought to be the model for the later magician (*goēs*).[201] The word for "magician" (*goēs*) is derived from the word "lament" (*goos*).[202] A formal funerary lament is also called *thrēnos* and follows a formal structure: (1) address of the dead, (2) narrative, and (3) renewed address. Formal laments are more regular but in many ways are parallel to folk laments women still sing in modern rural Greece.[203] Laments are characterized by antiphonal structure and antithetical thought; one singer leads the lament and calls to the rest of the women to follow her in song. This basic antiphonal structure still survives in formal laments in modern rural Greece.[204] These dirges serve as a form of communication with the dead and attest to a tradition of women's interpretation of death and suffering.[205]

As a form of communication with the dead, however, lamentation can also be described in literature as a form of necromancy. In Aeschylus's *The Persians*, for example, Darius's widow Atossa brings offerings to her husband's tomb. A chorus of lamenters come with her (in this case men). Their joint task? To summon the dead king from Hades. When Darius rises and speaks, it is on account of the force of their wailing lament. He declares:

> As I behold my consort hard by my tomb I feel alarm, and I accept her libations in kindly mood; while you [pl.], standing near my tomb, make lament (*thrēneō*) and with shrilling cries (*gooi*) that summon the spirits of the dead, invoke me piteously. Not easy is the path from out of the tomb.[206]

At the end of the play, it is Xerxes who leads a staged lament, calling to the chorus to respond: "Lift up your voice in the lament [*goos*]!" The antiphonal shouts this precipitates probably reflect what would have been a female lament in ancient Greek funerary practice.[207] A similar scene is found in Aeschylus's *The Libation Bearers,* where Electra brings offerings to her father Agamemnon's tomb, accompanied by a chorus (all women). She pours libations on the grave and laments. As wails of the chorus urge her on, she cries out to Hermes as a mediator of the spirits of the dead to return her brother Orestes from exile to help her avenge her father's death. Upon his return, both brother and sister (accompanied by the chorus) pour libations on their father's tomb together, invoking his spirit to empower them to avenge his murder and the mutilation of his corpse.[208] Thus, laments function in these stories as a powerful form of magic, stirring up the dead, especially to exact vengeance.[209] As such, they are meant to invoke fear in the audience (primarily male) and serve as a powerful vehicle for cultural catharsis.[210] This literary motif linking women, laments, tombs, and communication with the dead is a prominent theme in Greek tragedy,[211] which carries over into literature of the Roman period as well. For example, in Seneca's *Hercules Oeateus,* Hercules appears to his mother Alcmena following her lamentation. She witnesses his death, lamenting it both before and after. He then appears to her and tells her to be quiet.[212] Elsewhere, mourning wives are even translated into the air to be with their dead husbands. Immediately, their husbands tell them to quit crying.[213] Even the woman's lament in 4 Maccabees 16:5–11 retains this element of the address of the dead. In ancient Greek, Roman, and as we will see, even Jewish religion, women continued to be associated with tomb visitation, lamentation, and communication with the dead.

Women and Funerary Rituals in Judaism and Palestine

The "cult of the dead" has a long history in the ancient Near East.[214] As in Greek and Roman culture, women played a central role in Jewish funerary practices. Both men and women are described washing bodies for burial and expressing grief for the dead, but again women are still stereotypically associated with these roles.[215] Although there is little early evidence for Jewish burial preparation, in later rabbinic sources, men are allowed to prepare only men for burial, but women may prepare corpses of either sex.[216] The time between death and burial is unknown, although it is probable that burials took place on the same day as death. Deuteronomy 21:22-23 requires that the bodies of executed criminals be taken down and buried before dusk, and it may be safe to assume that all burials proceeded quickly due to the climate.[217] The period of mourning also varied, although in later Judaism seven days, thirty days, and one year are often specified.[218] Cremation was rare, except for the worst of criminals;[219] inhumation was the most common form of burial. For a person to go unburied was a great misfortune, and even ordinary criminals were buried.[220] Israelite gravesites have been discovered from various periods of Israelite history. The types of burials are diverse, including simple graves, cist tombs, natural caves, and tombs cut into soft rock.[221] In early times, bodies were placed on vertical ledges and later on narrow niches cut perpendicularly into the stone. After the remains had decomposed, skeletons were then given a second burial, either in special cavities or pits, and later, in ossuaries.[222] Bodies of poorer families who could not afford expensive tombs were often simply buried in the ground or in common trenches. Foreigners or criminals could also be buried in common pits.[223] Later rabbinic sources mention charitable societies that helped to care for the dead and help the bereaved.[224] For Israelites, to be buried was to "sleep with one's fathers" (šākab ʿim ʾăbōtayw), that is, the ancestors of the family clan.[225] The tomb was the "house" of the spirit of the departed.[226] Furthermore, Israelites had their own "heroes" and heroines," that is, their own special dead. Rituals were held at various monuments and tombs, such as the tombs of Rachel (Bethlehem) and the patriarchs (Hebron).[227]

Israelite mourning practices, particularly the practices of weeping or keening and the singing of formal laments, were similar to those of their neighbors.[228] To have one's death go unsung or unmourned was unfortunate.[229] Other mourning customs included fasting, scattering dust, tearing garments, wearing sackcloth, dancing, and funeral feasts (including feeding the dead) at tombs.[230] In later rabbinic Judaism, mourning also meant cessation from work, but this did not include housecleaning, making the bed, or dishwashing.[231] Death, as in many cultures, brought ritual uncleanliness.[232] However, Jewish concern for corpse impurity could not have been extreme in comparison with other ancient cultures, given that Jewish tombs were generally so well hidden that they could be walked over unnoticed.[233] Even in the Mishnah, graves are only to be marked for festival days like Passover, indicating that generally tombs and cemeteries were not avoided, even in the late second to early third centuries.[234] The connection of the marking of graves with Passover may reflect the origin of this custom in and around Jerusalem due to the large number of visitors in the city for this festival. Corpse impurity was primarily of significance for priests, but also for the many Israelites who visited the temple in Jerusalem many times throughout the year. The temple had ample ritual bathing facilities for visitors. In earlier times, however, the purity of the temple regarding corpse defilement was not scrupulously observed. According to Ezekiel, writing in exilic times, some kings were buried directly adjacent to the temple walls (Ezek 43:6-9). Joachim Jeremias suggests that Ezekiel must be referring to either the royal family tombs or to the tombs of Manasseh and Amon, which could easily be seen. It is probable that Herod's expansions, of the temple was built over the area of these ancient royal tombs.[235] It is also likely that the burial site of King Uzziah was disturbed during Herodian building programs in the time of Herod Agrippa (37–44 CE).[236] Thus, the ritual uncleanliness derived from death and burial in first-century Judaism should not be characterized as extreme, either for nonpriestly families or outside of Jerusalem. Greeks and Romans had similar concerns for ritual impurity derived from death and corpses. Greek and Roman houses were also cleansed following funerals, cemeteries were situated outside city limits, and individuals, both men and women, had to go through purity rituals before entering sacred places.[237]

Although both men and women are described as performing various expressions of grief, and although both men and women could be professional mourners, in the ancient Near East, as elsewhere, mourning the dead was more often done by women. To mourn or lament the dead was thus stereotypical of women's behavior, not men's.[238] Jeremiah uses the image of a weeping woman to lament the exile of the northern tribes. Rachel weeps (*bkh*) over the loss of Israel:

> Thus says the LORD:
> A voice is heard in Ramah,
>> lamentation and bitter weeping.
> Rachel is weeping for her children;
>> she refuses to be comforted for her children
>> because they are not. (Jer 31:15 RSV)

Jeremiah also assumes that professional mourners would be women, and that women would teach the skill of lamenting to their daughters (Jer 17:21). This imagery continues in later Jewish texts, as in 2 Esdras 9:26—10:54, where a weeping woman represents Zion in a vision.[239] Images of mourning women are found on the end panels of a tenth-century BCE sarcophagus of Ahiram.[240] Much later, after the fall of Jerusalem in 70 CE, defeated Israel is still portrayed as a weeping woman on the "Judaea Capta" coins struck by the Romans.[241] In laments, the dead themselves are usually addressed (2 Sam 1:26; 3:34; Ezek 32:2), although as in Greek lament tradition, the mourners could also call to one another to join in their song.[242] As mentioned above, Israelite women also performed yearly ritual lamentation for Tammuz (Ezek 8:14).[243] Ezekiel calls the women's rituals for Tammuz an "abomination." Another yearly rite is described in Judges 11:40, where women are said to lament the death of Jephthah's daughter. Scholars agree that this story of the lamentation of Jephthah's daughter is probably a cultic legend created to explain a yearly women's lamentation ritual, which would either function to dissociate the custom from the cult of Tammuz[244] or reflect a yearly rite of passage for adolescent girls approaching marriage.[245] In *Biblical Antiquities*, a first-century Jewish text probably written in Palestine, Jephthah's daughter is given a name, Seila, where she speaks a full dramatic lament.[246] This lament from the *Biblical Antiquities* stands out from the rest of the narrative as a passionate and lyrical piece of poetry that reflects the popular tone and style of later recorded poetry and funerary inscriptions, giving us a possible insight into the unrecorded popular laments of Hellenistic antiquity.[247] Themes from Seila's lament became part of Jewish epitaph tradition written in the Greek style.[248] De Ward suggests that the formal literary lament tradition arose from the popular tradition of women's laments.[249] Later formal rabbinic laments, however, are also characterized by the praise of the dead rather than mourning and loss, and may be a genre that developed along similar lines as the Greek eulogy. Both men and women could be eulogized.[250] Laments attributed to women are preserved in rabbinic literature. They are attributed to professional women mourners and are in Aramaic.[251]

Although mourning was considered a necessary part of care for the dead, we can also find limitations on mourning rites. Scholars have long associated the complex of rites involved in the cult of the dead with non-Israelite religions and cultures in the ancient Near East. Such practices would include feeding the dead, feasting at tombs and funeral houses, leaving offerings for the dead, frequent visits to tombs and gravesites, and even necromancy, which included the taking of bones for magical purposes and revivication of corpses.[252] Recent scholarship has reached a new consensus that continued attempts to limit various burial customs associated with the cult of the dead indicates a continuation of practices connected with the cult of the dead among Israelites, not just non-Israelites. Both readings of various biblical texts and archaeological evidence support this contention, to the extent that the previous consensus of De Vaux and others that there was no cult of the dead among Israelites has been overturned.[253] Many biblical writers attest to the continuation of common gravesite customs. For the Deuteronomist and many prophets, such practices were in conflict with Yahwism and centralized worship of Yahweh in the Jerusalem temple. Although not described in 1 and 2 Samuel, the prophets of Jezebel practiced lacerating the flesh (1 Kgs 18:28). This practice is condemned in Deut 14:1.[254] There were also attempts to curtail the custom of leaving food in tombs and funerary feasting with the dead.[255] Bread was a primary funerary food.[256] For example, Isaiah renounces the continued invocation of the spirits of the dead, as well as other customs such as eating with the dead in tombs.[257] Neither Jeremiah nor Ezekiel participated in funerals; Ezekiel did not even mourn the death of his wife.[258] It is also probable that a drinking club known as the *marzeah* gathered together for feasts with the dead in a special *marzeah* house set aside for this purpose.[259] In connection with Baalism, Israelites may have participated in these feasts.[260] Feasting in a *marzeah* house may also simply have been connected with funerary feasting generally.[261] The practice of funerary feasting in the *marzeah* house continued into the Second Temple period.[262] Archaeological evidence also indicates that the cult of the dead was regularly practiced among Israelites in spite of numerous attempts to suppress it. Pits for grave offerings are found in tombs,[263] and tomb apertures, storage jars over the heads of corpses, and cup holes found in tombs are consistent with periodic tomb visits for communication with the dead after the tomb had been sealed, as well as for food and drink offerings to the dead.[264]

Necromancy also flourished in spite of laws and pronouncements to the contrary. Both ancient Near Eastern texts and the Hebrew Bible describe men and women as performing these kinds of religious rituals.[265] The bones of the prophet Elisha, for example, were thought in the North to be powerful enough to raise the dead (2 Kgs 13:20-21).[266] According to Leviticus 20:27, both men and women could conjure spirits from the grave; both men and women could be put to death by stoning for doing so.[267] Divinized ancestors could also be invoked in times of trouble and given offerings (so Gen 28:17-18; 1 Sam 1:11).[268] Such texts attest to the powers that the dead were thought to have in regard to fortelling the future, reviving life, and exacting vengeance.[269] Reforms such as Josiah's were thus promonotheist programs directly antithetical to ongoing cult-of-the-dead practices among Israelites.[270]

The best-known story from the Hebrew Bible involving necromancy is about a woman, the so-called Witch of Endor, who raises the spirit of the dead prophet Samuel for Saul.[271] The woman's necromancy described in 1 Samuel must be a literary stereotype parodying women's religious rituals in the ancient Near East. Ancient Mesopotamian texts contain extant religious rituals performed by women "witches," including the placement of figurines representing individuals into graves with corpses.[272] A woman necromancer could also be likened to a harlot (Isa 57:3).[273] In Proverbs, Wisdom is said to protect one from this kind of whore who is connected with death cults.[274] Later Jewish writers repeat and discuss the tale of the Witch of Endor. Josephus has no trouble admitting that Samuel was raised by means of the woman's power.[275] However, in spite of maintaining a belief in the possibility of necromancy, the author of the *Biblical Antiquities* prefers to add that Samuel appeared by means of God's command, not the woman's.[276] Later rabbis considered necromancy possible, although sinful, but still acknowledge that the woman raised the prophet by magical means.[277] Rabbinic literature gives ample evidence that beliefs in the power and presence of the shades of the dead near graves, the existence of wandering spirits, as well as religious rituals considered magical or necromantic continued well into the Roman period despite rabbinic attempts to curtail or simply reinterpret them.[278] Thus, in many ways, the beliefs and practices of Israelites relating to the dead during the biblical period should be seen as consistent with the cultural environment of the ancient Near East and the larger Mediterranean world. Feeding the dead, feasting at tombs, and communication with the dead by meals of religious rituals were customs not easily eradicated.[279] In fact, certain modern Jewish women continue these ancient practices of ritual lamentation and mourning, as do women from all around the world.[280] In Palestine and the ancient Near East, as in other parts of the Mediterranean world, women especially practiced religious rituals that focused on the veneration of ancestors. Thus, limitations to these and other graveside rituals served to limit women's participation in traditional religion more than men's, both in early Israel and in later Hellenistic times.[281]

Excavations of late Hellenistic Palestinian tombs also suggest that certain so-called pagan customs persisted among Jews. For example, pre-Maccabean tombs betray the extent of Hellenization within Jewish society.[282] And, although later Second Temple tombs show a great deal of restraint in artistic representation and amount of grave goods,[283] coins placed in the mouth of the deceased (for the ferryman, Charon),[284] perfume bottles (*alabastra*),[285] signs of the anointing of remains,[286] dining benches,[287] tables and cups for water for the deceased,[288] as well as cooking pots[289] and lampstands[290] found in Jewish tombs reflect the persistence of certain gravesite customs and the continued influence of ancient Near Eastern or even Hellenistic burial rites.[291] "Jason's Tomb" near Jerusalem contains a lament over the death of Jason inscribed in Aramaic. The inscription calls visitors to the tomb to grieve for Jason's death and attests to the scribe's personal grief over his brother's death.[292] Also found in Jason's Tomb is a Greek inscription encouraging merrymaking (*euphrainō*), feasting (*esthiō*) and drinking (*pinō*).[293] In one tomb painting from Marissa, we find two funerary musicians, a man and a woman dressed in festive attire. The man leads, playing the flute, while the woman plays a harp.[294] This kind of evidence strongly suggests the continuation of laments, mourning rituals, funerary feasts, and family visits to tombs and burial grounds during the first century.[295] The restraint in grave goods and artistic representation may thus not be indicative of an overall change in basic religious practices. Rather, such restraint may simply indicate a change in mortuary fashion, as well as an increased Hebraic concern for idolatry.[296] Roman mortuary practices underwent a similar shift in fashion from elaborate burials and offerings to simpler family plots during the early imperial period.[297] Thus, there is little reason to conclude that grave gifts in Jewish tombs had no cultic or religious function for Jews.[298] Even Erwin R. Goodenough raises the possibility that the archaeological and literary evidence suggests that Jews continued ceremonies and feasts for the dead into later Second Temple times.[299]

However, the best archaeological evidence for the continuation of funerary rituals involving ancestor veneration from 30 BCE until at least the fourth century CE is the practice of secondary burial and the prevalent use of ossuaries.[300] Rather than being a sign of newer beliefs in the "resurrection of the dead,"[301] the popularity of secondary burial shows not only a continuation of previous forms of secondary burial among Israelites[302] but a renewed interest in a sense of continuity or connection with the dead. The shift to ossuaries in Second Temple Judaism has been called "the renaissance of the cult of ancestral tombs in the Herodian period."[303] The use of ossuaries in Palestine should not be considered limited to a small group of Jews like the Pharisees,[304] but seem rather to be a more pervasive fashion enjoyed by even higher-paid artisans.[305] Even the priestly family of the High Priest Caiaphas used ossuaries; one woman in the Caiaphas family, Miriam daughter of Simon, had a coin placed on her tongue for the ferryman Charon.[306] Furthermore, tombs and ossuaries even in Palestine could be protected by symbols that had magical functions,[307] if not by Jewish curse inscriptions, as found in the Diaspora.[308] Thus, secondary burial of dried bones in ossuaries did not differ in function from the storage of cremated remains in Greek funerary jars or Roman style urns.[309] Even the decorations found on ossuaries, though modified to meet Jewish cultural sensibilities, reflect common Greek funerary artistic fashions. Rosettes can be found on many funerary recepticals from ancient Greece, Mycenae, and Italy[310] as well as in the Orient.[311] From Helladic to Hellenistic times, funerary rosettes were even connected with the cult of Adonis, although their appearance in Palestine may again be mere mortuary fashion.[312] Since the tomb was elsewhere considered the "house" of the dead, Jewish ossuary and tomb decorations with roofs, houses, or depictions of tombs like those found in the Kidron Valley are not only standard, but furthermore show influence of Hellenistic and early Roman artistic tradition.[313] It was possible for Jews to vary their burial practices for sectarian reasons, but those buried in ossuaries did not. The one group that did vary from the common burial practices of first-century Palestine is the sectarians at Qumran, who practiced primary inhumation burials, not secondary burials, in communal graveyards, not family tombs.[314] The *Temple Scroll* in particular shows an interest in seeing temple purity laws concerning corpse impurity (originally intended for priests) extended to all of Israel, including the proper location for cemeteries. Still, the cemeteries at Qumran are not laid out according to the precepts of the *Temple Scroll*, but rather seemingly for the sake of convenience.[315]

There is also ample evidence that a Jewish equivalent of "hero" and "heroine" cults of the special or holy dead continued from ancient times through the Greek and Roman periods. Tombs extant at the time of Jesus include tombs dedicated to the patriarchs and matriarchs, Rachel, the Maccabean martyrs, the prophetess Hulda, the prophet Isaiah, the prophet Zechariah ben Judah, and a necropolis of kings near Jerusalem.[316] Throughout New Testament times there remained a deep-rooted belief among Jews in the incorruptibility of these special dead. Supplicants could seek after the Jewish holy dead for intercessory prayer on behalf of the living and to work wonders and magic. Jews made pilgrimages to their tombs and monuments.[317] It is precisely this custom that is being criticized in Q 11:47-51 (Luke 11:47-51 // Matt 23:29-36).[318] Several of these special tomb monuments, such as Zechariah's, are still standing in the Kidron Valley.[319] In Bethlehem, a tomb monument to Rachel still remains.[320] Busloads of pious Jewish women still visit these ancient tombsites as sacred places where they venerate Jewish saints, prophets, matriarchs and patriarchs, pray for healings of various sorts, and socialize with other women over elaborate picnics.[321] Depictions of these tombs of the special dead can be found as ossuary decorations, further attesting to their popularity during the first century.[322] The naming of children after fathers/grandfathers or mothers/grandmothers and other family names rather than previously popular biblical figures suggests both interest in Jewish ancestral lines during the Second Temple period as well as Hellenistic influence.[323]

Jewish literature from the second century BCE through the first century CE also attests to the continuation of practices connected with the cult of the dead, especially feeding the dead and requesting the prayers of dead ancestors, or "fathers," and prophets. When combined with archaeological evidence, literary evidence buttresses the argument that in postexilic times and into the Greek and Roman periods Jews continued these family religious practices. Most references to these rituals are negative; some are not. During the early Greek period, the book of Zechariah may reflect restrictions similar to those enacted in Solon's legislation, in that formal funerals require the segregation of the sexes (Zech 12:11-14). Second Maccabees attests to the acceptability of sacrifices for the dead and assumes that Onias and Jeremiah could perform intercessory prayer for Jerusalem.[324] Other Jewish writers dispute the efficacy of such prayer to prophets and "fathers." Deborah is portrayed in the first-century *Biblical Antiquities* as saying right before her death, "Do not hope in your fathers [*patres*]," which ironically would discourage veneration of herself as a dead prophetess and matriarch.[325] In 2 Baruch, the writer envisions a future in which such prayers to the ancestors and prophets will cease.[326] There may have been cause for concern among stricter monotheists in regard to the invocation of the prophets. The prophet Ahijah was even eventually identified with Adonis.[327] The book of Tobit recommends feeding the dead, but only the righteous dead.[328] Other writers, however, were not so supportive of such customs. The author of Wisdom considers the cult of the dead to be the source of idolatry,[329] and Ben Sira, writing around 180 BCE in Jerusalem, says, "Good things poured upon a mouth that is closed are like offerings of food [*brōma*] placed upon a grave [*taphos*]" (Sir 30:18 RSV).[330] In *Jubilees*, a book written in Palestine and also found in the library of Qumran, Gentiles are to be avoided since they feed the dead in tombs.[331] In another book found in the library of Qumran, the Epistle of Jeremiah, the author decries various idolatrous practices, including the ritual lamentation of women and men for other gods:

Women serve meals for gods of silver and gold and wood; and in their temples the priests sit with their clothes rent, their heads and beards shaved, and their heads uncovered. They howl and shout before their gods as some do at a funeral feast [*perideipnon*] for a man who has died. (Ep Jer 30-32 RSV)[332]

Not only could this refer to the ritual lamentation of Tammuz or other gods in the mysteries, but this author assumes the continued practice of lamentation in the context of funeral feasts. Although written in the Hellenistic period ostensibly about Gentile idolatry, the author may also have continued concern for potential Jewish involvement in these rites, given the history of Jewish attraction to the cult of Tammuz. Finally, ever the apologist, in *Against Apion*, Josephus records the orderly, conservative nature of the majority of Jewish funerals, a description that matches the conservative ideal of the imperial age.[333] He does note that all observers join in the funeral procession and that the family of the deceased and their home are purified following the funeral.[334] The many negative references to cult-of-the-dead practices reflect not only a continued concern for the compatibility of various religious funerary rites with certain forms of Judaism but also function to restrict such customs.[335]

Later funerary restrictions in rabbinic sources from the second to fourth centuries show a more detailed interest in the control of both the expenses of funerals as well as women's mourning rituals.[336] Rabbinic restrictions thus reflect the growing conservatism of the Roman period and are comparable to similar Greek and Roman legislation.[337] Rabbinic literature also shows an increased stress on the impurity caused by death, corpses, and tombs, which also functions to limit the frequency of tomb visitation, especially after the first year.[338] In general, the rabbis tried to modify customs they could not eradicate. In comparison with Greek and Roman legislation, the rabbis made weeping for the dead obligatory for both men and women and encouraged verbal expressions of grief. Within limits, even excessive expressions of grief honored the dead.[339] They did not forbid certain common customs, like throwing grave goods on the coffin, as long as the practice did not become overly wasteful.[340] They attempted to limit alcoholic excesses at funeral feasts.[341] When the third-day visit persisted, they gave it the purpose of confirming the death.[342] Still, both the *Mishnah* and the later tractate *Semahot* have funeral restrictions that limit women's behavior at funerals. The *Mishnah* prohibits setting funeral biers down in the open street in order to curtail funerary lamentation, prohibits mourning by women at certain yearly festivals, and prohibits women from mourning the dead after the corpse has been buried.[343] The *Mishnah* also reports that criminals executed by the religious court may not be buried in a family tomb but should be buried in separate burial grounds set up by the court for this purpose.[344] The tractate *Semahot* prohibits certain mourning gestures for those not next of kin,[345] denies funeral rites to suicides,[346] and denies funeral rites to those executed by the (religious) court. Such a condemned person may be buried but is not to be mourned.[347] However, all mourning rites are to be fully observed for those executed by the (presumably Roman) state. In such cases, the family is discouraged from trying to steal the body.[348] In light of these restrictions, it is reasonable to assume that in the centuries preceding the compilation of these texts, women continued various mourning rituals particular to their own religious experience, which precipitated a concern for their control. In light of the function of laments suggested for ancient Greek cultural contexts,[349] the lack of restrictions on mourning following state executions betrays an awareness on the part of certain rabbis of the potential for national protest through the vehicle of family mourning (especially women) following a state (presumably Roman) execution. The banning of mourning following executions carried out by the religious court, as well as the burial of executed criminals in court-organized burial grounds, shows a similar awareness of the potential opposition to religious court decisions that could be expressed by women lamenting over the graves of their dead.[350]

It is difficult to determine the applicability of these later regulations to first-century Palestine. We have only the remains of one crucified individual from Roman Palestine, in spite of the thousands that were no doubt put to death during Roman occupation.[351] This alone suggests that criminals were buried in common plots rather than family tombs; most families may never have recovered bodies. Further, it seems reasonable to conclude that executed criminals were buried in common plots due to the application of Deuteronomy 21:22-23. A pesher from Qumran (4QpNah) and a passage from the Temple Scroll (11QTemple 64:6-13) illustrate a pre-Christian association by certain Jews in first-century BCE or CE Palestine of death by "hanging on a tree" (Deut 21:22-23) with crucifixion.[352] Furthermore, comments by Josephus suggest that although Roman officials might refuse to comply, generally there was a continued interest in burying not only social and religious outcasts, but criminals executed by Roman authorities.[353] The story of Tobit's burial of (presumably) executed Jews encourages Jewish readers that an ideal of Jewish piety can prevail even under the forces of hostile occupation (Tob 1:18-20; 2:3-10). The burial of Yehohanan from Givat Ha Mivtar in an ossuary shows that it was possible for a family with good connections to recover the remains of a family member for at least an honorable second burial.[354] In this instance, it seems reasonable to assume that some families did recover the remains of their loved ones from common plots set aside for such burials. That the only remains of a crucified person come from Palestine, rather than elsewhere in the Roman world, may indicate ancient Jewish predilection for burial, even burial of criminals. Primary (and honorable) burials of criminals in family plots, however, were probably very rare exceptions, and limited to wealthier families like Yehohanan's.[355] The possibility of a family recovering a body at any time would depend on the temperament of the Roman authority in question.[356] It seems unlikely that family members would be allowed to gather in close proximity to the crucifixion site itself,[357] although spectators could probably gather at a distance given the continued human fascination with such spectacles. Proceedings for crucifixions seem engineered to make public mourning and normal burial practices difficult, which is not surprising given the inherent potential for vocal opposition in women's lamentation of the dead. This would particularly be the case in Roman-occupied Palestine.[358] However, women and families no doubt strained for a glimpse of arrested relatives, attempted to secure the remains of their loved ones, and continued to mourn their dead and visit their gravesites, if known. The custom of tomb and graveyard visitation by women and family lamenting their loved ones and bringing them food and gifts had thousands of years of tradition on its side. Women-led rituals remained sanctioned as stable and traditional features of Greek, Roman, and even Jewish religion.

Women, the Cult of the Dead, and Early Christianity

There is little doubt that the cult of the dead flourished among early Christian groups. Early Christians met at tombs and gravesites for

funerals of family and friends, but also for the eucharist.[359] There is
a long tradition of women's lamentation of the dead in the liturgical
tradition of the church. Women lamented the dead for their adjura-
tion and for the purposes of liturgical singing.[360] Women also participated fully in funerary meals of Christians, led the funerary meals, and
raised a cup at funerary meals to toast the dead and lead the group in
liturgical recitations.[361] Thus, there were really two places of meeting for early Christians: the "house church" (domus ecclesiae) and the
cemetery.[362] Evidence for the earliest material culture for early Christianity is a matter of dispute. In 1947, E. L. Sukenik, then one of
the foremost experts on Jewish ossuaries, published inscriptions from
Jewish ossuaries found in a tomb in a suburb of Jerusalem, Talpioth.
Sukenik claimed to have discovered first-century evidence for the
crucifixion of Jesus and the Jerusalem church.[363] Several ossuaries were
inscribed with names familiar to the New Testament, such as "Simon
Barsaba" and "Miriam the daughter of Simon," and "Mattai." In two
cases, Sukenik read the Talpioth ossuary inscriptions as referring to
the lamentation of Jesus' death. On ossuary number seven, Sukenik
read "Jesus, woe!" (Iesous oui). On ossuary number eight, Sukenik
read "Jesus, alas!" (Iesous aloth).[364] These inscriptions, combined with
the cross signs scratched on the ossuaries and a coin dated to 41–42 CE
found in the tomb, led Sukenik to conclude that these were early
Christian ossuaries. A lively debate ensued.[365] Ossuary inscriptions
usually give the name of the person whose bones are contained in the
ossuary. A second reading for the inscription from ossuary number
seven has been generally accepted as "Jesus (son of) Ju(das)."[366] The
second disputed inscription could refer to a place name: "Jesus (of)
Aloth."[367] However, the context of funerary rituals supplies the missing cultic context in which to understand the Talpioth inscriptions as
Sukenik understood them. The Talpioth ossuaries could therefore well
be evidence for the ongoing lamentation of Jesus' death among early
Christians in first-century Jerusalem. The cross marks found on these
ossuaries are probably protective taus rather than Christian crosses,
which function to protect the burial from being disturbed by evil spirits. These cross marks are also found in Jewish funerary inscriptions,
including Jewish inscriptions found in Roman catacombs.[368]

Other tombs have similarly been suggested as containing early
Jewish Christian ossuaries, particularly the Dominus Flevit tomb

on the Mount of Olives, in which were found over forty ossuaries inscribed with many names from the New Testament, cross marks, and at least one ChiRho symbol.[369] Near Bethany, on the Mount of Offence, archaeologists discovered a tomb chamber that appeared to be a storehouse for ossuaries in which there were found approximately thirty ossuaries with familiar New Testament names, including Mary, Martha, Simon, and Salome. One Mount of Offence ossuary of a woman, probably named Hedea, is inscribed with a Latin cross.[370] Given that both the ChiRho symbol and the Latin cross are post-Constantinian developments in Christian art and iconography,[371] it may well be that fourth-century Christians visited the tombs on the Mount of Offence and the Mount of Olives, and understood these to be early Christian tombs.[372] The burial of the woman Hedea would then have a clear precursor in ancient tomb cult practices, in which a notable tomb was reused.[373]

Although these are clearly late first-century tombs, the identification of the Dominus Flevit and Mount of Offence ossuaries as Jewish Christian, however, remains difficult. Early Christians had very common Jewish names. The cross symbols in most cases can be found in other clearly Jewish tombs. Ossuaries were in limited use in Palestine until the fourth century.[374] Thus, the material remains of Jewish burials and the proposed Christian burials are indistinguishable from one another. Byron McCane has shown that Christian burials in Palestine cannot be clearly distinguished from Jewish burials until the late fourth century.[375] Notably, two Syrian documents, the third-century *Didascalia Apostolorum* and the fourth-century *Apostolic Constitutions* encourage Christians to continue to worship in cemeteries without concern for ritual corpse impurity as observed by Jews.[376] It is these texts that should be considered as contemporaneous with rabbinic literature, not the New Testament. These texts reflect the later increased concern for corpse impurity among the general Jewish population outside of Jerusalem and the temple found in later Jewish literature. The *Didascalia Apostolorum* and the *Apostolic Constitutions* thus attest to a third-to-fourth-century change in Jewish practice as well as a change in Christian practice.[377] This means that at the same time as the Christian cult of the special dead and the cult of martyrs was growing in popularity, rabbinic writers were encouraging increased distance from the dead and from cemeteries. The cult of the martyrs eventually led to a major reorganization of cemeteries and the special dead in late antiquity, in that bones and relics were relocated within city limits and placed in church buildings.[378] However, if any of the Talpioth, Dominus Flevit, or Mount of Offence ossuaries are indeed Jewish Christian, this means that standard Jewish burial practices continued among Jewish Christians for hundreds of years in Palestine. This conclusion calls into question the common assumption of a decisive sectarian break between Judaism and Christianity in the late first century, at least in Palestine.[379]

The clearest archaeological evidence for early Christian culture is from other parts of the Roman Empire, including Italy (especially Rome), Dura-Europos, Ostia, Spain, Egypt, Asia Minor, and North Africa, and dates from 180 CE. This evidence is also funerary.[380] Pre-Constantinian catacomb art depicts Christians gathered for meals, but for meals that include not bread and wine but bread and fish (with or without wine), accompanied by cups and other utensils.[381] Fish is often found as a funerary offering in other ancient funerary art.[382] Given the funerary character of the evidence, it seems more likely that the fish depicted on tables with bread and or wine in Christian catacomb meal scenes is derived from the ancient use of fish in funerary offerings, which was eventually combined with eucharistic motifs due to the celebration of the eucharist as part of funerary meals.[383] Thus, the communal meals depicted in early Christian tombs and cemeteries should rather be seen as a continuation of the non-Christian meal for the dead, which was later interpreted as a eucharist in light of Jesus' feeding of thousands in the New Testament.[384] Graydon Snyder writes:

> The most powerful community developing force in the ancient world was the cult of the dead. It based the present and future on past loyalties and relationships. Early Christianity entered a social matrix where this was so. Early Christianity also continued that force.[385]

In fact, very recently, Ramsey MacMullen has well documented the continued popularity of the cult of the dead through the fourth century CE in spite of ecclesiastical hierarchies' efforts to eradicate such popular practices.[386] Christians continued these funerary practices, and Christian art shows that Christians continued the practice of the *Totnemahl*—the meal for the dead. The scenes in catacombs of meals with offerings of bread and fish are probably funerary meals. These meals lasted long into the night, with the telling of stories about the deceased. Sometimes these meals would become bawdy with inebriated excess. Again, church officials tried to limit these practices. Such attempts met with great resistance. Still, in spite of efforts to the contrary, Christians spent a lot of time banqueting with their dead in cemeteries and tombs. Finally, "the eucharist itself never really ceased to be a certain kind of funeral meal—a meal at which the once-dead hero is now living and present."[387]

Later church writers also continue to complain about the behavior of women at Christian wakes and funerals, including the participation of non-Christian women in funeral lamentation.[388] Again, writers express concern for controlling women mourners, both "virgins" and non-Christian women hired to sing dirges for funerals.[389] Eventually, churches gained control of funerals by bringing them into the church proper. Laments were eventually replaced with the singing of Psalms.[390] Eventually, the church eradicated the very singing of women, even of Psalms, in their liturgies.[391] However, later Christian leaders did not discourage their women constituents from identifying Christ with the dead god Adonis, which means that women lamented him.[392] In fact, Montanist Christian virgins continued a practice of prophetic lamentation that merged the annual grieving for Apollo/Attis with the idea of Jesus' passion and death.[393] In spite of Justin Martyr's claim that Christians did not bring offerings to their dead,[394] later church leaders also had trouble with continued feasting for the dead, both at graveyards and in church sanctuaries.[395] Early Christian apologists defended their communities against accusations that their meetings for the eucharist were drunken funeral orgies, complete with dogs leashed under the table to knock out the lights.[396]

We find the earliest reference to the celebration of the eucharist in a tomb in an early Christian novel called the *Acts of John* about the travels of the apostle John. The *Acts of John* was probably written in Syria around 150 CE.[397] In fact, much of the action in the *Acts of John* takes place in tombs, which further suggests the author's familiarity with tombs as a venue for Christian gatherings. Even a woman named Drusiana reports an appearance to her of the risen Lord as a "young man" as occurring in a tomb.[398] Significantly, however, the *Acts of John* also includes a very ancient piece of early Christian liturgy often called the "Round Dance" or "Hymn of Christ," which certain scholars argue was inserted into the *Acts of John*.[399] The hymn begins with Christ calling to his disciples to form a circle around him and to follow his song, answering "Amen." Midway through the antiphonal hymn, however, there is a break, and the lead seems to shift to a feminine figure: "Grace dances" (*charis*, fem.). This feminine figure then invites others present in the circle to join her in piping, mourning, praising, and dance:

> I will pipe,
> Dance, all of you—Amen
> I will mourn (*thrēneō*),
> Beat you all your breasts (*koptō*)—Amen
>
> He who does not dance
> does not know what happens.—Amen
>
> I am a door to you
> <who> knock on me.—Amen
> I am a way to you
> the traveller.—Amen
>
> Now if you follow my dance,
> see yourself
> in Me who am speaking,
> and when you have seen what I do,
> keep silence about my mysteries.
> You who dance, consider
> what I do, for yours is to suffer
> this passion of Man
> which I am to suffer.[400]

Following this "Hymn of Christ," the *Acts of John* continues with the story of the crucifixion. Here the second liturgical leader of the dance calls to the others to respond to (probably her) song, which begins with a call to lament. Although this hymn may indeed contain materials from revelation discourses that have been secondarily been incorporated into a round dance hymn,[401] it seems likely that such a hymn would have been composed more specifically for early Christian worship in funerary contexts rather than as a more general dance accompanied by song.[402] That the section of the hymn immediately following "Grace dances" contains references to lamentation and piping, as well as allusions to the mysteries, may be no coincidence. We can compare this kind of lamentation to laments sung in the *Isia* liturgy as well as with other hymns of Isis that follow a similar repetitious "I am" motif.[403] It is significant that this lament from the *Acts of John* includes allusions to the sayings tradition, both from the Gospel of John and the Synoptics (Q).[404] Augustine also quotes fragments of this lament liturgy.[405] The presence of this hymn combined with the repeated setting of scenes in tombs in the *Acts of John* suggests that some Christians in Syria met in tombs for the eucharist and passed on church traditions in the context of funerary liturgy. Further, combined with the evidence for women's roles in Isis lamentation liturgy, this evidence strongly suggests that the remythologization of Jesus as Wisdom by means of an interaction with Isis-like theology occurred within grassroots liturgical contexts, not just scribal ones. This liturgical interaction would better explain the early parallel to Isis mythology in pre-Pauline christological hymns found in the New Testament itself.[406] Finally, it should be remembered that early Christian martyrs were revered as early as the time of Polycarp, and by post-Constantinian times, the cult of the martyrs was well established. Women, the poor, and demoniacs were frequent visitors to the shrines of the martyrs.[407]

In spite of the tremendous cultural diversity distinguishing funerary practices within Greek, Roman, and Jewish religious practices at the grave, the continuity of women's roles of ritual lamentation within these cultures both at the grave and within other related liturgical contexts suggests that the location of the tomb or graveyard is an unexplored *Sitz im Leben*, or "life setting," for the development of early traditions about Jesus found in the Gospels and about early Christian liturgical traditions found in Paul. In fact, scholars have assumed that the usual assumed location for the development of oral traditions about Jesus was oral memorization in rabbinic schools, but this has only been documented for the third and fourth centuries CE. They have merely assumed the context of late rabbinic literature for the first century CE.[408] In comparison, the religious rituals of the cult of the dead and the mysteries have a history that spans thousands of years, including ritualized liturgy in which women played a documentable leadership role and formal meals that included both men and women. Funerary meals allowed for the free exchange of information between the sexes and provided an institutionalized context for the telling of stories of the departed loved one on a regular basis. Related ritual contexts allowed for the liturgical leadership of women in the ritual lamentation of dead gods and heroes. In particular, we can show that women's lament traditions have been transferred into literary and scribal contexts in Greek, Roman, Jewish, and Christian literature. Judaism in particular has a long tradition of formal laments that scholars suggest originated in popular lamentation.[409] Thus, the role of women in the cult of the dead and other occasions of ritual lamentation provide an alternative background for understanding the development of Gospel traditions such as the passion narrative and the empty tomb stories.

CHAPTER 3

CELEBRATORY MEALS OF THE KINGDOM OF GOD AND MEALS OF JESUS' PRESENCE

From Jesus to Q, the Didache, *and the Eucharist*

Open Commensality and the Parable of the Feast:
Celebratory Meals in the Movement of the Historical Jesus

Jesus met with his followers for meals. This seems to be a fact about the historical Jesus upon which historians may rely. There is various evidence for this in the Gospels, in the parables, in the tradition that Jesus ate and drank with "tax collectors and sinners/courtesans," and in the tradition that Jesus was a "glutton and a drunkard" who "feasted," whereas John the Baptist "fasted." The major parable that indicates this joining for an inclusive celebratory meal is the parable of the feast, found in the Gospel of Matthew, the Gospel of Luke, and the *Gospel of Thomas*. When read in conjunction with the tradition that Jesus welcomed "tax collectors and sinners" to his table, this parable does seem to suggest the invitation of women and the poor to the kingdom of God (Matt 22:2-13; Luke 14:16-24). Here, the theme of the unexpected nature of the kingdom of God has its clearest expression. In this parable, Jesus overturns ancient social paradigms of honor and wealth in a depiction of a feast for the lowly and the derelict rather than one for the customary guests of rank and privilege. Borg, Crossan, and Schüssler Fiorenza all focus on the message of the parable of the feast and Jesus' table practice as a sign of his egalitarian ethic.[1] Both Borg and Schüssler Fiorenza see Jesus as opening up the banquet of the kingdom to the unclean; Jesus overturns purity regulations by eating with women.[2] Crossan and Luise Schottroff see Jesus' egalitarianism as reflective of a peasant mentality or a consequence of his impoverishment. Jesus' parable of the feast thus portrays the kingdom of God as a large inclusive meal to which people from all levels of society are invited, including women (Matt 22:1-14; Luke 14:16-24; *Gos. Thom.* 64:1-12).[3]

Such arguments require some nuance. First, the argument that Jesus here challenges purity regulations is unlikely since, as was noted earlier, Jews may not have been overly concerned with purity outside of the temple and because rabbinic sources emphasizing purity issues postdate the New Testament. Recent reconstructions of the Qumran community suggest that even the purity-conscious sectarians at Qumran could have allowed women to join certain ritual meals. Thus, concern over Jesus' table practice is more likely to have been a matter of propriety than purity.[4]

Second, the point of the parable of the feast does not hinge on the issue of gender but on that of class or rank. Any application of the parable to the situation of women would therefore have been strictly secondary. One could argue that women are invited as being among the poor, the sick, and the street people, but the point of the parable is not to invite *women* to the feast, but to invite the underclasses. Jesus here does not defend the right of women to join him at table. Given the strong likelihood that Greco-Roman culture pervaded Palestine, and with it the customary presence of women at meals with men, it seems more plausible that inclusion of women at Jesus' meals reflects progressive (although controversial) cultural practices found throughout

Greco-Roman society and in Hellenistic Judaism rather than a peasant egalitarian ideology or Sophia-inspired prophetic vision.

In fact, later Gospel portrayals of Jesus at meals do not show him taking a particularly radical stance. For example, in the story of his meal with Mary and Martha (Luke 10:38-42), Jesus does encourage Mary, who is seated at his feet. However, although such a position does indicate that Mary is receiving instruction, her posture reflects a more conservative, matronly role, and she remains silent throughout the scene. The more radical stance would have been to invite Mary to recline with him like an equal on a banquet couch, as Jesus does with Salome in the *Gospel of Thomas* (*Gos. Thom.* 61). In these Lukan stories, Jesus does not appear radical in his relationships with women; it is the women who are bold, not Jesus.

In order to derive from the feast parable an egalitarian meaning, we must read it in conjunction with one other piece of evidence from the Jesus tradition, the accusation that Jesus dined with "tax collectors and sinners" (Mark 2:15; Q 7:34). This accusation reflects typical characterizations of those known for banqueting with tax collectors, pimps, and prostitutes. The very imagery of disreputable banquet behavior calls to mind the presence of lewd women, slaves, and courtesans—the kind of women present in a typical Hellenistic banquet scene. We should thus view this accusation as a standard charge of Hellenistic rhetoric and not necessarily indicative of the occupations or morals of Jesus' actual table companions. Both Mark and Q imply that Jesus ate with women, and thus was a participant in the social progressivism of his day.[5] Again, however, the force of this tradition maintains between Jesus and his dining companions a distinction that remains one of class, not necessarily sex differentiation. Jesus is here accused of dining with those who are beneath his station. Dennis E. Smith writes:

> The strongest evidence for the open commensality theme in the Jesus tradition is the theme that Jesus dined with tax collectors and sinners. Yet, this theme only works best if Jesus is not of the same social level with tax collectors and sinners. If all parties involved, including Jesus, are peasants, then the motif fails, for there is no experience of social stratification at table.[6]

If Jesus or all of his followers are of the same low social class, then the force of the insult leveled against him is lost. Smith argues that John Dominic Crossan, although having made a good case for an egalitarian table ethic in Jesus' movement, undercuts his proposition by turning Jesus into a peasant.[7] Still, it is possible to maintain a lower social location for Jesus as long as it is recognized that there would have been those even beneath his social station in ancient Palestine, particularly slaves.[8] The feast parable would then reflect Jesus' resistance to authority on behalf of those beneath his station, including perhaps women of the lower classes, even though they are not the focus of the feast parable proper.

That said, it is still possible to identify one tradition, which some scholars consider both early and authentic, that suggests Jesus himself defended the presence of women among his followers by deflecting slander leveled against them. Probably going back in some form to Q[9] is the statement of Jesus that links women to both his movement and to that of John the Baptist:

> Truly I say to you, the tax collectors and the harlots go into the kingdom of God before you. For John came to you in righteousness, and you did not believe him, but the tax collectors and the harlots believed him; and even when you saw it, you did not afterward repent and believe him (Matt 21:31b-32 RSV).

Here Jesus calls the women entering the kingdom of God "whores." As I have suggested, taken as a repeated form of slander leveled against Jesus and his table companions rather than as a social description of some of his followers, this would indicate that he was well aware of the controversial nature of his group, including the presence of women. He accepted the label of the women around him as "whores," possibly in bitter jest, even as the basis of a bitingly sarcastic riposte. His opponents accused him of consorting with "tax collectors and whores," but he responds that those so labeled will enter the kingdom of God first. To claim an insult robs it of its power. Of course, Jesus' use of snide humor implies discomfort as well as acceptance. By using the gender-stereotypical label of "whores" for the women in his group, Jesus identifies the underlying cause of the tension aroused by the presence of women among his followers—their difference. So employed, humor seeks to relieve tension through laughter while at the same time serving to incorporate women in a predominantly male group.[10] In sum, this saying does not identify the women in Jesus' group as actual prostitutes but merely repeats a slander leveled against women whose bad reputations are due either to their socially progressive behavior or to their low social status.[11] That Jesus could have expressed his discomfort with the presence of women in his company by means of snide humor suggests either the resistant attitude of lower-class peasants or a wit informed by the currents of Greco-Roman philosophy present in first-century Palestine, or both.[12] Thus, the parable of the feast, in combination with the typical characterization of his dining companions as "tax collectors, sinners, and whores," suggests that Jesus' teaching on open commensality was inclusive of women and those beneath Jesus' station, such as domestic servants and slaves.

Meals with "Tax Collectors and Sinners"
(Q 7:33-34)

Another major tradition that links Jesus to celebratory meals is his eating and drinking with "tax collectors and sinners." In Q 7:34, Jesus is insulted for his table practice, one that supposedly features "wine bibbing and gluttony." He is also accused of being a "friend of tax collectors and sinners." This characterization of Jesus' activities appears also in Mark 2:14-17; most historical Jesus scholars consider it to be an authentic tradition,[13] since they are persuaded that these passages involve groups that can be identified within the social environment of first-century Palestine.[14] "Tax collectors" (or "toll collectors")[15] are usually identified as despicable because of their relationship with the Roman occupational forces,[16] their connection with "robbers,"[17] or their basic dishonesty.[18] For Jews to eat with them would therefore have been considered scandalous, not only in view of their occupation and lifestyle, but out of concern for becoming ritually impure in their company.[19] Or such behavior could simply have been considered immoral.[20] The term "sinners" is similar. Many scholars identify "sinners" with those who would have been considered ritually impure, particularly by Pharisees. These would have been the ʿammê hāʾāreṣ, that is, all non-Pharisees with whom Pharisees would have been prohibited from eating, though the number of Pharisees actually affected by such restrictions would have been small.[21] Narrower definitions of "sinners" have also been suggested, such as those known for habitual sin or those unwilling to repent.[22] Still others suggest that these "sinners" were Jews who lived like Gentiles or rejected the practice of the law.[23] "Sinners" were also associated with all those involved in lower-class service occupations, including former slaves.[24] Some scholars have even argued that the category of "sinners" would have included women generally, or particularly those with bad reputations, or prostitutes.[25] However, it cannot be substantiated that the practice of eating with those characterized as "sinners" would in and of itself have been contrary to Jewish purity regulations.[26] It is further unlikely that the mere presence of women at meals would have violated Jewish purity regulations, and especially not in the context of everyday or celebratory meals.[27] Rather, as previously noted, the complaint of Jewish envoys to Caesar that Herod allowed their women to participate in Roman orgies suggests that their concern was not purity but propriety.[28]

In fact, since eating with "tax collectors and sinners" was probably less a purity issue than a matter of propriety, "tax collectors and sinners" may not have been a designation for two historically identifiable groups at all. Rather, "eating with tax collectors and sinners" may simply have been a stereotypical way of insulting someone's way of life regarding customary behavior at meals.[29] The accusation in Q may simply be a swipe at Jesus' table etiquette. For example, that Jesus is "friends" with tax collectors and sinners certainly implies that he eats with them. "Friendship" is a common banquet theme.[30]

Such a characterization also reflects typical depictions of those known for banqueting with "promiscuous" women and pimps, for in antiquity, tax collectors were often linked to prostitution. In ancient Greece, special tax gatherers known as *pornotelōnai*, who kept lists of licensed harlots, collected state revenue.[31] Prostitutes were not taxed during the Roman period until the reign of Caligula (37–41 CE), but they were still required to register to ply their trade.[32] Thus, tax collecting and keeping a brothel still remained linked in Hellenistic literature. We can also find this association in first-century Palestine.[33] Because of these stereotypical associations, rhetoricians and others used tax collecting and brothel keeping as a means to slander groups or individuals. Thus, Plutarch remarks that the Spartans slighted the Athenians for collecting taxes and keeping brothels,[34] and Dio Chrysostom remarks of rulers, "Is it not plain to see that many who are called kings (*basileis*) are only traders, tax collectors (*telōnai*), and keepers of brothels (*pornoboskoi*)?"[35] Brothel keepers, of course, would have been expected to have prostitutes in their company.[36]

Not only was the term *tax collector* associated with those who kept company with promiscuous women, prostitutes, and pimps, but the term *sinner* likewise held connotations of sexual impropriety. Certain behavior identified Hellenistic persons as "sinners," and the term was particularly applied to those who participated in sexual misconduct, such as drunkards, male prostitutes, men who chased women, and adulterers.[37] In Hellenistic literature, *hamartōlos* usually designated either a person's lack of education or a moral failure of some kind,[38] and as such appears in Hellenistic catalogues of virtues and vices, where it is roughly equivalent to the Latin *sceleste*.[39] Plutarch uses it in the first sense as slander against his Stoic opponents.[40] Luke uses the term to designate a "woman of the city" (a prostitute) who anoints Jesus at a meal (Luke 7:37).[41]

This background reinforces the recent suggestion that "sinners" (*hamartōloi*) is best understood in the context of Jewish sectarianism and philosophical debate, where it was used as rhetorical slander to denounce fellow Jews who did not belong to one's particular sect.[42] Dennis Smith has suggested that both "sinners" and "tax collectors" should be understood in this manner. Thus, according to Smith, the entire phrase "tax collectors and sinners" should be categorized as a *topos* in Greco-Roman Jewish polemic.[43] Although the use of the term *sectarian* to describe first-century Jewish groups may not be helpful for understanding the relationship of these groups to one another,[44] it remains the case that these groups engaged in polemic and verbal exchange.[45] Thus, the accusation that Jesus associated with "tax collectors and sinners" is an example of the caricature of polemic rather than social description.[46]

As noted above, the connection between these two terms and their use together as slander against Jesus' or his followers' table practice is apt, as tax collectors are connected in Greco-Roman literature to those who trafficked in prostitution and slavery, particularly to brothel keepers and pimps, those most responsible for supplying women and slaves for banquets.[47] And it was common for demeaning portraits of individuals to include insults leveled against their table practice and dining companions. To malign Verres, for example, Cicero pictures his degenerate behavior at banquets with lewd women.[48] In view of such a model, it is hardly surprising to find *telōnai* combined with *pornai* (Matt 21:31), nor is it startling that Luke should portray a prostitute at a meal in staging his dramatic narrative about Jesus' attitude toward "sinners" (Luke 7:36ff.).[49]

Certain Q scholars have remarked that Q 7:34 makes Jesus out to be some kind of "party boy" or "party animal."[50] However, the Hellenistic evidence suggests that this kind of language in Q 7:34 is merely the language of insult and tells us little about Jesus' actual behavior, nor can it be used to identify Jesus' table companions in Q as real "tax collectors" or "sinners."[51] Even the accusation against Jesus' lifestyle in Q 7:31-35 as a "wine bibber and glutton" reflects the Deuteronomic theme of the "rebellious son" who keeps company with "harlots." Far from a trivial allegation, being a "rebellious son" is a serious indictment.[52] The "wine bibber and a glutton" charge and the accusation of eating with "tax collectors and sinners" are similar insults. The force of "tax collectors and sinners" is connotative rather than denotative, and mainly identifies Jesus or his followers as opponents.[53] It is said of John, "He has a demon." No one has ever taken seriously the reported claim that John had a demon (Luke 7:33), or speculated about what kind of demon he had.[54] Both attacks are simply insults disparaging the respective lifestyles of Jesus and John.[55]

Given the links between "tax collectors" and prostitution, "sinners" and sexual impropriety, and banqueting and consorting with lewd women at meals, such slander also suggests that Jesus is here being accused of eating with "promiscuous" women. Women were often accused of promiscuity for public behavior generally, particularly when they participated in unorthodox table etiquette or engaged in free association with men in the public sphere.[56] In fact, we also find the accusation of meretricious behavior in the context of philosophical repartee, in particular as a term bandied about by philosophical groups in the habit of slandering one another when debating the relative merits of one another's philosophical systems.[57] The use of this kind of slander reveals the presence of women in certain philosophical groups. The Cynic school in particular was notable for its inclusion of women like Hipparchia and for their defense of women's ability to study philosophy and achieve moral virtue.[58] Epicureans included women in their circles[59] who had diverse social backgrounds; some were slaves and courtesans, others were respectably married.[60] The Stoic philosopher Musonius Rufus also encouraged teaching women philosophy, albeit for the purpose of making them better housewives and mothers.[61] Given the rivalry between philosophical groups and the controversial nature of the presence of women in groups usually restricted to men, it is not surprising that these groups used cultural stereotypes of women to insult each other. Since the attainment of a philosophical education was common among ancient Greek courtesans, women in these groups could have been called "prostitutes" by rival philosophical sects.[62] Various religious groups in antiquity were also accused of sexual immorality, particularly in regard to women members. Groups so accused included early Christianity and Judaism, as well as adherents to the cults of Isis and Dionysius.[63] The term *prostitute*, then, as well as the general accusation of sexual promiscuity in regard to women in a group, should be recognized as a common form of insult leveled against women in antiquity, and therefore numbered among the Hellenistic *topoi* of Greco-Roman polemics.[64]

Hence, the report in Q 7:34 implies that Jesus was slandered for eating with women, and thus was a participant in the social progressivism of his day, as were Cynics, Epicureans, Stoics, and others who allowed women to attend philosophical symposia and other public or religious meals. It further betrays the presence of women in the Q community and identifies the Jesus movement as one of the numerous Jewish and other Hellenistic groups that was affected by changing Greco-Roman meal customs. The meals of Jesus were thus known for celebration, drinking, and socially mixed company.

The Children of the Marketplace
(Q 7:31-32)

Another passage found in Q that further associates Jesus with banquet revelry and thus women is the so-called "children of the marketplace" pericope in Q 7:31-32. This passage immediately precedes the
accusation of Jesus' dining with "tax collectors and sinners." The
rejection of Jesus and John reported in Q 7:33-34 is also implicit in Q
7:31-32. John came fasting, and he was not accepted; Jesus came "eating and drinking," and he was not accepted. Again, this implies that
the criticism of John and Jesus was a criticism not of their preaching
but of their respective lifestyles.[65]

The Q redactor uses the marketplace pericope to elaborate this
comparison:

To what will I compare this generation?

They are like children sitting in the marketplace
[*paidiois tois en agora kathēmenois*] and calling to one another:

"We played the flute for you and you did not dance;
we wailed [*thrēneō* and you did not weep [*klaiō*]." (NRSV)

The word "children" in both 7:32 and 7:35 has been variously interpreted. However, in spite of the lack of parallelism between the two
sections, it seems clear that the activities of the children in 7:32 (piping and mourning) roughly correspond to the activities of Jesus and
John in 7:33-34 (feasting and fasting), at least in this Q context.[66]
In Q, however, Jesus and John are the "children" (*tekna*) of Wisdom
(v. 35).[67] Thus, those who refuse to respond are "this generation,"
that is, the same opponents who accuse John of having a demon and
Jesus of being a "wine bibber" and "glutton." Likewise, the followers
of Jesus and John are "children" of Wisdom who "call" out to others
who also refuse to respond.[68] In Luke, those who respond to the call of

Jesus and John are likened to the woman "sinner" who "weeps" (*klaiō*) at the feet of Jesus (Luke 7:38).[69] Thus, according to Luke, implicit in the marketplace pericope is some kind parallel between women such as this sinner/prostitute and the followers of Jesus and John.

Although it must be admitted that without the necessary historical and social background the image seems anomalous, Luke's understanding of this section of Q can be easily explained. First, it is unlikely that the image in Q 7:32 is meant to call to mind children acting like adults seated in judgment in the marketplace, as Wendy Cotter has suggested.[70] Although the diminutive of *pais* can indeed mean "child," either a boy or a girl up to the age of seven or so, the activities of these "children" do not really suggest children at play so much as banquet or funeral musicians. These could be men or women, free or slave. In Judaism, hired mourners were more commonly women.[71] In fact, one could expect to find slaves or day laborers waiting in the marketplace to be hired, especially since slave owners often sent their unoccupied slaves to the marketplace to look for extra work.[72] Here they display their wares, as it were, by piping and wailing. The tomb painting from Marissa discussed in chapter 2 nicely illustrates this social custom. The painting depicts two funerary musicians, a man and a woman, both dressed in funerary attire. The man leads, playing the flute, while the woman follows with a harp.[73] The activities of these "children" (piping and mourning) certainly explain the use of the diminutive of *pais* (*to paidion*, "young child" but also "servant" or "slave") in this instance.[74]

Flute playing and mourning were stereotypically associated with women,[75] who often performed public mourning of this nature.[76] Many of them came not only from the family of the deceased but from the ranks of prostitutes, and were especially found among the lower class of skilled slavewomen or day laborers often hired to serve, entertain, and play musical instruments for banquets.[77] However, such women would similarly be hired to play instruments and mourn at funerals.[78] Flute players could also be men.[79] This kind of banquet or funeral help may have been young, but it is it not their youth that catches the attention of the Q redactor, rather the similarities of their activities (piping and mourning) to Jesus' and John's (eating and drinking/fasting). Thus, although *tekna* in 7:35 tends to indicate young children,[80] the *paidia* of 7:32 are still best understood as slaves or day laborers waiting in the marketplace to be hired for banquets or funerals. Furthermore, even if this group of musicians and mourners is understood as children and not hired adults or slaves, the mixed-gendered nature of this image still remains: boys *and girls* pipe and mourn in the marketplace, not simply boys.[81] The redactor of Q has used this parable as an example of the contrast between the lifestyles of Jesus and John: Jesus "feasts" (pipes), whereas John "fasts" (mourns) (cf. Mark 2:18-19). Jesus' activity is likened to that of flute players awaiting hire to play at a dinner party, whereas John's is likened to professional mourners awaiting hire to mourn at a funeral.[82]

The accusation leveled against Jesus in Q 7:34 fits neatly with the characterization of the situation of the opposition to Wisdom's envoys by "this generation" in Q 7:32. Both sections of this Q passage employ stereotypical banquet imagery. Subsequently, as the "children/servants" of Wisdom can also be understood to include those who have responded to the message of Wisdom's prophets, especially Jesus, these new envoys of Wisdom, or the Q "mission," are likewise compared to those hired either to play music for a dinner party or mourn at a funeral. Thus, both John and Jesus are here tacitly accused of having women, hirelings, and slaves among their followers, John in the context of a funeral, Jesus in the context of a banquet. As this implies the presence of women among their followers, it subsequently associates women, hirelings, and slaves with both "envoys" of Wisdom—Jesus and John. Q 7:33-34 thus already presupposes the parallel between Jesus and John found in Luke 7:29 // Matt 21:31-32.[83] The controversial nature of the image notwithstanding, it is one that is inclusive of—and, one could argue—even more characteristic of women's roles than men's. It must be admitted, however, that the Q redactor shows little interest in the gendered overtones of the marketplace parable, nor does he use this parable explicitly to identify Jesus' followers or the Q prophets with women. The attention in the text falls on the similarity of the activities described in Q 7:31-32 and Q 7:34-35, not its gendered overtones. The mourners suggest fasting (John's activity), the pipers represent feasting (Jesus' activity). Both Jesus and John are emissaries ("children," *tekna*) of Wisdom.

Still, the fact that the parable likens the activity of these children/servants to "this generation," which is usually a designation of Jesus' opponents in Q as well as a sign of the Q redactor's hand, is problematic.[84] Scholars often take the lack of parallelism between Q 7:31-32 and Q 7:34-35 as an indication that the placement of this parable in Q is secondary.[85] This case can be strengthened if the parable is taken out of its Q context entirely and considered on its own terms. Without Jesus' "eating and drinking" and John's "fasting" (Q 7:34-35), the image of the pipers and mourners becomes an image of mourning activities alone, not banqueting and mourning activities respectively. The antiphonal nature of the piping and mourning may be the key to its original meaning. We can better understand the lack of response inherent in the image of the parable in the context of ritual lamentation, in which calling back and forth between mourners was commonplace. Seen in this light, there are two sides to this encounter in the marketplace.[86] One side of the mourners criticizes the other for refusing to participate in antiphonal mourning: "We piped to you, and you did not dance, we wailed and you did not weep" (Q 7:31-32). The stronger term for mourning found in the Matthean version (Matt 11:17, "you did not beat your breast in grief" [koptō]), long a problem for translators and interpreters in relationship to the play of children, is thus probably earlier, original to Q, and a designation for mourning, not childplay.[87] "This generation," usually a designation of those opposed to Jesus and the Q prophets, objects to those who do not participate in mourning rituals. Although the Q redactor has used this parable for another purpose, once it is removed from its Q context, its meaning is clear, for it corresponds nicely with early traditions that indicate Jesus (and his subsequent followers) rejected certain burial customs (Q 9:60). Thus, rather than mourning and fasting, Jesus and his followers were known for their celebratory meals of the kingdom of God. These meals did not emphasize Jesus' presence at the meal, but rather community inclusivity and celebration.

"Let the Dead Bury Their Own Dead" and the Fatherhood of God

Few dispute that Jesus addressed God as Father.[88] Based on the work of Joachim Jeremias, many Christian scholars have affirmed the special nature of Jesus' relationship to God on the basis of this title and have argued that Jesus' use of the term *abba* set him apart from both Hellenistic Judaism and the early church.[89] Robert Hamerton-Kelly further asserted the antipatriarchal nature of Jesus' theology in the wake of feminist critiques of the use of titles like *father* for God.[90] Certain feminist scholars followed Hamerton-Kelly's example in their reconstructions of the message of Jesus.[91] Mary Rose D'Angelo has documented this discussion and successfully called all aspects of it into question.[92] Jewish texts in first-century Palestine, most notably from Qumran,[93] give evidence for the use of the term *father* as an address to God both in general declarative statements and in prayer. Further, linguistic analysis of the use of the Aramaic *abba* does not support a specialized meaning conveying the intimacy between father and child.[94] Rather, the title *father* evoked the power, divine authority, and kingship of the Jewish God in the face of Roman Imperial propaganda.[95] D'Angelo argues that presupposing as it does the superiority of men within society, it cannot convey an antipatriarchal meaning. *Father* is the highest title of authority only within a social system in which privileged men have power over women, children, and such lesser males such as slaves, freedmen and, clients.[96] Therefore, if Jesus addressed God as his father, he did so within the context of a Hellenistic Judaism that revered its God as king in an empire that demanded fealty to the emperor (cf. Mark 12:17 // Luke 20:25 // Matt 22:21; *Gos. Thom.* 100:2-3).

Yet the evidence that Jesus applied the title *Father* to God is slight. It is limited to Mark 14:36, when Jesus prays to God in the Garden of Gethsemane, the Lord's Prayer in Q (Luke 11:2b // Matt 6:9), and also from Q the so-called Johannine Thunderbolt (Luke 10:21-22 // Matt 11:25-27).[97] But only with great difficulty can one ascribe to Jesus the use of *abba* for God in Mark 14:36, given that it occurs in a section of Mark that is undeniably a Markan composition. For one thing, Jesus is alone; no one can witness to his words. Second, Mark casts Jesus as one in a line of Jewish martyrs.[98] Further, since *abba* was used liturgically in the early church (the spirit causes believers to cry out "Abba, father!" [*abba ho patēr*] [Gal 4:6; Rom 8:15]),[99] the use of Aramaic does not suggest that here we have Jesus' actual words. Thus, the cry of Jesus in the Garden of Gethsemane almost certainly does not go back to Jesus. Similarly, Jesus' claim of a special relationship with the Father in Luke 10:21-22 // Matt 11:25-27 reflects Q's identification of Jesus with the figure of Wisdom and is therefore not likely to represent

Jesus' understanding of God or himself.[100] The Lord's Prayer, derived from Q, thus remains the only identification of God as *patēr* ("father") that can reasonably be attributed to Jesus himself. Yet there is no compelling reason to assume that the Aramaic "Abba" lies behind this address. No recensions of the Lord's Prayer read "Abba," nor is there any evidence that the Lord's Prayer was composed in anything but Greek.[101] Given that *Father* appears as an address in Jewish prayer of the period, D'Angelo is right to conclude that "it is not surprising to find Jesus employing in prayer an address to God that called Caesar's reign into question and made a special claim on God's protection, mercy, and providence."[102]

Still, D'Angelo's discussion accounts neither for the absence of fathers from Jesus' ideal family nor for the generational nature of the dispute fostered by Jesus' message. The context of a Jewish anti-imperial theology does not by itself explain either Jesus' address of God as father or the incidence of family conflict created by his message.

However, another controversy within Judaism could well explain Jesus' interest in God as the true father. In Judaism, as in other religions of the ancient Mediterranean, there existed a complex of family rituals surrounding the burial of family members: it is commonly referred to as the cult of the dead. Women usually dominated this family cult, although within Judaism, men were also active in mourning rites. Ceremonies included funeral liturgies and feasts, frequent visits to the burial place, and the offering of foodstuffs to the deceased, who was thought to be in need of sustenance following death.[103] These practices were condemned by a number of Jewish prophets and assailed in other biblical writings, as I discussed in chapter 2.

In Jesus' day, care of the dead included rites of reburial. After the body of a loved one had decayed, the bones were carefully placed in a bone box called an ossuary, which was then placed in a niche in the family tomb. Rather than being restricted to a particular group of Jews such as the Pharisees or the upper classes, such reburials are now considered to have been performed more generally.[104] Even the high priest Caiaphas and his family were reburied in ossuaries.[105] Recall that, as we saw in chapter 2, evidence in inscriptions that parents named their children after family members rather than popular biblical figures may reflect Hellenistic influence, but it also clearly shows that Palestinian Jews in the Second Temple period were interested

in Jewish ancestral lines.[106] We also saw in chapter 2 that the veneration of special prophets and patriarchs was a well-established practice in first-century Palestine. Evidence includes tombs dedicated
to the Patriarchs and Matriarchs, Rachel, the Maccabean martyrs,
the prophetess Hulda, the prophet Isaiah, the prophet Zechariah ben
Judah, and a necropolis of kings near Jerusalem, all of which were
extant at the time of Jesus.[107] Making pilgrimages to these tombs and
monuments[108] is precisely the custom that is being criticized in Q
11:47-51 (Luke 11:47-51 // Matt 23:29-36).[109] Several of these special tomb monuments, such as Zechariah's, are still standing in the
Kidron Valley,[110] and in Bethlehem, a tomb monument to Rachel still
remains.[111] Depictions of these tombs of the special dead can be found
as ossuary decorations, further attesting to their popularity during
the first century.[112] Jewish writers are found debating the efficacy
of prayer to prophets and "fathers." So, for example, Deborah was
portrayed in the first-century *Biblical Antiquities* as exhorting, "Do
not hope in your fathers (*patres*)." I observed in chapter 2 that this
exhortation would have discouraged veneration of Deborah herself
as a dead prophetess and matriarch.[113] In 2 Baruch, the writer envisions a future in which such prayers to the ancestors and prophets will
cease.[114] John the Baptist warns his contemporaries not to depend on
Abraham as their Father (Matt 3:7-10 // Luke 3:7-9).

Within this context, I would like to place a series of sayings attributed to Jesus that suggest both a generational dispute over burials and
disapprobation of practices involving veneration of the dead:

> To another [Jesus] said, "Follow me." But he said, "Lord, let me go
> first and bury my father." But he said to him, "Leave the dead to bury
> their own dead; but as for you, go and proclaim the kingdom of God."
> (Luke 9:59 // Matt 8:21)[115]

> Where the corpse is, there the eagles with be gathered together. (Luke
> 17:37 // Matt 24:28)[116]

> Become passersby. (*Gos. Thom.* 42)[117]

> Woe to you! for you are like unmarked graves, and people who walk
> over them do not know it. (Luke 11:44 // Matt 23:27)[118]

Woe to you! for you build the tombs of the prophets but it was your fathers that killed them. (Luke 11:47 // Matt 23:29)[119]

Call no man your father on earth. (Matt 23:6-11)[120]

Scholars usually consider the saying on the dead burying their dead authentic. Since burial rites for parents were a special responsibility, this saying would have been particularly offensive to many. Accordingly, most scholars have interpreted it to mean "let the (spiritually) dead bury the (physically) dead."[121] However, Byron McCane has argued persuasively that this saying refers not to initial burial but to reburial, particularly the practice of reburial in ossuaries. Jesus would then be saying, "Let the dead (in the tombs) rebury their own dead," and thus denouncing special attention to the dead as contrary to his teaching of the kingdom of God.[122] The saying from the *Gospel of Thomas* (42) can also be read to betray a similar critique of the over-attention to graves: "Become passersby" (*sope etet n rparage*) may well allude to the phrase *passersby* common in ancient grave epitaphs. The point would be to keep on walking.[123] The saying on eagles and corpses (Q17:37) seems to express a similar distaste for burials: vultures were birds of carrion, in the same class with ravens and crows.[124] This teaching of Jesus is the most likely to foster a family generational dispute, as it denies the legitimacy of burial practices that children traditionally owed to their parents. Biblical writers and prophets regularly censured excessive concern with tombs, corpses, and burials—to one's "fathers" or ancestors—as being at odds with true Hebraic monotheism. Jesus' concern was similar.

But this does not fully explain the witty harshness of these sayings, which fit better in a Hellenistic context. We have seen that Theodore the Atheist's comment when threatened with death without burial, "What matters it if I rot on the earth or under it?" was popular among Cynics, Epicureans, and Stoics, who considered solicitude for the dead a matter of superstition.[125] And Socrates was similarly indifferent to his own burial: to the question how he would like to be buried he replied, "However you please, if you can catch me."[126] Other philosophers, especially Cynics, expressed a similar lack of concern for the disposal of their remains.[127] Thus, Jesus' saying has a clear Hellenistic flavor to it, although the underlying concern is Hebraic, not Greek.

Likely enough, Jesus also rejected the practice of venerating the dead at tombs. The woes against the Pharisees involving graves and the tombs of the prophets should be reconsidered as evidence for the historical Jesus. Many scholars reject these sayings because they betray the influence of a Deuteronomic view of history and therefore tend to presuppose the situation following Jesus' death.[128] While that is certainly the case for Luke 11:49-51 // Matt 23:34-36, there are several reasons to consider the less complex sayings in Luke 11:44, 49 // Matt 23:27, 29 as authentic. First, Q 11:47-48 is not so obviously Deuteronomic and is detachable from Q 11:49-51.[129] Second, O. H. Steck has argued that by the first century CE two themes in prophetic thought had coalesced: (1) the Deuteronomic view of history that assumed that God's judgment was precipitated by Israel's disobedience to God's law and (2) the notion that prophets were habitually killed by Israel (cf. Neh 9:26). According to Steck, this blended theme was an oral tradition readily widespread in Palestinian Judaism between 200 BCE and 100 CE.[130] Hence, Jesus' words in Q 11:47-48 do not presuppose his death, and may make good sense for the situation following the death of John the Baptist. It is therefore not necessary to consider the entire section of the woes against the Pharisees in Matt 23:27-36 // Luke 11:44-51 inauthentic. Jesus could well be reproaching the Pharisees for participating in a documentable and popular institution from first-century Palestine, the veneration of popular prophets and patriarchs at special tombsites. This scenario accords well with the widespread view that Jesus was a prophetic figure who defended a strict view of Hebraic monotheism.

Clearly, Matthew understood these imprecations. As a precursor to the woes against the Pharisees, Matthew quotes Jesus as saying:

> Call no man your Father on earth, for you have one Father who is in heaven. (Matt 23:9 RSV)

This is a Matthean addition to Mark 12:37b-40, the question concerning the greatest commandment, which Matthew connects to one of the Q passages in which Jesus attacks the popular veneration of the prophets (Q 11:47-48). This suggests a concern not for family, marriage, or patriarchy, but for monotheism. Here, emphasizing and expanding on a theme that I suggest was fundamental to Jesus' own teaching, Matthew reasserts Hebraic monotheism according to classic prophetic style: God sends prophets who preach repentance, but Israel persecutes and subsequently kills them.

Jesus' concern for the veneration of prophets at tombsites readily comports with the saying "Let the dead bury their own dead," which criticized the reburial of "fathers" as contrary to the vision of the kingdom of God. Both would reflect an ongoing concern within Judaism going back to exilic times. The presence of such a prophetic theme in Jesus' teaching would best explain the repeated characterization of Jesus as a prophet[131] without denying the Hellenistic flavor of many of his sayings.[132] Further, according to Q, Jesus taught that the judgment would come unnoticed in the midst of everyday activities (Luke 11:26-32 // Matt 24:37-39; Luke 17:34-35 // Matt 24:40-41).[133] That is, most would not notice that there was anything amiss. Similarly, burial customs were so much a part of the culture it is easy to imagine that few would have considered them objectionable.

That Jesus repudiated extravagant burial practices for parents and the veneration of patriarchs and special prophets at tombs makes better sense of his omission of fathers from the ideal family (Mark 3:33-35) and the generational nature of family divisions fostered by his message as found in Q (Luke 12:52-53 // Matt 10:35-36; Luke 14:25-27; Matt 10:37). Burial customs are essential to the workings of any culture, and Jesus' challenge to traditional practices, even ancient practices considered at odds with Jewish monotheistic tradition, would have been highly offensive and caused deep divisions within households.[134] This theme of Jesus' teachings demonstrates both the Hebraic aspects of his message, but also its Hellenistic flavor, reflecting as it does both prophetic monotheistic interests and the mordant wit of Hellenistic aphorisms expressing a lack of interest in burial. The easy intertwining of these two influences in Jesus' message should warn us against glibly characterizing him as either a prophetic character or a Cynic, but it does allow for his assimilation in the culturally eclectic environment of Palestine and Lower Galilee. These celebratory meals that did not invoke Jesus' presence persisted in Galilee and Syria after Jesus' death, as evidenced by the feast parables found in Q and the *Gospel of Thomas*. Further, both communities persisted in Jesus' command not to attend to the dead. Neither community celebrated the resurrection of Jesus.

Meals of Jesus' Presence: From the Didache to the Eucharist

The *Didache* contains what is probably the most archaic form of the early Christian communion meal. It has long puzzled commentators, as it contains no words of institution, and the loaf and cup sequence is inverted from other eucharistic prayers. It also has Jewish elements, such as prayer elements that scholars believe originated from the Jewish *Birkat Ha-Mazon*. Various places of origin have been suggested for this ancient document, which dates from the mid-first century to the mid-second century. Scholars have suggested Antioch in Syria, Egypt, and Northern Galilee, or simply Palestine. It is so archaic that Jonathan Draper considers its rituals to come from the Q community.[135] That would make the meal rituals in the *Didache* archaic indeed. There has also been much comparison of the *Didache* with the Gospel of Matthew,[136] suggesting a strong Jewish-Christian milieu for this text.

Rather than having just one meal tradition, however, the *Didache* probably contains two parallel meals and two separate liturgies. Alan J. P. Garrow has suggested this, and his argument is strong.[137] The two prayers can be seen to "correspond structurally, verbally and conceptually. In both cases there is a three strophe pattern. In both cases there are exact verbal parallels and parallel imagery. In both cases a full meal is followed by a transitional prayer leading into a eucharist of spiritual food and drink, or cup and fragment. In both cases there is a prohibition with respect to the members of the community who may or may not take part in the following event."[138] The parallel meals would be as follows. Note, verbal parallels are underlined; the thematic parallel of "knowledge. . . revealed" is italicized; and references to cup and fragment and to "spiritual food and drink" are underlined with a thick line:

Did. 9

Did. 10

9.1 Concerning the eucharist, give thanks thus:

10.1 After you have had your fill, give thanks thus:

9.2 First, concerning the cup: We give thanks to you, our Father for the holy vine of David your servant which you have revealed to us through Jesus your servant:

10.2 We give thanks to you holy Father for your holy Name which you have made to dwell in our hearts and for the *knowledge,* faith and immortality *which you have revealed to us through Jesus your servant.*

To you be glory for ever.

To you be glory for ever.

9.3 And concerning the fragment: *We give thanks to you, our Father,*

10.3a You Lord Almighty have created everything for the sake of your Name; you have given human beings food and drink to partake with enjoyment so that they might give thanks:

For the life and *knowledge, which you have revealed* to us *through Jesus your servant:*

10.3b but to us you have given the grace of spiritual food and drink of eternal life through Jesus your servant.

To you be glory forever.

10.4 Above all we give you thanks because you are mighty: To you be glory for ever.

9.4 As this fragment was scattered upon the mountains and been gathered to become one,

so gather your Church from the four corners of the earth into your kingdom.
For yours is the glory and the power through Jesus Christ for ever.

9.5 Let no one eat or drink of your eucharist save those baptized in the name of the Lord,

For the saying of the Lord applies, "Do not give to the dogs what is holy."

10.5 Remember, Lord, your Church, to preserve it from all evil and to make it perfect in your love. And sanctified,

gather it from the four winds into your kingdom which you have prepared for it.

For yours is the power and the glory for ever.

10.6 Let grace come and let this world pass away. Hosanna to the God of David.

If anyone is holy let him come, if anyone is not let him repent. Maranatha. Amen.[139]

Garrow considers the first liturgy the earlier.[140] I would like to argue the opposite, that the second is the earlier, as it is a simpler meal and invites the Lord to attend (*maranatha*, "our Lord come") to the meal. This would then be a simple meal of the presence of Jesus with its precursor in women's memorial meals for the dead Jesus, where his presence would have been expected as well as felt. It is not yet called *eucharist*. The meal of *Didache* 9, which is called *eucharist*, would then be secondary, with cup and fragment clearly delineated. These parallel meal traditions can be explained on the basis of their being two types of meals, one a eucharist and one an agape meal, or due to the continued redaction of the *Didache* proper, which contains earlier materials overlapped with newer ones while retaining the earlier materials. I would thus propose a trajectory: first, the celebratory meals of Jesus and his followers while he was alive; second, the memorial meals for the dead Jesus held by women as part of ordinary funerary rites, where his presence was felt; third, the more formal meals of the *Didache*, the first of which, *Didache* 10, welcomes Jesus to the meal—Maranatha— then the meal of *Didache* 9, which uses the term *eucharist* for the meal with the cup and fragment of the bread. All were practiced in first-century Palestine, probably concurrently.

But there is a fourth kind of meal that believers were practicing in first-century Palestine and Antioch, a more formalized "last supper" based on the etiological legend of Jesus having instituted a meal on the eve of his death. This is found in Mark 14:22-24 and in Paul (1 Cor 11:23b-25). The texts read thus:

MARK 14:22-24

[*Jesus*] *taking bread*, blessing *he broke* [*it*] and gave [it] to them and said: "Take: this is my body."

[23] And taking [*the*] *cup* giving thanks he gave [it] to them,
    and they all drank from it,
[24] and he *said* to them:
"*This is the blood of the covenant*, which is poured out for many."

1 COR 11:23b-25

The Lord *Jesus* on the night which he was handed over took bread
[24] and giving thanks
He broke [*it*] *and said*:

"*This is my body* for you. DO this for my memorial."
[25] Likewise also *the cup*

after they had dined

saying:
"*This* cup is *the* new *covenant* through *my blood*.
Do this as often as you drink for my memorial."

There is a remarkable list of verbatim agreements between the two recitations:

[Jesus] *took a loaf,*
[he said a prayer]
he broke it,
and he said,
"This is my body."
and [Jesus] took *a cup,*
and he said,
"This is [something to do with *my blood* and *the covenant*]."[141]

Jonathan Schwiebert believes that Paul and Mark here retain an early oral tradition of the Jesus movement.[142] This would mean that in the first century the various Jesus movements concurrently practiced several ongoing types of meals: the celebratory meals of the kingdom of God, still practiced by the Q community and the Thomas community, the two separate meals of the *Didache*, the memorial meals for the dead Jesus that women practiced in ordinary funerary rites, and the meals with the words of institution crediting a memorial meal to Jesus himself before his death. This attests to the diversity of meals of the earliest Christians of the first century and does not suggest a linear development of meals of any kind during this formative stage of Christian churches.

CHAPTER 4

THE EUCHARIST
AND MEALS FOR THE DEAD

Jesus, Women, and Meals:
Social Conflict at Table and Funerary Rituals

The appearance of women at communal meals is characteristic
of Greco-Roman times. That means that gender-inclusive meals,
although noteworthy, were not unique in the social world of the Gospels. I have suggested that such meals, which were characteristic of
Christian groups generally, show that early Christians were participants in the innovative culture of their times. Thus, gender-inclusive
meals were not distinctively Christian but were rather the result of an
Empire-wide social innovation beginning in the Late Republican era,
wherein women began having increased access to the "public" sphere

of men and began attending public meals. This innovation in the meal practices of Greco-Roman women was met with strong resistance, as it undermined the social and gender-based hierarchy of Greco-Roman society. Such behavior had long been associated with the less-restricted behavior of lower-class women, slave women, prostitutes, and courtesans. Women who ventured out into public in this manner or attended public meals with men were labeled "slaves," "courtesans" or "prostitutes," regardless of their actual social status, occupation, or social position. This fluctuation in Greco-Roman meal etiquette was found throughout the Hellenized Mediterranean world, even in Palestine.[1] Gospel stories featuring women and meals reflect these fluctuations in Greco-Roman etiquette, associating the women around Jesus with social progressivism and sometimes surprising behavior. Gospel stories about women and meals also reflect the themes of funerary rituals, betraying the existence of funerary meals at an early layer of the Gospel tradition.

Feedings of Thousands: Eucharists and Funerary Meals

The feeding miracle occurs in all four Gospels, but it is Matthew who includes women in the group eating the meal, so we will consider his account. This shows Matthew's openness to the presence of women in his community. Men, woman, and children gather to receive bread and fish—common funerary offerings to the dead[2]—from Jesus' disciples, giving these meals the feel of a large family celebration. Moreover, Matthew clearly recasts these meals as eucharistic feasts, and his working of this miracle alludes to the institution of the Lord's Supper in chapter 26. Matthew's feeding stories thus look forward to the messianic banquet, which he characterizes as a wedding celebration (Matt 22:1-14), the kind of meal for which even unmarried virgins prepare (Matt 25:1-13). Thus, of all the Synoptics, it is Matthew who allows for a more egalitarian presence of women at public meals, not only within the time of the Jesus movement, but in the time of the

Matthean community itself. Note that the meal has both funerary and eucharistic overtones, with the offerings of bread and fish.

The first feeding miracle begins with a reference to the lateness of the time of day, "when evening came" (*opsias de genomenēs*; 14:15). This makes the meal an evening meal, further connecting the meal to the Lord's Supper, or eucharist. The late hour is also mentioned in the opening of the Last Supper in Matt 26:20.[3] Matthew here also emphasizes the crowds (*ochloi*; 14:13-15, 19) that gather for the meal, which foreshadows the eventual numbers that will gather for the eucharistic feasts of the church.[4] Jesus, as the host of the Lord's Supper "takes" (*lambanō*), "blesses" (*eulogeō*), "breaks" (*klaō*), and "gives"(*didōmi*) the bread, which the disciples then distribute to the crowds. This very vocabulary is repeated in Matthew's rendition of the Lord's Supper in Matt 26:26-29. Since the Lord's Supper does not include fish, Matthew deemphasizes it in this scene (14:16, 20).[5] However, the presence of the fish is a vestige of the original feasts of the earliest Christians, which were memorial funerary meals for the dead Jesus.[6]

Not only does this meal foreshadow the eucharist and reflect funerary themes, Matthew also depicts the gathering as a large family meal, not a symposium just for men, as in Mark. Matthew omits the arrangement of the men "symposia by symposia" (*symposia symposia*; Mark 6:39). Rather, in his feeding scene "men" (*andres*), "women" (*gynaikes*), and "children" (*paidia*; 14:21) all "recline" (*anaklinō*) together for the meal. This terminology could suggest that "husbands" and "wives" recline together.[7] Thus, the group here represented is like a household, reminiscent of the holy family of Joseph (*anēr*), Mary (*gynē*), and Jesus (*pais*), found in Matt 1–2.[8] A household would also include servants and slaves. Noting this identification of the gathering as a household, Robert Gundry remarks, "Thus Matthew portrays the crowds as the church, a gathering of Christian families."[9] The group in Matthew is reclining for a family meal more akin to a Jewish Passover celebration or a wedding feast or a funerary feast, which always included women and children.[10]

The interest here for Matthew is apologetic. Women and children did not usually attend public banquets unless they were servants, courtesans, or slaves, whereas in feasts for weddings and funerals, the whole family would join in the meals and celebrations.[11] For the Matthean community, women attended the meals around Jesus and subsequently eucharistic and funerary feasts not because they were promiscuous but because the church is like a large household that joins together for festive meals, even nocturnal ones.

Matthew also records the feeding of the four thousand. This second scene likewise has the presence of "women" (*gynaikes*) and "children" (*paidia*) in a similar family group (Matt 15:32-39). Again, eucharist language is present, as Jesus, the host of the Lord's Supper, "takes" (*lambanō*), "blesses" (*eulogeō*), "breaks" (*klaō*), and "gives" (*didōmi*) the bread, which the disciples then distribute to the crowds. In chapter 15, however, Jesus is in Gentile territory and the crowds are Gentiles rather than Jews.[12] As in Mark, the second feeding follows the story of the Syro-Phoenician woman, whom Matthew calls a Canaanite. After healing a Gentile girl, Jesus is pictured feeding a large Gentile group.[13] Again, the large numbers here symbolize the large numbers that will join the church. In this case, Gentile members are pictured, which includes women proselytes and their children. Matthew here again represents an open, more egalitarian and inclusive household meal, more akin to a wedding or funerary feast. Thus, all are welcomed to the table fellowship of the Matthew community, whether they be Jew or Gentile, slave or free, male or female.

Dogs on the Floor with the Syro-Phoenician Woman
(Mark 7:24-30; Matt 15:21-28)

The most audacious story of a woman in relationship to Jesus is that of the Syro-Phoenician woman and her demon-possessed daughter. This story combines the themes of both miracle and funerary meal in that it reflects typical banquet imagery as well as involving the exorcism of a young girl. The story is very ancient, as it comes from a collection of pre-Markan miracle stories that cast Jesus as Elijah.[14] This story thus reflects two stories of two different women from Jewish tradition: the story about the widow who shares her bread with Elijah

(1 Kgs 17:7-16) and the story of the healing of the widow of Zarephath's son (1 Kgs 17:17-24). We know from the murals of Dura-Europos that Jewish miracle tradition concerning Elijah utilized such images of banqueting heroes. One panel in the Dura-Europos synagogue depicts the story of Elijah's raising of the widow of Zarephath's son (1 Kgs 17:8-24). The widow approaches Elijah with her son while Elijah reclines on a banquet couch.[15] The story of the Syro-Phoenician woman and her daughter thus has clear literary and artistic anteced-ents, precluding an easy identification of the story as historical, in spite of the surprising behavior of the woman.

Mark places this early story between the two miraculous feeding narratives cast as all-male symposia (Mark 6:30ff.; 8:1ff.).[16] The story is the only Markan narrative involving the healing of a Gentile. Its parallel Gospel tradition is the healing of the centurion's servant (Matt 8:5-10 // Luke 7:1-10; John 4:46-54). The story also immediately follows material dealing with ritual purity (Mark 7:1-23), in which the narrator interprets Jesus as declaring "all foods clean" (Mark 7:19). After the narratives involving purity, Mark brings Jesus into the Gen-tile territory of Tyre.[17] There he is approached by a women seeking the healing of her daughter who is afflicted by an "unclean spirit" (*pneuma akatharton*). In this Markan context, the story speaks to the mixed social arrangement of Mark's community (Jews and Gentiles) as well as his community's mission to Gentiles.[18] The woman appears to rep-resent only non-Jewish Christians.[19] The designation of the woman as a Syro-Phoenician is rare. In Jewish tradition, women from the city of Tyre or the area of Phoenicia were associated with struggles with foreign religious influences, such as the cults of Ba'al and Astarte, and particularly the practice of temple prostitution. The most notable of these women is Jezebel, who was a fierce supporter of her own reli-gious tradition in the Northern Kingdom and successfully attracted many to join her at Ba'al's "table."[20] As cities associated with foreign religious practices, Tyre and Sidon became objects of Yahweh's wrath in ancient Hebrew tradition.[21]

The woman is also identified as a "Greek." Mark may intend this designation to identify the woman as wealthy.[22] However, by Mark's day, the term *Greek* may simply have identified a member of a group distinct from Jews in the context of early Christian missionary activity.[23] Mark emphasizes her Gentile origins by describing her as Syro-Phoenician "by birth" (*to genei*). As Mark narrates it, a Gentile woman, now appropriately located in a house where Jesus (probably) reclined for a meal,[24] falls at his feet (probably the foot of his dining couch) and begs his help for her daughter.

Jesus' response remains problematic. In short, he refers to the Syro-Phoenician woman and her daughter as "little bitches," albeit indirectly: "Let the children first be fed, for it is not good to take the children's bread and throw it to the dogs" (Mark 7:27). Interpreters, anxious to preserve Jesus' image, usually assert that the scene here is one of a cozy household, where children's little "puppies" can expect to be fed from the abundance of the messianic banquet.[25] Such interpretations fail to take into account the use of the diminuative term "dog" (*kynarion*) in reference to a woman. When used of women it is a term of reproach for shameless and audacious behavior, not an endearment. It can also be used of maids and other servants, especially in the context of Greek mythology.[26] Thus, in spite of her possible social status, Jesus insults the woman by calling her a "dog." As Burkill has noted, "As in English, so in other languages, to call a woman 'a little bitch' is no less abusive than to call her a 'bitch' without qualification."[27] This language, far from including the woman and her daughter in any messianic feast, functions to exclude her, for the dogs are not part of the family, but under the table; they receive scraps of food only as they fall—they are not entitled to be fed. It is therefore not "good" (*kalos*, here probably "proper") to give food meant for the family to the dogs scavenging under the table. That the "children" should first be fed (implying the Gentiles will be fed second) may be a secondary softening of Jesus' retort by Mark.[28] The scene reflects stereotypical Christian funerary feasts where dogs on the floor were present to knock out the lights:[29]

> These people gather together illiterates from the very dregs of society and credulous women who easily fall prey because of the weakness of their sex. They organize a mob of wicked conspirators, who join together in nocturnal assemblies and ritual fasts and inhumane dinners. . . . Everywhere they share a kind of religion of lust, and promiscuously call one another brothers and sisters so that even ordinary

sexual intercourse becomes incest by the use of the sacred name. . . .
On holy days they gather for a banquet with all their children, sisters, and mothers, people of both sexes and all ages. There, after many
courses of food, the party heats up and the passion of incestuous lust
inflames those who are drunk. . . . In the shameless darkness they are
indiscriminately wrapped in shocking embraces.

It is precisely this kind of stereotype Matthew is trying to avoid in
his depiction of the miraculous feedings. In its present context, Mark
intends the story to locate the eventual mission to the Gentiles within
Jesus' own ministry: eventually all will be filled. The admittance of
Gentiles into the community comes about due to Jesus' contact with a
Gentile woman. Following this story, Jesus travels further in the Gentile areas of the Decapolis (Mark 7:31).

Thus, the inclusion of Gentiles into the Markan community and
its table fellowship is prefigured by Jesus' granting of this woman's
request, albeit from a distance (v. 29). What is striking is that it is
the woman's wit and quick retort to Jesus' insult that persuades Jesus
to perform the healing.[30] It is she who gives the surprising completion to the chreia, "Lord,[31] but even the dogs under the table feed on
the children's crumbs" (Mark 7:28). It is because of her deft answer
(*logos*) that Jesus casts the demon out of her daughter. Her witty retort
and willingness to stand up to Jesus further suggests a higher level of
education and probably social class.[32] However, women stereotyped
as courtesans were also depicted as having the ability to participate
in philosophical repartee. Even aristocratic women could be accused
of promiscuity and audaciousness for such behavior. Cynic women
in particular could be characterized as "dogs" for their prowess in
philosophical debate.[33] Thus, the Syro-Phoenician woman fits a "public" rather than "private" cultural stereotype of women's behavior in
antiquity. Mark, however, seems uninterested in the woman's female-
ness or her relationship to men. Rather, her story represents a rationale
for the inclusion of Gentiles in Mark's own community.[34]

Matthew is the only other Gospel writer to repeat this strange
story. Luke, probably offended by the behavior of the woman, omits
it.[35] Matthew follows Markan order by splicing the story of the Syro-
Phoenician woman between the two miraculous feedings (Matt

14:13-21; 15:32-39). Since Matthew adds "women and children" to
the feeding narratives, particularly to the second account in 15:29-38,
the intent here is probably to highlight the story as involving a woman
and her child (who are Gentiles) rather than just Gentiles alone.[36]
Unlike Mark, Matthew did have the story of the centurion and his
son from Q (Matt 8:5-13), yet he here still follows Markan order.
Thus, set between the two feeding narratives, the story of the Syro-
Phoenician woman gives a precedent within Jesus' own ministry for
the inclusion of women and Gentiles in community meals.

Matthew further connects this pericope with the preceding discussion of Jewish dietary laws (Matt 15:1-20) by means of a continua-
tive *kai* ("and," 15:21). Matthew also adds "and Sidon" to the Markan
"Tyre" (v. 21). Here Jesus withdraws into the districts of Tyre (*eis ta
merē Tyrou*), rather than remaining along its outskirts as in Mark.[37] The
combination of "Tyre and Sidon" recalls even more the stereotypical
language concerning such sinful cities worthy of the judgment of God
in Jewish biblical tradition.[38] Here the woman is labeled with the out-
dated term *Canaanite*, rather than as a Syro-Phoenician.[39] This apellation recalls at least two of the women in Matthew's genealogy accused
of harlotry, Tamar and Rahab, both Canaanites. However, Matthew
removes the setting of the scene in a house, setting the encounter more
naturally in the open air.[40] This lessens the association of the scene
with a meal. Still, here the woman remains an example of a marginal
woman to whom Jesus ministers.

In spite of her Canaanite background, the woman addresses Jesus
by a messianic title, "son of David" (Matt 15:22). This title occurs
elsewhere in Matthew in healing miracles.[41] By combining "son of
David" with the declaration of Jesus as "Lord," the woman makes a
confession of faith in Jesus even before he grants her request.[42] Her
faith contrasts the lack of faith among many Jews, especially the Pharisees. She is thus like the women "prostitutes" who enter the kingdom
by faith before the Pharisees (21:31-32). Following her acknowledg-
ment of Jesus as Lord and Messiah, the Canaanite women cries loudly
for Jesus to cast the demon out of her daughter. This makes such a
racket that the disciples are annoyed (15:23). Jesus at first ignores her;
his disciples encourage him to send her away. Jesus' lack of an ini-

tial direct response casts him as even ruder to the woman than he is in Mark.[43] He says nothing at all, then gives a flat refusal: "I was sent only to the house of Israel" (15:24). Still the woman persists, kneeling in worship before him (15:25). Jesus' further reply is not to the woman but to the disciples and contains the only negative remark found in Mark: "It is not good to take the children's bread and give it to the dogs" (15:26). Again, Jesus describes the woman and her child as "little dogs" or "bitches." In Matthew, this is more likely to be a derogatory term for Gentiles[44] or simply an ethnic insult.[45] The woman persists but agrees with Jesus's statement and requests the scraps of food beneath the table. Finally, Jesus relents. However, he no longer relents due to the woman's wit, but because of her great faith in his miracle-working power: "Oh woman, great is your faith! Be it done for you as you desire" (15:28). Matthew accentuates the woman's faith by heightening Jesus' refusal. The woman's great faith becomes the justification of the inclusion of Gentiles into the eucharistic meals of the Matthean church.[46]

The story of the Syro-Phoenician woman is unarguably strange and suggests its authenticity and antiquity on the basis of the criterion of dissimilarity.[47] Here Jesus is depicted as acting with both rudeness and prejudice. Given the multicultural environment of Palestine, it is not impossible that Jesus may have met with foreign women. Further, Jesus was known for his exorcisms and for casting out demons from several women (Luke 8:1-3). The story does originate in a very early collection of six miracle stories, three of which involve women. However, the story also betrays literary and artistic stereotypes that cast Jesus as a hero in a Hellenistic mode, especially in a banquet setting, and reflects an Elijah typology. Just as the mural at Dura-Europos depicts Elijah healing the widow of Zarephath's son while reclining on a banquet couch, in the earliest Markan version of the story, the Syro-Phoenician woman approaches Jesus in a house. The conversation between Jesus and the woman suggests a similar funerary banquet setting for the scene; the culinary themes of the dogs under the table and the impending messianic feast make this clear. The story is thus very likely the product of early Christian storytelling, albeit audacious storytelling.

The Woman, Anointing, Burial, and a Meal: The End of Mourning?

The story of the unnamed woman who anoints Jesus is one of the few Gospel stories in which Jesus appears in the company of a woman at a meal. The scene has both banquet and funerary themes. A version of the story occurs in all four Gospels (Mark 14:3-9; Matt 26:6-13; Luke 7:36-50; John 12:1-8) and is corroborated by one extrabiblical source (Ign. *Eph.* 17:2). Several elements of the story remain constant in all four Gospel accounts: Jesus is anointed with expensive perfume by a woman in the context of a meal; others present object to her action; Jesus rises to defend her. I have argued elsewhere that this image brings to mind one who dines in the company of disreputable people, including women accused of promiscuity.[48]

Tradition History of the Anointing Story

Other scholars have previously done overviews of theories of the transmission of the anointing story.[49] Until the 1950s, the scholarly consensus seemed to be that behind the Gospel accounts was one incident, and that variations arose in the course of oral transmission and the evangelists' redactions.[50] For a period of time, however, some scholars reconsidered the possibility of there being two separate incidents or stories behind the Gospel accounts, one event in Bethany and a second in Galilee.[51] Further discussions, however, reaffirm that there lies one single incident or story behind the four accounts.[52] Scholars have been equally divided over both the development of the Gospel tradition as well as over which account of the anointing should be given priority. Most assume the priority of the Markan account,[53] but many consider Luke's version the more primitive.[54] Even the priority of John's account has a few adherents.[55] Most recently, Burton Mack has argued that behind both Mark and Luke is a single chreia, which was subsequently elaborated in different ways by the two evangelists.[56]

One story/incident behind the various versions best explains the many unlikely coincidences among them.[57]

On the issue of historicity, scholars have long assumed that a historical core lies behind one account or the other.[58] However, given the preference for Markan priority, the connection in Mark of the woman's act with Jesus' burial has always been a problem, assuming as it does a post-Easter Christology.[59] Furthermore, the objections to the woman's action have always been suspected as being contrived.[60] Unfortunately, little sense has been made of the story without them.[61] A few scholars have correctly suspected that the scandal behind the story is to be found in the impropriety of the woman's action.[62] Despite the fact that Mark's account does not suggest that the woman is unvirtuous, the presence of a woman at a meal scene alone would indeed have signaled sexual innuendo to ancient readers. During Hellenistic times, those women present for dinner parties with men were stereotypically considered to be prostitutes of some kind, or at the least promiscuous, whatever their social status or occupation. This ideology concerning women's proper behavior at meals can be found throughout Hellenistic literature, even Jewish Hellenistic literature.[63] Thus, the Lukan version may indeed retain the essential conflict over the woman's presence at the meal.[64] The core story behind the anointing accounts could therefore be considered as historically reliable on the grounds of dissimilarity. However, the scene arguably reflects both literary and artistic stereotypes, which preclude any easy identification of a historical core behind this story.[65]

The Anointing of Jesus in Mark and Matthew
(Mark 14:3-9; Matt 26:6-13)

Mark's account of the anointing is one of several Markan stories connecting women to meals with men. Although Mark's casting of the story serves in some ways to obscure it, the characterization of the woman as a stereotype from literary and artistic depictions of such women remains.[66] The meal setting is probably original,[67] although the setting in the "house of Simon the leper," is more questionable. The designation of Simon as a "leper," however, is certainly odd, and thus this name may be the original to the tradition.[68] First, the setting of a meal or dinner party itself would bring to mind possible frivolous behavior. There is no indication from the text that the woman is a relative of Jesus, and yet she is present at a meal with a large group (presumably) of men. Second, the very service she performs would have had sexual connotations, as anointings were often performed in banquet settings by sexually available slave women or young male servants. Anointings of upper-class men and kings at banquets by courtesans or other servants are ancient, and the connection between perfumes and the sexually available slaves who frequented such meals can be found throughout literature from the ancient Near East and the Greco-Roman world.[69] Furthermore, according to ancient Greek customs, wives regularly performed anointings for their husbands before sexual intercourse, and the alabastron was often portrayed in private scenes with women. Hetaerae were also pictured with such vessels.[70] Moreover, the perfume the woman uses (*myrou nardou pistikēs*—often rendered "spikenard") may have been connected to those perfumes used by prostitutes or courtesans.[71] Scholars often note the incredible cost of such perfumes.[72] However, the cost of the perfume may indicate that she is a woman of some means rather than a servant. Not only does Mark not indicate that she is a slave or unvirtuous, but she remains unnamed. This contributes to the likelihood that she is a respectable woman, as respectable women's names were not mentioned in public.[73] Moreover, she is silent and is not described as reclining at table with the men in the manner of a courtesan or liberated woman. I would therefore concur with other scholars who consider the name "Mary" in John 12:3 to be secondary.[74] Thus, given the meal setting, the action of the woman, and her probable social class,[75] her action would have been viewed as improper, even scandalous. Furthermore, men who accepted such ministrations at banquets too often could be accused of being "soft" or "effeminate."[76] As is the case in the story of the Syro-Phoenician woman, here the woman's approach to Jesus is mirrored in literary and artistic depictions of banqueting men of leisure and heroes who accept ministrations from women and servants. In typical artistic banquet scenes, a single woman approaches the man reclining for his meal, sometimes climbing onto his banquet couch while offering food on plates, oil in alabastra, or simply joining him for his meal. In Mark, the woman's stance is that of a servant providing the niceties of banquet etiquette for Jesus.[77]

In light of this background, the objection of those present in Mark 14:4-5 due to cost (or "waste") seems even more contrived and is therefore probably an addition, as many scholars have suggested.[78] Furthermore, the connection of the anointing in Mark to Jesus' burial shifts attention away from the impropriety of the scene. This relieves the problem of the respectability of the woman's action, as women were often sent to anoint a dead body for burial.[79] Finally, as not only kings were anointed at banquets in this manner (it was primarily an indication of general wealth or leisure), there is no need to suppose that the original story contained overtones of a messianic Christology.[80] These considerations, combined with the presupposition of a post-Easter Christology inherent in the interest in Jesus' death and burial, increase the probability that the concern for the cost of the perfume, the connection of the woman's act to Jesus' burial, and the overtones of a kingly "messianic" anointing are later additions. However, Jesus' defense of the action as "good" or "proper" (*kalos*) (14:6) may indeed have been part of the original story, not only because it fits nicely into a reconstructed chreia,[81] but because it would have completely reversed an ancient reader's expectations. Jesus declares an action—which in light of all Hellenistic standards of meal etiquette was considered improper for a respectable woman—to be "proper."[82] Mark subsequently incorporates this image of the woman into his ideal of a true discipleship of service.[83] The story brings together themes of burial and meal, as the women's service prefigures Jesus' burial and hence funeral.

Matthew records the Markan anointing story with only a few select changes, which nevertheless often leads to its neglect.[84] Matthew omits the parallel story about the poor widow and emphasizes the cost of the perfume in the anointing scene proper.[85] The identification of the perfume as "spikenard" drops out. Matthew simply calls the ointment "very expensive" (*barytimos*, Matt 26:7)[86] and shortens the detail concerning the cost of the ointment to "a large sum" or "for much" (*pollou*; Matt 26:9). Matthew further stresses the connection of the woman's action to the burial of Jesus (Matt 26:12), heightening the funerary theme of the story,[87] and the unnamed woman sufficiently performs the requisite anointing for burial. In Matthew, the women do not take spice to the tomb (Matt 28:1).[88] Those who object to the woman's action are not an indefinite "some" (Mark 14:4), but are rather the "disciples" (*mathētai*; Matt 26:8).[89] Mark's version is probably more original in this case, which leaves the identity of the objectors ambiguous.[90] All of the sexual innuendo inherent in the action of anointing and the meal setting itself, as well as the probable class of the woman, remain.[91] In Matthew, however, this is less of a problem, as he embraces the scandal of Jesus' connections to stereotypically "promiscuous" women, and is comfortable adding women even to large meal scenes.[92]

The Anointing of Jesus in Luke and John
(Luke 7:36-50; John 12:1-8)

Luke's version of the anointing story is remarkably different from Mark and Matthew's, which has caused certain scholars to suggest that Luke's story records an entirely different event, or at least a separate source.[93] However, we may still account for the differences between Luke and Mark on the basis of Lukan redaction.[94] The setting of the meal in the house of a Pharisee is undoubtedly Lukan,[95] as is the addition of the parable of the two debtors[96] and the subsequent discussion of love and forgiveness.[97] The basic setting of the meal, however, probably predates Luke, in spite of Luke's tendency to set scenes of Jesus' teaching at meals.[98]

A major emphasis missing in Luke is the clear connection between the woman's action and the burial of Jesus (including its connection with the passion narrative). However, there still remains some connection in Luke between the action of the woman and Jesus' death.[99] Luke also omits the objection to the woman's action on the basis of its being a "waste."[100] Rather, Luke records that the objection to the anointing is based on the impropriety of the woman and her behavior. As we have seen, the impropriety of the woman and her action is implicit in the Markan version as well, even though his casting of the story serves to obscure it. Thus, it is not necessary to posit a separate Lukan source in order to explain Luke's description of the woman. In Luke, however, the woman (still unnamed) is clearly called "a woman who was a sinner in the city" (*gynē hētis ēn en tē polei hamartōlos*), that is, a woman with a bad reputation. The combination of the term *sinner* with her identification as a woman known in the city makes it more than likely that Luke intends his readers to identify her as a prostitute of some sort, or more colloquially, a "streetwalker" or "public woman."[101] She is therefore known for her sexual promiscuity. This might indicate that Luke intends his readers to identify her as a lower-class working woman or a freedwoman who has earned her freedom by prostituting herself.[102] This is surely the tension underlying the original story and may explain why certain scholars suspect that Luke retains an earlier version.[103] However, given that women who frequented dinners with men could be accused of promiscuous behavior regardless of their true social status or occupation, it is unlikely that Luke here preserves historical information about the actual woman herself, but rather only the true motivation behind the objection to her presence and action.

The action of anointing in Luke differs somewhat from that in Mark. In Luke, the woman first washes Jesus' feet with her tears (7:38). After drying them with her unbound hair, she kisses them, and then anoints them with costly perfume. The reference to tears occurs only in Luke, and is probably Lukan.[104] This further connects the woman's action to Jesus' burial, and the keening and weeping (*thrēneō*; *koptō*; Luke 23:27) of the daughters of Jerusalem at Jesus' death scene. The funerary connections of the story here are even clearer than in the other Synoptics. Whether the anointing of the feet is more historical or not is a matter of further debate. Although anointings of the head and face were more common in banquet settings,[105] both male and female slaves' anointing the feet of wealthy individuals was not unheard of.[106] Suffice it to say that the anointing of the head has a slight historical advantage, given that anointings of the head and face were more commonly associated with banquet settings. Such anointings were not connected to only "royal" anointings, and the other early extrabiblical witness to the anointing records that it was of Jesus' head.[107] Whether or not the anointing was of the head (Mark and Matthew) or of the feet (Luke and John) may not be that significant.[108] The sensual connotations of either kind of anointing are clear, as is the association of this kind of activity to (sexually available) slaves, prostitutes, and the like.[109] It is possible that the earliest tradition merely recorded that Jesus was anointed by a woman at a meal, and either the anointing of the head or the feet could be imagined in that context.[110]

The Pharisee Simon present for the occasion, mentally rebukes Jesus for allowing such a woman to touch him. Jesus defends the woman's action by noting the lack of meal propriety on the part of his host (vv. 44-46). Simon had neglected the basic customs of banquet hospitality for his guest: he neither washed Jesus' feet, greeted Jesus with a kiss, nor anointed him with oil. Thus, the woman's actions are defensible: she provides these basic services for Jesus; Simon did not. She has washed his feet with her tears, dried them with her hair, and then anointed his feet with perfume.

In spite of the many variations in the story between Mark and Luke, we can still account for the Lukan version on the basis of Luke's editing of his Markan source. The setting of the meal in the house of Simon "the Pharisee" is undoubtedly Lukan, as is the addition of the parable of the two debtors and the subsequent discussion of love and forgiveness. The "sinful" woman/prostitute represents one of the many repentant sinners who accept Jesus' message; Luke here underscores the overtones of stereotype and scandal from the Markan scene.[111]

John's version of the anointing is generally considered independent of both Mark and Luke; both rely on common oral tradition for the anointing story.[112] However, the occurrence of the extremely rare phrase describing the perfume, *myrou nardou pistikēs* (*pistikēs*, probably "pure" or "liquid" occurs only here and in Mark 14:3 in reference to oil or ointment) and the general description of the ointment's cost (it could have been sold for three hundred denarii: a year's wages) may indicate literary dependence on Mark rather than oral tradition.[113] Given John's probable dependence on Mark's passion cycle, which begins with the story of the anointing, we cannot rule out John's dependence on Mark for this story either, despite some scholars' usual claim that the so-called Markan passages in John (2:14-22; 5:1-9; 6:1-13; 6:16-21; 12:1-8) are independent.

John resets the anointing scene in Bethany and peoples it with popular characters from his own Gospel. Lazarus owns the house, and the women present for the meal are his sisters, Martha and Mary (11:1-43). In John's version, one of Jesus' closest women friends, Mary of Bethany, anoints his feet, while Mary's sister serves the meal (11:2). The sequence of events in John's version is somewhat convoluted. Rather than washing and drying Jesus' feet and then anointing them, as in Luke (Luke 7:38), here Mary of Bethany pours on the perfume and then wipes it off with her hair. This rearrangement of the narrative, although common among storytellers, is nonsensical. As in Mark 14:3-9, this anointing is done in advance of Jesus' embalming before burial (12:7), although it is by no means the final or even kingly embalming, as in Matthew (28:1). In John, Joseph of Arimathea and Nicodemus later virtually smother Jesus' body in dry spices when they place him in the tomb (19:39). Rather than seeing the anointing of Jesus as his final burial rite, John connects Mary's "wiping" of Jesus' feet to Jesus' "wiping" of the disciple's feet in the footwashing scene in 13:5. Thus, Mary here provides a menial service for Jesus, which he will also provide for his disciples (13:2-17), thus becoming the model for Jesus' own actions. Mary of Bethany is the first to follow Jesus' admonishment to "do as I have done for you" (13:15). The anointing could signal the end of mourning rituals.[114]

The origins of this story remain unknown. The criterion of dissimilarity could favor its historicity, given its scandalous overtones. It could be argued that it is unlikely that the early church would have created a scandalous story involving a woman's improper anointing of Jesus at a banquet. If historical, the story would cohere with the accusation that Jesus was known for consorting with tax collectors, sinners, and even prostitutes at meals (Mark 2:14-17; Q 7:34; Matt 21:31-32). Or Christian storytellers, remembering it as a precursor to Jesus' death and burial, later embellished an incidental anointing of Jesus at a meal.[115] However, the scene is overwhelmingly stereotypical and clearly reflects literary and artistic portrayals of banquet revelry and etiquette. This suggests that the story is pure fiction and a fabrication of either Mark or early Christian storytellers. The stereotypical nature of the story, the lack of clear signs of oral tradition in even the Markan version, and the variation of the tradition in both Luke and John suggest that the story reflects early Christian idealization of Jesus as a hero in a stereotypical banquet setting.[116] In many ways, the earliest account of the anointing in Mark creates a narrative memorial to Jesus in a manner similar to the last supper scene (Mark 14:17-25) by bringing together the themes of meal, death, and memorial. Both the last supper and the anointing narratives in Mark memorialize Jesus' death in the context of a meal; both employ stock banquet motifs. Neither of these stories is a historical report; both are Mark's imaginative fiction.

Last Supper Traditions: Memorial Meals for the Dead

There are two recitations of last supper traditions from the night before Jesus' death. I use the term *recitation* to indicate the oral nature of these traditions.[117] In Paul (1 Cor 11:23-26) and Mark (14:22-26), we find these two versions of the last supper tradition. As we saw in chapter 3, these are probably two versions of a single oral tradition.[118]

MARK 14:22-24

[*Jesus*] *taking bread*, blessing *he broke* [*it*] and gave [it] to them and said: "Take: this is my body."

[23] And taking [*the*] *cup* giving thanks he gave [it] to them,
    and they all drank from it,
[24] and he *said* to them:
"*This is the blood of the covenant*, which is poured out for many."

1 COR 11:23b-25

The Lord *Jesus* on the night which he was handed over took bread
[24] and giving thanks
He broke [*it*] *and said*:

"*This is my body* for you. DO this for my memorial."
[25] Likewise also *the cup*

after they had dined

saying:
"*This* cup is *the* new *covenant* through *my blood*.
Do this as often as you drink for my memorial."

And as we saw in chapter 3, there is a remarkable list of verbatim agreements between the two recitations:

[Jesus] *took a loaf,*
[he said a prayer]
he broke it,
and he said,
"This is my body."
and [Jesus] took *a cup,*
and he said,
"This is [something to do with *my blood* and *the covenant*].*"*[119]

In Mark's version there is a degree of parallelism: (1) "taking bread," "blessing" (*labōn arton eulogēsas*) // "taking a cup," "giving thanks" (*labōn potērion eucharistēsas*); (2) "he gave [it] to them" (*edōken autois*) // "and he said to them" (*kai eipen autois*); (3) "and he said" *(kai eipen)* // "and he said to them" (*kai eipen autois*); and (4) "This is my body" (*touto estin to sōma mou*) // "This is my blood" (*touto estin to aima mou*). These parallels are well suited for oral recitation.[120] Further, Jesus' actions in Mark and Paul are similar and indicate that the same oral tradition lies behind both.

JESUS' ACTIONS (MARK)	JESUS' ACTIONS (PAUL)
A	A
[Jesus] taking a loaf, blessing, he broke [it] and gave [it] to them	The Lord Jesus . . . Took a loaf and giving thanks He broke [it]

JESUS' SAYINGS (MARK)	
B	A1
And he said, "Take; this is my body"	Likewise also the cup after they had dined

	JESUS' SAYINGS (PAUL)
A1	B
And taking [the] cup, giving thanks,	And said,
	"This is my body for you
He gave [it] to them,	
And they all drank from it,	Do this
	For my memorial."
B1	B1
and he said to them	saying,
"This is my blood of the cov-enant,	"This is the new covenant through my blood.
which is being poured out for many,	Do this, as often as you drink [it]
Amen, I say to you . . . "	For my memorial.

In both recitations, Jesus both does something and says something with respect to the bread or cup, and the actions and words parallel one another.[121]

Further, both recitations locate the event of the last supper on the night before Jesus' death. In light of their being two different literary genres, one a letter, the other a narrative, this is noteworthy. Both place the event in a special past with significance for the cultic ritual in view. Further, both connect the ritual to both the death of Jesus and the coming Parousia. In Paul, eating the loaf and drinking from the cup anticipate the coming of the Lord (1 Cor 11:26), whereas in Mark, it is when the "kingdom of God" comes that Jesus will "drink [the fruit of the vine]" again. Here a mythic past event is linked to an eschatological future.[122] Both ground the authority of the tradition in Jesus. It is Jesus who institutes this meal, not women or underlings in the community. As an etiological legend, these recitations ground the cult of the eucharist in the life and deeds of Jesus. Thus, a memorial meal originally founded by women and the poor is here attributed to a man (Jesus).

The Eucharist and Meals for the Dead: Some Conclusions

In the context of Greco-Roman literature, the Gospel traditions contain an abundance of unusual stories concerning women, funerals, and meals. As a collection, all of these stories reflect clear literary and artistic stereotypes that idealize Jesus as a heroic figure and should therefore not be considered as historical but rather as the products of early Christian storytelling. However, there is a marked contrast of the audacity and scandal of these later stories about women, funerals, and meals in comparison to earlier materials concerning the historical Jesus. Only the hint of scandal at Jesus' association with "tax collectors," "sinners," and/or "prostitutes" remains at the level of Q, for example. Jesus' teaching nowhere directly addresses the issue of women or their presence among his followers or table companions. This strongly suggests that Jesus' himself did not broach the question of the presence of women in community meals, but that the direct controversy surrounding these matters arose after his death.[123] In contrast, these traditions highlight several perspectives concerning the role of women. The Syro-Phoenician woman uses philosophical wit to gain the healing of her daughter while convincing Jesus to extend his ministry to the Gentiles in the process. A woman boldly anoints Jesus at a meal announcing his impending death, arousing controversy among Jesus' male disciples. As a collection, these stories suggest the active role of creative women and ordinary people in the community and in the formation of tradition. The role of women in their creation remains conjecture, but tantalizing conjecture. However, these stories still betray the amazing ways in which the Gospel communities chose to remember not only Jesus, but more importantly, the women around him. The last supper traditions, however, focus the beginnings of the most important ritual meal in the person of Jesus himself, leaving women out of the tradition entirely.

CHAPTER 5

THE PASSION STORY
AS A LAMENT STORY FOR THE DEAD

Scholars have long considered both the passion narrative and the empty tomb stories to have been produced within scribal networks; in other words, by elite men. Further, in the context of historical-critical inquiry, the tradition linking Mary Magdalene to a resurrection appearance of Jesus usually takes a back seat to Paul's earlier description of an appearance to Peter mentioned in the early Christian creed found in 1 Cor 15:3-11. However, assumptions concerning the origin of these traditions are altered when we consider them in light of literary and social historical evidence for women's and ordinary people's roles in ancient funerary practices. I will suggest that the empty tomb stories, although arguably late and driven by fictional narrative themes, were in part suggested by the creedal formulation that Jesus was "buried" and then "raised on the third day," due to the common connection in antiquity of women to tomb visitation and lamentation on the third day after death. Further, although the entire passion narrative as it first appears in Mark is arguably a late scribal product driven by scriptural *testimonia* and literary models from noble death scenes, it does contain elements that suggest its origins in an earlier oral lament. Evidence for women's roles in liturgical lamentation and the performance of oral poetry thus alter our understanding of how both the passion narrative and resurrection traditions developed in early Christian tradition.

Women Witnesses at the Cross and the Tomb

The question of the historicity of the presence of women at the crucifixion found in all four canonical Gospels is a complex one. In these narratives, the women serve as an important witness linking the stories of Jesus' death, burial, and the empty tomb. However, in light of ancient women's roles in death and burial rituals, especially their role in lamenting the dead, the behavior of the women as described in most of these Gospel scenes is implausible. Furthermore, the presence of the women in these scenes can be compared to ancient descriptions of the death of heroic individuals, particularly those influenced by the stories of the "noble" deaths of Socrates and Hercules. However, the behavior of the women at the crucifixion does not fit the stereotypical role of the *women* in these stories, but that of the close associates—disciples or friends of the dying hero—who are usually men. Although literary models do not fully account for every aspect of the portrayal of women in these narratives, attention to the function of gender in ancient descriptions of dying heroes and to the roles of women in ancient burial rites can contribute to the overall task of testing the historicity of the passion narratives.

Jesus' Death as a Heroic and Noble Death

Ancient literary portrayals of deaths reflect stereotypes of men's and women's appropriate expressions of grief and emotion, particularly deaths of notable individuals, the Latin *exitus illustrium virorum*.[1] As we have seen, that New Testament portrayals of Jesus reflect certain literary motifs or themes found in stories about heroes, immortals, so-called divine men, great philosophers and the like, is not a new idea.[2] Such images were no doubt available in both popular folklore and artistic representations as well as in literature. There is no need to posit an exact literary model or type of a "divine man," given the general tendencies of popular folklore traditions to create and re-create heroes in a Hellenistic mode.[3] As in the last chapter, discussions have focused on miracle traditions in the Gospels and the relationship of Jesus to other Hellenistic wonder-workers.[4] Scholars usually juxtapose the passion narrative with traditions of the miraculous in Mark and John to make the point that Christian understandings of Jesus' death served as a critique of primitive divine-man theologies.[5] However, John's passion account serves John's interests in the glorification of Jesus, not just through the many signs he performs, but through his death on the cross.[6] The power of Jesus as a great thaumaturge is also no doubt the point of Mark's portrayal of Jesus' last cry, which forcefully rends the temple curtain and elicits the declaration of the centurion, "Truly this man was the Son of God."[7] Furthermore, the desertion of Jesus' disciples during the passion week follows a common aretalogical theme.[8] Finally, once we understand (properly) Hellenistic and Jewish martyrological literature to be the genre behind Mark's passion account,[9] then Mark's description of Jesus' death must also be analyzed in light of the Hellenistic concepts of the noble and heroic deaths, which these martyrologies presuppose.[10] This has in fact already been done.[11] What has not been done is an analysis of the function of gender in the Markan passion and subsequent passion accounts.[12] Attention to the gender of the characters in each Gospel story and their expressions of grief (or lack thereof) clarifies how these stories of Jesus' death fit into the larger theological interests of the evangelists.

As we saw in chapter 2, women generally play minor roles in "noble death" stories, many of which derive from the most classic case, the death of Socrates. The general pattern is that men (women already having been escorted from the room for their stereotypically feminine displays of grief) must exhibit characteristics culturally defined as feminine and then overcome them. Too much grief is "womanish" and "irrational." Similarly, in scenes of the death of Hercules, only men or his mother are featured prominently. Jewish death scenes follow this mode as well, such as the death of Moses in Josephus. Other Jewish stories follow a set pattern, a genre established by George Nickelsburg, of the person suffering as "righteous," as well as "noble,"[13] Although absent from Nickelsburg's model for the Markan passion, the Psalms also imply the presence of family and friend as onlookers, if only from a distance.[14] Thus, there is good precedent in Jewish Hellenistic tradition for the martyrological themes in the passion narratives. The presence of family and friends is expected, and expressed grief is a prerequisite for the scene. Generally, women are expected to weep, whereas men should restrain their grief in the face of death. If a woman does not mourn but shows restraint, she can be described as a "man."

He Was Buried, He Was Raised on the Third Day

In light of literary and social historical evidence, the women followers of Jesus in both the passion and empty tomb accounts are remarkably silent. Generally, they do not lament (*thrēneō*), they do not cry or weep (*klaiō*), they do not beat their breasts (*koptō*). When they come to the tomb, they do anything but lament, coming rather to anoint (*aleiphō*) (Mark 16:1; Luke 24:1), to sit (*kathēmai*) (Matt 27:61), to watch or see (*theoreō*) (Matt 28:1), or they just simply come (*erchomai*) (John 20:1). If they do come to lament (*Gos. Pet.* 13:55-57), they never get the chance, but are interrupted by angels. In Mark, they at least come to anoint the body, which is a burial custom, but they are much too late.[15] Only in John is Mary Magdalene described as weeping (klaiō, John 20:11), but she is alone. In other words, the women do not do the one thing ordinarily expected of them under such circumstances: lament the dead. In light of the Hellenistic evidence, this is suspicious. If the women are at the cross and the tomb, why do they not weep? What keeps the authors from portraying this common custom? Susan Heine and Carolyn Osiek have also suggested that the women in Mark 16:1-8 could only have gone to the tomb to mourn. Heine clearly connects this with women's obligations to visit the tombs of the dead.[16] The women should weep, but they do not. There must be a reason for this. I am going to make the bold suggestion that the association of women with the death and burial of Jesus was suggested by the creedal tradition that Jesus "was buried" (thaptō) and then "was raised on the third day" (egēgertai tē hēmera tē tritē) (1 Cor 15:4),[17] due to the commonly known Hellenistic custom of tomb visitation, often three days after death. Attempts to explain the "third day" tradition as a reference to Hos 6:2 have been unsuccessful. There is no clear evidence that early Christians used Hos 6:2 as proof text or testimonia.[18] However, even though women's lament rituals "on the third day" were quite orderly, their rites were often considered theologically suspect due to their necromantic associations. Thus the implications of 1 Cor 15:4b had to be modified, and the empty tomb tradition was the result. The association of followers of Jesus (particularly women) going to a tomb on the third day following Jesus' death to commune with the dead through their mournful cries could too closely associate Jesus with everyday "divine men" or heroes, and his followers with magic. The overall effect of the empty tomb tradition, which featured women in this stereotypical role of tomb visitation, functioned to marginalize women followers of Jesus more than men, thus weakening their claim to having seen (oraō) the risen Christ. Women could be seen in the role of witches or magicians, their lamentations as a powerful form of magic, stirring up the dead, especially to exact vengeance.[19] In ancient Greek, Roman, and Jewish popular religion, women continued to be associated with tomb visitation, lamentation, and communication with the dead.[20]

Seen in a funerary context, the empty tomb story is a modification of a strong literary and cultural connection between women, tomb cults, and magic. It should be considered as sort of an antideification story that employs a common narrative device of an "empty tomb." This fictional device was common in deification or translation stories in antiquity and can also be found in Hellenistic romances.[21] Cleomedes leaves behind an empty chest,[22] Hercules an empty pyre,[23] Romulus an empty chair,[24] Aristeas an empty house,[25] and when Chaereas goes to mourn the death of his beloved Callirhoe, he finds the tomb empty:

> At the crack of dawn [*periorthon*] Chaereas turned up at the tomb, ostensibly to offer wreaths and libations, but in fact with the intention of doing away with himself. . . . When he reached the tomb, he found that the stones had been moved [*eupe tous lithous kekinemenous*] and the entrance was open [*phaneran ten eisodon*]. He was astonished [*ekplesso*] at the sight and overcome with fearful perplexity [*upo deines aporias*] at what had happened. Rumor—a swift messenger—told the Syracusans this amazing news. They all quickly crowded round the tomb, but no one dared go inside until Hermocrates gave an order to do so. . . . It seemed incredible that even the corpse was not lying there. Then Chaereas himself determined to go in, in his desire to see Callirhoe again even dead; but though he hunted through the tomb, he could find nothing [*ouden eurein edunato*].

Later, Chaereas finds Callirhoe's grave goods from the tomb on a pirate's ship:

> Ah, Callirhoe! These are yours! This is the wreath I put on your head! Your father gave you this, your mother this; this is your bridal dress! . . . But—I can see your things but where are you? The tomb's contents are all there—except the body!

We eventually learn that poor Callirhoe has been seized by tomb robbers after being awakened from a drug-induced sleep.[26] Many such "empty tombs" (*kenotaphion*) of the special dead were known.[27] The

Hellenistic translation tradition is certainly the best literary context in which to understand the "empty tomb" tradition found in Mark.[28] Logically, such translation stories are more likely to have evolved when the real grave of the special dead was unknown.[29] As it stands, Mark 16:1-8 is a fictional antitranslation or deification story.[30]

However, to say this is not enough. The gender of the characters plays more of a role in the story than previous commentators have allowed. The flight of the women from the tomb should also be understood in light of Mark's interest in debunking the disciples, also an aretalogical commonplace.[31] First the men flee, then the women. That the women flee from a *tomb* is no doubt due to the common connection of women to such activities. The women go to the tomb to do what women were supposed to do, but they fail miserably. Burton Mack, commenting on the empty tomb account in Mark, sees the real implications of Mark's narrative when he writes:

> The story of the empty tomb is a poor appearance story since Jesus does not appear. It is also a poor cultic legend of any kind. The young man explains that the women have come to the wrong place. "He is not here." "Go." (Don't come back.)[32]

Tombs are, after all, where one picks up demons (Mark 5:1-5). This is no doubt why Mary Magdalene picks up a few demons herself (Mark 16:9; Luke 8:2). Despite feminist scholars' current interest in the empty tomb tradition, the cumulative effect of these stories is hardly affirming of women or women's religious rituals in antiquity.[33] Celsus certainly gets the overall effect of these Gospel accounts. He says that Jesus' resurrection was confirmed by one hysterical female[34] who no doubt hallucinated[35] or saw a ghost.[36] Origen responds that Jesus appeared to others too.[37] It is not the case that women could not be legal witnesses to such events,[38] but the negative associations of women with death, burial, and mourning fuels Celsus's criticism. However, the continued marginalization of women in death and mourning scenes coincides with a continuing significant role for women in the cult of the dead. Gregory Riley has recently suggested a similar theological function for the Thomas appearance tradition in the *Gospel of John*. By portraying the physicality of Jesus' resurrection, John intends to counteract notions of nonphysical resurrections presupposed in the cult of heroes and the dead.[39] Gerd Lüdemann has suggested that Peter's resurrection experience presupposes an experience of extreme grief.[40] Although Peter's grief following Jesus' death is nowhere narrated in the New Testament, Mary Magdalene's is (John 20:4).[41] Furthermore, dreams, waking dreams, and visions following deaths were commonly linked to the founding of cults in antiquity.[42] The Gospel empty tomb and physical appearance stories are attempting to obscure this as a possible origin for Christian belief and practice by replacing it with a bodily resurrection or translation theology. These stories also function to discourage any current practice of the cult of the dead, which although practiced among Jews and Christians, remained problematic.

This tradition certainly did not encourage any kind of tomb cult of the special dead in earliest Christian groups. There is little evidence that early Christians had much interest in the location of Jesus' tomb until post-Constantinian times.[43] This strongly suggests that the location of Jesus' burial place was simply unknown, considered unimportant, or in an unlocatable mass grave. Given the strong ancient traditions associating Jesus with powerful, magical figures, it seems reasonable to conclude that if his tomb had been known early on, it would have been venerated, particularly if it had actually been found empty or if Jesus had actually been spotted in the vicinity of a tomb, as later Gospel stories claim. Early Palestinian Christians could also have built a tomb monument; such monuments to special prophets and patriarchs were common in first-century Palestine.[44] Given that there is no evidence for a tomb cult among early Christians, an early identification of his tombsite is unlikely and precludes the origin of the empty tomb story in pre-Constantinian Christian worship at the location of Jesus' tomb.[45] This explains the vague place-references in Mark's empty tomb story: "He is not here. Go!" (Mark 16:6-7).[46] There is ample evidence, however, that pre-Constantinian Christians continued a tradition of the cult of the dead unconnected to a particular location of Jesus' tomb, gathering to meet in communal tombs, much like associations.[47] The evidence for this kind of cultic practice is the earliest evidence for Christian worship in antiquity.[48]

I believe that Mark 15:40-41 and 16:1-8 both serve to modify the implications of 1 Cor 15:4, placing the women at the cross and the tomb where they do not mourn. In light of this common background, the variations of women's names in Mark 15:40, 47 and 16:1 suggests that these two stories were linked secondarily.[49] Since both a "suffering dikaios" model and a literary "noble death" theme presuppose the presence of women, albeit weeping women, this favors including them in any posited pre-Markan account. Thus, although the empty tomb tradition does not contain an oral narrative tradition passed through women's networks,[50] it may have arisen in response to a tradition that implied women's cultic experience: "he was buried, he was raised on the third day" (1 Cor 15:4).

Women at the Crucifixion

We find the earliest account of the crucifixion in the Gospel of Mark, from which notions about Matthew's and Luke's should naturally follow. John S. Kloppenborg has dealt sufficiently with Luke's passion narrative in this regard.[51] Scholars sometimes consider the general report of the women at the cross (Mark 15:40-41) as coming from a traditional passion source.[52] An analysis of John's version supports the claim that Mark's is the one story from which the rest are derived. It seems unlikely that John gives us independent accounts of the crucifixion, burial, and empty tomb for the following reasons: (1) John's account of the crucifixion, empty tomb, and appearances presuppose the Markan account, which places only women at the cross and the tomb. Like the Gospels of Luke and Peter, John secondarily inserts male characters into these traditions, especially the "beloved disciple" (John 19:26-27). (2) In the burial scene, women's roles are further co-opted by male characters in that Nicodemus brings spices rather than the women (John 19:39-40). (3) In the list of women at the cross, Mary Magdalene is listed last rather than in her usual primary position. This presupposes the Markan lists in which she is placed first and serves to weaken her importance (John 19:25; compare Mark 15:40, 47; 16:1). (4) The women do not weep at the cross in John, which is a Markan theme of feminine failure in the case of Jesus' women disciples

(John 19:25). John does, however, reintroduce feminine weeping at the tomb (John 20:4). John's account of these events thus reflects further developments that distance the women from the narrated burial events and include the reintroduction of a weeping woman.[53] The nearness of the women to the cross and the emphasis on Jesus' mother are often considered Johannine construction, theologically motivated and historically implausible (19:25-27).[54] And, although the women are near the cross, they do not mourn there, and they are not described as following Joseph and Nicodemus to the tomb (John 19:38-42).

In light of an analysis of the function of gender, the *Gospel of Peter* is also arguably late.[55] In fact, in light of the Hellenistic evidence, the novelistic developments of the *Gospel of Peter* become almost comical. Women are not present for the crucifixion. The men continually mourn before and after the empty tomb scene (*Gos. Pet.* 7:26-27; 14:58-59). Crowds, Jewish authorities, soldiers, and angels all witness the empty tomb before the women (8:28-33; 9:34-39). Although the women go to the tomb to mourn, they never get the chance but are interrupted by angels (15:55-57).[56] Although the omission of the silent women at the cross and the lack of a reference to Galilee are often taken to be a sign of Petrine independence from Mark,[57] the addition of mourning (*lypeō*) men immediately following the crucifixion scene (7:26-27) makes this unlikely. The comment by the women when they go to the tomb in fact presupposes knowledge of the Markan account (Mark 15:40-41): "We could not weep or lament on the day he was crucified" (*Gos. Pet.* 12:56). This also shows more development than either Luke or John. Men are not only added but entirely replace the women in and around the crucifixion. The removal of the women from the crucifixion scene is thus a late development in the tradition, not a sign of an independent tradition. The reduction of the number of the women at the tomb to Mary Magdalene and friends (12:50-51), rather than being a sign of primitive tradition,[58] merely shows the author's abandoned effort to sort out the competing traditions in the Synoptic records and John. Mary Magdalene is most uniformly identified.[59] The inserted epiphany scene (8:28—10:41) also has late elements.[60] The cross motif (10:39) is a tremendously late development in Christian iconography and tradition.[61] The two shorter characters that sustain the taller one as they exit the tomb (10.39) reflects a Roman processional practice that did not influence church liturgy until post-

Constantinian times.[62] The crowds at the tomb (9:34) no doubt also reflect a post–Constantinian veneration of Jesus' designated tomb.[63] The mourning of the men at the end of the fragment presupposes the longer ending of Mark (Mark 16:10, *pentheō/klaiō*; *Gos. Pet.* 14:59, *klaiō/ lypeō*; cf. 7:26-27, *pentheō/klaiō*). Furthermore, P. Oxy. 2949 (usually identified as a second-to third-century scrap of the *Gospel of Peter*) has such substantial variations from the eighth- to ninth-century Akhmim fragment of Peter that it may not even be a piece of the same text at all, and at the very least is a different version of the text. It cannot be used to confirm the narrative of the Akhmim fragment, nor does it firmly establish an early date for the *Gospel of Peter*.[64] Thus, the *Gospel of Peter* should be considered a late novelistic account of the crucifixion and the empty tomb.

Mark's account of the crucifixion should still be considered the earliest. However, Mark comes not to mourn Jesus, as women eye-witnesses would, but to praise him. His overall report thus has little in it that reflects the characteristics of women's interpretation of death and suffering found in formal or folk laments. The basic structure of Mark's passion narrative reflects both the Hellenistic noble death tradition and the suffering and righteous martyrdom tradition, which presumes noble death themes.[65] Both of these paradigms presuppose the presence of lamenting women, family, and friends. In Hellenistic noble death scenes, women and friends are usually present or nearby before being asked to leave the scene.[66] In the Psalms, we find two possible antecedents for the distance of these family and/or friends from the scene, Psalm 38:11 and Psalm 88:8.[67] Psalm 38:11 in particular sounds similar to Mark 15:40-41: "My friends and companions stand aloof from my affliction, and my neighbors stand far off" (RSV) (LXX, *apo makrothen*).[68] Mark records that a group of women watch (*theōreō*) the crucifixion "from afar," or "at a distance," (*apo makrothen*), including "Mary Magdalene, Mary the mother of James and Joseph, and Salome," as well as "many other women" (*allai pollai*). Mark says that these women "followed" (*akoloutheō*) and "served" (*diakoneō*) Jesus from Galilee to Jerusalem (Mark 15:40-41). However, it is striking that in Mark, the women are silent, both at the cross and at the tomb.

Most scholars argue that the reference to the women was not in a pre-Markan passion source but is rather from the hand of the evangelist.[69]

Others argue that Mark refers to a pre-Markan source and here shares traditional material with the Gospel of John.[70] The introduction of the women in Mark 15:40 is arguably quite abrupt, and the lists of the women vary: 15:40-41 (three women), 15:47 (two women), and 16:1 (three women). This suggests some source may lie behind these stories, or perhaps separate pre-Markan traditions.[71] Mark's abruptness in mentioning the women so late in his narrative has sparked a lively debate among feminist scholars.[72] This abruptness supports the view that the reference to the women is pre-Markan. In neither John nor Mark do these women, particularly Mary Magdalene, play further important roles. Further, the lists of the women in Mark and John do show some correspondence (Mark 15:40; John 19:25). However, given that lists of three and two are common in folk narratives,[73] the variations in Markan lists may be accounted for on the basis of simple narrative style rather than pre-Markan written tradition.[74] John subsequently has expanded this number to four.[75] Moreover, names like Mary and Salome were so common in first-century Palestine that any definite identification of these women may be impossible, except for the mother of Jesus and Mary Magdalene (Mark 15:40; John 19:25).[76] It seems more logical to conclude that Mark made the connection of women to the cross and the tomb due to the more general connection of women to death, burial, and tombs, the early tradition that Jesus "was raised on the third day" (1 Cor. 15:4), combined with an oral tradition linking women to these events. Mark 15:47 serves as a Markan narrative link between these two stories.[77] Finally, there is reason to doubt Johannine independence for the traditions concerning the women, both here and in his empty tomb narrative (John 19:25; 20:1-18).[78] This further weakens arguments for a pre-Markan written source, either for the crucifixion scene proper or the tale of the empty tomb (16:1-8). Given Markan reticence over the associations of Mary Magdalene and women with mourning rituals and the cult of the dead, Winsome Munro may be correct in her assumption that Mark deliberately postpones reference to these women to suppress or obscure their role in the Jesus movement.[79] Since both the "suffering *dikaios*" (righteous one) genre and other literary models for death scenes requires women, Mark may have had ample reason to include them without reference to a source.[80] However, the question of a pre-Markan source in this instance is relatively moot when it comes to determining the historicity of the entire narrative. Whether included in a pre-Markan source modeled on the motif of a "suffering righteous one" or written by Mark's own hand, this aspect of the Markan narrative has clear antecedents in both the genre of the "suffering *dikaios*" and in Hellenistic death scenes. Mark differs from these models only in the silence of the women. However, if his portrayal relied only on literary models, he could easily have the women lament, wail, and leave. But he does not. This suggests a strong oral tradition and that not only literary and scriptural models linked women and lamentation to these events. Mark therefore writes women into both the crucifixion scene and his story of the empty tomb;[81] he keeps them in the story in spite of his obvious discomfort with the tradition, but he keeps them silent.

Further, what is interesting about Mark's placement of the women in the narrative is that it is clear that he considers them disciples. Like their masculine counterparts, the women form a triumvirate subset (Peter, James, and John/Mary Magdalene, Mary the mother of James and Joseph [cf. Mark 15:40, 47; 16:1], and Salome). Like the men, once they are introduced into the narrative, they subsequently flee the scene, show fear of epiphany, and do not do as they are instructed.[82] Comparison of Mark 15:40-41 in the context of ancient death scenes strengthens the argument that the women here have the role of disciples. Usually, the women are dismissed from the death scene proper, and the male disciples or companions who remain. In Mark, this order is reversed; the men flee before the crucifixion scene, the women remain to observe the death (Mark 14:50-51, 66-72). Later the women too will flee, but from the tomb (16:8). Adela Yarbro Collins misses this parallel between the men and the women once the women are introduced. She sees the flight of the men (Mark 14:50-51) as referring to Psalm 38:11, that is, the friends are "far off" in that the men are entirely absent.[83] This ignores the clear parallel to Psalm 38:11, *apo makrothen*, which describes the stance of the women (Mark 15:40). Notably, following the flight of the men, Peter "follows" (*akoloutheō*) Jesus "from a distance" (*apo makrothen*) (Mark 14:54).[84] Mark's portrayal of the women as disciples is clear and deliberate. The motif of "service" (*diakoneō*) (Mark 15:41) also implies that the women are present at meals with Jesus even though they are absent from scenes like the last supper (cf. 14:3-9; 14:12-25).[85] We should therefore view

Mark's negative portrayal of the women as corresponding to his negative portrayal of the men rather than as a positive portrayal that juxtaposes them.[86] The women fit into the larger theme of discipleship in Mark,[87] since failure of disciples is a larger Markan and aretalogical theme.[88] Given the theme of failure in Mark and the later fleeing of the women from the tomb (16:8), it seems unlikely that the silence of the women is here meant to be a sign that the women are noble in the sight of death. Thus, although it seems improbable that the Markan narrative presupposes an early written account, it is notable that in Mark the women fill the slot of "disciple" along with the men, and he includes them in the crucifixion and burial scenes. Mark waits to mention them, and after he does, he modifies their claim to have seen the risen Jesus, but they are there nonetheless. It seems reasonable to conclude that there is at least a pre-Markan oral tradition linking women followers of Jesus to the crucifixion and burial of Jesus.[89] Scribal activity alone does not account for the portrayal of women in the Markan passion narrative.

Oral Lamentation and the Passion Narrative

Given the concern for women's lamentation in all Gospel accounts and the common practice of women's lamentation of the dead in antiquity, the most logical oral tradition presupposed by the passion narrative would be oral laments. The passion narrative itself could have its roots in the formal context of repeated sung storytelling, which could have preserved basic details of the tale of Jesus' death. Both folk and formal laments contained the element of narrative and followed set oral patterns. Lament traditions were transferred into literary and scribal contexts in Greek, Roman, and Jewish literature. Judaism in particular has a long tradition of formal laments that scholars suggest originated in popular lamentation.[90] The earliest evidence for Christian liturgical practice is funerary. Oral lament traditions thus do make imaginable some plausible context in which oral traditions about Jesus' death may have been transmitted by early Christian men and women.

In fact, this context explains several things, particularly the use of lament Psalms (especially Psalm 22) in the development of a written passion narrative. Further, Aramaic words are preserved in the Markan narrative, *Golgotha* (Mark 15:22) and *Eloi, Eloi, lama sabachthani?* ("My God, my God, why have you forsaken me?") (Mark 15:34, cf. Ps 22:1). Rather than preserving Jesus' actual words or representing Markan attempts at local color, we can explain the Aramaic in Mark 15 as remnants of an early sung lament by women, given that fragments of women's laments are preserved in Aramaic in rabbinic sources.[91] It would be natural to assume that not only scribes knew how to quote the Psalms. Further, allusions to biblical passages and the Psalms are also preserved in rabbinic laments.[92] Place-names, geographical references, and proper names occur in biblical laments, although not in rabbinic laments.[93] It is also the case that evidence very close in age to the Gospels themselves, the *Epistle of Barnabas*, which contains many of the scriptural "proofs" used in the passion narrative in the discussion of the crucifixion, contains no narrative, no *story*.[94] Evidently, scriptural proofs and scribal activity alone were not enough to create the impetus for narrative that lies behind the creation of the passion story of the death of Jesus.

This contention can be reinforced with cross-cultural examples. In many parts of the world, such as Greece, Ireland, Central America, Finland, China, the Middle East, Africa, New Guinea, and Spain, women have in past and present times habitually keened and mourned the dead. Many of these lament traditions in fact sustain a poetic genre that goes back in some cases hundreds, or in the case of rural Greece, thousands of years.[95] Certain women in these areas are well-known for their gifts of lamentation and are much sought after to sing well known and popular stories at various funerals, or to create new songs of lamentation for a particular or notable person who has died. Lamentation also retains its power as a vehicle for social and political protest, and in areas like Ireland or Greece, for example, these laments sung at funerals can serve to inflame crowds present for funerals to seek vengeance for the deaths of those unjustly killed. Such laments contain the details of the story of the death of the deceased. Hence there has been an attempt in modern times to limit this art form at public funerals.

It is the case, however, that these songs contain an important narrative element, including details of the life and death of the deceased that can be compared to certain elements of the passion story that cannot be accounted for on the basis of literary and scriptural models. Laments recording events of a very distant past are less likely to contain valuable historical details than laments recording events within a generation of a death.[96] Laments, as an oral genre intended to fix memories for a community, fix the event of a death in time and space. They usually contain reference to the mode of death, whether by murder, execution, failed medical operations, horsing accidents, or death by natural causes. They also often open with a phrase that sets the death in time: "Early one Monday morning," "On a holiday," "on Sunday," "One Saturday at nine," "One night right at midnight." The time of year can also be mentioned, such as Eastertide, and so on. This custom of fixing the mode of death and setting it in time is common to laments from many cultures.[97] Besides fixing the death in time, laments also contain many proper names and place-names, often set by the singer's or the dead's walk through a landscape.[98] References to family members are also common.[99] The blame for the death is often assigned to a specific individual or group.[100] Embellishment of facts and romanticizing of the event, however, can begin early, such as the association in Christian cultures of a murder with the time of Jesus' death at Easter.[101] These laments are worked at slowly, over a period of days or even months, before they are performed in public.[102]

The passion narratives in the Gospels all betray a likely beginning in a lament in that they contain similar settings in time, place-names, proper names, and other details found in laments. The mode of death is uniformly crucifixion, the blame for which is given to Pilate or the Jewish authorities (Mark 15:24; John 19:18; Gos. Pet. 4:10). The time of year is set at Passover (Mark 14:1; John 19:14; Gos. Pet. 2:6), the times of day for Jesus' crucifixion, death, and burial are noted (Mark 15:25, 33-34, 42; John 19:14; Gos. Pet. 5:15), the day is the day before the Sabbath (Mark 15:42; John 19:31; Gos. Pet. 2:5), the Aramaic place-name of the site of the crucifixion is fixed (Golgotha, Mark 15:22; John 19:17), and the titulus remembered (Mark 15:26; John 19:1-20; Gos. Pet. 4:11). Lists of family and friends present are supplied (Mark 15:40-41; John 19:25). The association of Jesus' death with the Passover and his death with the time of the slaughtering of a lamb in preparation for the Passover feast are similar to common embellishments of death stories found in popular laments. A more general association of Jesus' death with the Passover in an oral lament would better explain the many detailed discrepancies between John and the Synoptics, which vary considerably on the exact relation of the crucifixion to the Passover.[103] The written versions of the passion story found in Mark, John, and the *Gospel of Peter* thus contain details common to oral laments.

However, both John and the *Gospel of Peter*, although dependent on Mark for their written narratives, also show signs of the variation in tradition that is common in oral materials, and we can show them to reflect independent oral traditions from that of Mark that could be explained on the basis of independent performances of a lament of Jesus' death. John's narrative contains a doubling of the tradition of a Jewish official assisting in the burial (Nicodemus, John 19:39), as well as a second Aramaic place-name (the judge's bench, *Gabbatha*, 19:13); he also expands the wording of the titulus to "Jesus of Nazareth, King of the Jews," the knowledge of which in several languages must be explained (John 19:19-20); he lists a fourth woman at the foot of the cross, Mary Clopas (John 19:25); and he identifies a new tomb for Jesus in a garden (John 19:21). Thus, although John does show literary dependence on Mark for much of his passion narrative, there are varied elements that can be explained on the basis of an alternative oral source such as a lament. The *Gospel of Peter* shows similar variations that are better explained on the basis of a common liturgical context of ritual lamentation. The cry from the cross is varied—"My power, my power why have you forsaken me?" (*Gos. Pet.* 5:19), the list of women shortened to one (*Gos. Pet.* 12:50), the place of burial named as "Joseph's Garden" (*Gos. Pet.* 6:24), and the titulus changed to "King of Israel" (*Gos. Pet.* 4:11). All of these minor alterations are better explained on the basis of varied but similar oral performances of the story of Jesus' death rather than on the basis of three independent written versions of the story known to Mark, John, and Peter. Rather, John and Peter would have been drawing on both Mark and current oral versions of the passion story still being performed in their community rather than a written pre-Markan source.

These observations alter the current understanding of the probable origin of the passion narrative itself. Rather than being exclusively a scribal product and originally a written document from a subculture dominated by well-educated men as virtually all scholars suppose, I am suggesting that the passion narrative had its origins in a grassroots liturgical context dominated by women and ordinary people, even possibly day laborers. Thus, its origins are in an oral genre found among ordinary people who visited over and over again the gravesites of their loved ones and sang and sang again the stories of notable deaths in their community, in this case, Jesus'. This would mean that the kernel of tradition behind the passion narrative would be very, very ancient indeed. Certain details and embellishments of the story of Jesus' crucifixion could go back to the first few days and months following Jesus' death. The antiquity of the passion story that I am suggesting undermines the extreme skepticism now present in the discussion of the passion narrative itself.[104] The passion narrative becomes basic evidence for the mode of Jesus' death (crucifixion) as well as potentially providing certain ancient details concerning his death and burial found in the passion narrative that cannot be explained on the basis of literary models of noble deaths available to the evangelists. Further, the existence of a popular liturgical tradition concerning Jesus' death could preclude the existence of an original written version of the passion narrative altogether. Just as there was probably no original written version of the Lord's Prayer, there may have been no original written version of the passion narrative, but rather all early versions reflect a common liturgical context.[105] This lamentation tradition would have naturally predated the empty tomb tradition, and even the creed in 1 Cor 15:3-8, which both evolved in part to undermine the ramifications of the connecting women's lamentation to Jesus' death and resurrection. This would mean that there was a stage of heroization of Jesus in Palestine that did not presuppose a cult, but grew out of a repeated, well-known song heroizing Jesus' death that invoked the opening lines of the lament Psalm 22.

Resurrection Traditions and Continuing Conflict

The significance of this theory is that if Jesus was mourned over and over by means of liturgical lamentation, he was not at first considered resurrected in any special way by some, perhaps for many years. Rather, the development of resurrection theology could have followed a normal course of development from a lament for the dead Jesus without a formal cult of any kind to an ideology supporting a cult based in part on visionary experiences of Jesus as he gained postmortem popularity, to the fictional empty tomb stories, and finally to bodily resurrection narratives. A number of factors probably worked together to undergird the development of Easter faith within early Christian communities. It is possible that the popularity of his sung story increased his postmortem significance. It is possible that close friends and family experienced a series of grief-induced visions. Such experiences on the part of loved ones have been documented weeks, months, and even years following family deaths.[106] Dreams, waking dreams, and visions were also known to occur following deaths in antiquity and were commonly linked to the founding of cults.[107] Gerd Lüdemann, as mentioned above, has already suggested that Peter's vision of Jesus was a grief hallucination.[108] Marianne Sawicki has also associated Mary Magdalene's resurrection experience with women's mourning rites in antiquity.[109] It is further possible that liturgies involving grief and resurrection motifs from the mysteries, especially from the Isis religion or that of Tammuz, influenced early Christian thinking concerning the resurrection of Jesus and contributed to the development of a full-blown resurrection theology. We know that Isis hymns paralleled hymns to Christ in the pre-Pauline period.[110] However, in light of the first description of resurrection appearances recorded in 1 Cor 15:3-8, whenever their occurrence before the development of the creedal tradition Paul transmits, the experiences of early Christians were spiritual visions of Jesus or ecstatic experiences, not experiences of a bodily risen Lord.[111] At some point, certain of these visions became associated with a third-day funerary ritual. What remains unlikely is that a tomb was found empty. Not only do the empty tomb narratives betray obvious fictional themes, but the lack of any sign of a tomb cult in Palestine until the fourth century precludes this. Given the popularity of tombsites for well-known prophets and patriarchs in first-century Palestine, a literal "empty tomb" would have increased the likelihood of a physical site commemorating Jesus' resurrection, not decreased it. Perhaps Jesus' own reticence concerning such sites lived on in the minds of early Palestinian Christians, further precluding the development of a tomb cult. The empty tomb traditions thus show prejudice against the development of such a cult as well as reflect cultural stereotypes linking women to necromancy, magic, and tomb visitation. These associations led to the erasure of the women's and the lower classes' contribution to the development of resurrection theology in early Christian communities. Only the hint of women's funerary rituals associated with Jesus' burial remain in the earliest tradition: "he was buried, on the third day he was raised" (1 Cor 15:4). At some point, however, grief gave way to joy. An ongoing lament tradition would have been at odds with a clear resurrection theology (1 Thess 4:13; Heb 11:35).

To be clear, I do not mean to imply by this that Mary Magdalene was a magician or that she conjured Jesus' spirit by magical means; rather, I mean to suggest that the stereotypical connection of women to magic and conjuring the dead at tombs served to marginalize her claim to having seen a vision of the resurrected Lord in a way that it did not for the men, even though Peter and the other male disciples are also associated with the "third day" tradition. Mary Magdalene's experience was understood within a particular cultural, literary, and cultic context. Thus, although it becomes difficult to define exactly what Mary Magdalene's experience was, it is clear that her claim to having had such an experience became theologically problematic at a very early level of the tradition.

Could Women's Lamentation and Grief Lead to "Resurrection Faith"?

In spite of the fact that Mary Magdalene and women figure prominently in the empty tomb and resurrection narratives in the Gospels, women are omitted from the earliest tradition of the beginnings of "resurrection faith" in 1 Corinthians 15. No women's names appear in the list of those who had seen the risen Lord. This omission is glaring and belies the later traditions of the Gospels, which feature women. Elsewhere, Paul is not bothered to name a woman an apostle (Romans

16). Scholars often argue that Paul has simply omitted the women due to gender prejudice. However, there is no reason to think that lamenting women and day laborers would have thought that the dead Jesus was somehow alive in any real way other than in the sense of his presence at the memorial meal for his death and in their lament. The empty tomb stories are late and fictional, and the resurrection accounts of Matthew and John are even later additions to the Markan narrative and clearly ficticious and unhistorical. The paradigm for Christian origins I am suggesting does not allow for supernatural experiences on the part of these early women and lower-class followers of Jesus, but instead allows for the ordinary experiences of grieving women and the lower classes in the community in the context of memorial meals for the dead Jesus. Grief hallucinations are common experiences of those who have lost a loved one.

Jesus, History, and Lament

Given the tenacity of women's lament traditions, as well as the interest in family retrieval of executed family members, it seems plausible that a few women, including Mary Magdalene, and even some of the men,[112] would have tried to find Jesus' body after he died in spite of the risks that such actions might have entailed. It seems probable that Jesus was buried, as 1 Cor 15:4 affirms, since we may assume the application of Deut 21:22-23 to crucifixions in first-century Palestine. It seems more likely that Jesus was buried in a mass grave set aside for criminals than in a special tomb. Given the fictional elements in the "empty tomb" narratives, that he was buried in a tomb seems more problematic. We can assume that either Jesus was from a social class that brought him political connections[113] or that his visibility as a public figure gave him friends in high places[114] since "empty tomb" stories are more common when the location of the remains of the special dead are unknown.[115] In any case, the song of Jesus' death would have been more naturally resung after the first year following his death at the funeral locations of other Jews, Jewish Christians, and others in Palestine. In spite of—or because of—the glaring omission of any lamenting women from Mark's earliest account of Jesus' death and burial, and because the literary models he assumes in fact include them, it seems more likely that Jesus' women and lower-class followers indeed mourned his death, given the pervasiveness of cultic lamentation by ancient women and the lower classes in the ongoing family rites of the cult of the dead. For clearly theological reasons, the Gospel accounts avoid portraying women's lamentation of Jesus at the tomb. "He was raised on the third day" implies that Jesus' followers, especially women, probably mourned his death the third day following his burial and may have commemorated his presence, probably with a meal, in spite of Jesus' declaration, "Let the dead bury their own dead!" (Matt 8:22 // Luke 9:60). Such attempts to restrict popular funerary rites were everywhere ignored. The empty tomb and physical-appearance stories were developed to correct the assumption that visions of Jesus' resurrection were associated with the religious rites of women and the lower classes going to the gravesite to commune with the spirit of the deceased, as women and the lower classes had done in the context of popular Greek, Roman, and ancient Near Eastern religious ritual for thousands of years. Since women and the lower classes in antiquity had thousands of years of tradition on their side, their rituals associated with the cult of the dead remained sanctioned as traditional features of popular religion, and thus contributed to the preservation of details of the story of Jesus' death in oral poetic form.

CONCLUSION

Commensality and meals have become the focus of the study of Christian origins. This book has proposed that the liturgical context of women's funerary meals and lament was the best situation in life (*Sitz im Leben*) to solve many vexing problems of Christian origins. The creative work of ordinary women generated the formation of the earliest Christian community. It is women's funerary rituals, or the cult of the dead, that create community by creating continuity with the living and the deceased, in this case, Jesus. Jesus became the special dead of the community whose presence was memorialized and felt in women's and ordinary people's mortuary meals and laments. It is the storytelling of women and ordinary people that gives us many of the miracle stories that feature the themes of funeral, miracle, and meal, and it is women's laments that lie at the heart of the narrative core of the passion story.

New Testament texts betray the debate over the place of women in public meals or banquets. This is because women's meal etiquette was undergoing flux and change from 300 BCE to 300 CE. Their posture and very presence at meals was being negotiated: should they be seated or reclining on the banquet couch like equals, present or separated in their own dining rooms, or remain absent altogether? Women who were present for public meals could be accused of promiscuity and errant sexual behavior, since in the ancient Greek East only prostitutes, courtesans, slaves, and flute girls were present for men's banquets. The banquet became the stereotypical location for erotic goings on, as the women present were assumed to be there for the sexual sport of the men. However, as early as 300 BCE, respectable women began to be present for public meals, and by Roman times, respectable women began to recline with men for formal banquets. Funerary meals were one meal context where women could be expected to attend, although they may have been seated separately or in a separate room.

Mark is the most ambiguous of the Gospels in this regard, as he portrays women in erotic locales and in gender stereotypical ways but does not suggest that the women are any less respectable. Luke maintains strict gender segregation in his literary meal scenes, and the one woman who appears at a formal banquet is a "woman known in the city as a sinner," that is, a prostitute of some sort. Matthew's is the most open of all the Gospels to women's place at meals, as he adds women to his miraculous feeding narratives, which are cast as funerary meals and eucharists. John has both respectable and unrespectable women in his meal scenes, like the respectable Mary of Bethany, who anoints Jesus at a meal, or the disreputable Samaritan woman who has had too many husbands and offers Jesus water at mealtime. In Paul, women are obviously present for community worship and community meals, although Paul wants the women to be respectably veiled and prefers gender-segregated seating during times of community worship.

Early Christian groups were therefore akin to Greco-Roman associations and clubs, which were gender-inclusive and held communal meals for social occasions as well as provided for members' funerals and banquets. Leadership and community terminology used by early

Christian groups is best seen as having antecedents in the terminology used by Greco-Roman associations or clubs. *Episkopos*, "bishop," *diakonos*, "deacon," and the term for the entire community, *ekklēsia*, "church," have their best reflection in terms used in the Greco-Roman associations and clubs. Like early Greco-Roman clubs, early Christians gathered for gender-inclusive meals, albeit often with gender-segregated seating; worshiped their god and celebrated liturgy; and provided for the funerals and funeral meals of community members.

Women were the primary actors and oral creators in funerary contexts in Greek, Roman, and Jewish traditions, even in first-century Palestine. Women washed the dead, anointed the dead with oil, sang oral laments retelling the story of the circumstances of the death of the individual, and repeatedly went to tombs and gravesites throughout the year to conduct liturgical rituals. These rituals included offering food to the deceased, especially bread and fish, and welcoming the presence of the deceased in their memorial meals and laments. Such rituals were conducted on the third day after death, the ninth day after death, the thirtieth day after death, and then annually, throughout the ancient Mediterranean world. With thousands of years of tradition on their side, women and ordinary people, in spite of attempts to limit and restrict their liturgical activities, continued to visit the graves and tombs of their loved ones and to sing laments over and over again. These rituals were central to Greek, Roman, and Jewish societies and, as such, were not easily changed or eradicated.

The New Testament reflects this common funerary practice and the connection of women to funerals and meals. The movement around Jesus, however, predates this connection. It held celebratory gender- and class-inclusive meals of the kingdom of God, which did not celebrate Jesus' presence. Jesus himself opposed excessive attention to the dead, declaring, "Let the dead bury their own dead!" and saying "Become passersby," in reference to passing by epitaphs on tombstones commemorating the dead. Only after Jesus' death did early Christians celebrate meals of Jesus' presence and memorialize his death. The *Didache* contains two meals of Jesus' presence, one that has the leader declare "Maranatha," "Our Lord come (to the meal)," and the other, which is called a eucharist, but does not have the words of institution over the cup and bread. It is Mark and Paul that contain recitations of the Lord's Supper with the full words of institution over the cup and bread and claim that a man, namely, Jesus himself, instituted this memorial meal for the dead Jesus, not women or ordinary people.

Women's storytelling may well lie behind several miracle stories that feature themes of burial, women, and meals. In the miraculous feeding narratives of Matthew, women and children gather with the men for eucharist and funerary meals featuring bread and fish. They are cast as family eucharists, the bread and fish being a vestige of the oral telling of the story about funerary meals in a funerary context. In the story of the Syro-Phoenician woman, Jesus casts a demon from the daughter of a stereotypical promiscuous woman who requests crumbs from the messianic banquet. This story reflects stereotypical Christian funerary meals with dogs under the table to knock out the lights. Jesus treats the woman and her daughter with extreme prejudice and calls them "little bitches" or "dogs." The audaciousness of the woman is the heart of the story: she earns her daughter's healing by her witty retort. That audaciousness suggests women's storytelling, not men's.

In the story of the unnamed woman who anoints Jesus at a meal, it is the woman who understands and proclaims the death of Jesus as she anoints him for his burial. Here she earns the ire of the male disciples for her audacious behavior. The scene has its roots in an early oral chreia and has erotic overtones in each Gospel, although only Luke's version makes this eroticism clear. The audacious behavior of the woman again suggests women's storytelling, not men's. Along with the miracle stories with their themes of burial, women, and meals, it is the passion story that can be shown to have its roots in women's grassroots oral storytelling in the context of women's lamentation for the dead Jesus. Cross-cultural studies of oral laments of women highlight the oral core behind the four passion accounts, whose differences can be accounted for on the basis of differing oral recitations in women's lament. Scriptural proofs and scribal activity are not enough to account for the narrative design of the passion narratives.

Further, we have seen that women's role in funerals, funerary meals, and laments began on the third day following the death of an individual and that it was on this third day that the dead were invoked and their presence felt. In this light, I asserted that the pre-Pauline tradition that Jesus was "raised" and "appeared," in the sense that his presence was felt, "on the third day" can be explained on the basis of women's funerary practices and laments "on the third day" after death.

Thus, the early attestation of the "raised and appeared" Lord has its roots in the rituals of a grassroots cult of the dead among women and ordinary people, not in the experience of an all-male group either of scribal elites or apostles. It is the liturgical experiences and practices of women and ordinary people that best explain the "third day" tradition in 1 Corinthians 15.

It is unlikely, however, that these women had a developed "resurrection faith" as is found in the later resurrection narratives in the Gospels, which feature a bodily resurrected Lord. Women who lament the dead feel the presence of the deceased in their memorial meals and laments for the dead, but this liturgical practice is part of the normal grieving process of ancient Mediterranean people and does not require divine intervention or supernatural experiences to explain. Even grief hallucinations are part of the normal process of human grieving. Thus, the origins of the earliest traditions of the New Testament concerning the origins of the Christian communities can be explained on the basis of the liturgical funerary rituals and meals and ordinary people, not elite men or an all male apostleship.

It is here, then—in the gatherings of ordinary women to mourn and lament the dead Jesus, not in the closed circle of male disciples—that we should seek the origins of the resurrection traditions.

NOTES

Chapter 1: Early Christian Meals and Associations

1. Keith Bradley, "The Roman Family at Dinner," in *Meals in a Social Context: Aspects of the Communal Meal in the Hellenistic and Roman World*, ed. Inge Nielson and Hanne Sigismund Nielson (Oxford: Aarhus University Press, 1998), 36–55; Joan Burton, "Women's Commensality in the Ancient Greek World," *Greece and Rome* 45 (1998): 143–65; Hanne Sigismund Nielson "Roman Children at Mealtimes," in *Meals in a Social Context: Aspects of the Communal Meal in the Hellenistic and Roman World*, ed. Inge Nielson and Hanne Sigismund Nielson (Oxford: Aarhus University Press, 1998), 56–66; John F. Donahue, "Toward a Typology of Roman Public Feasting," *American Journal of Philology* 124 (2003): 423–41; David Noy, "The Sixth Hour Is the Mealtime for Scholars: Jewish Meals in the Roman World," in *Meals in a Social Context: Aspects of the Communal Meal in the Hellenistic and Roman World*, ed. Inge Nielson and Hanne Sigismund Nielson (Oxford: Aarhus University Press, 1998), 134–44; Matthew Roller, "Horizontal Women: Posture and Sex in the Roman

Convivium," *American Journal of Philology* 124 (2003): 377–422; idem, *Dining Posture in Ancient Rome: Bodies, Values and Status* (Princeton, N.J.: Princeton University Press, 2006), 96–156; William J. Slater, ed., *Dining in a Classical Context* (Ann Arbor: University of Michigan Press, 1991); Dennis E. Smith, *From Symposium to Eucharist: The Banquet in the Early Christian World* (Minneapolis: Fortress Press, 2003); Hal Taussig, *In the Beginning Was the Meal: Social Experimentation and Early Christian Identity* (Minneapolis: Fortress Press, 2009); Michael L. White, "Regulating Fellowship in the Communal Meal: Early Jewish and Christian Evidence," in *Meals in a Social Context: Aspects of the Communal Meal in the Hellenistic and Roman World*, ed. Inge Nielson and Hanne Sigismund Nielson (Oxford: Aarhus University Press, 1998), 177–205.

2. Kathleen E. Corley, *Private Women, Public Meals: Social Conflict in the Synoptic Tradition* (Peabody, Mass.: Hendrickson, 1993).

3. See Jane S. Webster, *Ingesting Jesus: Eating and Drinking in the Gospel of John* (Atlanta, Ga.: Society of Biblical Literature, 2003).

4. Ibid., 180–82

5. Ibid., 182.

6. Ibid., 183.

7. Ibid., 183–84.

8. Ibid., 176.

9. Ibid., 176–77.

10. Ibid., 178.

11. Ibid.

12. Wayne Meeks, *The First Urban Christians: The Social World of the Apostle Paul* (New Haven, Conn.: Yale University Press, 1983).

13. Richard S. Ascough, "Greco-Roman Philosophic, Religious and Voluntary Associations," in *Community Formation in the Early Church and in the Church Today*, ed. Richard N. Longnecker (Peabody, Mass.: Hendrickson, 2002), 3–19; idem, "Matthew and Community Formation," in *The Gospel of Matthew in Current Study: Studies in Memory of William G. Thompson, S.J.*, ed. David E. Aune (Grand Rapids: Eerdmans, 2001), 96–126; idem, *Paul's Macedonian Associations* (Tübingen: Mohr Siebeck, 2003); idem, "A Question of Death: Paul's Community Building Language in 1 Thessalonians 4:13-18," *Journal of Biblical Literature* 123 (2004): 509–30; idem, "The Thessalonian Christian Community as a Professional Voluntary Association," *Journal of Biblical Literature* 119 (2000): 311–28; idem, "Voluntary Associations and the Formation of Pauline Christian Communities: Overcoming Objections," in *Vereine Synagogen und Gemeinden im kaiserzeitlichen Kleinasien*, ed. Andreas Gutsfeld and Dietrich-Alex Koch (Tübingen: Mohr Siebeck, 2006), 149–83; Philip Harland, *Associations, Synagogues, and Congregations* (Minneapolis: Fortress Press, 2003); John Kloppenborg and Stephen Wilson, Edited by *Voluntary Associations in the Graeco-Roman World* (New York: Routledge, 1996).

14. Ascough, "Overcoming Objections," 155–61; see also Wayne O. McCready, "Ekklesia and Voluntary Associations," in *Voluntary Associations*

in the Graeco-Roman World, ed. John Kloppenborg and Stephen Wilson (New York: Routledge, 1996), 59–73.

15. Ascough, "Overcoming Objections," 155–62.

16. Ibid., 162–69.

17. Ibid.

18. Ibid.

19. Ibid.

20. Ibid., 169–71.

21. Ibid., 171–76.

22. Jonathan Z. Smith, *Drudgery Divine: On the Comparison of Early Christianities and the Religions of Late Antiquity* (Chicago: University of Chicago Press, 1990).

23. Ascough, "Overcoming Objections," 171.

24. Ibid., 171–76.

25. Meeks, *First Urban Christians*.

26. Ascough, "Overcoming Objections," 171–76.

27. Harland, *Associations*, 206.

28. *In Flaccum* 4.136.

29. Harland, *Associations*, 200–12.

30. Ascough, "Overcoming Objections," 173.

31. Meeks, *First Urban Christians*.

32. Ascough, "Overcoming Objections," 179.

33. Ibid.

34. Ibid., 180.

35. Ibid.

36. Ascough, *Paul's Macedonian Associations*, 54–58; Corley, *Private Women, Public Meals*.

37. Ascough, "Overcoming Objections," 181.

38. Ibid., 182; Harland, *Associations*.

39. Tertullian, *Apology* 39.5-6.

40. Harland, *Associations*, 84.

41. Ibid., 86.

42. Ibid., 85.

43. Ibid.

44. Ibid., 86.

45. Joan Burton, "Women's Commensality in the Ancient Greek World," *Greece and Rome* 45 (1998): 143, 165, esp. 159.

46. Hugh Lindsay, "Eating with the Dead: The Roman Funerary Banquet," in *Meals in a Social Context: Aspects of the Communal Meal in the Hellenistic and Roman World*, ed. Inge Nielson and Hanne Sigismund Nielson (Oxford: Aarhus University Press, 1998), 67–80, esp. 67.

47. Ibid., 68.

48. Ibid.

49. Ibid., 68–69.

50. Robin M. Jensen, "Dining with the Dead: From the Mensa to the Altar in Christian Late Antiquity," in *Commemorating the Dead: Texts and Artifacts in Context*, ed Laurie Brink and Deborah Green (New York: Walter de Gruyter, 2008), 197–43, esp. 108–18.

51. Ibid., 117. See also Jonathan Z. Smith, *Drudgery Divine: On the Comparison of Early Christianities and the Religions of Late Antiquity* (Chicago: University of Chicago Press, 1990), 132–33.

52. Jensen, "Dining with the Dead," 120.

53. Ibid.

54. Ibid., 123–24.

55. Ibid., 128, 124.

56. Ibid., 128.

57. Ibid., 132–33

58. Ibid., 132–37.

59. Ibid., 141.

60. Ibid., 143.

61. I am greatly indebted to two papers presented at the SBL Meals Seminar in November 2006 by Ellen B. Aitken and Angela Standhartinger for recent bibliography on meals used in this chapter: Ellen B. Aitken, "Remembering and Remembered Women in Greco-Roman Meals," and Angela Standhartinger, "Women in Early Christian Meal Gatherings: Discourse and Reality."

Chapter 2: Funerary Rituals, Meals, and Lament

1. S. C. Humphreys, *The Family, Women and Death: Comparative Studies* (London: Routledge and Kegan Paul, 1983), 79.

2. Peter Brown, *The Cult of the Saints: Its Rise and Function in Latin Christianity* (Chicago: University of Chicago Press, 1981), 18–19. See also Aubrey Cannon, "The Historical Dimension in Mortuary Expressions of Status and Sentiment," *Current Anthropology* 30 (1989): 437–58.

3. Carla Antonaccio, "The Archaeology of the Ancestors," in *Cultural Poetics in Archaic Greece: Cult, Performance, Politics* (Cambridge: Cambridge University Press, 1993), 46–70, esp. 47–49; W. R. Halliday, "Cenotaphs and Sacred Localities," *Annual of the British School at Athens* 17 (1910–11): 182–92, esp. 183–84.

4. See ch. 5 below.

5. Susan Starr Sered, *Priestess, Mother, Sacred Sister: Religions Dominated by Women* (New York: Oxford University Press, 1994), 89–118; 120–33; Serinity Young, *An Anthology of Sacred Texts by and about Women* (New York: Crossroad, 1993), xxi.

6. Margaret Alexiou, *The Ritual Lament in Greek Tradition* (Cambridge: Cambridge University Press, 1974); Gail Holst-Warhaft, *Dangerous Voices: Women's*

Laments and Greek Literature (London: Routledge, 1992); Robert Garland, *The Greek Way of Death* (Ithaca, N.Y.: Cornell University Press, 1985).

7. Peter Brown remarks on the "massive stability of the Mediterranean care of the dead," *Cult of the Saints*, 24.

8. Brown, *Cult of the Saints*, 29, 31–32; Jonathan Z. Smith, *Drudgery Divine: On the Comparison of Early Christianities and the Religions of Late Antiquity* (Chicago: University of Chicago Press, 1990), 131–33. See below.

9. Here I adopt the terminology of Smith, *Drudgery Divine.*

10. On impurity in Greek religion, see Robert Parker, *Miasma: Pollution and Purification in Early Greek Religion* (Oxford: Clarendon, 1983), esp. 32–48; Jean-Pierre Vernant, *Myth and Society in Ancient Greece*, trans. Janet Lloyd (Sussex: Harvester; Atlantic Highlands, N.J.: Humanities, 1980), 110–28.

11. Alexiou, *Ritual Lament*, 4–7, 27; Walter Burkert, *Greek Religion* (Cambridge, Mass.: Harvard University Press, 1985), 192; Garland, *Greek Way of Death*, 23–24; Donna C. Kurtz and John Boardman, *Greek Burial Customs* (Ithaca, N.Y.: Cornell University Press, 1971), 143–44.

12. This may be another overgeneralization. Morris notes that only 66 of 644 graves exhumed from the fourth century BCE in Olynthus had a coin in them; none were found in the North Cemetery near Corinth. Some graves have more coins than others. See Ian Morris, *Death Ritual and Social Structure in Classical Antiquity* (Cambridge: Cambridge University Press, 1992), 105–6). See also Alfred C. Rush, *Death and Burial in Christian Antiquity* (Washington, D.C.: Catholic University of America Press, 1941), 92–99; J. M. C. Toynbee, *Death and Burial in the Roman World* (Ithaca, N.Y.: Cornell University Press, 1971), 44.

13. Burkert, *Greek Religion*, 192; Kurtz and Boardman, *Greek Burial*, 144; Garland, *Greek Way of Death*, 30.

14. Garland, *Greek Way of Death*, 30; Kurtz and Boardman, *Greek Burial*, 144.

15. Garland, *Greek Way of Death*, 30.

16. Burkert, *Greek Religion*, 192.

17. Alexiou, *Ritual Lament*, 4–7, 10–14, 29–31; Burkert, *Greek Religion*, 192; Holst-Warhaft, *Dangerous Voices*, 105–14; Garland, *Greek Way of Death*, 25–37; Kurtz and Boardman, *Greek Burial*, 144–45.

18. Holst-Warhaft, 103–14.

19. Ibid. See also Nicole Loraux, *The Experiences of Tiresias: The Feminine and the Greek Man* (Princeton, N.J.: Princeton University Press, 1995). Thus, in Homer, in order to show true manliness or courage (*andreia*) a warrior must exhibit characteristics culturally coded as feminine and then transcend them. "Or to put it another way, fear can be transcended, but without fear there is no epic" (Loraux, *Experiences of Tiresias*, 75). In Plato's ideal state, however, stories of men's grief are to be attributed to women, and poets should not be allowed to portray the gods as weeping or lamenting (*Republic* 387B–388C).

20. Garland, *Greek Way of Death*, 29; Pantel, *History of Women*, 163–72. For extensive discussions of women in vase-representations and illustrations, see

Gudrun Ahlberg, *Prothesis and Ekphora in Greek Geometric Art* (Göteborg, Sweden: Elanders Boktryckeri Aktiebolag, 1971), 72–87, 97, 102–8, 114–21, 129, 179, 225–27, 230–31; Christine Mitchell Havelock, "Mourners on Greek Vases: Remarks on the Social History of Women," in *The Greek Vase*, ed. Stephen L. Hyatt (Latham, N.Y.: Hudson-Mohawk Association of Colleges and Universities, 1981), 102–65, plates 26, 34, 35, 40, 41, 88, 89, 90, 91, 92, 93, 94, 95, 96, 97, 98; Emily Vermule, *Aspects of Death in Early Greek Art and Poetry* (Berkeley, Calif.: University of California Press, 1979), 11–23, figs. 6, 7, 8A, 9, 10, 13, 16; Kurtz and Boardman, *Greek Burial*, figs. 43, 44 (clay figurines of mourning women), 73 (sarcophagi with mourning women).

21. The men and women are often depicted on separate sides of the vase. See Ahlberg, *Prothesis and Ekphora*, 179–84.

22. Ibid., 99–101.

23. Garland, *Greek Way of Death*, 33.

24. Owners sent their domestic servants out into the marketplace to look for work on off days. Slaves and professionals hired for banquets would come from the same social class. See Kathleen E. Corley, *Private Women, Public Meals: Social Conflict in the Synoptic Tradition* (Peabody, Mass.: Hendrickson, 1993), 48–49, 129–30, 153. Matthew mentions a group of flute players (*tous aulētas*) in Matt 9:23, but in Greek, the masculine plural does not exclude the possibility that the group of professional mourners was mixed (correction to idem, 153). See Barbara Butler Miller, "Women, Death, and Mourning in the Ancient Eastern Mediterranean" (Ph.D. diss., University of Michigan, 1994), 61–62.

25. Alexiou, *Ritual Lament*, 108–9; Holst-Warhaft, *Dangerous Voices*, 131–33; Kurtz and Boardman, *Greek Burial*, 145.

26. Garland, *Greek Way of Death*, 34–35. Ian Morris suggests that inhumation may also have been practiced concurrently with cremation. Cremation has generally been considered a "Greek custom," and was so labeled in antiquity. See Morris, *Death Ritual*, 52–69.

27. Humphreys, *Family*, 87.

28. See Smith, *Drudgery Divine*, 132: "The dead remain dead, in a sphere other than the living; but there is contact, there is continuity of relationship, there is memorialization, there is presence."

29. F. van der Meer, "The Feasts of the Dead," in *Augustine the Bishop: The Life and Work of a Father of the Church*, trans. B. Battershaw and G. R. Lamb (New York: Sheed and Ward, 1961), 498–526, esp. 499–501.

30. See Garland, *Greek Way of Death*, 110–15; Oswyn Murray, "Death and the Symposion," *Annali. Sezione di archeologia e storia antica* 10 (1988): 239–57, esp. 246–47. Some artifacts found in tombs do not clearly indicate funeral feasting. Cooking pots, for example, might also indicate habitation in a tomb. See Carla M. Antonaccio, *An Archaeology of Ancestors: Tomb Cult and Hero Cult in Early Greece* (Lanham, Md.: Rowman & Littlefield, 1995), 256–57. On feasting with the dead, see also Marvin H. Pope, "Love and Death," in *Song of Songs* (Garden City, N.Y.: Doubleday, 1977), 210–29.

31. Burkert, *Greek Religion*, 193. Exactly when the *perideipnon* was held is difficult to determine, as is its relationship to the third day rites. Alexiou, *Ritual Lament*, 10, 209n55; Garland, *Greek Way of Death*, 40, 112; Kurtz and Boardman, *Greek Burial*, 146–47.

32. On *ta trita* (third day rites) and *ta enata* (ninth day rites), see Aeschines, 3.225; Aristophanes, *Lys.* 611–13; Isaios 2.37, 8.39; Hyperides, *Fr.* 110; *Poll.* 8.146. The view established by Rohde that funerary visits were made on the third and ninth days following burials (rather than death) has been widely accepted. See Erwin Rohde, *Psyche: The Cult of Souls and Belief in Immortality among the Ancient Greeks* (reprint; Chicago: Ares, 1925), 195n83. See also Burkert, *Greek Religion*, 194, 425n38. Other scholars have argued that third-day rites should be reckoned from the day of death, not burial (Alexiou, *Ritual Lament*, 7, 208n38; Kurtz and Boardman, *Greek Burial*, 145–47). Both Burkert (*Greek Religion*, 425n38) and Alexiou, (*Ritual Lament*, 7, 208n38) doubt the thesis of Kurtz and Boardman that *ta trita* coincided with the burial itself (Kurtz and Boardman, *Greek Burial*, 145–46). Only in Aristophanes, *Lys.* 611–13, are burial and *ta trita* mentioned together. Kurtz and Boardman do, however, reckon the *ta enata* from the day of burial (147). Alexiou comments on this inconsistency. Since *ta trita* and *ta enata* are twice mentioned together, it seems unlikely that they would be reckoned from different days (*Ritual Lament*, 208, 238). Garland considers the matter insolvable (*Greek Way of Death*, 40, 146).

33. Alexiou, *Ritual Lament*, 7–10; Burkert, *Greek Religion*, 194; 32–33; Garland, *Greek Way of Death*, 39–40; Rohde, *Psyche*, 167, 196n87.

34. Burkert , *Greek Religion*, 38; Garland, *Greek Way of Death*, 40.

35. On funerary feasts as familial gatherings, see Antonaccio, *An Archaeology of Ancestors*, 256; Franz Cumont, *After Life in Roman Paganism* (New Haven, Conn.: Yale University Press, 1922), 58–54; Graydon F. Snyder, *Ante Pacem: Archaeological Evidence of Church Life before Constantine* (Atlanta, Ga.: Mercer University Press, 1985), 91. On woman and family celebrations, see Corley, *Private Women, Public Meals*, 29.

36. Murray, "Death and the Symposion," 246.

37. LSG 97A. See Garland, *Greek Way of Death*, 37; S. C. Humphreys, "Family Tombs and Tomb Cult in Ancient Athens: Tradition or Traditionalism?" *Journal of Hellenic Studies* 100 (1980): 96–126, esp. 99.

38. See most recently Andrew Dalby, *Siren Feasts: A History of Food and Gastronomy in Greece* (New York: Routledge, 1996), 5–6.

39. Pope, "Love and Death," pl. 2 (woman seated), pl. 3 (woman seated), pl. 4 (woman standing). This is also the case for funerary scenes connected with hero cults. See Oscar Broneer, "Hero Cults in the Corinthian Agora" *Hesperia* 11 (1942): 128–61, esp. 131, fig. 1 (well-dressed woman seated next to reclining man, veiled woman and two men in attendance, dressed children (male and female?) in attendence to man's right, one naked boy to the man's left. For discussion of this well-known type and citations for other sites, see Broneer, "Hero Cults," 129n4.

40. Oswyn Murray, *Early Greece* (Atlantic Highlands, N.J.: Humanities, 1980), 199.

41. Pope, "Love and Death," 211–16; Corley, *Private Women, Public Meals,* passim.

42. As were weddings. Garland suggests that the women went to cook the meal, and the men remained to complete the construction of the tomb (*Greek Way of Death*, 37). An interest in the separation of the sexes seems more likely. See Corley, *Private Women, Public Meals*, 25–28; Humphreys, "Family Tombs and Tomb Cult," 100.

43. The ritual pollution caused by corpses is the main reason why ancient cemeteries were often outside the city, town, or village. Garland, *Greek Way of Death*, 38–47.

44. Although the best evidence comes from Athens, funerary legislation was also enacted in Ioulis on the island of Keos, at Delphi and Sparta, Nisyrus in the Sporades, Gortyn in Crete, Gambreion and Mytilene in Asia Minor, Cyrene in Libya, and Catana and Syracuse in Sicily. For a complete discussion of all of the pertinent legislation, see Robert Garland, "The Well-Ordered Corpse: An Investigation into the Motives behind Greek Funerary Legislation," *Bulletin for the Institute for Classical Studies* 36 (1989): 1–15. See also Alexiou, *Ritual Lament*, 14–23; Holst-Warhaft, *Dangerous Voices*, 114; Garland, *Greek Way of Death*, 29–30; Humphreys, *Family*, 85–86.

45. Alexiou, *Ritual Lament*, 21; Holst-Warhaft, *Dangerous Voices*, 114–15; Garland, "Well-Ordered Corpse," 4.

46. Plutarch, *Solon* 21; Cicero, *Leg.* 2.24.61-64. See Garland, "Well Ordered Corpse," 3–5.

47. Alexiou, *Ritual Lament*, 14–23; Holst-Warhaft, *Dangerous Voices*, 114–15; Garland, "Well Ordered Corpse," 8–9.

48. Thus the right to inherit was related to the right to mourn. To secure these rights, several men could appear to take responsibility for the funeral expenses. Alexiou, *Ritual Lament*, 17–22; Holst-Warhaft, *Dangerous Voices*, 115–17.

49. Alexiou, *Ritual Lament*, 21. Holst-Warhaft (*Dangerous Voices*) reinforces this argument with an analysis of the function of women's laments in twentieth-century Greece in similar contexts of blood feud and war. Garland follows Alexiou's discussion as well ("Well-Ordered Corpse," 4–5). He comments, "There can be no doubt that in Greece, as commonly throughout the Mediterranean to this day, the task of mourning the dead fell chiefly to the women, whose displays of grief, unless checked, might amount to a social nuisance" (5). Holst-Warhaft, however, has demonstrated that expressions of women's grief amounted to more than a simple "nuisance."

50. Helene P. Foley, "The Politics of Tragic Lamentation," in *Tragedy, Comedy and the Polis: Papers from the Greek Drama Conference, Nottingham, 18–20 July 1990*, ed. Alan H. Sommerstein et al. (Bari, Italy: Levante, 1993), 101–43.

51. Humphreys, *Family*, 121.

52. Alexiou, *Ritual Lament*, 104–11; Holst-Warhaft, *Dangerous Voices*, 119–26; Garland, "Well-Ordered Corpse," 15; Humphreys, *Family*, 88–94. See also Nicole Loraux, *The Invention of Athens: The Funeral Oration in the Classical City* (Cambridge, Mass.: Harvard University Press, 1986).

53. Havelock, "Mourners on Greek Vases," 112.

54. Cross-cultural studies show that women's lamenting is quite orderly and controlled. Men are much less likely to channel their grief into organized mourning than women (Holst-Warhaft, *Dangerous Voices*, 122).

55. On the unemotional quality of ritualized grief, see the overview of anthropological views on grief ritual in Gary A. Anderson, *A Time to Mourn and a Time to Dance: The Expression of Grief and Joy in Israelite Tradition* (University Park, Pa.: Penn State University Press, 1991), 3–9; Richard Huntington and Peter Metcalf, *Celebrations of Death: The Anthropology of Mortuary Ritual* (Cambridge: Cambridge University Press, 1979), 25–28.

56. Holst-Warhaft, *Dangerous Voices*, 123–24.

57. See, for example, Thucydides, *History of the Peloponnesian War* 2.46, where Pericles tells the women to mourn quickly and leave. Even the "Oration of Aspasia," supposedly by a woman, encourages moderation among women in their mourning and declares that the dead are better praised than mourned (Plato, *Menex.* 246D-249D). For the dismissal of mourning women from death scenes, see below.

58. Garland, *Greek Way of Death*, 29, 33–34, 110–13. Archaeological excavations of tombs and funerary art belie the assumption that such legislative measures had great effect on the actual behavior of women.

59. Foley, "Politics of Tragic Lamentation," passim; Holst-Warhaft, *Dangerous Voices*, 127–70. See also Anna Caraveli, "The Bitter Wounding: The Lament as Social Protest in Rural Greece," in *Gender and Power in Rural Greece*, ed. Jill Dubisch (Princeton, N.J.: Princeton University Press, 1986), 169–94; Anna Caraveli-Chavez, "Bridge between Worlds: The Greek Woman's Lament as Communicative Event," *Journal of American Folklore* 93 (1980): 129–57. There are dissenters to this view that women's laments could function to disrupt society. Women's lamentation also has a therapeutic and communal function that reinforces women's roles by helping women adjust to their suffering and oppression. See Fatima Mernissi, "Women, Saints and Sanctuaries," *Signs* 3 (1977): 101–12. This reading of women's rituals does not account for continued social interest in their control.

60. Garland, *Greek Way of Death*, 30–31, 112–13. As late as the fourth century BCE, Plato was still trying to forbid hired songs at funerals (*Leg.* 800e 1-3).

61. Toynbee, *Death and Burial in the Roman World*, 16–17.

62. Ibid., 43.

63. Rush, *Death and Burial in Christian Antiquity*, 101–5; Toynbee, *Death and Burial in the Roman World*, 43–44.

64. Cicero, *Verr.* 2.5.45.118; Rush, *Death and Burial in Christian Antiquity*, 101.

65. Rush, *Death and Burial in Christian Antiquity*, 106.

66. Ibid., 113–14, 117–25; Toynbee, *Death and Burial in the Roman World*, 44.

67. Rush, *Death and Burial in Christian Antiquity*, 133–37.

68. Ibid., 117–25.

69. Ibid., 108–9.

70. Ibid., 110–11. Young men in the early church, or clerics, took up this role. See Acts 5:6, 10; 8:2.

71. Toynbee, *Death and Burial in the Roman World*, 44–47. See especially pl. 9 and 11.

72. Rush, *Death and Burial in Christian Antiquity*, 109.

73. Ibid., 163.

74. Ibid., 168–70, 181–82, 228–31; Toynbee, *Death and Burial in the Roman World*, 44–47.

75. Rush, *Death and Burial in Christian Antiquity*, 168–69, 188–91. Corley, *Private Women, Public Meals*, 48–49; Plutarch mentions a man named Xenophantus as a renowned flute player who played at the funeral of Demetrius (Plutarch, *Demetrius* 53.2).

76. Rush, *Death and Burial in Christian Antiquity*, 165.

77. Ibid., 258–73. The early church used this time of oration for the preaching of doctrine to the Christian community rather than for a speech in praise of the dead (ibid., 262–73).

78. Ibid., 236–53; Toynbee, *Death and Burial in the Roman World*, 49–50. See also Arthur Darby Nock, "Cremation and Burial in the Roman Empire," in *Arthur Darby Nock: Essays on Religion and the Ancient World*, ed. Zeph Stewart (Cambridge, Mass.: Harvard University Press, 1972), 278–307.

79. Nock sees this as a mere shift in fashion rather than due to the influence of the mysteries ("Cremation and Burial," 306–7). For a full discussion of this shift in Roman practices in light of archaeological evidence and cross-cultural anthropological perspectives, see Morris, *Death Ritual*. Although generally in agreement with Nock, Morris still finds it significant that Roman burial practices became homogenized at the same time as "economic and political regionalism was increasing" (*Death Ritual*, 203).

80. Rush, *Death and Burial in Christian Antiquity*, 238.

81. Toynbee, *Death and Burial in the Roman World*, 54–55. See also G. R. H. Horsley, "Funerary Practice in Hellenistic and Roman Rhodes," *New Documents Illustrating Early Christianity* (Macquarie University: Ancient History Documentary Research Center, 1982), 2:48–52, esp. 2:49–50.

82. Toynbee, *Death and Burial in the Roman World*, 50.

83. The time between wake and burial is difficult to determine during Roman times (Rush, *Death and Burial in Christian Antiquity*, 150–51). Wakes in the home could last up to seven days before a burial (ibid., 153–54). Poorer people probably buried their dead more quickly, especially since they would not have been able to afford ointments and preservatives (ibid., 153).

84. Cumont, *After Life*, 56.

85. Van der Meer, "Feasts of the Dead," 500.

86. Toynbee, *Death and Burial in the Roman World*, 50–52, 61–64.

87. Ibid., 51, 136.

88. Van der Meer, "Feasts of the Dead," 499–501.

89. This trend may have begun in the late Hellenistic period. See now Joan B. Burton, "The Function of the Symposium Theme in Theocritus' *Idyll* 11," *Greek, Roman and Byzantine Studies* 33 (1992): 227–45, esp. 232–33, 235, 238; as well as Corley, *Private Women, Public Meals*, passim, and 29–30; Smith, "Social Obligation," 33ff. In funerary banquet scenes, women are either seated or standing. See Corley, *Private Women, Public Meals*, 35n10; Pope, "Love and Death," pl. 2–4.

90. Corley, *Private Women, Public Meals*, 35n60.

91. Murray, *Early Greece*, 199.

92. As in the "Fractio Panis" fresco of the catacomb of St. Priscilla, which is probably a picture of a group of women, not men. See Corley, *Private Women, Public Meals*, 76–77, as well as Snyder, *Ante Pacem*, 21–26, 64–65, 132–33.

93. Tertullian, *Apol.* 7–8; Minucius Felix, *Oct.* 9.5-6; See discussion by Pope, "Love and Death," 211–14.

94. Corley, *Private Women, Public Meals*, ch. 2.

95. Van der Meer, "Feasts of the Dead," 500.

96. Cumont, *After Life*, 55.

97. Brown, *Cult of the Saints*, 19–20.

98. Cicero, *Leg.* 2.25.64. Garland, "Well-Ordered Corpse," 3.

99. Cicero, *Leg.* 2.26.65-66.

100. A point emphasized by David Daube, *Roman Law: Linguistic, Social and Philosophical Aspects* (Edinburgh: Edinburgh University Press, 1969), 117–30. Curbing expenditure was also in the interest of close relatives and the upper classes as more property was left over to pass on to the next generation. On Roman funerary legislation, see also Rush, *Death and Burial in Christian Antiquity*, 176–86; Toynbee, *Death and Burial in the Roman World*, 54–55.

101. Paul Zanker, *The Power of Images in the Age of Augustus* (Ann Arbor: University of Michigan Press, 1990), 291–95. See also Morris, *Death Ritual*, passim, and 149–55.

102. Zanker, *Power of Images*, 338.

103. Lucian, *Luct.* esp. 12, 19, 20.

104. Ibid., 19. Translation and text by A. E. Harmon (LCL).

105. The theme of the theft of executed criminals became proverbial. See Martin Hengel, *Crucifixion in the Ancient World and the Folly of the Message of the Cross*, trans. John Bowden (Philadelphia: Fortress Press, 1977), 47–48; Rush, *Death and Burial in Christian Antiquity*, 123, 194.

106. Rush, *Death and Burial in Christian Antiquity*, 101–2, 123. See above on the patience of mothers who hoped to give the last kiss to their condemned children.

107. Raymond E. Brown, *The Death of the Messiah, From Gethsemane to the Grave: A Commentary on the Passion Narratives in the Four Gospels* (New

Haven, Conn.: Yale University Press, 1998), 2:1207–9; John Dominic Crossan, *The Historical Jesus: The Life of a Mediterranean Jewish Peasant* (San Francisco: HarperSanFrancisco, 1993), 391–94; idem, *Who Killed Jesus? Exposing the Roots of Anti-Semitism in the Gospel Story of the Death of Jesus* (San Francisco: HarperSanFrancisco, 1995), 160–68; Hengel, *Crucifixion*, 22–32.

108. Brown, *Death of the Messiah*, 2:1207–8; Hengel, *Crucifixion*, 39–45.

109. Brown, *Death of the Messiah*, 2:1207–9.

110. Crossan, *Historical Jesus*, 391–94; idem, *Who Killed Jesus?* 160–63.

111. For the execution of women and children, especially in the presence of husbands or parents, see Plato, *Gorgias* 473C; Herodotus, 9.120; Plutarch, *Agis and Cleomenes* 19.7; Josephus, *A.J.* 8.380, 15.232 *B.J.* 1.97-98. On the crucifixion of women, see Josephine Massyngbaerde Ford, "The Crucifixion of Women in Antiquity," *Journal of Higher Criticism* 3 (1996): 291–309; Hengel, *Crucifixion*, 81–82; comments by Luise Schottroff, *Let the Oppressed Go Free: Feminist Perspectives on the New Testament* (Louisville: Westminster John Knox, 1993), 172. Schottroff cites Josephus, *B.J.* 2.307 (196), to which I would add Xenophon, *An Ephesian Tale* 4.4 (free woman crucified) and 4.6 (the crucifixion of the heroine, Anthia, is considered); *Sem.* 2.11 (woman could hypothetically be crucified). In the New Testament, Paul meets Junia in prison (Rom 16:7) and Sapphira is executed (albeit by divine intervention) along with her husband (Acts 5:7-10). See also Tal Ilan, *Jewish Women in Greco-Roman Palestine: An Inquiry into Image and Status* (Peabody, Mass.: Hendrickson, 1996), 158–63; Nicole Loraux, *Tragic Ways of Killing a Woman* (Cambridge, Mass.: Harvard University Press, 1987).

112. N. Haas, "Anthropological Observations of the Skeletal Remains from Giv'at ha-Mivtar," *Israel Exploration Journal* 20 (1970): 38–59.

113. For further discussion of the remains of the crucified man from Giv'hat ha Mivtar, see Crossan, *Who Killed Jesus?* 167–68; J. Navneh, "The Ossuary Inscriptions from Giv'at ha-Mivtar," *Israel Exploration Journal* 20 (1970): 33–37; V. Tzaferis, "Crucifixion: The Archaeological Evidence," *Biblical Achaeology Review* 9.1 (1985) 44–53; idem, "Jewish Tombs at and near Giv'at ha-Mivtar," *Israel Exploration Journal* 20 (1970): 18–32; Y. Yadin, "Epigraphy and Crucifixion," *Israel Exploration Journal* 23 (1973): 18–22; J. Zias and E. Sekeles, "The Crucified Man from Giv'at ha-Mivtar: A Reappraisal," *Israel Exploration Journal* 35 (1985): 22–28.

114. See below.

115. Burkert, *Greek Religion*, 203; Arthur Darby Nock, "The Cult of the Heroes," *Harvard Theological Review* 37 (1944): 141–74. For Heroine Cults, see Jennifer Larson, *Greek Heroine Cults* (Madison: University of Wisconsin Press, 1995).

116. Gregory J. Riley, *Resurrection Reconsidered: Thomas and John in Controversy* (Minneapolis: Fortress Press, 1995), 43.

117. Antonaccio, *An Archaeology of Ancestors*, 46–70, esp. 47–49; Burkert, *Greek Religion*, 205; Halliday, "Cenotaphs and Sacred Localities," 183–84.

118. Nock, "Cult of Heroes," 142, 157.

119. Antonaccio, *An Archaeology of Ancestors*, 256–57.

120. Burkert, *Greek Religion*, 205; Broneer, "Hero Cults," 129–31; Larson, *Greek Heroine Cults*, 43–57.

121. Antonnacio, *An Archaeology of Ancestors*, 245; Corley, *Private Women, Public Meals*, 31–32; Smith, "Social Obligation," 109–10.

122. Smith, "Social Obligation," 108.

123. Ibid., 109–10. Correction to Corley, *Private Women, Public Meals*, 31n41. See also Benjamin D. Meritt, "A Decree of Orgeones," *Hesperia* 11 (1942): 282–87, esp. 287.

124. A woman is typically portrayed attending a hero at his feast. See Broneer, "Hero Cults," 129–31, esp. fig. 1, which shows the reclining man with a well-dressed woman seated by his side and one veiled woman standing with two men to the hero's right. One naked boy stands to the hero's left, who may be a slave.

125. The meaning of these dogs is disputed. See Broneer, "Hero Cults," 134; Pope, "Love and Death," 210–14; figs. 2–4.

126. Alexiou, *Ritual Lament*, 61; Burkert, *Greek Religion*, 205; Nock, "Cult of Heroes," 143.

127. Philostratus, *Heroicus* 20.22. See Alexiou, *Ritual Lament*, 61, 219.

128. Euripides, *Medea* 1379; Pausanius, Descr., 2.3.7; Philostratus, *Heroicus* 20.24. See Alexiou, *Ritual Lament*, 61, 219.

129. Zen. 5.8 in Leutsch Paroemiogr. 1, 117. See Alexiou, *Ritual Lament*, 61.

130. Alexiou, *Ritual Lament*, 61.

131. See also Athenaeus, *Deipn.* 14.619–20 (dirges sung for Bormus [Egyptian Maneros]; Herodotus, *Hist.* 5.67 (lamentation of Adrastus); Plutarch, *Mor.* 228E (lamentation in honor of Leukothea).

132. Recent research on the mysteries indicates that these religions focused less on "resurrection" as on confidence in the presence of the god. See especially the recent work by G. Sfameni Gasparro, *Soteriology and Mystic Aspects in the Cult of Attis and Cybele* (Leiden: Brill, 1985). See also Smith, *Drudgery Divine*, 126–27.

133. On the Dionysiac, Orphic, and Eleusinian traditions, see Alexiou, *Ritual Lament*, 61. For Adonis, Isis/Osirus, and Tammuz, see below.

134. Walter Burkert, *Structure and History in Greek Mythology and Ritual* (Berkeley, Calif.: University of California Press, 1979), 107. See below.

135. For translations and discussion of ancient Mesopotamian texts concerning Tammuz/Dumuzi, see Thorkild Jacobsen, *Toward the Image of Tammuz and Other Essays on Mesopotamian History and Culture* (Cambridge, Mass.: Harvard University Press, 1970), esp. 73–103; idem, *The Treasures of Darkness: A History of Mesopotamian Religion* (New Haven, Conn.: Yale University Press, 1976), 25–73; for the myth of Tammuz, see also Burkert, *Structure and History*, 108–11.

136. See also other references to the worship of Ishtar, the "Queen of Heaven," who was often identified with Inanna: 2 Kgs 21:1-18; 23:4-14; 23:36—24:7; Jer 7:16-18; 44:17-19. On the dirge singers to Tammuz, see S. D.

Goitein, "Women as Creators of Biblical Genres," *Prooftexts* 8 (1988): 21–23. On the "Queen of Heaven" as a melding of the Semitic goddesses Ishtar and Astarte, see Susan Ackerman, " 'And the Women Knead Dough': The Worship of the Queen of Heaven in Sixth-Century Judah," in *Gender and Difference in Ancient Israel*, ed. Peggy L. Day (Minneapolis: Fortress Press, 1989), 109–24.

137. Burkert, *Structure and History*, 106.

138. Ibid., 109.

139. Ibid., 106.

140. Ibid., 106–7.

141. For discussions of the *Adonia*, see Alexiou, *Ritual Lament*, 55–57; Marcel Detienne, *The Gardens of Adonis: Spices in Greek Mythology*, trans. Janet Lloyd (Sussex, UK: Harvester, 1977), 99–122; Frederick T. Griffiths, "Home before Lunch: The Emancipated Woman in Theocritus," in *Reflections of Women in Antiquity*, ed. H. P. Foley (New York: Gordon and Breach, 1981), 247–73; Kraemer, *Her Share of the Blessings*, 30–35;Pantel, *History of Women*, 188.

142. Sappho, fr. 168. Text in Edgar Lobel and Denys Page, Edited by, *Poetarum Lesbiorum* (Oxford: Clarendon, 1955), 166. See also fr. 140 (Lobel and Page, *Poetarum Lesbiorum* 95). Alexiou, *Ritual Lament*, 55; Burkert, *Structure and History*, 106.

143. *Lys.* 390–5. Text and trans. B. B. Rogers (LCL).

144. Theocritus, *Idyll* 15. See also Bion, *Epitaphios for Adonis*; See Griffiths, "Home before Lunch"; Kraemer, *Her Share of the Blessings*, 31–33.

145. See also Athenaeus, *Deipn.* 4.174f; Plutarch, *Nic.* 13.2, 7; Plutarch, *Alc.* 18.3; comments by Alexiou, *Ritual Lament*, 57. For other fragments of Greek poets and playwrights that attest to the popularity of the *Adonia*, see Alexiou, *Ritual Lament*, 217n2.

146. Alexiou, *Ritual Lament*, 57.

147. "The Songs of Isis and Nephthys" dates to the fourth century BCE, but an inscription that mentions the rites of Osiris dates to the Middle Kingdom. Sharon Kelly Heyob, *The Cult of Isis among Women in the Graeco-Roman World* (Leiden: Brill, 1975), 38–40; J. Gywn Griffiths, *Plutarch's Iside et Osiride* (Cardiff, UK: University of Wales Press, 1970), 38–40. Plutarch's description of the ceremonial mourning of Isis dates to the first century CE (*Mor.* 366D). See also Kraemer, *Her Share of the Blessings*, 74.

148. Papyrus Bremner-Rhind 7.24–8.1. Text, Raymond O. Faulkner, *The Papyrus Bremner Rhind*, Biblioteca Aegyptica 3 (Bruxelles: Édition de la fondation égyptologique reine Élisabeth, 1933), 14. Translated by R. O. Faulkner, "The Bremner Rhind Papyrus—I," *Journal of Egyptian Archaeology* 22 (1936): 121–40, esp. 126.

149. Cult centers for Isis and Osiris include Athens, Boetia, Phocis, Epirus, Thessaly, Macedonia, Thrace, the Peloponnese, and the islands in the Aegean, especially Delos. See Griffiths, *Iside*, 41. On Rome, see Heyob, *Cult of Isis*, 42.

150. Heyob, *Cult of Isis*, 54; Kraemer, *Her Share of the Blessings*, 72.

151. Herob, *Cult of Isis*, 56; Kraemer, *Her Share of the Blessings*, 73.

152. See, for example, Diodorus, 1.14.2; Ovid, *Metamorphoses* 9.693; Juvenal, *Sat.* 8.26-30; Firmicus Maternus, *Err. prof. rel.* 2.6, 2.9, 27.1-2; Minucius Felix, *Oct.*, 23.1; Tertullian, *Adv Marc.* 1.13.5; Augustine, *Civ.* 6.10. For further references, see Heyob, *Cult of Isis*, 55–56.

153. Smith, "Social Obligation," 89. Smith lists P. Oxy 1755, P.Fouad 76 and P.Columbia inv. 550a. For further discussion of all relevant texts, see J. F. Gilliam, "Invitations to the Kline of Sarapis," in *Collectanea Papyrologica: Texts Published in Honor of H. C. Youtie, Part One*, ed. Ann Ellis Hanson (Bonn: Rudolf Habelt, 1976), 315–24, esp. 322–23; G. H. R. Horsley, "Invitation to the *kline* of Sarapis," in *New Documents Illustrating Early Christianity* (Macquarie University: Ancient History Documentary Research Centre, 1981), 1:5–9.

154. See Corley, *Private Women, Public Meals*, esp. 59–62; Karen Jo Torjesen, *When Women Were Priests* (San Francisco: HarperSanFrancisco, 1993), esp. 111–32; 135–52.

155. *Moralia* 113A. Translation by F. C. Babbitt (LCL). According to Plutarch, women's quarters are also full of *lypē* (*Mor.* 465D). The cries of prisoners being led off to slavery is called "womanish" (Polybius, 1.56.7-9; Xenophon, *Hell.* 2.2.3). Grief and emotion (*pathos*) are therefore irrational (*Diog. Laert.* (Zeno), 7.110-11.

156. Plutarch, *Mor.* 449D-E.

157. Ibid., 608F.

158. Plutarch, *Sol.* 21.5. Text and trans. by B. Perrin (LCL). For a further discussion of Plutarch's views on grief, see Hubert Martin Jr. and Jane E. Phillips, "*Consolatio ad Uxorem* (*Moralia* 608A–612B)," in *Plutarch's Ethical Writings and Early Christian Literature*, ed. Hans Dieter Betz (Leiden: Brill, 1978), 394–441.

159. Cicero, *Tusc.* 3.26.63–3.30.73, esp. 3.29.72. Translation by J. E. King (LCL).

160. Porphyry, *Life of Pythagoras*, 35. Text by E. Des Places, *Porphyre* (Paris, 1982), 52.

161. Pliny, *Ep.* 8.12. For more on this genre, see Adela Yarbro Collins, "The Genre of the Passion Narrative," *Studia Theologica* 47 (1993) 3–28, esp. 6, 13, 23n22 and John S. Kloppenborg, "*Exitus clari viri*: The Death of Jesus in Luke," *Toronto Journal of Theology* 8 (1992): 106–20, esp. 106–8.

162. Plato, *Phaed.* 60A.

163. Ibid., 116B-C.

164. Ibid., 117C-E. Text and translation by H. N. Fowler (LCL).

165. Death of Aratus, companions present: Plutarch, *Arat.* 52–53; Caius Gracchus, followers keep watch the night before, sleeping on and off, wife enters crying, forbidden to mourn further, Caius leaves her, his friends follow: Plutarch, *Tiberius and Caius Gracchus* 14-15. See also death of Seneca: Tacitus, Annals, 15.61–64; death of Thraesea: Tacitus, Annals, 16.34-35; death of Otho: Plutarch, *Oth.* 16–18; death of Socrates: Xenophon, *Apol.* 27-28; death of Oedipus, Sophocles, *Oed. col.* 1570–1770 (mourning daughters asked to leave, Oedipus disappears, and he has no tomb); burial of Achilles, Homer, *Od.*

24.35-75 (mother present, daughters of the sea wail, but only warriors surround the funeral pyre).

166. Loraux, *Experience of Tiresias*, 116–39; 150–58. See also Nicole Loraux, "Herakles: The Supemale and the Feminine," in *Before Sexuality: The Construction of Erotic Experience in the Ancient Greek World*, ed. D. M. Halperin et al. (Princeton, N.J.: Princeton University Press, 1990), 21–52.

167. Kloppenborg, "*Exitus clari viri*," 111–12.

168. Euripides, *Iph. Aul.* 1368ff.

169. Seneca, *Herc. Ot.*, 1620–1970, esp. 1667–90, 1738–59. Translated by F. J. Miller (LCL).

170. Diodorus of Sicily, 4.38.4-5. This basic story is repeated in Apollodorus, 2.7.7. See also Sophocles, *Trach.* 1065–1275, where Hercules weeps himself, then calls weeping "womanish" and tells his son not to cry but to "be a man."

171. Lucian, *Peregr.* 37. Translated by A. M. Harmon (LCL).

172. *Sentences*, 98. This can also be translated, "set limits to [the grief] of your family [and friends]." The text is uncertain. See text and translation by P. W. Vander Horst, *The Sentences of Pseudo-Phocylides* (Leiden: Brill, 1978), 95, 180.

173. Sir 38:16-23. Sir 22:12 suggests mourning for seven days. Only a fool would weep any longer.

174. *A.J.* 17.174-78; *B.J.* 1.666.

175. *A.J.* 4.320-26.

176. See Miller, "Women, Death and Mourning," 168–70. See also Bar 4:23.

177. 2 Macc 7; 4 Maccabees, passim.

178. See also Plutarch, *Ag. Cleom.* 19.6-5, where a woman is executed after her son (but she weeps). In other accounts, men watch their wives and/or children executed before they die. See Herodotus, Hist., 9.120; Plato, *Gorg.* 473C; Josephus, *B.J.* 1.97, and of course the death of Eleazar in 2 Macc 6:18-31.

179. Sus 31-33.

180. See David Seeley, *The Noble Death: Graeco-Roman Martyrology and Paul's Concept of Salvation* (Sheffield: JSOT Press, 1990), 113–41.

181. Miller "Women, Death and Mourning," 150–52.

182. Ibid., 151.

183. See above.

184. George W. E. Nickelsburg, *Resurrection, Immortality, and Eternal Life in Intertestamental Literature* (Cambridge, Mass.: Harvard University Press, 1972), 48–111; idem, "The Genre and Function of the Markan Passion Narrative" *Harvard Theological Review* 73 (1980): 153–84.

185. Psalm 38:11; 88:8. See below.

186. Cumont, *After Life*, 45–56. On the tomb as the house of the dead, see J. H. M. Strubbe "Cursed Be He That Moves My Bones," in *Magica Hiera: Ancient Greek Magic and Religion*, ed. Christopher A. Faraone and Dirk Obbink (New York: Oxford University Press, 1991), 33–59, esp. 40.

187. Cumont, *After Life*, 60–61.

188. For an introduction to ancient magic and translations of various magical texts, see Hans Dieter Betz, *The Greek Magical Papyri in Translation*, 2nd ed. (Chicago: University of Chicago Press, 1992); Georg Luck, *Arcana Mundi: Magic and the Occult in the Greek and Roman Worlds* (Baltimore: Johns Hopkins University Press, 1985); Marvin Meyer and Richard Smith, *Ancient Christian Magic: Coptic Texts of Ritual Power* (San Francisco: HarperSanFrancisco, 1994).

189. Munich Coptic Papyrus 5. Text by W. Henstenberg, "Koptische Papyri." In *Beiträge zur Forschung: Studien und Mitteilungen aus dem Antiquariat Jacques Rosenthal, München*, ed. Jacques Rosenthal (Munich: Verlag von Jacques Rosenthal, 1915), 1:95–100, 1:8–11. Translated by Marvin Meyer in Meyer and Smith, *Ancient Christian Magic*, 188–90, esp. 190.

190. See *PGM* 4:1875–2240; A. Delatte, *La catoptromancie grecque et ses dérivés* (Liége and Paris: l'Université de Liége, 1932), 94, 106–7, 141; Luck, *Arcana Mundi*, 26, 166–68, 176–80, 184–85, 192–204, 212–17, 222–25.

191. Cumont, *After Life*, 64–69; Rohde, *Psyche*, 210–11 (nn. 144–48, 593–95; 603–5).

192. See Richard Lattimore, *Themes in Greek and Latin Epitaphs* (Urbana: University of Illinois Press, 1942); Strubbe, "Cursed Be He," 33–59.

193. Cumont, *After Life*, 65. Cumont unfortunately makes this citation without sources.

194. Plato, *Phaedo* 115C.

195. See *Diog. Laert.* 4.52, 4.79; *Cynic Epistles* 25; Cicero, *Tusc.* 1.104 (quoting Diogenes); Lucian, *Demon.* 35, 66. I would like to thank David Seeley for these references.

196. See discussion by Meyer and Smith of the definitions of "magic" vs. "religion," *Ancient Christian Magic*, 1–9.

197. Apuleius, *Met.* 2.20. Text and translation by W. Adlington (LCL).

198. Ibid., 2.21.

199. Ibid., 2.28.

200. Lucan, *Pharsalia*, 6.415–830. See also Heliodorus, *Aeth.* 6.14–15; Ovid, *Met.* 7.235–94. For another example of a man raising the spirit of the dead in a similar manner, see Seneca, *Oedipus* 548–650.

201. Vermule, *Aspects of Death*, 17, 215n31.

202. George Thompson with Walter G. Headlam, *The Oresteia of Aeschylus* (Cambridge: Cambridge University Press, 1938), 2:189.

203. Alexiou, *Ritual Lament*, 13; Holst-Warhaft, *Dangerous Voices*, 112.

204. Alexiou, *Ritual Lament*, 131–205; Holst-Warhaft, *Dangerous Voices*, 111–12.

205. Holst-Warhaft, *Dangerous Voices*, 127–28.

206. Aeschylus, *Pers.* 683–88. Translated by H. Weir Smythe (LCL); Holst-Warhaft, *Dangerous Voices*, 132.

207. Aeschylus, *Pers.* 1050–56. Translated by Holst-Warhaft, *Dangerous Voices*, 132–33. Text by H. Weir Smythe (LCL).

208. Aeschylus, *Cho.* 429–584; Holst-Warhaft, *Dangerous Voices*, 143–44, 151.

209. Holst-Warhaft, *Dangerous Voices*, 144–49. On necromancy and Aeschylus, see H. D. Broadhead, *The Persae of Aeschylus* (Cambridge: Cambridge University Press, 1960), 302–9; S. Eitrem, "The Necromany in the Persai of Aischylos" *Symbolae Osloenses* 6 (1928): 1–16; W. Headlam, "Ghost Raising, Magic and the Underworld," *Classical Review* 16 (1902): 52–61; Jacqueline de Romilly, *Magic and Rhetoric in Ancient Greece* (Cambridge, Mass.: Harvard University Press, 1975), 16–19; H. J. Rose, "Ghost Ritual in Aeschylus," *Harvard Theological Review* 43 (1950): 257–80. A negative response to Headlam may be found in J. C. Lawson, "The Evocation of Darius," *Classical Quarterly* 28 (1934): 79–89.

210. Holst-Warhaft, *Dangerous Voices*, 129, 133–34.

211. Ibid., passim.

212. Seneca, *Herc. Ot.* esp. 1863–1970.

213. Ovid, *Met.* 829–51; Ovid, *Fasti*, 459–516.

214. See Alan Segal, *Life after Death: A History of the Afterlife in the Western World* (New York: Doubleday, 2004), 97–98, 112–13, 115–18.

215. Washing of corpses is not mentioned in the Hebrew Bible, but rather in later Jewish sources. The most complete discussion of later customs of Jewish mourning can be found in the tractate "Mourning," or *Sem.* See translation and commentary by Dav Zlotnick, *The Tractate "Mourning" (Semaḥot)* (New Haven, Conn.: Yale University Press, 1966). The date of this source is a matter of debate. Suggestions range from the third to the eighth centuries CE. Many scholars would still argue that this source contains very ancient traditions (Zlotnick, *Tractate*, 4–5). For general discussions of Jewish burial and mourning practices, see Roland de Vaux, *Ancient Israel: Its Life and Institutions* (London: Darton, Longman and Todd, 1961), 56–61; Eileen F. de Ward, "Mourning Customs in 1, 2 Samuel," *Journal of Jewish Studies* 23 (1972): 1–27; idem, "Mourning Customs in 1, 2 Samuel II," *Journal of Jewish Studies* 23 (1972): 145–66; Emanuel Feldman, *Biblical and Post-Biblical Defilement and Mourning: Law as Theology* (New York: KTAV and Yeshiva University Press, 1977); S. Safrai, "Home and Family," in *The Jewish People in the First Century*, Edited by S. Safrai et al. (Philadelphia: Fortress Press; Assen/Maastricht: Van Gorcum, 1987), 2:728–92, esp. 773–87.

216. *Sem.* 12:10. The Mishnah requires that the corpse be washed (*m. Shabbat* 23:5). In Acts 9:36–37, women prepare the body of Tabitha in Joppa by washing it. There is no mention of the washing of corpses in the Hebrew Bible (de Ward, "Mourning Customs II," 148).

217. De Vaux, *Ancient Israel*, 57; de Ward, "Mourning Customs," 2–3; Safrai, "Home and Family," 774.

218. De Ward, "Mourning Customs," 3. For further references to Mishnaic sources and the tractate *Sem.*, see Safrai, "Home and Family," 774.

219. The cremation of Saul and his sons is considered an exception (1 Sam 31:12). See also Gen 38:24; Lev 20:14; 21:9; de Vaux, *Ancient Israel*, 57; de Ward, "Mourning Customs II," 146. Annanias and Sapphira are also buried quickly in Acts 5:6–10; Safrai, "Home and Family," 774. Later sources require

burial on the same day as death. (For further references, see Safrai, "Home and Family," 774.)

220. De Ward, "Mourning Customs II," 146–47; see Deut 21:22ff.; Ezek 32:18-32; and 1 Sam 31:12.

221. See recently Elizabeth Bloch-Smith, *Judahite Burial Practices and Beliefs About the Dead* (Sheffield: Sheffield, 1992), 133–46.

222. On Jewish burial practices and tombs, see L. Y. Rahmani, "Ancient Jerusalem's Funerary Customs and Tombs," parts 1–4 in *Biblical Archaeologist* 44, no. 3 (1981): 171–77 (Part 1); 44, no. 4 (1981): 229–35 (Part 2); 45, no. 1 (1981) 43–53 (Part 3); 45, no. 2 (1982): 109–19 (Part 4); and Erwin R. Goodenough, "Jewish Tombs of Palestine" in *Jewish Symbols in the Greco-Roman Period* (New York: Pantheon, 1953), 1:61–84. See also de Vaux, *Ancient Israel*, 57; de Ward, "Mourning Customs II," 145–46.

223. Jer 26:23; 2 Kgs 23:6; de Vaux, *Ancient Israel*, 57–58.

224. Safrai, "Home and Family," 775.

225. Gen 47:30; 50:25; 1 Sam 17:44; 2 Sam 17:23; 19:37; 21:14; 2 Chr 16:13; Ezek 29:5. Lewis Bayles Paton, *Spiritism and the Cult of the Dead in Antiquity* (New York: Macmillan, 1921), 239; Nicholas Tromp, *Primitive Conceptions of Death and the Nether World in the Old Testament* (Rome: Pontifical Biblical Institute, 1969), 168–71.

226. Gen 15:2; 1 Sam 25:1; 1 Kgs 2:34; Job 17:13; 30:23; Ps 49:12; Isa 14:18; 26:19; Neh 2:3. See also Bernard Goldman, *The Sacred Portal: A Primary Symbol in Ancient Judaic Art* (Detroit: Wayne State University Press, 1966), 101–24; Tromp, *Primitive Conceptions*, 77–79.

227. Halliday, "Cenotaphs and Sacred Localities," 188–89; Joachim Jeremias, *Heiligengräber in Jesu Umwelt (Mt. 23, 29; Lk. 11, 47): eine Untersuchung zur Volksreligion der Zeit Jesu* (Göttingen: Vandenhoeck and Ruprecht, 1958), 114; Charles A. Kennedy, "Cult of the Dead," *Anchor Bible Dictionary*, ed. David Noel Freedman (New York: Doubleday, 1992), 2:106; Paton, *Spiritism*, 238; See below.

228. De Ward, "Mourning Customs II," 155; Goitein, "Women as Creators," 23–27.

229. Job 27:15; Ps 78:64; de Ward, "Mourning Customs II," 153.

230. Bloch-Smith, *Judahite Burial Practices*, 105–8, 120–21, 122–26, 141; de Ward, "Mourning Customs"; idem, "Mourning Customs II"; de Vaux, *Ancient Israel*, 59–60.

231. *Sem.* 11:9.

232. Lev 22:4-5; Num 19:14

233. Byron McCane, "Jews, Christians and Burial in Roman Palestine," (Ph.D. diss., Duke University, 1992), 139–40. Hence, McCane's reference to Jewish beliefs in the "virulence of corpse impurity" seems exaggerated, at least for first-century Palestine.

234. *m. Seqal.* 1:1; *m. Ma'as. S.* 5:1; *m. Mo'ed Qat.* 1:2.

235. Josephus, *B.J.* 1.21.1 (401); Jeremias, *Heiligengräber*, 53–56.

236. Josephus, *B.J.* 2.11.5–6; Meyers, *Jewish Ossuaries*, 84.

237. See above and Shaye J. D. Cohen, "Menstruants and the Sacred in Judaism and Christianity," in *Women's History and Ancient History*, ed. Sarah B. Pomeroy (Chapel Hill: University of North Carolina Press, 1991), 273–99.

238. De Vaux, *Ancient Israel*, 59–61; de Ward, "Mourning Customs II," 154–59; Goitein, "Women as Creators," 23–27; Ilan, *Jewish Women*, 189–90; Safrai, "Home and Family," 775. For Ancient Near Eastern images of weeping women, see Samuel Noah Kramer, "The Weeping Goddess: Sumerian Prototypes of the *Mater Dolorosa*," *Biblical Archaeologist* 46 (Spring 1983): 69–80; idem, "BM 98396: A Sumerian Prototype of the *Mater-Dolorosa*," *Eretz-Israel* 16 (1982): 141–46; T. Dothan, "A Female Mourner Figure from the Lachish Region," *Eretz-Israel* 9 (1966): 43–47 (Hebrew); Miller, "Women, Death and Mourning," passim; Karel van der Toorn, *From Her Cradle to Her Grave: The Role of Religion in the Life of the Israelite and the Babylonian Woman* (Sheffield: JSOT Press, 1994), 119–21. For a further discussion of women's roles in mourning, including later Judaism, see Léonie J. Archer, *Her Price Is Beyond Rubies: The Jewish Woman in Greco-Roman Palestine* (Sheffield: JSOT Press, 1990), 280–90.

239. On Rachel's lament and the debate over the presence of professional mourners in ancient Israel, see de Ward, "Mourning Customs II," 159; Miller, "Women, Death and Mourning," 83–84; 135–38. Professional mourners are only explicitly mentioned in later rabbinic texts. In the tannaitic literature, only women mourners/keeners are mentioned (Safrai, "Home and Family," 775, esp. nn. 1, 4). Safrai cites *m. Ketub* 4:4; *Sem.* 14:7; *m. Mo'ed Qat* 3:9; and other texts.

240. Bloch-Smith, *Judahite Burial Practices*, 96.

241. Yigael Yadin, *Masada* (London: Weidenfeld and Nicolson, 1966), 214–15.

242. De Ward, "Mourning Customs II," 157; Goitein, "Women as Creators," 21–23. See also discussion of ancient Near Eastern women's laments by van der Toorn, *From Her Cradle*, 119.

243. See also concern for rites done for the "Queen of Heaven," or Ishtar: 2 Kgs 21:1-18; 23:4-14; 23:36-24:7; Jer 7:16-20; 34:5; 44:17-19. The worship of Tammuz/Ishtar or Dumuzi/Inanna was particularly popular among women.

244. See also Zech 12:11, which alludes to the "lamentation for Hadadrimmon in the Valley of Megiddo" in Northern Israel. Hadad-rimmon is the Aramean god of fertilizing rain. Van der Toorn, *From Her Cradle*, 117. The singing of dirges for Jephthah's daughter is also discussed by Jeremias, *Heiligengräber*, 138.

245. Athalya Brenner and Fokkelien van Dijk-hemmes, *On Gendering Texts: Female and Male Voices in the Hebrew Bible* (Leiden: Brill, 1993), 88–90; Peggy L. Day, "From the Child Is Born of Woman: The Story of Jephthah's Daughter," in *Gender and Difference in Ancient Israel*, ed. Peggy L. Day (Minneapolis: Fortress Press, 1989), 58–74. A few scholars assume the historicity of the story: see Goitein, "Women as Creators," 22–23; Weems, *Just a Sister Away*, 53–69.

246. Pseudo-Philo, *L.A.B.* 40.6. See also Josephus, *A.J.* 5.264–66. See Margaret Alexiou, "The Lament of Jephtha's Daughter: Themes, Traditions,

Originality," *Studi Medievali* 12 (1971): 819–63; Cheryl Anne Brown, *No Longer Be Silent: First Century Portraits of Biblical Women* (Louisville: Westminster John Knox, 1992), 93–127.

247. Alexiou, "The Lament of Jephtha's Daughter," esp. 851.

248. P. W. van der Horst, *Ancient Jewish Epitaphs* (Kampen: Kok Pharos, 1991), 48.

249. De Ward, "Mourning Customs II," 159.

250. See the contrast of a "woman's" lament and a "noble" or "manly" lament in 4 Macc 16, which is discussed by Miller, "Women, Death and Mourning," 149–57. Miller has demonstrated that the first lament (which the narrator denies the mother spoke) (16:5-12) contains elements typical of women's lament traditions. There is also a later rabbinic tradition of stylized laments that praise the dead for their nobility (Feldman, *Biblical and Post-Biblical Defilement*, 110–19, esp. 125–29). On funeral eulogies for men and women, see Safrai, "Home and Family," 779.

251. Feldman, *Biblical and Post-biblical Defilement*, 129–32.

252. On the ancient Near Eastern cult of the dead, see Miranda Bayliss, "The Cult of Dead Kin in Assyria and Babylonia," *Iraq* 35 (1973): 115–25; Marvin H. Pope "The Cult of the Dead at Ugarit," in *Ugarit in Retrospect*, ed. Gordon Douglas Young (Winona Lake, Ind.: Eisenbrauns, 1981), 159–79; idem, "Love and Death," 210–29; E. L. Sukenick, "Arrangements for the Cult of the Dead in Ugarit and Samaria," in *Mémorial Lagrange* (Paris: Librairie Lecoffre, 1940), 59–64. On necromancy, see Y. Avishur, "A Ghost-Expelling Incantation from Ugarit," *Ugarit -Forschungen* 13 (1981): 13–25; Irving L. Finkel, "Necromancy in Ancient Mesopotamia," *Archiv für Orientforschung* 29–30 (1983–84): 1–17.

253. Prominent scholars in this debate have been W. F. Albright, who argued for the funerary character of the "high places," and Marvin Pope, who has argued forcibly for funeral feasts among Israelites. Elisabeth Bloch-Smith's recent study of the archaeological record confirms recent readings of the textual evidence (*Judahite Burial Practices*, 105–8, 120–21, 122–26, 141). See W. F. Albright, *Yahweh and the Gods of Canaan* (Winona Lake, Ind.: Eisenbrauns, 1968), 230ff.; Kennedy, "Cults of the Dead," 105–8; Theodore J. Lewis, *Cults of the Dead in Ancient Israel and Ugarit*, Harvard Semitic Monographs 39 (Atlanta: Scholars Press, 1989); Mark S. Smith, *The Early History of God: Yahweh and Other Deities in Ancient Israel* (San Francisco: Harper and Row, 1990), 126–32; Sukenik, "Arrangements for the Cult of the Dead," 62; Paton, *Spiritism*, 232–307; J. Alberto Soggin, "Child Sacrifice and Cult of the Dead in the Old Testament," in *Old Testament and Oriental Studies* (Rome: Biblical Institute Press, 1975), 84–87; Ribar John Whalen, "Death Cult Practices in Ancient Palestine" (Ph.D. diss., University of Michigan, 1973).

254. De Ward, "Mourning Customs II," 165–66; de Vaux, *Ancient Israel*, 59. For the cutting of flesh and hair, see also Job 1:20; Isa 22:21; Ezek 7:18; Amos 8:10.

255. 1 Sam 28:39; Deut 26:14; Hos 9:4; Amos 6:10; Jer 16:7; Ezek 24:17; Ps 106:28; see also Cant 2:4; 5:1. See de Ward, "Mourning Customs II," 166;

de Vaux, *Ancient Israel*, 59–60. Later Hellenistic sources probably reflect Greek tendencies (Tob 4:17; 2 Macc 12:38-46), although these customs are also native to the ancient Near East as well. See Pope, "Love and Death," passim; Smith, *Early History of God*, 128–29.

256. Hos 9:4; Jer 16:16; Tob 4:17; Sir 7:3.

257. Isa 8:19; 19:3; 28:15, 18; 29:4; 57:9; 65:4.

258. Jer 16:1-13; Ezek 24:15-18. Priests are directed to go only to funerals of those who are next of kin. See Lev 21:1-3.

259. Lewis, *Cults of the Dead*, 80–74; Pope, "Love and Death," passim; Segal, *Life after Death*, 98, 112, 113, 115–18.

260. Ps 106:28; Pope, "Song of Songs," 217. For a dissenting opinion on Pope's analysis of Ps 106:28, see Lewis, *Cults of the Dead*, 92.

261. See discussion of Jer 16:5ff., Lewis, *Cults of the Dead*, 137–39; and also Bloch-Smith, *Judahite Burial Practices*, 125, 129.

262. Segal, *Life after Death*, 126, 131–34, 156.

263. Kennedy, "Cult of the Dead," 107; Sukenik, "Arrangements for the Cult of the Dead," 62.

264. These are probably not "air shafts," but conduits for food and liquids for the refreshment of the dead. See Bloch-Smith, *Judahite Burial Practices*, 105–8; Kennedy, "Cult of the Dead," 1–7; Lewis, *Cults of the Dead*, 179–80; Paton, *Spiritism*, 233; Whalen, "Death Cult Practices," 72–73.

265. For concern about necromancy in biblical texts, see Deut 18:9-11; Lev 19:31; 1 Sam 28:6-25; 2 Kgs 21:6; Isa 8:19; 19:3; 29:4. On the prevalence of necromancy among Israelites, see Avishur, "Ghost-Expelling Incantation from Ugarit," 22–23; W. A. M. Beuken, "1 Samuel 28: The Prophet as Hammer of Witches," *Journal for the Study of the Old Testament* 6 (1978): 3–17; John Barclay Burns, "Necromancy and the Spirits of the Dead in the Old Testament," *Transactions of the Glaskow University Historical Society* 26 (1976): 1–14; Kennedy, "Cult of the Dead," 106; Lewis, *Cults of the Dead*, 111–17, 126–27, 132, 137; Paton, *Spritism*, 237; Athalya Brenner, *The Israelite Woman: Social and Literary Type in Biblical Narrative* (Sheffield: JSOT Press, 1985), 67–77; Smith, *Early History of God*, 127–29.

266. See also Sir 48:13-14; Smith, *Early History of God*, 131.

267. See also Deut 18:10-11.

268. For further discussion, see Bloch-Smith, *Judahite Burial Practices*, 122–25.

269. Ibid., 121–22.

270. Ibid., 130–31.

271. 1 Sam 28:6-25. See also 1 Chr 10:13-14. Beuken, "The Prophet as the Hammer of Witches"; Bloch-Smith, *Judahite Burial Practices*, 121–22; Brenner, *Israelite Woman*, 34–35; 72–74; Lewis, *Cults of the Dead*, 111–17; Goitein, "Women as Creators," 14–15; K. A. D. Smelik, "The Witch of Endor: 1 Samuel in Rabbinic and Christian Exegesis Till 800 A.D.," *Vigiliae christianae* 33 (1977): 160–79; Smith, *Early History of God*, 127.

272. Sue Rollin, "Women and Witchcraft in Ancient Assyria (900–600 BC)" in *Images of Women in Antiquity,* ed. Averil Cameron and Amélie Kuhrt, (Detroit: Wayne State University Press, 1983), 34–45, esp. 41.

273. See also Lev 20:6; Ezek 43:7-9. See discussion by Lewis, *Cults of the Dead,* 146–47, 152, 157–58, 162–63.

274. Prov 2:16-18; Lewis, *Cults of the Dead,* 158.

275. Josephus, *A.J.* 6.327–42.

276. Pseudo-Philo, *L.A.B.* 64.1–3. See Smelik, "The Witch of Endor," 162. For Josephus and Pseudo-Philo's discussions of the "Witch of Endor," see also C. Brown, *No Longer Silent,* 181–211.

277. See Smelik, "Witch of Endor," 162–63, for numerous references to rabbinic discussions of the "Witch of Endor" and 1 Sam 28.

278. Saul Lieberman, "Some Aspects of After Life in Early Rabbinic Literature," in *Harry Austryn Wolfson: Jubilee Volume* (Jerusalem: American Academy for Jewish Research, 1965), 494–532; idem, *Greek in Jewish Palestine* (New York: Jewish Theological Seminary of America, 1942), 97–114, 103–6; Finkel, "Necromancy in Ancient Mesopotamia," 13–15; Eric M. Meyers, *Jewish Ossuaries: Reburial and Rebirth* (Rome: Biblical Institute Press, 1971), 88–89. On the power of dead prophets and heroes, see Jeremias, *Heiligengräber,* 126–37.

279. Herbert Chanan Brichto, "Kin, Cult, Land and Afterlife—A Biblical Complex," *Hebrew Union College Annual* 44 (1973): 1–54, esp. 48–49.

280. On Yemenite women, see Goitein, "Women as Creators," 3, 23–27. On European women settled in Israel, see Susan Starr Sered, *Women as Ritual Experts: The Religious Lives of Elderly Jewish Women in Jerusalem* (New York: Oxford University Press, 1992), 18–22, 28–29. For a cross-cultural study of women's lamentation in reference to the development of the passion narrative, see below, ch. 5.

281. Van der Toorn, *From Her Cradle,* 119.

282. Goodenough, "Jewish Tombs," 63–78.

283. Ibid., 79–83.

284. Evidence that coins were placed in the mouths of the deceased has been found in Second Temple Jewish tombs in both Jerusalem and Jericho, including the one found in the skull of an adult woman placed in an ossuary inscribed "Miriam, daughter of Simon" from the family tomb of the High Priest Caiaphas. Although their significance is a matter of heated debate, I am in agreement with Zvi Greenhut, "Burial Cave of the Caiaphas Family," *Biblical Archaeology Review* 18, no. 5 (1992), 29–36, 79, that many coins found in Second Temple Jewish tombs reflect this Greek custom. For a further discussion of coins, see R. Hachlili, "Ancient Burial Customs Preserved in Jericho Hills," *Biblical Archaeology Review* 5, no. 4 (1979): 28–35, esp. 34; L. Y. Rahmani, "Jason's Tomb," *Israel Exploration Journal* 17 (1967): 61–100, esp. 92–93. Morris's cautions on making immediate generalizations about the significance of all coins found in graves are germane here. Although two skeletons have one or two coins in the skull, in other graves, coins are not in the general vicinity of human remains. In "Jason's Tomb," 42 coins from 30–31 CE were found in

a single *kokh* (Rahmani, "Jason's Tomb," 92–93). See Morris, *Death-Ritual*, 105–6.

285. Rahmani, "Jason's Tomb," 81–85; James F. Strange, "Late Hellenistic and Herodian Ossuary Tombs at French Hill Jerusalem," *Bulletin of the American Schools of Oriental Research* 219 (1975): 39–67, esp. 60–61, on alabastra found in tombs.

286. Haas, "Anthropological Observations," 39–40.

287. Goodenough, "Contents of Jewish Tombs in Palestine" in *Jewish Symbols in the Greco-Roman Period* (New York: Pantheon, 1953), 1:103–39, esp. 107.

288. Goodenough, "Contents of Jewish Tombs," 108.

289. Hachlili, "Ancient Burial Customs," 34; Rahmani, "Jason's Tomb," 85–87; Strange, "Late Hellenistic," 49–58.

290. Goodenough, "Contents of Jewish Tombs," 105–7.

291. So Greenhut, "Burial Cave," 35–36. See also Hachlili, *Ancient Jewish Art*, 97.

292. N. Avigad, "Aramaic Inscriptions in the Tomb of Jason," *Israel Exploration Journal* 17 (1967): 101–11. Avigad suggests that the lament follows a Hellenistic formula (105–6). Most Jewish funerary inscriptions are in Greek, although many are bilingual (Greek and Aramaic). See Pieter W. van der Horst, "Jewish Funerary Inscriptions: Most Are in Greek," *Biblical Archaeology Review* 18, no. 5 (1992): 46–57; R. A. Kearsley, "The Goliath Family at Jericho," *New Documents Illustrating Early Christianity*, ed. S. R. Llewelyn and R. A. Kearsley (Macquarie University: Ancient History Documentary Research Centre, 1992), 6:162–64. For a further discussion of Jason's Tomb, see Rahmani, "Jason's Tomb."

293. The inscription contains the common formula *euphrainesthe hoi zōntes* found in tomb inscriptions in Athens, Rome, Thessalonica, Phrygia, and Syria. See Baruch Lifshitz, "Notes d'épigraphie palestinienne," in *Revue biblique* 73 (1966): 248–57.

294. Found in Tomb 2. See Finegan, *Archaeology*, 301–5. Goodenough, *Jewish Symbols*, vol. 3, pl. 14.

295. The interpretation of burial remains is a vexed one, but it is still possible to detect some patterns of rituals from them. See Morris, *Death-Ritual*, 12–15. I agree that the complete abandonment of all evidence is not helpful.

296. Cannon, "Historical Dimension," 438.

297. Zanker, *Power of Images*, 292.

298. Hachlili comments that Jews followed the custom of placing grave gifts in tombs but "gave it their own interpretation by ignoring the connotation of an offering to the dead" (*Ancient Jewish Art*, 92).

299. He also suggests that the artifacts may have had symbolic significance for Jews, but he affirms that some cultic significance for tomb staples such as the small water cisterns, tables, and benches cannot be denied. Goodenough, "Contents of Jewish Tombs," 107–8.

300. Meyers dates the use of ossuaries from approximately 40–30 BCE to the fourth century CE (*Jewish Ossuaries*, 37–44).

301. Rahmani, "Ancient Jerusalem's Funerary Customs," part 1, 174–76. Meyers does not see the abrupt shift of ossuaries as indicative of a simple shift

to beliefs in "resurrection" (*Jewish Ossuaries*, 85–86), but he does suggest that its appeal to Jews is related to their continued belief in the "totality of the individual" and shows interest at least in spiritual resurrection (*Jewish Ossuaries*, 89–92).

302. Meyers, *Jewish Ossuaries*, 70.

303. Kennedy, "Cult of the Dead," 107.

304. Rahmani, "Ancient Jerusalem's Funerary Customs," part 4, 110.

305. Against Rahmani, see Meyers, *Jewish Ossuaries*, 85–86. On the ossuary of "Simon, Builder of the Sanctuary," see Naveh, "Ossuary Inscriptions from Giv'at ha-Matar," 33–34.

306. Greenhut, "Burial Cave of the Caiaphas Family," 79.

307. The *tau* mark found on ossuaries is no doubt apotropaic (protective). See Finegan, *Archaeology of the New Testament*, 339, 343–45. For further discussion, see Erich Dinkler, "Comments on the History of the Symbol of the Cross," trans. Gerhard Krodel, in James M. Robinson et al., *The Bultmann School of Biblical Interpretation: New Directions?* (Tübingen: J. C. B. Mohr (Paul Siebeck); New York: Harper and Row, 1965), 124–46; Robert Houston Smith, "The Cross Mark on Jewish Ossuaries," *Palestine Exploration Quarterly* 106 (1974): 53–66. Since it is not possible to distinguish between Jewish and Christian ossuaries in first- and second-century Palestine, it is unlikely that this cross sign is a Christian symbol. See Byron R. McCane, "Jews, Christians and Burial in Roman Palestine" (Ph.D. diss., Duke University, 1992), esp. 95–111.

308. Adolf Deissmann, *Light from the Ancient Near East*, trans. L. R. M. Strachan (London: Hodder and Stoughton, 1927), 413ff.; van der Horst, *Ancient Jewish Epitaphs*, 54–60.

309. Robert Hertz, *Death and the Right Hand* (Glencoe, Ill.: Free Press, 1960), 42–43.

310. Ahlberg, *Prothesis,* 152; Elderkin, "Architectural Detail," 517–22.

311. Meyers, *Jewish Ossuaries*, 45–47.

312. Elderkin, "Architectural Detail," 522–23.

313. N. Avidad, "The Rock Carved Facades of the Jerusalem Necropolis," *Israel Exploration Journal* 1 (1950–51): 96–106; Elderkin, "Architectural Detail," 518; B. A. Masten, "Chalcolithic Ossuaries and 'Houses for the Dead' " *Palestine Exploration Quarterly* 97 (1965): 153–60; Meyers, *Jewish Ossuaries*, 19–20; L. Y Rahmani, "Jerusalem's Tomb Monuments on Jewish Ossuaries," *Israel Exploration Journal* 18 (1968): 220–25; van der Horst, *Jewish Epigraphs*, 42–43;

314. McCane, "Jews, Christians and Burial," 85n110.

315. Lawrence H. Schiffman, "The Impurity of the Dead in the Temple Scroll," in *Archaeology and History in the Dead Sea Scrolls*, ed. Lawrence H. Schiffman (Sheffield: JSOT Press, 1990), 135–56, esp. 153n21.

316. Jeremias, *Heiligengräber*, 114. Jeremias discusses over forty cult sites in Palestine and the surrounding areas, which he views as precursors to the later Christian cult of the martyrs (5). Peter Brown also finds a similar precursor to the cult of the saints in Jewish veneration of martyrs and prophets (*Cult of the Saints*, 3, 10, 33). See also Halliday, "Cenotaphs," 188–89; Meyers, *Jewish Ossuaries*, 54n31; Paton, *Spiritism*, 238.

317. Jeremias, *Heiligengräber*, 126–41.

318. It was the purpose of Jeremias's study to confirm the historical background to the "woe" attributed to Jesus against the Pharisees for building and beautifying the tombs of the prophets and the righteous (*Heiligengräber*, 5). On Q and Jesus, see below.

319. See Jack Finegan, *The Archaeology of the New Testament*, rev. ed. (Princeton, N.J.: Princeton University Press, 1992), 305–10.

320. Finegan, *Archaeology*, 38–39; Jeremias, *Heiligengräber*, pl. 4.

321. Sered, *Women as Ritual Experts*, 114–20.

322. Rahmani, "Jerusalem's Tomb Monuments."

323. Ilan, *Jewish Women*, 53.

324. 2 Macc 12:43-45; 15:12-16. Jeremias discusses Jewish belief in intercessory prayers of the dead, *Heiligengräber*, 126–29. See also the prayers to the "fathers" at the graves of the patriarchs in *b. Sotah* 34b and the translation of Enoch to the dwelling place of the ancestors in 1 Enoch 70:4.

325. Pseudo-Philo, *L.A.B.* 33:5. Translated by D. J. Harrington, in *The Old Testament Pseudepigrapha,* ed. James H. Charlesworth (Garden City, N.Y.: Doubleday, 1985), 348. Daniel J. Harrington, *Pseudo-Philon*, vol. 1 (Source chrétiennes 229; Paris, Editions du cerf, 1976), 2:256.

326. 2 Bar 85:1, 12.

327. 1 Kgs 11:29; 12:15; 14:2-16. See Jeremias, *Heiligengräber*, 42–43, 138.

328. Tob 4:17.

329. Wis 14:15.

330. See also Sir 38:21, 23. Text in *Septuaginta,* ed. A. Rahlfs (Stuttgart: Deutsche Bibelgesellschaft, 1979), 429.

331. *Jub.* 22:17. See also *Sib. Or.* 8:377-98.

332. Text in *Septuaginta,* 768.

333. Zanker, *Power of Images,* 291–95.

334. *Against Apion,* 2.205.

335. Goodenough also suggests that the literary injunctions against such cultic practices indicated their possible continuation ("Contents of Jewish Tombs," 107).

336. Thus, the burial of Gamaliel was supposedly a simple affair. See *b. Ket.* 8b; *b. Mo'ed Qat.* 27b.

337. Again, most scholars focus on the concern for the reduction of expenses. See Safrai, "Home and Family," 777. See also Zlotnick, *Tractate*, 22–26.

338. *Sem.* 4:7, 10; *m. Ohol.* 1.1, 17.5; McCane, "Jews, Christians and Burials," 82–84.

339. Zlotnick, *Tractate,* 23–24.

340. Ibid., 25.

341. Pope, "Love and Death," 216.

342. *Sem.* 8:1. Certain manuscripts read "thirty." The reading "three" is supported by many medieval commentators and corresponds more to the purpose of the visit suggested: confirmation of death. See Zlotnick, *Tractate,* 135. Visits to the tomb on both the third day and the thirtieth day were common in antiquity (Garland, *Greek Way of Death,* 104).

343. *m. Mo'ed Qatan* 3:8-9.

344. *m. Sanh.* 6:5.

345. *Sem.* 9, passim.

346. *Sem.* 2:1-3.

347. *Sem.* 2:6.

348. Which, of course, implies that the family might try to steal it. See *Sem.* 2:9.

349. See above.

350. Byron R. McKane's discussion of these later rabbinic regulations assumes that all in the community would have agreed with decisions by the religious court and would therefore have meekly followed such restrictions. However, this seems to be an unreasonable assumption, given apparent ineffectiveness of most funerary restrictions in antiquity. See "'Where No One Had Yet Been Laid': The Shame of Jesus' Burial," *SBL 1993 Seminar Papers*, ed. E. H. Lovering, (Atlanta: Scholars Press, 1993), 473–84, esp. 478–79.

351. On the remains of the crucified man from Giv'at ha-Mivtar, see Navneh, "The Ossuary Inscriptions from Giv'at ha-Mivtar"; Tzaferis, "Crucifixion: The Archaeological Evidence"; idem, "Jewish Tombs at and Near Giv'at ha-Mivtar"; Yadin, "Epigraphy and Crucifixion"; Zias and Sekeles, "The Crucified Man from Giv'at ha-Mivtar." See also Crossan, *Who Killed Jesus?* 168.

352. Joseph M. Baumgarten, "Hanging and Treason in Qumran and Roman Law," *Eretz-Israel* 16 (1982): 7–16; Joseph A. Fitzmyer, "Crucifixion in Ancient Palestine, Qumran Literature, and the New Testament," *Catholic Biblical Quarterly* 40 (1978): 493–513. See also Hengel, *Crucifixion*, 85.

353. Josephus, *B.J.* 3.8.5 (377); 4.5.2 (317); *A.J.* 4.8.24 (264–65). See also Philo, *In Flacc.* 83; Brown, *Death of the Messiah*, 2:1209–11; Crossan, *Who Killed Jesus?* 167.

354. Brown, *Death of the Messiah*, 2:1210; Crossan, *Who Killed Jesus?* 167.

355. And they, of course, may not even have accomplished that. What we have evidence for is secondary burial in the family tomb, not primary burial. Crossan, *Who Killed Jesus?* 168.

356. Philo, *In Flacc.* 83; Brown, *Death of the Messiah*, 2:1209–10; Crossan, *Historical Jesus*, 391–94; idem, *Who Killed Jesus?* 167.

357. C. K. Barrett is certainly correct in this instance. The rabbinic sources that Strack and Billerbeck cite, as well as others commonly marshaled to support such a contention, either deal with such hypothetical situations that they are hardly germane or describe religious and not state executions. See C. K. Barrett, *The Gospel according to St. John* (London: SPCK, 1978), 551; H. L. Strack and P. Billerbeck, *Kommentar zum neuen Testament* (Munich: C. H. Beck, 1922–1956), 2:580. Commonly cited as evidence are *y. Git.* 7:1 (330) or *b. B. Mes.* 83b. For example, *b. B. Mes.* 83b describes R. Eleazar weeping under the gallows of a man hanged for violating religious law (rape of an engaged woman); *y. Git .* 7:1 describes a wildly hypothetical situation involving divorce.

358. Here Holst-Warhaft's discussion of the function of women's lament in times of political change and unrest in antiquity as well as in modern times seems most applicable (*Dangerous Voices*, passim).

359. Rush, *Death and Burial in Christian Antiquity*, 17, 160. Sometimes the eucharist was given to the corpse (Rush, *Death and Burial in Christian Antiquity*, 99–100). For the Christian cult of the dead, see Brown, *Cult of the Saints*; Kennedy, "Cult of the Dead," 107–8; Smith, *Drudgery Divine*, 129–32; Rush, *Death and Burial in Christian Antiquity*, passim; James Stevenson, *The Catacombs: Life and Death in Early Christianity* (Nashville: Thomas Nelson, 1978), 13; van der Meer,"The Feasts of the Dead," passim; Pope, "Love and Death," 211–14.

360. Johannes Quasten, *Music and Worship in Pagan and Christian Antiquity* (Washington, D.C.: National Association of Pastoral Musicians, 1973), ch. 6.

361. Janet Tulloch, "Women Leaders in Family Funerary Banquets," in *A Woman's Place: House Churches in Earliest Christianity*, ed. Carolyn Osiek and Margaret Y. MacDonald (Minneapolis: Fortress, 2006), 164–93.

362. Snyder, *Ante Pacem*, 83.

363. E. L. Sukenik, "The Earliest Records of Christianity," *American Journal of Archaeology* 51 (1947): 351–65.

364. Sukenik, "Earliest Records," 358.

365. Berndt Gustafsson, "The Oldest Graffiti in the History of the Church?" *New Testament Studies* 3 (1956–57): 65–69; Dinkler, "Comments on the History of the Symbol of the Cross," 124–46; Duncan Fishwick, "The Talpioth Ossuaries Again," *New Testament Studies* 10 (1963–64): 49–61; J. P. Kane, "By No Means 'The Earliest Records of Christianity' with an Emended Reading of the Talpioth Inscription *Iesous oui*," *Palestine Exploration Quarterly* 103 (1971): 103–8; Carl H. Kraeling, "Christian Burial Urns?" *Biblical Archaeologist* 9 (1946): 16–20; Smith, "The Cross Marks on Jewish Ossuaries," 53–66.

366. Kane, "By No Means," passim. See also G. H. R. Horsley, "The 'Early Christian' Ossuary Inscriptions from Jerusalem," in *New Documents Illustrating Early Christianity* (Macquarie University: Ancient Documentary Research Centre, 1981), 1:112; Finegan, *Archaeology*, 365; McCane, "Jews, Christians, ands Burial," 99–100. Jack T. Sanders considers the matter insovable and suggests the person buried here was a Roman Jew named "Jesus something." See *Schismatics, Sectarians, Dissidents, Deviants: The First One Hundred Years of Jewish-Christian Relations* (Valley Forge, Pa.: Trinity Press International, 1993), 31.

367. McCane finds *alaōth* as a place-name in the Septuagint: Jer 31:5 (MT Jer 48:5) (personal correspondence, October 31, 1995). It is unlikely that "Aloth" is an abbreviation for the name "Alothis" as Kane and Dinkler suggest (Dinkler, "History of the Symbol of the Cross," 130–31; Kane, "By No Means," 105). The suggested reading of "Aloth" as a name based on a possible reference to "Alothis" in P.Fay 68.2 is no longer tenable. The most recent editor of P.Fay 68 renders the name in 68.2 as "Ammonis." See P. J. Sijpesteijn, *Customs Duties in Greco-Roman Egypt* (Zutphen: Terra, 1987), 112. Fishwick suggests that "Aloth" is a magical phrase ("Talpioth Ossuaries," 55–59). See also Finegan, *Archaeology*, 365; McCane, "Jews, Christians and Burial," 100–101. I would like to thank Byron McCane for his help with this inscription.

368. Dinkler lists ten Jewish inscriptions with similar cross markings ("History of the Symbol of the Cross," 135–41). See also Finegan, *Archaeology*,

343–44; Fishwick, "Talpioth Ossuaries," 59; McCane, "Jews, Christians and Burial," 101–2; Snyder, *Ante Pacem*, 28, 139.

369. For a tentative conclusion of these tombs as early Christian burials, see Gaalyah Cornfeld, *Archaeology of the Bible: Book by Book* (San Francisco, 1976), 306–8; Finegan, *Archaeology*, 355–74. For arguments against this conclusion, see McCane, "Jews, Christians and Burials," 104–11; Meyers, *Jewish Ossuaries*, 53–54; Snyder, *Ante Pacem*, 28–29; Smith, "Cross Marks," 60–65.

370. Finegan, *Archaeology*, 359–61; Snyder, *Ante Pacem*, 28–29.

371. Dinkler, "History of the Symbol of the Cross"; Snyder, *Ante Pacem*, 27–29.

372. Also suggested by J. T. Sanders for the Dominus Flevit tomb (*Schismatics*, 36).

373. Antonaccio, *An Archaeology of Ancestors*, 47–49.

374. Meyers, *Jewish Ossuaries*, 53, and personal correspondence, October 10, 1995.

375. McCane, "Jews, Christians and Burial."

376. *Did. Apos.* 6.22; *Apos. Const.* 6.30. See McCane, "Jews, Christians and Burial," 208–11.

377. McCane assumes that it is the Christians who are changing their customs rather than the Jews. See "Jews, Christians and Burial," 212.

378. Brown, *Cult of the Saints*.

379. McCane, "Jews, Christians and Burial," 227–31.

380. Smith, *Drudgery Divine*, 131–33; Snyder, *Ante Pacem*, passim.

381. Stevenson, *Catacombs*, 90–91, 94–95.

382. The debate over the background of the fish in early Christian art is a vexing one. Snyder identifies two separate motifs, a nautical fish motif and the meal-with-fish motif (*Ante Pacem*, 24–26). Snyder rightly rejects Goodenough's suggestion that the fish in the meal is derived from a Jewish *cena pura*, or meal of preparation (*Jewish Symbols*, 1:31–61; see *Ante Pacem*, 25). The bulk of Goodenough's discussion is based on late rabbinic evidence. For early Christian meals and catacomb art, see Corley, *Private Women, Public Meals*, 74; Snyder, *Ante Pacem*, 21–26, 64–65, 132–33.

383. For the by-laws of a funerary society that lists wine and fish (sardines) as part of dues for the society, see *CIll.* vol. 14, no. 2112. Text, H. Dessau, *Inscriptiones Latinae*, vol. 2, part 2 (Chicago: Ares, 1979), no. 7212 (737–46); N. Lewis and M. Reinhold, eds., *Roman Civilization* (New York: Harper and Row, 1955), 2:272–75, esp. 275..

384. Of the catacomb meal scenes, only two of twenty-seven reflect the multiplication of loaves theme from the Gospels. For a discription of the twenty-seven meal scenes, see John Dominic Crossan, *The Essential Jesus: Original Sayings, Earliest Images* (San Francisco: HarperSanFrancisco, 1994), 180–91. See also Snyder, *Ante Pacem*, 64.

385. Snyder, *Ante Pacem*, 91–92.

386. Ramsey MacMullen, *The Second Church: Popular Christianity AD 200–400* (Atlanta: Scholars Press, 2009.

387. Robin M. Jensen, "Dining with the Dead: From the *Mensa* to the Altar in Christian Late Antiquity," in *Commemorating the Dead: Texts and Artifacts*, ed. L. Brink and D. Green (Berlin and New York: Walter de Gruyter, 2008), 107–43, esp. 143.

388. Brown, *Cult of the Saints*, 70–71; Rush, *Death and Burial in Christian Antiquity*, 174–86, 108–9; Quasten, *Music and Worship*, 160–64.

389. Rush, *Death and Burial in Christian Antiquity*, 182–94.

390. Ibid., 174–86. See also 108–9. Certain orders of nuns were even instructed to keep complete silence at funerals while the chanting of psalms was done by monks (Rush, *Death and Burial in Christian Antiquity*, 183), and the number of nuns in funeral processions was limited to a few old women (Rush, *Death and Burial in Christian Antiquity*, 204–5). See also Quasten, *Music and Worship*, 167–68.

391. Rebecca Rollins, "The Singing of Women in the Early Church: Why It Occurred, Why It Disappeared" (D.Mus. diss., Claremont Graduate School, 1988). Singing by boys choirs continued.

392. Alexiou, *Ritual Lament*, 57.

393. Epiphanius, *Panarion* 49.2; Firmicus Maternus *Err. prof. rel.* 3.1. See Susanna Elm, "Montanist Oracles," in *Searching the Scriptures: A Feminist Commentary*, ed. Elisabeth Schüssler Fiorenza (New York: Crossroad, 1994), 2:131–38, esp. 35.

394. Justin Martyr, *First Apology* 24.

395. Brown, *Cult of the Saints*, 34–35; Pope, "Love and Death," 211–13; van der Meer,"Feasts of the Dead," 510–25.

396. Minucius Felix, *Octavius* 9.5-6; Tertullian, *Apol.* 7.1-2, 7.8; Pope, "Love and Death," 211–13.

397. Schäferdiek, "Acts of John," 166. Some sections of Acts of John may be later. The section containing the round dance (*Acts of John* 94-96, 97) is ancient. See also Stevenson, *Catacombs*, 13.

398. *Acts of John* 85.

399. Schäferdiek, "Acts of John," 164.

400. Excerpts from *Acts of John*, 94-96. Text by Eric Junod and Jean-Daniel Kaestli, *Acta Iohannis. Praefatio—Textus*, Corpus Christianorum, Series Apocryphorum 1 (Brepols: Turnhout, 1983), 200–07. Translated by Knut Schäferdiek, in *New Testament Apocrypha*, ed. Wilhelm Schneemelcher (Louisville: Westminster John Knox, 1992), 2:182–83.

401. Arthur J. Dewey, "A Hymn in the Acts of John: Dance as Hermeneutic," *Semeia* 38 (1986): 67–80.

402. As suggested by Dewey, in Ibid.

403. The most famous example is the aretalogy of Isis from Cyme in Asia Minor. See brief discussion by Marvin W. Meyer, *The Ancient Mysteries: A Sourcebook* (San Francisco: Harper and Row, 1987), 172–74.

404. See the "children of the marketplace" pericope in Luke 7:31-23 // Matt 11:16-17 and the "I am" sayings in John, esp. 10:9 and 14:6.

405. Augustine, *Ep.* 237.5-9. See Schäferdiek, "Acts of John," 206n27.

406. Elisabeth Schüssler Fiorenza, *Jesus: Miriam's Child, Sophia's Prophet: Critical Issues in Feminist Christology* (New York: Contiuum, 1994), 147–48; idem, "Wisdom Mythology and the Christological Hymns of the New Testament," in *Aspects of Wisdom in Judaism and Early Christianity*, ed. Robert Louis Wilkin (Notre Dame: University of Notre Dame Press, 1975), 17–42. For suggestions concerning the cult of the dead in the Corinthian context, see Richard E. Demaris, "Corinthian Religion and Baptism for trhe Dead (1 Cor. 15:29): Insights from Archaeology and Anthropology," *Journal of Biblical Literature* 114 (1995): 661–82; Charles A. Kennedy, "The Cult of the Dead in Corinth," in *Love and Death in the Ancient Near East: Essays in Honor of Marvin H. Pope*, ed. John H. Marks and Robert M. Good (Guilford, Conn.: Four Quarters, 1987), 227–36.

407. Brown, *Cult of the Saints*, 43–46, 48, 113.

408. Jacob Neusner, *Rabbinic Literature and the New Testament* (Valley Forge, Pa.: Trinity Press International, 1994), 8. The common assumption of the applicability of rabbinic literature for understanding first-century Judaism has been challenged not only by Neusner, but also by Stemberger and Saldarini, as well as by feminist scholars such as Brooten, Kraemer, Amy-Jill Levine, and others engaged in the reconstruction of ancient Jewish women's lives (see ch. 1).

409. De Ward, "Mourning Customs II," 159.

Chapter 3: Celebratory Meals of the Kingdom of God

1. Marcus Borg, *Jesus: A New Vision: Spirit, Culture, and the Life of Discipleship* (San Francisco: HarperSanFrancisco, 1987), 133–35; idem, *Meeting Jesus Again for the First Time: The Historical Jesus and the Heart of Contemporary Faith* (San Francisco: HarperSanFrancisco, 1994), 57–58; John Dominic Crossan, *The Historical Jesus: The Life of a Mediterranean Jewish Peasant* (San Francisco: HarperSanFrancisco, 1991), 261–64; Elisabeth Schüssler Fiorenza, *In Memory of Her: A Feminist Theological Reconstruction of Christian Origins* (1983; repr., New York: Crossroad, 1994), 118–22; idem, *Jesus: Miriam's Child, Sophia's Prophet: Critical Issues in Feminist Christology* (New York: Crossroad, 1994), 93–94.

2. Borg, *Jesus: A New Vision*, 133–35; idem, *Meeting Jesus*, 57–58; Schüssler Fiorenza, *In Memory of Her*, 118–22. In *Miriam's Child*, Schüssler Fiorenza does not mention purity (93–94).

3. Crossan, *Historical Jesus*, 261–64; Luise Schottroff, *Let the Oppressed Go Free: Feminist Perspectives on the New Testament* (Louisville: Westminster John Knox, 1995), 93–94, 104.

4. See comments by Paula Fredriksen, *From Jesus to Christ: The Origins of the New Testament Images of Jesus* (New Haven, Conn.: Yale University Press, 1988), 105–6.

5. On Mark, see above, ch. 2; on Q, see ch. 4; Kathleen E. Corley, *Private Women, Public Meals: Social Conflict in the Synoptic Tradition* (Peabody, Mass.: Hendrickson, 1993), 89–95; Corley, "Jesus' Table Practice: Dining with Tax

Collectors and Prostitutes, Including Women," in *Society of Biblical Literature 1993 Seminar Papers*, ed. Eugene H. Lovering (Atlanta: Scholars Press, 1993), 444–59.

6. Dennis E. Smith, "Table Fellowship and the Historical Jesus," in *Religious Propaganda and Missionary Competition in the New Testament World: Essays Honoring Dieter Georgi*, 135–62, ed. Lkan Bormann et al. (Leiden: Brill, 1994), 160–61.

7. Smith, "Table Fellowship and the Historical Jesus," 161.

8. Kathleen E. Corley, *Women and the Historical Jesus: Feminist Myths of Christian Origins* (Sonoma, Calif.: Polebridge, 2002), ch. 2.

9. Corley, *Women and the Historical Jesus*, ch. 4.

10. I thank Jack Kugelmass for his comments on the function of humor. Jack Kuglemass, "Undser Shtik: The Meaning of Humor for American Jews," Institute for Research in the Humanities Seminar, University of Wisconsin-Madison, Spring 1996.

11. See also Robert Funk, *Honest to Jesus: Jesus for a New Millennium* (San Francisco: HarperSanFrancisco, 1996), 194.

12. On Jesus and humor, see Funk, *Honest to Jesus*, 158–62; Burton L. Mack, *A Myth of Innocence: Mark and Christian Origins* (Minneapolis: Fortress Press, 1988), 61–62, on Jesus' probable "playful mode of response"; and Wayne D. Sandifer, "The Humor of the Absurd in the Parables of Jesus," in *Society of Biblical Literature 1991 Seminar Papers*, ed. Eugene Lovering (Atlanta: Scholars Press, 1991), 287–97.

13. See Robert Funk and the Jesus Seminar, *The Acts of Jesus: What Did Jesus Really Do?* (San Francisco: HarperSanFrancisco, 1998), 66–67. For an overview of this discussion, see Dennis E. Smith, "The Historical Jesus at Table," *in The Society of Biblical Literature Seminar Papers*, ed. David Lull (Atlanta: Scholars Press, 1989), 466–86; idem, "Table Fellowship and the Historical Jesus," 135–62. Smith argues that the association of Jesus at meals is a literary motif and presupposes enough of a social formation to render it inauthentic. See Corley, *Women and the Historical Jesus*, ch. 2, on Mark 2:16. Here I follow closely my discussions in Corley, *Private Women, Public Meals*, 89–93, 130–33, 152–58. Material reused here is with the permission of Hendrickson Publishers.

14. I. Abrahams, "Publicans and Sinners," in *Studies in Pharisaism and the Gospels* (New York: KTAV, 1967), 54–61; John R. Donahue, "Tax Collectors and Sinners: An Attempt at Identification," *Catholic Biblical Quarterly* 33 (1971): 39–60; James D. G. Dunn, "Pharisees, Sinners and Jesus," in *The Social World of Formative Christianity and Judaism: Essays in Tribute to Howard Clark Kee*, ed. Jacob Neusner et al. (Philadelphia: Fortress Press, 1988), 264–89; William R. Farmer, "Who Are the 'Tax Collectors and Sinners' in the Synoptic Tradition?" in *From Faith to Faith: Essays in Honor of Donald G. Miller on His Seventieth Birthday*, ed. D. Y. Hadidan (Pittsburgh: Pickwick, 1979), 167–74; J. Gibson, *"Hoi Telōnai kai hai Pornai,"* *Journal of Theological Studies* 32 (1981): 429–33; Joachim Jeremias, *Jerusalem in the Time of Jesus* (Philadelphia: Fortress Press, 1975), ch. 14; idem, *New Testament Theology* (New York: Scribner's, 1971), 108–12; Delores

Osborne, "Women: Sinners and Prostitutes" (Paper presented at the Society of Biblical Literature Pacific Coast Region, Long Beach, Calif., April 1987); Norman Perrin, *Rediscovering The Teaching of Jesus* (New York: Harper and Row, 1967), 102–8; E. P. Sanders, *Jesus and Judaism* (Philadelphia: Fortress Press, 1990), 182–99; Smith, "The Historical Jesus at Table," 466–86; idem, "Table Fellowship and the Historical Jesus." See Corley, *Private Women, Public Meals*, 89–93, and Smith, "Historical Jesus at Table," 474–84.

15. Donahue, "Tax Collectors and Sinners," 59–61. So also Richard A. Horsley, *Jesus and the Spiral of Violence: Popular Jewish Resistance in Roman Palestine* (Minneapolis: Fortress Press, 1987), 212. F. Herrenbrück has suggested that the "tax collectors" were Hellenistic tax farmers rather than Roman *publicani* or part of the Roman tax gathering system. See F. Herrenbrück, "Wer waren die 'Zöllner'?" *Zeitschrift fuer die neutestamentliche Wissenschaft* 78 (1987): 178–94.

16. Abrahams, "Publicans and Sinners"; Farmer, "Who Are the 'Tax Collectors and Sinners'?"; Gibson, "*Hoi Telōnai*," 430. This thesis is disputed by Herrenbrück, "Zum Vorwurf der Kollaboration des Zöllners mit Rom," *Zeitschrift fuer die neutestamentliche Wissenschaft* 78 (1987): 186–99. Herrenbrück suggests that the Pharisees, who were the social and political rivals of tax collectors, coined the phrase *sinful tax collectors*.

17. Abrahams, "Publicans and Sinners," 54; Donahue, "Tax Collectors and Sinners," 52; Jeremias, *New Testament Theology*, 110–11.

18. Horsley, *Jesus and the Spiral of Violence*, 213.

19. Farmer, "Who are the 'Tax Collectors and Sinners'?" 168; Perrin, *Rediscovering*, 103. Horsley doubts that either tax or toll collectors were regarded as "sinners" or Gentiles, that is, outside of the Jewish community (*Jesus and the Spiral of Violence*, 213–14).

20. Donahue, "Tax Collectors and Sinners."

21. Jeremias, *New Testament Theology*, 109–13. See Sanders, *Jesus and Judaism*, 182–99.

22. Sanders, *Jesus and Judaism*, 177.

23. John P. Meier, *A Marginal Jew: Rethinking the Historical Jesus* (New York: Doubleday, 2001), 3:28.

24. Abrahams, "Publicans and Sinners," 55; Schüssler Fiorenza, *In Memory of Her*, 128.

25. Borg, *Jesus: A New Vision*, 129–35; idem, *Meeting Jesus*, 55–56; Corley, "Jesus' Table Practice"; Crossan, *Historical Jesus*, 335; Schüssler Fiorenza, *In Memory of Her*, 118–30; idem, *Miriam's Child*, 93–94 (she cites Alan F. Segal).

26. See especially Paula Fredriksen, "Did Jesus Oppose the Purity Laws?" *Bible Review* 11, no. 3 (1995), 18–25, 42–45, esp. 23; idem, *Jesus of Nazareth* (New York: Knopf, 2000), 67; E. P. Sanders, *Jesus and Judaism* (Philadelphia: Fortress Press, 1990), 182–85.

27. Corley, *Women and the Historical Jesus*, ch. 1. This is the basis of the reconstruction Schüssler Fiorenza presents in *In Memory of Her*, where she juxtaposes Jesus' open table praxis with "sinners" (characterized by "wholeness") to that of the Pharisees' table practice of cultic purity (characterized by

"holiness") (118–22). Her discussion of Jesus' meals in *Miriam's Child*, however, is devoid of this distinction (93–94). Borg's reconstruction mirrors Schüssler Fiorenza's original premise in his *Jesus: A New Vision*, 129–35; see also *Meeting Jesus*, 55–56, where he places Jesus within a diverse Judaism, offering "compassion" as opposed to "purity" and "holiness." This common distinction between Jesus and Judaism follows a Lutheran historiographical pattern, "law vs. grace," and uses Judaism as a negative foil (Jonathan Z. Smith, *Drudgery Divine: On the Comparison of Early Christianities and the Religions of Late Antiquity* [Chicago: University of Chicago Press, 1990], 79–81).

28. Josephus, *A.J.* 17.11.2 (304–9); *B.J.* 1.25.6 (511). See Freyne, "Geography, Politics, and Economics of Galilee," in *Studying the Historical Jesus: Evaluations of the State of Current Research*, ed. Bruce Chilton and Craig Evans (Leiden: Brill, 1994), 102–3.

29. The accusation is assumed to be false. See Horsley, *Jesus and the Spiral of Violence*, 215–21; Smith, "Historical Jesus at Table," 482, 484.

30. Smith, "Jesus at Table," 477–79; idem, "Table Fellowship as a Literary Motif in the Gospel of Luke," *Journal of Biblical Literature* 106 (1987): 613–38, esp. 634.

31. Aeschines, *Tim.* 117-20; Cicero, *Verr.* 2.1.39.101; Dio Chrysostom, *Or.* 4.97-98; *Or.* 14.14; Lucian, *Men.* 11; Plutarch, *Apoph. Lac.* 236B–C; Theophrastus, *Char.* 6.5-6; F. Hauck and S. Schultz, "πορνη, κτλ," *TDNT* 6:579–95, esp. 582; Hans Licht, *Sexual Life in Ancient Greece* (New York: Barnes and Noble, 1953), 334; Vern and Bonnie Bullough, *Prostitution* (New York: Crown, 1978), 48; Corley, *Private Women, Public Meals*, 40–41.

32. Suetonius, *Tib.* 35; Bullough and Bullough, *Prostitution*, 48, 52–53; Corley, *Private Women, Public Meals*, 40–41, 64–65.

33. See Dio Chrysostom, where these two trades are "unseemly" or "base" (*Or.* 14.14); In Lucian, tax collectors are linked to pimps, adulterers, and other despised individuals (*Men.* 11). In Theophrastus, a character called "Willful Disreputableness" looks for various kinds of jobs, including innkeeping, brothelkeeping, and tax collecting (*Char.* 6). For this association in Palestine, see Gibson, "*Hoi Telōnai,*" 431–33.

34. *Mor.* 236C.

35. *Or.* 4.98. See Corley, *Private Women, Public Meals*, 40–41, 89–93.

36. For one example, see Cicero, *Verr.* 2.1.39.101; for further discussion, see Corley, *Private Women, Public Meals*, 38–48.

37. Ronald Hock, "The Will of God and Sexual Morality" (paper presented at the Society of Biblical Literature Annual Meeting, New York, 1982), 35; K. H. Rengstorf, "ἁμαρτωλος, κτλ," *TDNT* 1:317–35, esp. 317–18. The use of *hamartōlos* in inscriptions is probably not pertinent (Rengstorf, *TDNT,* 1:318). For a contrary view, see Adolf Deismann, *Light from the Ancient Near East* (London: Hodder and Stoughton, 1927), 113–15.

38. Rengstorf, 317. It may also have been an insulting designation for slaves (Rengstorf, *TDNT* 1:318).

39. Deismann, *Light*, 113–15.

40. *Aud. Poet.* 7 [ii, 25C]; Rengstorf, *TDNT* 1:319.

41. For full discussion, see Corley, *Private Women, Public Meals*, 121–30.

42. Dunn, "Pharisees, Sinners and Jesus," 276–80; followed by Smith, "Jesus at Table," 482–84. See also Luke Timothy Johnson, "The New Testament's Anti-Jewish Slander and the Conventions of Ancient Polemic," *Journal of Biblical Literature* 108 (1989): 438–39.

43. Smith, "Jesus at Table," 482–84; Corley, *Private Women, Public Meals*, 63–66.

44. See James Charlesworth, "The Foreground of Christian Origins," in *Jesus' Jewishness: Exploring the Place of Jesus within Early Judaism*, 63–83 (New York: Crossroad, 1991), 68–69; Jacob Neusner's critique of Shaye Cohen, *From the Maccabees to the Mishnah* (Louisville: Westminster John Knox, 1987), in *Wrong Ways and Right Ways in the Study of Formative Judaism* (Atlanta: Scholars Press, 1988), 141–50; and more recently Anthony Saldarini's discussion of Matthew's group (not "community") in *Matthew's Christian-Jewish Community* (Chicago: Chicago University Press, 1994), 13–18, 84–123.

45. Saldarini, *Matthew*, 17.

46. Corley, *Private Women, Public Meals*, 93; Johnson, "The New Testament's Anti-Jewish Slander," 441; Smith, "Historical Jesus at Table," 486. See also James Robinson, "The Jesus of Q as Liberation Theologian," in *The Gospel behind the Gospels: Current Studies on Q*, ed. R. Piper (Leiden: Brill, 1995), 268. Thus, it is highly unlikely that this tradition can be used to identify real prostitutes, sinners, or tax collectors among Jesus' followers as is commonly assumed by Borg, *Jesus: A New Vision*, 130–35; idem, *Meeting Jesus*, 55–58; Schüssler Fiorenza, *In Memory of Her*, 118–30; idem, *Miriam's Child*, 93–94.

47. Corley, *Private Women, Public Meals*, 40–41.

48. *Verr.* 2.3.68.159-60; 2.5.12.30–13.31; 2.5.13.34; 2.5.32.83; 2.5.36.94; Corley, *Private Women, Public Meals*, 36–38; 42–53.

49. See Alfred Plummer, "The Woman That Was a Sinner," *Expository Times* 27 (1915–19), 42–43, and Luke 15:11-32, where the prodigal son is similarly an example of a "sinner" who wastes his money on "loose living," which includes prostitutes. Thus Walker's suggestion that what we have here is an image of "sporter," "pimps," or "playboys" is not far from the truth, although his positing of a mispelled word to make this conclusion is unnecessary (Wm. O. Walker, "Jesus and the Tax Collectors," *Journal of Biblical Literature* 97 (1978): 221–38, esp. 237).

50. Leif Vaage, *Galilean Upstarts: Jesus' First Followers According to Q* (Valley Forge, Pa.: Trinity Press International, 1994), 88. Ivan Havener sees this as a label given to Jesus by his opponents. See *Q: The Sayings of Jesus* (Wilmington, Del.: Michael Glazier, 1987), 66. Cotter and Vaage also assume this accusation reflects Jesus' actual conduct. See Wendy Cotter, "Yes, I Tell You, More Than a Prophet," in *Conflict and Invention: Literary, Rhetorical, and Social Studies on the Sayings Gospel Q*, ed. John S. Kloppenborg (Valley Forge, Pa.: Trinity Press International, 1995), 147; Leif E. Vaage, "More Than a Prophet," in *Conflict and Invention: Literary, Rhetorical, and Social Studies on the Sayings Gospel Q*, 181–202,

ed. John S. Kloppenborg (Valley Forge, Pa.: Trinity Press International, 1995), 190. Funk calls Jesus an "urban partygoer" (*Honest to Jesus*, 192).

51. Smith, "Historical Jesus at Table."

52. Deut 21:18-21; Prov 23:19-25; 28:7; 29:1-3. C. Brown, "The Parable of the Rebellious Son(s)" (unpublished manuscript used by permission). See also Funk, *Honest to Jesus*, 193.

53. Johnson, "Anti-Jewish Slander," 441. Smith suggests that the most it might suggest is that Jesus is not ascetic ("Jesus at Table," 486). See also comments by Horsley, *Jesus and the Spiral of Violence*, 215; Patrick Hartin, "Yet Wisdom Is Justified by Her Children," *Conflict and Invention: Literary, Rhetorical, and Social Studies on the Sayings Gospel Q*, ed. John S. Kloppenborg (Valley Forge, Pa.: Trinity Press International, 1995), 154.

54. Vaage sees this accusation of demon possession against John as similar to insults leveled by philosophers against other philosophers but does not consider a similar origin for the insult against Jesus. See Vaage, "More Than a Prophet," 191.

55. John S. Kloppenborg, *Formation of Q: Trajectories in Ancient Wisdom Collections* (Philadelphia: Fortress Press, 1987), 111; Robinson critiques Vaage in a similar manner ("Jesus of Q as Liberation Theologian," 268–69). See also Horsley, *Jesus and the Spiral of Violence*, 215.

56. Corley, *Private Women, Public Meals*, 24–77.

57. Johnson, "Anti-Jewish Slander," 431–32; Corley, *Private Women, Public Meals*, 63–65.

58. See the Cynic Epistles, especially the letters of Crates addressed to Hipparchia. In Lucian's *Fugitivi*, a woman Cynic leaves her husband and runs away with two of her slaves. See F. Gerald Downing, *Jesus and the Threat of Freedom* (London: SCM, 1987), 115–21; idem, *Christ and the Cynics* (Sheffield: Sheffield Academic Press, 1988), 1–5.

59. Wayne Meeks, "The Image of the Androgyne: Some Uses of a Symbol in Earliest Christianity," *History of Religions* 13 (1974): 172.

60. Catherine J. Castner, "Epicurean Hetairai as Dedicants to Healing Deities?" *Greek, Roman and Byzantine Studies* 23 (1982): 51–57; Smith, "Social Obligation in the Context of Communal Meals: A Study of the Christian Meal in 1 Corinthians in Comparison with Graeco-Roman Meals" (Th.D. diss., Harvard Divinity School, 1980), 57.

61. William Klassen, "Musonius Rufus, Jesus and Paul: Three First Century Feminists?" in *From Jesus to Paul: Studies in Honor of Francis Wright Beare*, ed. P. Richardson and J. Hurd (Ontario: Wilfred Laurier University Press, 1984), 185–206. See also Anna Lydia Motto, "Seneca on Women's Liberation," *Classical World* 65 (1972): 155–57, for Seneca's encouragement of women to follow Stoic discipline, and comments by Kathleen Wicker, "Mulierum Virtutes," in *Plutarch's Ethical Writings and Early Christianity*, ed. Hans Dieter Betz (Leiden: Brill, 1978), 114.

62. Johnson, "Anti-Jewish Slander," 431; Corley, *Private Women, Public Meals*, 63–66.

63. David L. Balch, *Let Wives Be Submissive: The Domestic Code in 1 Peter* (Chico, Calif.: Scholars Press, 1981), chs. 5–6. See also Corley, *Private Women, Public Meals*, 64–65.

64. Corley, *Private Women, Public Meals*, 64–65.

65. Schüssler Fiorenza, *In Memory of Her*, 119; Kloppenborg, *Formation of Q*, 111; Robinson, "The Jesus of Q as Liberation Theologian," 268–69, esp. n. 61.

66. Jacobson admits that this correspondence is somewhat clumsy. Another interpretation is that the "piping" and "mourning" activities do not correspond to Jesus and John's, but to those of "this generation." See Arland Jacobson, *The First Gospel* (Sonoma, Calif.: Polebridge, 1992), 123, esp. n. 183, as well as Kloppenborg, *Formation of Q*, 111. Cotter argues that it is "this generation" that does the calling in "Parable of the Children in the Marketplace," 295.

67. Matthew's *erga*, "deeds" (Matt 11:19), is undoubtedly secondary. See Kloppenborg, *Formation of Q*, 110; idem, *Excavating Q: The History and Setting of the Sayings Gospel Q* (Minneapolis: Fortress Press, 2000), 123, 126; Jacobson, *The First Gospel*, 124.

68. Hartin, "Yet Wisdom Is Justified by Her Children," 155; Jacobson, *The First Gospel*, 123–25; Kloppenborg, *Formation of Q*, 111; Cotter also argues that Jesus and John are the "children of Wisdom" (Wendy Cotter, "The Parable of the Children in the Marketplace: An Examination of the Parable's Meaning and Significance," *Novum Testamentum* 29 [1987]: 289–304, esp. 303; idem, "Yes, I Tell You," 146).

69. Corley, *Private Women, Public Meals*, 121–30.

70. Cotter, "Parable of the Children," who focuses on the possible connotations of the phrase *tois en agora kathēmenois* and argues that these children (who are equated with "this generation") are sitting in judgment of their peers (as if they were adults), but their youth exposes the self-righteousness of their behavior ("Parable of the Children," 299–302). See also Cotter, "Yes, I Tell you," 146–47.

71. Corley, *Women and the Historical Jesus*, ch. 4; idem, *Private Women, Public Meals*, 48–49, 128–30, 153, esp. n. 26. Even poorer families hired at least two flute players and one woman mourner for funerals. See Matt 9:23; *b. Ketub.* 46b; Robert Gundry, *Matthew: A Commentary on His Literary and Theological Art* (Grand Rapids: Eerdmans, 1982), 175; Samuel Tobias Lachs, *A Rabbinic Commentary on the New Testament* (Hoboken, N.J.: KTAV; New York: Anti-defamation League of B'nai B'rith, 1987). 172.

72. Milton Meltzer, *Slavery from the Rise of Western Civilization to the Renaissance* (New York: Cowles, 1971–72), 72–75; Yvon Garlan, *Slavery in Ancient Greece* (Ithaca, N.Y.: Cornell University Press, 1988), 62, 68, 70; John Kells Ingram, *A History of Slavery and Serfdom* (London: Adam and Charles Black, 1895), 21. See discussion in Corley, *Private Women, Public Meals*, 48–49.

73. Found in Tomb 2 at Marissa. See Jack Finegan, *The Archaeology of the New Testament* Princeton, N.J.: Princeton University Press, 1992), 301–5; Erwin R. Goodenough, *Jewish Symbols in the Greco-Roman Period* (New York: Pantheon, 1953), vol. 3, pl. 14.

74. For further discussion, see Mark Golden, *"Pais,* 'Child' and 'Slave,'" *L'antique classique* 54 (1985): 91–104; G. H. R. Horsley, *"paidarion,"* in *New Documents Illustrating Early Christianity,* ed. G. R. H. Horsley (Macquarie University: Ancient History Documentary Research Centre, 1981), 1:87.

75. Men were also flute players and musicians, but women more often fulfilled this role. Corley, *Private Women, Public Meals,* 26–28, 48–49.

76. Corley, *Women and the Historical Jesus,* ch. 5. For mourners in the Gospels, see, for example, Matt 9:23 (flute players) and Luke 23:27 (the "daughters of Jerusalem" who mourn the death of Jesus).

77. Corley, *Private Women, Public Meals,* 26–28; 48–49; Chester G. Starr, "An Evening with the Flute-Girls," *La parola del passato* 33 (1978): 401–10; on the connection between flute-players and the term *porné,* see also *BAGD* 700.

78. Corley, *Private Women, Public Meals,* 48–49, 128–30, 153n26; see discussion above.

79. Ibid., 26–27, 48–49, 153n26.

80. This Wisdom saying therefore may have circulated independently and was attached to this cluster at some compositional stage of Q. Kloppenborg, *Formation of Q,* 110–11. Jacobson argues the opposite (*The First Gospel,* 124). However, the possibility that the term *tekna* (v. 34) interprets *paidiois* (v. 32) in a way inconsistent with the sense of the parable itself is an argument in favor of Kloppenborg's position.

81. Amy-Jill Levine ignores the possibility that some of the "children" could be girls ("Second Temple Judaism, Jesus, and Women: Yeast of Eden," *Biblical Interpretation* 2 (1994): 8–33, esp. 27n54). Levine cites Arthur Dewey to support the notion that the distinction between male and female slaves in other Q passages is Lukan (Arthur Dewey, "A Prophetic Pronouncement: Q12:42-46," *Forum* 5, no. 2 (1989): 99–108, esp. 100). However, that both men and women are portrayed as slaves in various household contexts and service capacities can hardly be attributed merely to Luke. See LSJ 1287. It must be admitted that children could be assigned household roles similar to those as slaves, both in fields and at meals (Golden, *"Pais,* 'Child,' and 'Slave,' " 98–99), but this does not seem to have included participation in musical entertainment.

82. Earlier scholars suggested the contrast was weddings and funerals. See Olaf Linton, "Parable of the Children's Game," *New Testament Studies* 22 (1976): 159–79, esp. 174.

83. See below. There is therefore no "tension" between John and "tax collectors" in Q as Hoffmann suggests (juxtaposing Q 7:27 to Q 7:33-35, "Q 7:29-30: Fourth Response" [paper presented to the International Q Project. Claremont, Calif., May 1994], 3–4). "Tax Collectors" along with the "children of wisdom" are among the "envoys of Wisdom," and are not to be equated with "this generation."

84. Kloppenborg, *Formation of Q,* 107. See also Linton, "The Parable of the Children's Game," 171–75, for comments on earlier discussions.

85. Jacobsen, *The First Gospel,* 122–23.

86. See Linton, "Parable of the Children's Game," 162, 173.

87. See discussion of past scholarship in Linton, "Parable of the Children's Game," 162.

88. Jesus Seminar vote: red. See also comments by Hans Dieter Betz, *The Sermon on the Mount* (Minneapolis: Fortress Press, 1995), 372.

89. Jeremias, *Abba* (Göttingen: Vandenhoeck and Ruprecht), 15–67; idem, *The Prayers of Jesus* (Naperville, Ill.: Allec Allenson, 1967), 11–65.

90. Robert Hamerton-Kelly, *God the Father: Theology and Patriarchy in the Teaching of Jesus* (Philadelphia: Fortress Press, 1979); idem, "God the Father in the Bible and in the Experience of Jesus: The State of the Question," in *God as Father?* ed. Johannes Baptist Metz and Edward Schillebeecks (Edinburgh: T. & T. Clark; New York: Seabury, 1981).

91. Schüssler Fiorenza, *In Memory of Her*, 145–51; Rosemary Radford Ruether, *Sexism and God-Talk: Toward a Feminist Theology* (Boston: Beacon, 1993), 64–68; Sandra Schneiders, *Women and the Word* (Mahwah, N.J.: Paulist, 1986), 48–49.

92. Mary Rose D'Angelo, "Theology in Mark and Q," *Harvard Theological Review* 85 (1992): 149–74; idem, "*Abba* and 'Father,'" *Journal of Biblical Literature* 111 (1992): 611–30. See also critique of Jeremias by James Charlesworth, "A Caveat on Textual Transmission and the Meaning of the Lord's Prayer," in *The Lord's Prayer and Other Prayer Texts from the Greco-Roman Era*, ed. J. Charlesworth et al. (Valley Forge, Pa.: Trinity Press Intereco International, 1994), 1–14.

93. The use of God as Father in Jewish prayer is more common than has previously been supposed. See 4Q372 1; 3 Macc 6:3; *Apoc. Ezek.* frag. 3; Wis 14:3; Sir 23:1. On the biblical and Jewish precedents to the appelation of God as "father," see Charlesworth, "Caveat," 5–10; D'Angelo, "Theology in Mark and Q," 152–56; idem, "Abba and Father," 618–19; Alfonz Deissler, "The Spirit of the Lord's Prayer," in *The Lord's Prayer and Jewish Liturgy*, ed. J. J. Petuchowski and M. Brocke (New York: Seabury, 1978), 5–6; Hamerton-Kelly, *God the Father*, 20–51; Jeremias, *Prayers of Jesus*, 11–29; Vernon S. McCasland, "Abba, Father," *Journal of Biblical Literature* 72 (1953): 79–91, esp. 83–84; John M. Oesterrecher, "Abba, Father: On the Humanity of Jesus," in *The Lord's Prayer and Jewish Liturgy*, ed. J. J. Petuchowski and M. Brocke (New York: Seabury, 1978), 130–33; Eileen Schuller, *Post-Exilic Prophets* (Wilmington, Del.: Michael Glazier, 1988), 70–79. On 4Q372 1 and "father" in Jewish prayer, see Schuller, "4Q372 1: A Text about Joseph," *Revue de Qumran* 55 (1990): 349–76, esp. 355, 362–63; idem, "The Psalm of 4Q372 1," *Catholic Biblical Quarterly* (1992): 67–79, esp. 68, 71. Honi the Circle-Drawer also prayed "Father, Father, give us rain." See Charlesworth, "Caveat," 9; Geza Vermes, *Jesus the Jew* (Philadelphia: Fortress Press, 1973), 211.

94. D'Angelo, "Theology in Mark and Q," 151; idem, "Abba and Father," 614. See James Barr, "Abba Isn't 'Daddy,'" *Journal of Theological Studies* 39 (1988): 28–47; idem, "Abba, Father," *Theology* 91 (1988): 173–79; Charlesworth, "Caveat," 5–10.

95. D'Angelo, "Theology in Mark and Q," 173–74; idem, "Abba and Father," 623–30.

96. D'Angelo, "Theology in Mark and Q," 174.

97. So D'Angelo, "Abba and Father," 630.

98. So D'Angelo, "Theology in Mark and Q," 159. Against Jeremias, *Prayers of Jesus*, 55–56; Oesterreicher, "Abba, Father," 121–22.

99. D'Angelo, "Abba and Father," 615.

100. D'Angelo, "Theology in Mark and Q," 167–73; see also Kloppenborg, *The Formation of Q*, 197–203.

101. Betz, *Sermon on the Mount*, 374–75.

102. D'Angelo, "Theology in Mark and Q," 174.

103. See Corley, *Women and the Historical Jesus*, ch. 5.

104. See ibid.; Byron R. McCane, "Let the Dead Bury Their Own Dead," *Harvard Theological Review* 83 (1990) 31–43, esp. 32–34.

105. Zvi Greenhut, "Burial Cave of the Caiaphas Family," *Biblical Theological Review* 18, no. 5 (1992): 29–36.

106. Tal Ilan, *Jewish Women in Greco-Roman* Palestine (1995; repr., Peabody, Mass.: Hendrickson, 1996), 53.

107. Joachim Jeremias, *Heiligengräber in Jesu Umwelt* (Göttingen: Vandenhoeck and Ruprecht, 1958), 114. Jeremias discusses over forty cult sites in Palestine and the surrounding areas, which he views as precursors to the later Christian cult of the martyrs (5). Peter Brown also finds a similar precursor to the cult of the saints in Jewish veneration of martyrs and prophets (*The Cult of the Saints* [Chicago: University of Chicago Press, 1981], 3, 10, 33). See also W. R. Halliday, "Cenotaphs and Sacred Localities," *Annual of the British School of Athens* 17 (1910–11): 182–92, esp. 188–89; Eric Meyers, *Jewish Ossuaries: Burial and Rebirth* (Rome: Biblical Institute Press, 1971), 54n31; Lewis Bayles Paton, *Spiritism and the Cult of the Dead in Antiquity* (New York: Macmillan, 1921), 238. See also Corley, *Women and the Historical Jesus*.

108. Jeremias, *Heiligengräber*, 126–41.

109. It was the purpose of Jeremias's study to confirm the historical background to the "woe" attributed to Jesus against the Pharisees for building and beautifying the tombs of the prophets and the righteous (*Heiligengräber*, 5). On Q and Jesus, see below, ch. 4.

110. See Finegan, *The Archaeology of the New Testament*, 305–10.

111. Finegan, *Archaeology*, 38–39; Jeremias, *Heiligengräber*, pl. 4.

112. Portions of this chapter are used by permission of Polebridge. L. Y. Rahmani, "Jerusalem's Tomb Monuments," *Biblical Archaeologist* 4, no. 3 (1981): 171–77 (Part 1); 44, no. 4 (1981): 229–35 (part 2); 45, no. 1 (1981): 43–53 (Part 3); 45, no. 2 (1982): 109–19 (part 4).

113. Pseudo-Philo, *L.A.B.* 33.5. Translated by D. J. Harrington.

114. 2 Bar 85:1, 12.

115. RSV. Jesus Seminar vote on the saying "Let the dead bury their own dead": pink.

116. RSV. Jesus Seminar vote: grey.

117. Jesus Seminar vote: pink.

118. RSV. Jesus Seminar vote: black.

119. NRSV. Jesus Seminar vote: black.

120. RSV. Jesus Seminar vote: grey.

121. See overview in McCane, "Let the Dead," 38–39. He notes one exception: Robert Gundry, *Matthew*, 153–54. See also discussion in Herbert W. Basser, "Let the Dead Bury Their Dead," in Approaches to Ancient Judaism, ed. Herbert W. Bassser and Simcha Fishbane (New Series; Atlanta: Scholars Press, 1993), 5:84–85; Vernon Robbins, "Foxes, Birds, Burials, and Furrows," in *Patterns of Persuasion in the Gospels*, ed. Burton L. Mack and Vernon K. Robbins (Sonoma, Calif.: Polebridge, 1989), 72–73.

122. McCane, "Let the Dead," 38–39.

123. Philip Sellew came to this conclusion independently of me. See Sellew, "Death, Body, and the World," *Studia Patristica* 31, ed. Elizabeth A. Livingstone (Leuven: Peeters, 1996), 530–34. On ancient epitaphs, see Richard Lattimore, *Themes in Greek and Latin Epitaphs* (Urbana: University of Illinois Press, 1942).

124. See Aristotle, *History of Animals* 7.592b; 11.615a; 30.618b-619b; Prov 30:17. On the authenticity of this saying, see Heinz O. Guenther, "When 'Eagles' Draw Together," *Forum* 5 (1989): 140–50.

125. Franz Cumont, *After Life in Roman Paganism* (New Haven, Conn.: Yale University Press, 1922), 65. Unfortunately, Cumont makes this citation without sources.

126. Plato, *Phaedo* 115C.

127. See *Diog. Laer.*, 4.52; 4.79; *Cynic Epistles*, 25; Cicero, *Tusc.* 1.104 (quoting Diogenes); Lucian, *Demon.* 35; 66. I would like to thank David Seeley for these references.

128. See Corley, *Women and the Historical Jesus*, ch. 4.

129. See Ibid. I would like to thank John Kloppenborg for his remarks in this regard in a personal correspondence dated June 7, 1996.

130. See O. H. Steck, *Israel und das gewaltsame Geschick der Propheten.* WMANT 23 (Neukirschen-Vluyen; Neukirchner-Verlag, 1967). See David Seeley, "Jesus' Death in Q," *New Testament Studies* 38 (1992): 222–34, esp. 223; idem, "Blessings and Boundaries," *Semeia* 55 (1991): 131–46, esp. 135. See also Michael Knowles, *Jeremiah in Matthew's Gospel* (Sheffield: JSOT Press, 1993), 96–109; on Q see ibid., 116–17; Jacobsen, *The First Gospel*, 72–76; Kloppenborg, *Formation*, ch. 4; R. Miller, "The Rejection of the Prophets in Q," *Journal of Biblical Literature* 107 (1988): 225–40, esp. 226–33.

131. For Jesus as a prophet, see Mark 8:28 // Matt 16:14 // Luke 9:19; Matt 21:11; 21:46; Mark 6:14-15 // Matt 14:1-2 // Luke 9:7-9; Luke 7:16; 7:39-50; 13:33; John 4:19; 7:52; 9:17. See discussion in N. T. Wright, *Jesus and the Victory of God* (Minneapolis: Fortress Press, 1996), 164–65.

132. Mack, *Myth of Innocence*, 53–77.

133. The "days of Noah" warning in Q does not disparage patriarchal marriage, as Luise Schottroff has suggested, but reflects the ordinariness and therefore unexpected nature of the time of judgment. See Luise Schottroff, "Itinerant Prophetesses: A Feminist Analysis of the Sayings Source Q" (Institute for Antiquity and Christianity, Occasional Papers 21, August, 1991), 349.

134. Arland Jacobsen, "Divided Families and Christian Origins," in *The Gospel behind the Gospel: Current Studies on Q*, ed. Ronald A. Piper (Leiden: Brill: 1995), 361–80, esp. 361–63.

135. Jonathan Draper, "Torah and Troublesome Apostles in the Didache Community," *Novum Testamentum* 33 (1991): 347–72; "Recovering Oral Performance from Written Text in Q," and "Wandering Charismatics and Scholarly Circularities," in R. A. Horsley and J. A. Draper, *Whoever Hears You Hears Me: Prophets, Performance, and Tradition in Q* (Harrisburg, Pa.: 1999), 29–45; 175–94.

136. H. van de Sandt, ed. *Matthew and the Didache: Two Documents from the Same Jewish-Christian Mileu?* (Assen: Royal van Gorcum; Minneapolis: Fortress Press, 2005).

137. Alan J. P. Garrow, *The Gospel of Matthew's Dependence on the Didache* (New York: T. and T. Clark, 2004), 25–28.

138. Ibid., p. 27.

139. This chart is drawn from ibid., 26–27.

140. Oral comment at the *Didache* section of the Society of Biblical Literature Meeting, Washington, D.C., November, 2006.

141. Following the analysis of Jonathan Schwiebert, *Knowledge and the Coming Kingdom: The Didache's Meal Ritual and Its Place in Early Christianity* (New York: T. and T. Clark, 2008), 24–25.

142. Ibid., 26.

Chapter 4: The Eucharist and Meals for the Dead

1. Kathleen E. Corley, *Private Women, Public Meals: Social Conflict in the Synoptic Tradition* (Peabody, Mass.: Hendrickson, 1993), passim; idem, "Were the Women around Jesus Really Prostitutes? Women in the Context of Greco-Roman Meals," in *Society of Biblical Literature 1989 Seminar Papers*, ed. David J. Lull (Atlanta: Scholars Press, 1989), 487–521.

2. See chapter 2.

3. Many commentators acknowledge that the feeding meals are characterized as eucharists in Matthew. See Heinz Joachim Held, "Matthew as Interpreter of the Miracle Stories," in *Tradition and Interpretation in Matthew*, Günther Bornkamm, Gerhard Barth, and Heinz-Joachim Held (Philadelphia: Westminster, 1963), 187; W. F. Albright and C. S. Mann, *Matthew*, Anchor Bible (Garden City, N.Y.: Doubleday, 1971), 178–79; Robert H. Gundry, *Matthew: A Commentary on His Literary and Theological Art* (Grand Rapids: Eerdmans, 1982), 291; Samuel Tobias Lachs, *A Rabbinic Commentary on The New Testament: The Gospels Matthew, Mark, and Luke* (Hoboken, N.J.: KTAV; New York: Anti-Defamation League of B'nai B'rith, 1987), 241; Ulrich Luz, "Disciples in the Gospel according to Matthew," in *The Interpretation of Matthew*, ed. G. Stanton (Philadelphia: Fortress Press, 1983), 105; Eduard Schweizer, *The Good News according to Matthew*, trans. David Green (Atlanta: John Knox, 1975), 319.

4. Gundry, *Matthew*, 291.

5. Held, "Matthew as Interpreter," 185–86; Gundry, *Matthew*, 293–94.

6. See chs. 2 and 3 above.

7. Gundry, *Matthew*, 295; Michael H. Crosby, *House of Disciples: Church, Economics, and Justice in Matthew* (Maryknoll, N.Y.: Orbis, 1988), 115.

8. Matthew 1:19-20, 24; 2:2, 8-9, 11, 13-14, 20-21). See Gundry, *Matthew*, 295; Crosby, *House of Disciples*, 115; Jack Dean Kingsbury, "The Title 'Son of David' in Matthew's Gospel," *Journal of Biblical Literature* 95 (1976): 591–602, esp. 594–96.

9. Gundry, *Matthew*, 295.

10. See Corley, *Private Women, Public Meals*, 75–78, and above, ch. 2.

11. Corley, *Private Women, Public Meals*, 162.

12. Gundry, *Matthew*, 319–21.

13. Ibid., 320–22.

14. Paul J. Achtemeier, "The Origin and Function of the Pre-Markan Miracle Catenae," *Journal of Biblical Literature* 91 (1972): 198–221; idem, "Toward the Isolation of Pre-Markan Miracle Cantenae," *Journal of Biblical Literature* 89 (1970): 265–91.

15. André Grabar, *The Beginnings of Christian Art 200–395*, trans. Stuart Gilbert and James Emmons (London: Thames and Hudson, 1967), 79, fig. 69.

16. See Corley, *Private Women, Public Meals*, 97–102.

17. "And Sidon," which occurs in some manuscripts, is an assimilation from Matt 15:21 and Mark 7:31. See Bruce M. Metzger, *A Textual Commentary on the Greek New Testament* (New York: United Bible Society, 1975), 95.

18. T. A. Burkill, "The Historical Development of the Story of the Syro-Phoenician Woman (Mark 7:24-31)," *Novum Testamentum* 9 (1967): 161–77, esp. 173ff.; J. D. M. Derrett, "Law in the New Testament: The Syro-Phoenician Woman and the Centurion of Capernaum," *Novum Testamentum* 15 (1973): 161–86; Elisabeth Schüssler Fiorenza, *In Memory of Her: A Feminist Theological Reconstruction of Christian Origins* (1983; repr., New York: Crossroad, 1994), 137; Barnabas Flammer, "Die Syro-Phoenizerin: Mark 7:24-30," *Theologische Quartalschrift* 148 (1968): 463–78, esp. 20ff.; Robert A. Guelich, *Mark 1–8:26*, Word Biblical Commentary 34 (Dallas: Word, 1989), 383.

19. Winsome Munro, "Women Disciples in Mark?" *Catholic Biblical Quarterly* 44 (1982): 227; Gerd Theissen, *The Miracle Stories of the Early Christian Tradition*, trans. Francis McDonagh (Philadelphia: Fortress Press, 1983), 254.

20. 1 Kgs 16:31; 18:4, 13; 2 Kgs 9:7ff. For Jezebel's "table," see 1 Kgs 18:19.

21. Isa 23:12; Jer 25:22; 47:4; Ezek 27:8; 28:21-22; Joel 3:4. See also remarks by Hisako Kinukawa, *Women and Jesus in Mark: A Japanese Feminist Perspective* (Maryknoll, N.Y.: Orbis, 1994), 53.

22. F. Gerald Downing, "The Woman from Syro-Phoenicia and Her Dog-gedness: Mark 7:24-31 (Matthew 15:21-28)," in *Women in the Biblical Tradition*, ed. George J. Brooke (Lewiston, N.Y.: Edwin Mellen, 1992), 129–49, esp. 138; Guelich, *Mark 1–8:26*, 385; Judy Gundry-Volf, "Spirit, Mercy, and

the Other," *Theology Today* 51 (1995): 508–23, esp. 516; Theissen, *Miracle Stories*, 126; idem, "Lokal-und Soziolkolorit in der Geschichte von der syrophönikischen Frau (Mark 7:24-30)" *Zeitschrift für neutestamentischen Wissenshaft* 75 (1984): 202–25; P. Porkorny, "From a Puppy to the Child: Some Problems of Contemporary Biblical Exegesis Demonstrated from Mark 7.24-30/Matt 15.21-8," *New Testament Studies* 41 (1995): 321–37, esp. 323; See also comments by Schüssler Fiorenza on the version of this story in the Pseudo-Clementines: Elisabeth Schüssler Fiorenza, *But She Said: Feminist Practices of Biblical Interpretation* (Boston: Beacon, 1992), 100.

23. Guelich, *Mark 1–8:26*, 385; Theissen, *Miracle Stories*, 126.

24. Hal Taussig, "Dealing under the Table: Ritual Negotiation of Women's Power in the Syro-Phoenician Woman Pericope," in *Reimagining Christian Origins: A Colloquium Honoring Burton L. Mack*, ed. Elizabeth Castelli and Hal Taussig (Valley Forge, Pa.: Trinity Press International, 1996), 264–79, esp. 270.

25. Derrett, "Law and the New Testament," 169; Flammer, "Die Syro-Phoenizerin," 20; Gundry-Volf, "Spirit, Mercy, and the Other," 517; J. Ireland Hasler, "The Incident of the Syro-Phoenician Woman (Matt 15:21-28; Mark 7:24-30)," *Expository Times* 45 (1933–34): 459–61, esp. 460–61; Bruce J. Malina and Richard Rohrbaugh, *Social Science Commentary on the Synoptic Gospels* (Minneapolis: Fortress Press, 1992), 225; E. A. McNamara, "The Syro-Phoenician Woman," *American Ecclesiastical Review* 127 (1952): 360–69, esp. 363, 368; Sharon H. Ringe, "A Gentile Woman's Story," in *Feminist Interpretation of the Bible*, ed. Letty R. Russell (Philadelphia: Fortress Press, 1985), 65–72, esp. 68; James D. Smart, "Jesus, the Syro-Phoenician Woman, and the Disciples," *Expository Times* 50 (1939): 469–72, esp. 469. Francis Dufton argues that the woman speaks of dogs kept inside the house, whereas Jesus speaks of dogs kept outside a house ("The Syro-Phoenician Woman and Her Dogs," *Expository Times* 100 [1989]: 417). For a full lexical discussion, see A. L. Connolly, "kynarion," in *New Documents Illustrating Early Christianity*, ed. G. R. H. Horsley (Macquarie University: Ancient History Documentary Research Centre, 1987), 4:157–59.

26. Corley, *Private Women, Public Meals*," 99; Taussig, "Dealing under the Table," 265, 275n2; Marianne Sawicki, *Seeing the Lord: Resurrection and Early Christian Practices* (Minneapolis: Fortress Press, 1984), 156–59. Kinukawa finally decides the remark is offensive (*Women and Jesus*, 59), as does Ringe, "Gentile Woman's Story," 69. See also Emma Tufarina, "Women in Cultural Life. Mark 7:24-30: Jesus and the Syro-Phoenician Woman," *Pacific Journal of Theology* (March 1990): 48–50. Porkorny considers Jesus' apellation a way of identifying the woman as a defiled animal ("Puppy," 324). Downing sees the term as an insult ("Woman," 137).

27. Burkill, "Historical Development," 173.

28. Flammer, "Die Syro-Phoenizerin," 20ff.; Schüssler Fiorenza, *In Memory of Her*, 137; Guelich, *Mark 1–8:26*, 385: Kinukawa, *Women and Jesus*, 56; Porkorny, "Puppy," 325.

29. Minucius Felix, *Octavius* 8.4–12.5; Translation from Jo-Ann Shelton, *As the Romans Did: A Sourcebook in Roman Social History* (Oxford: Oxford University Press; New Haven, Conn.: Yale University Press, 1984), 15–47.

30. Downing, "Woman," 139; Guelich, *Mark 1–8:26*, 388; McNamara, "The Syro-Phoenician Woman," 368; Ringe, "Gentile Woman's Story," 65, 69, 71; Schüssler Fiorenza, *In Memory of Her*, 137. Kinukawa doubts that this is the important characteristic of the woman (*Women and Jesus*, 59).

31. "Yes," (*nai*) omitted on p. 75.

32. So Guelich, *Mark 1–8:26*, 385; Theissen, *Miracle Stories*, 126.

33. Taussig and Downing go so far as to identify the woman here as a Cynic like Hyparchia. See Downing, "Woman," passim; Taussig, "Dealing under the Table," 266–67.

34. Corley, *Private Women, Public Meals*, 102. See also Schüssler Fiorenza, *But She Said*, 97.

35. See Corley, *Private Women, Public Meals*, 165–69.

36. In contrast to Gundry, *Matthew*, 317.

37. Ibid., 310.

38. Derrett, "Law in the New Testament," 164; Gundry, *Matthew*, 310; Schweizer, *Matthew*, 330.

39. Lachs, *Rabbinic Commentary*, 248.

40. Hasler, "The Incident," 459.

41. Kingsbury, "The Title 'Son of David,'" 591–602, esp. 592, 598. Amy-Jill Levine doubts that the woman makes a confession of faith (*The Social and Ethnic Dimensions*, 139–40).

42. Gundry, *Matthew*, 311; Kingsbury, "The Title 'Son of David,'" 600–01.

43. Ringe, "Gentile Woman's Story," 69; Schweizer, *Matthew*, 313–14.

44. Derrett, "Law in the New Testament," 165n3; Ringe, "Gentile Woman's Story," 66.

45. Levine, *Social and Ethnic Dimensions*, 150.

46. Corley, *Private Women, Public Meals*, 168–69.

47. The Jesus Seminar, for example, voted that the story had a historical core. See also Downing, "Woman," 146.

48. Corley, *Private Women, Public Meals*, 89–93; 130–33; 152–58; Corley, "Jesus' Table Practice."

49. André Legault, "An Application of the Form-Critique Method to the Anointings in Galilee (Lk 7, 36-50) and Bethany (Mt 26, 6-13; Mk 14, 3-9; Jn 12, 1-8)," *Catholic Biblical Quarterly* 16 (1954): 131–45; Robert Holst, "The One Anointing of Jesus: Another Application of the Form-Critical Method," *Journal of Biblical Literature* 95 (1976): 435–46; Burton L. Mack, "The Anointing of Jesus: Elaboration within a Chreia," in *Patterns of Persuasion in the Gospels*, Burton L. Mack and Vernon K. Robbins (Sonoma, Calif.: Polebridge, 1989), 85–106. See also extensive recent overview of opinion in Robert H. Gundry, *Mark: A Commentary on His Apology for the Cross* (Grand Rapids: Eerdmans, 1993), 805–20.

50. So C. H. Dodd, F. Strauss, Bultmann, Klosterman. Redefended by Holst, "The One Anointing of Jesus."

51. So Benoit, Taylor, McNeile, Beare, R. Brown, Vawter, Schnackenburg, and Lindars. Affirmed by Legault, "An Application of the Form-Critique

Method." Holst notes that this was also the view of Origen, Tatian, and Chrysostom ("One Anointing of Jesus," 435n2). In the 1980s, Thomas L. Brodie suggested that Luke 7 was indeed independent of the other anointing accounts but was a fictional account constructed from two stories about women in the LXX. See "Luke 7, 36-50 as an Internalization of 2 Kings 4, 1-37: A Study of Luke's Use of Rhetorical Imitation," *Biblica* 64 (1983): 457–85.

52. J. F. Coakley, "The Anointing at Bethany and the Priority of John," *Journal of Biblical Literature* 107 (1988), 241–56, esp. 241; Corley, *Private Women, Public Meals*, 103; J. Duncan M. Derrett, "The Anointing at Bethany and the Story of Zacchaeus," in *Law in the New Testament* (London: Darton, Longman and Todd, 1970), 266–85; J. K. Elliott, "The Anointing of Jesus," *Expository Times* 85 (1973–74): 105–7; Joseph A. Fitzmyer, *The Gospel according to Luke* (Garden City, N.Y.: Doubleday, 1981–85), 1:686; Gundry, *Mark*, 810; Holst, "The One Anointing of Jesus"; Mack, "The Anointing of Jesus."

53. Luke and John being considered more "developed." So Haenchen, Schweizer, Schnackenburg, Storch, J. K. Elliott, Delobel (see Holst, "The One Anointing of Jesus," 436–37), as well as Gundry, *Mark*, 810.

54. So Goodenough, Drexler, Holst (see Holst, "The One Anointing of Jesus," 436–37), as well as Derrett, "The Anointing at Bethany."

55. J. N. Sanders, "'Those Whom Jesus Loved' (John 11.5)," *New Testament Studies* 1 (1954): 29–41; more recently, Coakley, "The Anointing at Bethany and the Priority of John." Several scholars at least consider John to be an independent witness to the one anointing. See David Daube, "The Anointing at Bethany and Jesus' Burial," *Anglican Theological Review* 32 (1950): 186–99; Winsome Munro, "The Anointing in Mark 14:3-9 and John 12:1-8," *Society of Biblical Literature 1979 Seminar Papers*, ed. Paul J. Achtemeier (Missoula, Mont.: Scholars Press, 1979), 127–30.

56. Mack, "The Anointing of Jesus."

57. The similar story elements are as follows: (1) the location (a house), (2) the setting (a meal), (3) the owner of the house (Simon), (4) the timing of the action (during the meal, not before it), (5) the doer of the action (a woman), (6) the anointing with perfume, (7) the reference to an alabaster jar, (8) the objection to the action, and (9) Jesus' defense of the woman. See Gundry, *Mark*, 810; Mack, "Anointing of Jesus," 90.

58. Even Bultmann considered the version in Mark up to 14:8 a "biographical apophthegm" with a claim to historical reliability (*History of the Synoptic Tradition*, trans. John Marsh (New York: HarperCollins, 1963), 37; Dibelius called the Markan account a "paradigm" (*From Tradition to Gospel* [Greenwood, S.C.: Attic, 1982], 43). See Mack, "The Anointing of Jesus," 87; Holst, "The One Anointing of Jesus," 436–37. John Dominic Crossan marks this tradition with a + (indicating that it is historical) but spends little time on the story in his treatment of the historical Jesus. He does, however, consider dining with women to be one aspect of Jesus' socially revolutionary program and suggests that such women would have been accused of acting like "whores" (*The Historical Jesus: The Life of a Mediterranean Jewish Peasant* [San Francisco: HarperCollins, 1991], 261–64, 335, 443, 416).

59. Mack, "The Anointing of Jesus," 87. David Daube goes so far as to consider even the earliest written accounts of the anointing to be fictionalized explanations to counter the charge that Jesus had been buried without proper ministrations ("The Anointing at Bethany and Jesus' Burial"). Marianne Sawicki also suggests that Jesus' death was the point of departure for the construction of the anointing story. She suggests that it was composed by women in order to come to terms with the death of Jesus ("Making the Best of Jesus" [paper presented to the joint meeting of the Social Science and New Testament Interpretation and Rhetoric and the New Testament Sections of the SBL Annual Meeting, San Francisco, Calif., November, 1992]). See now Sawicki, *Seeing the Lord*, 153. More conservative scholars do not have trouble envisioning the event as an actual passion week occurrence. See discussion by Mack, "Anointing of Jesus," 87.

60. Bultmann, *Synoptic Tradition*, 37; Derrett, "Anointing at Bethany," 267–70; Elliott, "Anointing of Jesus," 106; Holst, "One Anointing of Jesus"; Mack, "The Anointing of Jesus," 86–87; and also idem, *A Myth of Innocence* (Philadelphia: Fortress Press, 1988), 200.

61. Mack, "The Anointing of Jesus," 87.

62. Derrett, "Anointing at Bethany"; Mack, "The Anointing of Jesus."

63. Corley, *Private Women, Public Meals*, ch. 2. See also Corley, "Were the Women around Jesus Really Prostitutes?"

64. Hence, suspicions that Luke somehow retains a more primitive tradition are not entirely unfounded.

65. So Dennis E. Smith, "The Banquet of the King: Meal and Irony in Mark" (Presidential Address of the SBL, Southwest Region, 1995). See also Joël Delobel, "Lk 7,47 in Its Context: An Old Crux Revisited," in *The Four Gospels: Festschrift Frans Neirynck*, ed. R. Van Segbroeck et al. (Leuven: Leuven University Press; Peeters, 1992), 1581–90, esp. 1585.

66. See Corley, *Private Women, Public Meals*, 102–6.

67. Elliott, "Anointing of Jesus," 105; Holst, "One Anointing of Jesus," 439; Legault, "Form-Critique Method," 131; Mack, "Anointing of Jesus," 90; idem, *Myth of Innocence*, 200; C. J. Maunder, "A Sitz im Leben for Mark 14:9," *Expository Times* 99 (1987): 78–80, esp. 78.

68. Holst, "One Anointing of Jesus," 438; see also Gundry, *Mark*, 812.

69. Banquet anointings were generally of the head and face, but anointings of the feet of wealthy individuals by male and female slaves was not unheard of (see references in Coakley, "The Anointing at Bethany," 246–48). For a further discussion of the issue of whether the anointing was of the feet or the head, see below. On the connection of anointings of the wealthy by women and young male slaves at banquets, see Emily Cheney, "Honor and Shame: From Whose Point of View?" (paper presented to the joint meeting of the Social Science and New Testament Interpretation and Rhetoric and the New Testament Sections of the SBL Annual Meeting, San Francisco, Calif., November, 1992), 3–6; Derrett, "Anointing at Bethany," 274, 275n1, 277n2; Legault, "Form-Critique Method," 137; Malina and Rohrbaugh, *Social Science Commentary*, 264–65;

W. Michaelis, "μυρον, κτλ," *TDNT* 8:800–01, esp. n. 3. For further references, see Corley, *Private Women, Public Meals*, 104, esp. n. 105.

70. Eva C. Keuls, *The Reign of the Phallus: Sexual Politics in Ancient Athens* (New York: Harper and Row, 1985), 117–20, 170ff. Confirmed by Cheney, "Honor and Shame," 8–9; Sawicki, "Making the Best of Jesus," 9–13.

71. MM notes that the perfume spikenard is connected with "women of luxury," which I assume is a euphemism for prostitutes. Sawicki's suggestion that the term *pistikēs* means "persuasive" or "faith-inducing" in this context is unlikely ("Making the Best of Jesus," 11–13). See now Sawicki, *Seeing the Lord*, 165.

72. See, for example, Derrett, "The Anointing at Bethany," 267–68; Holst, "One Anointing of Jesus," 440.

73. Here I differ from Mack, who considers the unnamed woman to have been identified in the original chreia as disreputable (*Myth of Innocence*, 200). It would not have been all that unexpected for women servants or otherwise sexually available women to be present for meals or performing such services for men. The ancient conflict centered on the presence of matrons or married women at meals, or women considered otherwise respectable. Corley, *Private Women, Public Meals*, 43–44; see especially David Schaps, "The Women Least Mentioned: Etiquette and Women's Names," *Classical Quarterly* 27 (1977): 323–30, as well as Munro, "The Anointing in Mark," 130; Sawicki, "Making the Best of Jesus," 17.

74. The addition of names has long been considered part of the development of Gospel traditions (Holst, "One Anointing of Jesus," 437–38).

75. Highly placed but not necessarily aristocratic. Members of the retainer class, for example, would still have been (in terms of income) in the highest 5–10 percent of the ancient population. In the ancient world this would have included even some freedmen and women. See discussion of the women in Luke 8:1-3 in Corley, *Private Women, Public Meals*, 110–11, esp. n. 13. See also Corley, "Jesus' Table Practice," 452–59.

76. Cheney, "Honor and Shame," 10–13.

77. See above, and Dentzer, *Le motif du banquet couché*; N. Himmelmann, *Typologische untersuchungen an römischen Sarkophagareliefs des 3. und 4. Jarhunderts n. Chr.* (Mainz: Philipp von Zabern, 1973), figs. 24a; 25; 26; 35a; 36a, b; 37a, b; 38a, b; 39a, b; Larson, *Greek Heroine Cults*, 43–57; Pope, *Song of Songs*, 212–15; Zaphiropoulou, "Banquets funéraires," figs. 22, 24, 25.

78. Corley, *Private Women, Public Meals*, 103; Crossan, *Historical Jesus*, 416; Derrett, "The Anointing at Bethany," 267–70; Elliott, "Anointing of Jesus," 106; Holst, "One Anointing of Jesus," 444–45; Mack, "The Anointing of Jesus," 88; idem, *Myth of Innocence*, 200.

79. Corley, *Private Women, Public Meals*, 105; Derrett, "Anointing at Bethany," 270–71; Elliott, "The Anointing of Jesus," 106; Michaelis, *TDNT* 8:801n13; Sanders, "Those Whom Jesus Loved," 37. For further references to the connection of women to burial practices and mourning in both Hellenistic

and Jewish contexts, see Sawicki, "Making the Best of Jesus," 18–19, 24; and see above.

80. So Holst, "One Anointing of Jesus," 442–43; Gundry, *Mark*, 813, who doubts that the anointing has this implication even in Mark; Maunder, "A Sitz im Leben for Mark 14:9," 78; D. A. S. Ravens, "The Setting of Luke's Account of the Anointing: Luke 7:2—8:3," *New Testament Studies* 34 (1988): 282–92, esp. 283; Sanders, "Those Whom Jesus Loved," who remarks that the messianic implications of Mark's version are absent in Luke and are secondary to the tradition (37–38); against Elliott, "Anointing of Jesus," 105–7.

81. Mack, "The Anointing of Jesus," 89, 94–96; idem, *Myth of Innocence*, 200.

82. The unnamed woman therefore fits the description of those women I have suggested as numbering among the "sinners" known for "eating and drinking" with Jesus and "tax collectors" (Mark 2:14-17). She may be wealthy and respectable, and yet she is described as behaving in a manner beneath her station and is therefore "improper."

83. Corley, *Private Women, Public Meals,* 102–6. See also Stephen C. Barton, "Mark as Narrative: The Story of the Anointing Woman (Mk 14:3-9)," *Expository Times* 102 (1991): 230–34, esp. 233.

84. Ronald F. Theimann, "The Unnamed Woman at Bethany," *Theology Today* 44 (1987): 179–88, esp. 183, and n. 11.

85. Gundry, *Matthew,* 519–20; Elizabeth E. Platt, "The Ministry of Mary of Bethany," *Theology Today* 34 (1977): 29–39, esp. 31.

86. Following the editors of the UBS, the reading *barytimos* should be preferred to *polytimou.* It is supported by B, W, and Byzantine text types, and by the Matthean insertion of *barys* in Matt 23:4, 23. See Wiloughby Allen, *A Critical and Exegetical Commentary on the Gospel according to St. Matthew* (Edinburgh: T. and T. Clark, 1965), 268; Gundry, *Matthew,* 520.

87. Daube, "The Anointing at Bethany," 193; Elliott, "The Anointing of Jesus," 107; Legault, "An Application of the Form-Critique Method," 142; Platt, "Mary of Bethany," 31; Theimann, "The Unnamed Woman," 183.

88. Daube, "The Anointing at Bethany," 193; Elliott, "The Anointing of Jesus," 106; Theimann, "The Unnamed Woman," 183.

89. Gundry, *Matthew,* 520.

90. Matthew's emphasis on the disciples is well known. Although Matthew portrays them as being more aware of the significance of events than they are in Mark, Jesus still characterizes the disciples as those of "little faith," which is in contrast to women in the narrative who have greater faith, such as the Canaanite woman (Matt 15:21-28) and the *pornai* who believe (Matt 21:31-32). See Corley, *Private Women, Public Meals,* 170n125, 174–76.

91. Cheney, "Honor and Shame," 3–13.

92. Corley, *Private Women, Public Meals,* 147–79.

93. See Brodie, "Luke 7, 35-50," 458; Fitzmyer, *Luke,* 1:685; Holst, "One Anointing of Jesus," 436; Legault, "Form-Critique Method," 140, and above,

n. 5. I will rely again on my earlier discussion of Luke 7:36-50 from *Private Women, Public Meals*, 121–30.

94. Fitzmyer, *Luke*, 1:685–86; Gundry, *Mark*, 810; Mack, "Anointing of Jesus," 84; However, given that the story was well known, some reliance on oral tradition cannot be ruled out. See Legault, "Form-Critique Method," 144; Mack, "Anointing of Jesus," 85.

95. Luke's interest in Pharisees is well known. Derrett, "Anointing at Bethany," 275; Holst, "One Anointing of Jesus," 438; Dennis Smith, "Table Fellowship as a Literary Motif in the Gospel of Luke," *Journal of Biblical Literature* 106 (1987): 613–38, esp. 622n28; J. A. Zeisler, "Luke and the Pharisees," *New Testament Studies* 25 (1978–79): 146–57. Fitzmyer agrees that the identification of Simon as a Pharisee is secondary to the tradition, but not that it is Lukan (*Luke*, 1:688).

96. Some even suggest that Luke composed the parable for insertion here. See Fitzmyer, *Luke*, 1:687, 690; Mack, "Anointing of Jesus," 101; Sanders, "Those Whom Jesus Loved," 38; Smith, "Table Fellowship," 622–23. Bultmann thought that the opposite was the case, that is, that the parable was the original nucleus to which the rest was added (*Synoptic Tradition*, 20–21).

97. Derrett, "Anointing at Bethany," 276–78; Holst, "One Anointing of Jesus," 443; Mack, "Anointing of Jesus," 102–3. See also the connection in Luke between the woman's forgiveness and the "tax collectors and others" (7:29-30) who have previously been forgiven by the baptism of John. Corley, *Private Women, Public Meals*, 125–28; following John J. Kilgallen, "John the Baptist, The Sinful Woman, and the Pharisee," *Journal of Biblical Literature* 104 (1985): 675–79.

98. J. Delobel suggests that it is Luke who gives the story its mealtime setting, but this is probably incorrect ("L'onction par la pécheresse: la composition littéraire de Lc. VII, 36-50," *Ephemerides theologicae lovanienses* 42 [1966]: 415–75, esp. 460). See Fitzmyer, *Luke*, 1:685; Holst, "One Anointing of Jesus," 439; Legault, "Form-Critique Method," 144; Mack, "Anointing of Jesus," 85. See Corley, *Private Women, Public Meals*, 123.

99. Note the "weeping" of the "daughters of Jerusalem" at the end of the Gospel (Luke 23:27) (*Private Women, Public Meals*, 127–28).

100. Given Luke's interest in the poor, an emphasis on financial waste (even on Jesus) becomes awkward. See Corley, *Private Women, Public Meals*, 124; Holst, "One Anointing of Jesus," 440.

101. See Corley, *Private Women, Public Meals*, 38–39, 124. Several scholars hold this view. See Delobel, "L'onction," 425–26; Derrett, "Anointing at Bethany," 278; David Esterline, "Jesus and the Woman: Luke 7:36-50," *Pacific Journal of Theology* 7 (1992): 64–68; Schüssler Fiorenza, *In Memory of Her*, 129–30; Mack, "Anointing of Jesus," 88; Delores Osborne demonstrated how such a designation would identify a woman as a prostitute in Jewish Literature ("Women: Sinners and Prostitutes" [paper presented at the SBL Pacific Coast Region, Long Beach, Calif., April, 1987]); A. Plummer, "The Woman That Was a Sinner," *Expository Times* 27 (1915–19): 42–43; A. R. Simpson, "Mary of Bethany,

Mary of Magdala and Anonyma," *The Expositor* 8 (1909): 307–18, esp. 316. Legault suggests that her sin was known only to friends and family members ("Form-Critique Method," 141). Fitzmyer doubts she is a harlot (*Luke*, 1:689). So also Evelyn R. Thibeaux, "'Known to Be a Sinner': The Narrative Rhetoric of Luke 7:36-50," *Biblical Theology Bulletin* 23 (1993): 151–60, esp. 155.

102. Corley, *Private Women, Public Meals,* 52.

103. Daube, "Anointing of Jesus"; Holst, "One Anointing of Jesus"; Derrett, "Anointing at Bethany"; Mack, "Anointing of Jesus."

104. Delobel ("L'onction," 430) considers the term *klaiō* to be a term favored by Luke. See Luke 6:21, 25; 7:13, 32; 8:52; 23:28, and Holst, "One Anointing of Jesus," 441. I have suggested that Luke uses the tears of the woman to link her to the "servants" who wail in the marketplace on the one hand (7:31-32) (*Private Women, Public Meals*, 128–30) and the women who mourn Jesus' death on the other (23:28-31) (*Private Women, Public Meals* 127–28).

105. Derrett, "Anointing at Bethany," 274, 275n1; 277n2; Gundry, *Mark*, 813; Legault, "Form-Critique Method," 137, 145; Michaelis, *TDNT* 8:800–01, esp. n. 3. See additional references in Corley, *Private Women, Public Meals*, 104, esp. n. 105.

106. Coakley, "Anointing at Bethany," 246–48.

107. Ign. *Eph.* 17:2. See Gundry, *Mark*, 815; Elliott, "The Anointing of Jesus," 107; Ravens suggests that the anointing of feet was suggested by a (later) Lukan reading of Isa 52:7 ("Setting of Luke's Account"). Those who favor as earlier the tradition that Jesus' feet were anointed include Coakley, "Anointing at Bethany," 246–48; Elliott, "The Anointing of Jesus," 105–7; Holst, "One Anointing of Jesus," 439; and Sanders, "Those Whom Jesus Loved," 38, 40.

108. Derrett, "Anointing at Bethany," 267; Mack, "Anointing of Jesus," 88.

109. Richard I. Pervo, "Wisdom and Power: Petronius' Satyricon and the Social World of Early Christianity," *Anglican Theological Review* 67 (1985): 307–25, esp. 314; Smith, "Table Fellowship," 632. See also above, n. 22 (esp. references in Coakley, "The Anointing at Bethany," 246–48, and *Private Women, Public Meals*, 104, esp. n. 105) and comments by Esterline, "Jesus and the Woman," 65.

110. See Derrett, "Anointing at Bethany," 267; Mack, "Anointing of Jesus," 88; *Myth of Innocence*, 200.

111. Corley, *Private Women, Public Meals*, 121–30.

112. Coakley, "Anointing," 241–42.

113. John Amedee Bailey, *The Traditions Common to the Gospels of Luke and John* (Leiden: Brill, 1963), 2. Against suggestion by Sawicki that the term *pis tikēs* means "persuasive." See *Seeing the Lord*, 165.

114. Jane S. Webster, *Ingesting Jesus: Eating and Drinking in the Gospel of John* (Atlanta: Scholars, 2003), 92–93.

115. The opening of the scene during Passover time could suggest the origins of the story in a lament about Jesus' death. See below, ch. 5.

116. So Smith, "The Banquet of the King."

117. Jonathan Schwiebert, *Knowledge and the Coming Kingdom: The Didache's Meal Ritual and Its Place in Early Christianity* (New York: T. and T. Clark, 2008), 23; Ellen Bradshaw Aitken, *Jesus' Death in Early Christian Memory: The Poetics of the Passion* (Göttingen: Vandenhoeck and Ruprecht: 2004), 14–16.

118. Schwiebert, *Knowledge and the Coming Kingdom*, 23.

119. Following the analysis of Jonathan Schwiebert, *Knowledge and the Coming Kingdom: The Didache's Meal Ritual and its Place in Early Christianity* (New York: T. and T. Clark, 2008), 24–25.

120. Ibid., 27.

121. Ibid., 27–29.

122. Ibid., 34

123. Taussig, "Dealing under the Table," 267, 277n11.

Chapter 5: The Passion Story as a Lament Story for the Dead

1. Portions of this chapter are used by permission of Poebridge Press. Pliny, *Ep.* 8.12. For more on this genre, see Adela Yarbro Collins, "The Genre of the Passion Narrative," *Studia Theologica* 47 (1993): 3–28, esp. 6, 13, 23n22, and John S. Kloppenborg, "*Exitus clari viri*: The Death of Jesus in Luke," *Toronto Journal of Theology* 8 (1992): 106–20, esp. 106–8.

2. The section is a summary of ch. 2, pp. 32–35.

3. David E. Aune, "Heracles and Christ: Heracles Imagery in the Christology of Early Christianity," in *Greeks, Romans, and Christians: Essays in Honor of Abraham Malherbe*, ed. Abraham J. Malherbe et al. (Minneapolis: Fortress Press, 1990), 19; Eugene V. Gallagher, *Divine Man or Magician? Celsus and Origen on Jesus* (Chico, Calif.: Scholars Press, 1982), passim. See also Lord Raglan, "The Hero of Tradition," in *The Study of Folklore*, ed. Alan Dundes (Englewood Cliffs, N.J.: Prentice-Hall, 1965), 140–57; J. M. C. Toynbee, *A Study of History*, (London: Humphrey Milford; Oxford University Press, 1939), 4:444–57, esp. 454, on the "jetsam of 'folklore,'" and Marcel Simon, *Heracle et le Christianisme* (Paris: University of Strasbourg, 1965), 62.

4. See above, ch. 2.

5. Hans Dieter Betz, "Jesus as Divine Man," in *Jesus the Historian*, ed. F. T. Trotter (Philadelphia: Westminster, 1968), 124–25; Helmut Koester, "One Jesus and Four Primitive Gospels," *Harvard Theological Review* 61 (1968): 232–33; Weeden, *Mark: Traditions in Conflict* (Philadelphia: Fortress Press, 1971), passim. See also Hans Conzelmann, "History and Theology in the Passion Narratives," *Interpretation* 2 (1979): 178–97, esp. 183–84.

6. Robert T. Fortna, "Christology in the Fourth Gospel: Redaction-Critical Perspectives," *New Testament Studies* (1975): 489–504.

7. Howard M. Jackson, "The Death of Jesus in Mark and the Miracle from the Cross," *New Testament Studies* 33 (1987): 16–37.

8. Jonathan Z. Smith, "Good News Is No News: Aretalogy and Gospel," in *Christianity, Judaism, and Other Greco-Roman Cults: Studies for Morton Smith at Sixty*, ed. Jacob Neusner (Leiden: Brill, 1975), passim.

9. George W. E. Nickelsburg, "The Genre and Function of the Markan Passion Narrative," *Harvard Theological Review* 73 (1980): 153–84; and idem, *Resurrection, Immortality, and Eternal Life in Intertestamental Judaism* (Cambridge, Mass.: Harvard University Press, 1972), 48–111.

10. Sherman E. Johnson, "Greek and Jewish Heroes: Fourth Maccabees and the Gospel of Mark," in *Early Christian Literature and the Classical Intellectual Tradition*, ed. W. R. Schoedel and Robert L. Wilken (Paris: Éditions Beauchesne, 1979), 155–75; David Seeley, *The Noble Death: Graeco-Roman Martyrology and Paul's Concept of Salvation* (Sheffield: JSOT Press, 1990), esp. 84–141; Arthur J. Droge and James D. Tabor, *A Noble Death: Suicide and Martyrdom among Christians and Jews in Antiquity* (San Francisco: HarperSanFrancisco, 1992). See also Toynbee, *Study of History*, 4:444–45; and Nickelsburg, *Resurrection*, 48–111.

11. Adela Yarbro Collins, "From Noble Death to Crucified Messiah," *New Testament Studies* 40 (1994): 481–503; idem, "Genre of the Passion Narrative"; idem, *The Beginning of the Gospel: Probings of Mark in Context* (Minneapolis: Fortress Press, 1992), 92–118. See also John J. Pilch, "Death with Honor: The Mediterranean Style of Death of Jesus in Mark," *Biblical Theology Bulletin* 25 (1995): 65–70; David Seeley, *Deconstructing the New Testament* (Leiden: Brill, 1994): 53–79; On Luke's passion account, see Kloppenborg, "*Exitus clari viri.*"

12. For example, since Collins doesn't see the parallel between the men and the women in the passion narrative, she mistakenly applies the use of Psalm 38:11, "My friends and companions stand aloof from my affliction, and my neighbors stand far off" (NRSV) only to the fleeing of Peter and the disciples, but not to the women ("Genre of the Passion," 14). Nickelsburg's discussion of the passion narrative does not mention the women near the cross. Kloppenborg, however, does notice the motif of mourning women in Luke's addition of the weeping "Daughters of Jerusalem" ("*Exitus clari viri,*" 113–15).

13. Nickelsburg, *Resurrection*, 48–111; idem, "The Genre and Function of the Markan Passion Narrative."

14. Psalms 38:11; 88:8. See below.

15. Carolyn Osiek, "The Women at the Tomb: What Are They Doing There?" *Ex Auditu* 9 (1993): 97–107, esp. 98.

16. Osiek, "Women at the Tomb," 100–101; Susan Heine, "Eine Person von Rang und Namen: Historische Konturen der Magdalenerin," in *Jesus Rede von Gott und ihre Nachgeschichte im frühen Christentum* (Gütersloh: Mohn, 1989), 179–94, esp. 185.

17. A facsimile of this has been suggested before. See John Dominic Crossan's review of literature in "Empty Tomb and Absent Lord (Mark 16:1–8)," in the *Passion in Mark: Studies on Mark 14–16*, ed. W. H. Kelber (Philadelphia: Fortress Press, 1976), 135–52, esp. 137–38. However, no adequate antecedent, scriptural or otherwise, has ever been suggested for the "raised (*egeiro*) on the third day" tradition. Any connection with Hos 6:2 is quite doubtful, even a

"loose connection," given the parallelism between "three days" and "two days" (Gundry, *Mark*, 447–48). There is little evidence that the story of Jonah (see Jonah 1:17) was ever interpreted in pre-Constantinian Christianity to be about "resurrection from the dead." See, Graydon F. Snyder, *Ante Pacem: Archaeological Evidence of Church Life before Constantine* (Macon, Ga.: Mercer University Press, 1985), 45–49.

18. See discussions by Edward Lynn Bode, *The First Easter Morning: The Gospel Accounts of the Women's Visit to the Tomb of Jesus* (Rome: Biblical Institute Press, 1970), 113–16; W. L. Craig, "The Historicity of the Empty Tomb of Jesus," *New Testament Studies* 31 (1985): 39–67, esp. 44–45; Reginald H. Fuller, *The Formation of the Resurrection Narratives* (Philadelphia: Fortress Press, 1980), 24–25; Bruce M. Metzger, "A Suggestion Concerning the Meaning of 1 Cor 15:4b," *Journal of Theological Studies* 8 (1957): 118–23; Pheme Perkins, *Resurrection: New Testament Witness and Contemporary Reflection* (Garden City, N.Y.: Doubleday, 1984), 89–91. For an argument on the basis of rabbinic sources that Hos 6:2 is the scriptural basis for the "third day" tradition, see Harvey K. McArthur, "On the Third Day," *New Testament Studies* 18 (1971–72): 81–86. McArthur acknowledges, however, that Hos 6:2 is never quoted in the New Testament, which he finds curious (85).

19. Gail Holst-Warhaft, *Dangerous Voices: Women's Laments in Greek Literature* (London: Routledge, 1992), 144–49. See ch. 2 above.

20. See ch. 2 above.

21. Erwin Rohde, *Psyche: The Cult of the Souls and Belief in Immortality among the Greeks* (New York: Harcourt, Brace; London: Kegan Paul, Trench, Trubner, 1925), 42–43. This was, of course, first mentioned by Celsus (Origen, *Cels.* 3.33. Celsus also compared the Gospel stories to the translations of Aristeas (3.26), Heracles, and others (2.55). See Simon, *Hercule*, 67–71. Justin Martyr also contended with the similarities of Jesus to heroes like Hercules (*1 Apol.* 1.21; *Dial.* 69). On Origen and Justin Martyr, see Simon, *Hercule*, 67–71. See also Adela Yarbro Collins, "The Empty Tomb in the Gospel according to Mark," in *Hermes and Athena: Biblical Exegesis and Philosophical Theology*, ed. E. Stump and T. P. Flint (Notre Dame: University of Notre Dame Press, 1993), 107–40, esp. 123–28; idem, *Beginning of the Gospel*, 138–48; R. Pesch, *Das Markusevangelium* (Freiburg: Herder, 1970), 2:522–25, 2:536–38.

22. *Paus.* 2.9.7.

23. Diodorus of Sicily, 4.38.5.

24. Livy, 1.16.2-3.

25. Herodotus, *Hist.* 4.14.

26. À la Juliet. *Chariton, Chaereas and Callirhoe* 3.3. Translation by B. P. Reardon, in *Collected Ancient Greek Novels* (Berkeley, Calif.: University of California Press, 1989). Text by G. Molinié, *Chariton. Le roman de Chairéas et Callirhoé* (Paris: Belles lettres, 1979).

27. Achilles Tatius, *Leuc. Clit.* 5.14.4. Text and translation by S. Gaselee (LCL).

28. Collins, "Empty Tomb"; idem, *Beginning of the Gospel*, 119–48; See also Toynbee, *Study of History*, 4:474–75.

29. Rohde, *Psyche*, 144n43.

30. This of course has been suggested before. See Collins, "Empty Tomb"; idem, *Beginning of the Gospel*, 119–48; See also Toynbee, *Study of History*, 4:474–75. Collins thinks that Mark wrote his empty tomb account under the influence of these stories, but she stops short of saying that Mark 16:1-8 is an example of one: "In his composing the story of the empty tomb, the author of Mark interpreted the proclamation that Jesus had been risen" (*Beginning of the Gospel*, 145).

31. Smith, "Good News Is No News."

32. Burton L. Mack, *A Myth of Innocence: Mark and Christian Origins* (Minneapolis: Fortress Press, 1988), 308. John Dominic Crossan's instincts on this matter are certainly correct. See "Empty Tomb and Absent Lord (Mk 16:1-8)," 135–52. Note also Pheme Perkins's comments on Mark's ambiguity concerning the women's testimony in "I Have Seen the Lord (John 20:18): Women Witnesses to the Resurrection" *Interpretation* 46 (1992): 31–41, esp. 35.

33. Osiek, "Women at the Tomb," 104–5; Schaberg, "The Feminist Contribution," 284; Elisabeth Schüssler Fiorenza, *Jesus, Miriam's Child, Sophia's Prophet: Critical Issues in Feminist Christology* (New York: Crossroad, 1994), 90.

34. *Cels.* 2.55, 59.

35. Ibid., 2.60.

36. Ibid., 3.22.

37. Ibid., 3.59. Celsus had surely read John. Translation by H. Chadwick (Cambridge: Cambridge University Press, 1953).

38. So also Osiek, "Women at the Tomb," 104–5; Ben Witherington, *Women in the Ministry of Jesus: A Study of Jesus' Attitudes to Women and Their Roles as Reflected in His Earthly Life* (Cambridge: Cambridge University Press), 1984, 9. It is commonly affirmed that women could not be witnesses in Judaism. See Bode, *First Easter Morning*, 41–42; W. L. Craig, "Historicity of the Empty Tomb of Jesus," *New Testament Studies* 31 (1985): 39–67, esp. 42, 58; Stephen T. Davies, "Was the Tomb Empty?" in *Hermes and Athena: Biblical Exegesis and Philosophical Theology*, ed. E. Stump and T. P. Flint (Notre Dame: University of Notre Dame Press, 1993), 77–105, esp. 87; Jeremias, *Jerusalem in the Time of Jesus* (Philadelphia: Fortress Press, 1975), 375; Perkins, "I Have Seen the Lord," 40–41; Walter Wink, " 'And the Lord Appeared First to Mary': Sexual Politics in the Resurrection Witness," in *Social Themes of the Christian Year: A Commentary on the Lectionary*, ed. Dieter T. Hessel (Philadelphia: Geneva, 1983), 177–82, esp. 178, 180. On women as witnesses in Qumran assemblies, see above, ch. 1.

39. Gregory J. Riley, *Resurrection Reconsidered: Thomas and John in Controversy* (Minneapolis: Fortress Press, 1995).

40. Gerd Lüdemann, *The Resurrection of Jesus: History, Experience, Theology* (Minneapolis: Fortress Press, 1994), 84–114.

41. In light of the Hellenistic evidence for the role of women in mourning rituals at the gravesite and the cultic context of "feeding the dead" in earliest Christian groups, the documentation of visions of deceased love ones in the context of natural grieving can therefore not be so easily dismissed as pertinent to this discussion. Stacy Davids, M.D., "Appearances of the Resurrected Jesus

and the Experience of Grief" (paper presented to the Jesus Seminar, Spring 1995); idem, "What Is the Truth about the Resurrection of Jesus? The Testimony of Mary Magdalene" (unpublished paper).

42. E. R. Dodds, *The Greeks and the Irrational* (Berkeley, Calif.: University of California Press, 1968), 108–11, 117, 118–19, 127n52.

43. Mack, *Myth of Innocence*, 308; Nock, "Cremation and Burial," 303–4; Jonathan Z. Smith, *Drudgery Divine: On the Comparision of Early Christianities and the Religions of Late Antiquity* (Chicago: Chicago University Press, 1990), 142, esp. n. 43; idem, *To Take Place: Toward Theory in Ritual* (Chicago: University of Chicago Press, 1987), 74–95. See also Perkins, *Resurrection*, 93–94.

44. See above, ch. 2.

45. So Wolfgang Nauck, "Die Bedeutung des leeren Grabes für den Glauben an den Auferstandenen," *Zeitschrift für die neutestamentliche Wissenschaft und die Kunde der Älteren Kirche* 47 (1956): 243–67; Gottfried Schille, "Das Leiden des Herrn: Die evangelische Passionstradition und ihr 'Sitz im Leben,'" *Zeitschrift für Theologie und Kirsche* 52 (1955): 161–205. See Bode, *First Easter Morning*, 130–45; Perkins, *Resurrection*, 93–94; Smith, *Drudgery Divine*, 142n43.

46. Usually taken to be a sign of Mark's shift away from a source. See Collins, "Composition of the Passion Narrative," 64; idem, *Beginning of the Gospel*, 117.

47. Smith, *Drudgery Divine*, 131–33.

48. On early Christian "feeding the dead" and catacomb art, see ibid.; see also Snyder, *Ante Pacem*, passim.

49. So Rudolf Bultmann, *History of the Synoptic Tradition*, trans. John Marsh (New York: HarperCollins, 1963), 280.

50. As Osiek has suggested, "Women at the Tomb," 103–4.

51. Kloppenborg, "*Exitus clari viri,*" passim.

52. On a possible pre-Markan source, see below. On a pre-Johannine source for the women, see Raymond E. Brown, *The Death of the Messiah: A Commentary on the Passion Narratives in the Four Gospels* (New York; Doubleday, 1994), 2:1019; Anton Dauer, *Die Passionsgeschichte im Johannesevangelium* (Munich: Kösel-Verlag, 1972), 195–96; Joel B. Green, *Death of Jesus: Tradition and Interpretation in the Passion Narrative* (Tübingen: J.C.B. Mohr, 1988): 309–10; Robert T. Fortna, *The Fourth Gospel and Its Predecessor* (Minneapolis: Fortress Press, 1988), 177, 185. For a chart listing elements of a possible pre-Gospel passion narrative and commentators' views, see also Brown, *Death of the Messiah*, 2:1502–17; Green, *Death of Jesus*, 294.

53. Luke 23:27-31. See Kloppenborg, *Exitus clari viri,* 111–13; Jerome H. Neyrey, "Jesus' Address to the Women of Jerusalem (Lk 23:27-31)—A Prophetic Judgment Oracle," *New Testament Studies* 29 (1983): 74–86. See also *Acts of Pilate* 284-85.

54. C. K. Barrett, *The Gospel according to St. John* (London: SPCK, 1978), 551; Brown, *Death of the Messiah*, 2:1019, 2:1028–29, idem, "Roles of Women in the Fourth Gospel," *Theological Studies* 36 (1975): 688–99, esp. 698; Dauer, *Passionsgeschichte*, 192–93; Fortna, *John*, 177, 181. Rudolf Schnackenburg, *The Gospel according to John* (New York: Crossroad, 1982), 3:277, 3:279–82; Even

Joel B. Green notes that John moves this tradition forward so that Jesus' family and friends are not pictured as aloof (*Death of Jesus*, 310). See also Turid Karlsen Seim, "Roles of Women in the Gospel of John," in *Aspects on the Johannine Literature*, ed. L. Hartman and B. Olsson (Uppsala: Almqvist and Wiksell, 1986), 56–73, esp. 61. For more caution in regard to the symbolism of the scene, see Ernst Haenchen, *John* (Philadelphia: Fortress Press, 1984), 2:193; George Beasley-Murray, *John* (Waco, Tex.: Word, 1987), 350–51. For the argument that John's account is independent, see Joachim Jeremias, *The Eucharistic Words of Jesus* (London: SCM, 1966), 89–96.

55. *Gos. Pet.*, text by H. B. Swete, *The Apocryphal Gospel of St. Peter: The Greek Text of the Newly Discovered Fragment* (London: MacMillan, 1893); trans. Christian Maurer, "The Gospel of Peter," in *New Testament Apocrypha*, ed. Wilhelm Schneemelcher (Louisville: Westminster John Knox, 1991), 1:223–27.

56. There is reason to suspect that Jesus' appearance to the men occurs in the context of their mourning. It is unfortunate that the story breaks off at that point. Translation by C. Mauer (NTA).

57. Benjamin A. Johnson, "Empty Tomb Tradition in the Gospel of Peter," (Ph.D. diss., Harvard University, 1965), 34. See also John Dominic Crossan, *The Cross That Spoke: The Origins of the Passion Narrative* (San Francisco: HarperSanFrancisco, 1988), which argues for early written traditions in the *Gospel of Peter*.

58. Johnson, "Empty Tomb Tradition," 32.

59. See below.

60. Against Helmut Koester, *Ancient Christian Gospels* (Philadelphia: Trinity Press International; London: SCM, 1990), 233.

61. Snyder, *Ante Pacem*, 26–29.

62. Josef Jungmann even cites the *Gospel of Peter* as an example of this influence. See Josef A. Jungmann, *The Early Liturgy to the Time of Gregory the Great*, trans. F. A. Brunner (Notre Dame, Ind.: University of Notre Dame Press, 1959), 131–33. Now acknowledged by Crossan, *Who Killed Jesus? Exposing the Roots of Anti-Semitism in the Gospel Story of the Death of Jesus* (San Francisco, HarperSanFrancisco, 1995), 196.

63. Smith, *Drudgery Divine*, 142–43; idem, *To Take Place*, 74–95.

64. Jay C. Treat, "The Two Manuscript Witnesses to the Gospel of Peter," *Society of Biblical Literature 1990 Seminary Papers*, ed. David Lull (Atlanta: Scholars Press, 1990): 191–99. See also P. Oxy. 2949 in G. M. Browne et al., *The Oxyrhynchus Papyri* (London: Egypt Exploration Society, 1972), 41:15–16.

65. Collins, "From Noble Death to Crucified Messiah"; Nickelsburg, "Genre of the Markan Passion Narrative."

66. Toynbee, *Study of History*, 4:403–4, 4:524–25; and discussion above in ch. 2.

67. Collins, "Genre of the Passion," 14; idem, *Beginning of the Gospel*, does not include this reference; Winsome Munro, "Women Disciples in Mark?" *Catholic Bilblical Quarterly* 44 (1982): 225–41, esp. 226; Toynbee, *Study of History*, 4:421.

68. Luke reinforces this connection with Psalm 38:11 by the addition of *hoi gnostoi* (friends) (Luke 24:49).

69. Many scholars do not include the reference to the women at the cross in a pre-Markan passion. For a convenient list of scholars' views, see Brown, *Death of the Messiah*, 2:1516–17; Green, *Death of Jesus*, 295. See also Adela Yarbro Collins, "Composition of the Markan Passion Narrative," *Sewanee Theological Review* 36 (1992): 57–77, esp. 76; idem, *Beginning of the Gospel*, 116–17; Crossan, *Cross That Spoke*, 281–90, idem, *Who Killed Jesus?* 171; Frank J. Matera, *The Kingship of Jesus: Composition and Theology in Mark 15* (Chico, Calif.: Scholars Press, 1982), 52.

70. In his commentary on the Gospel of John, Bultmann remarks that here Mark agrees with John in mentioning women witnesses to the crucifixion; it is early tradition (*Gospel of John: A Commentary* [Philadelphia: Westminster Press, 1971], 666–67). In his *Synoptic Tradition*, he remarks that the reference to the women is patently unhistorical, both in Mark 15:40-41 and in 15:47. The women are only mentioned because the men are not available (274-75). Some scholars argue the presence of the women is traditional, in a pre-Gospel passion account, and/or historical. See Barrett, *John*, 551; Brown, *Death of the Messiah*, 2:1194–96; Dauer, *Passionsgeschichte*, 194–95; Green, *Death of Jesus*, 310; Lüdemann, *Resurrection of Jesus*, 160.

71. So Bultmann, *Synoptic Tradition*, 276; Martin Dibelius, *From Tradition to Gospel* (Greenwood, S.C.: Attic, 1982), 190–92; Matera, *The Kingship of Jesus*, 51. See also Bode, *First Easter Morning*, 20, 23.

72. Munro, "Women Disciples in Mark?" which was followed by Elizabeth Struthers Malbon, "Fallible Followers: Women and Men in the Gospel of Mark," *Semeia* (1983): 29–48; Marla Selvidge, "And Those Who Followed Feared," *Catholic Biblical Quarterly* (1983): 396–400, and others. For a full bibliography, see Kathleen E. Corley, *Private Women, Public Meals: Social Conflict in the Synoptic Tradition* (Peabody, Mass.: Hendrickson, 1993), 84n2, as well as recent discussion by Hisako Kinukawa, *Women and Jesus in Mark: A Japanese Feminist Perspective* (Maryknoll, N.Y.: Orbis, 1994), 90–106.

73. Axel Olrik, "Epic Laws of Folk Narrative" in *The Study of Folklore*, ed. Alan Dunde (Engelwood Cliffs, N.J.: Prentice-Hall, 1965), 133–34.

74. Mark likes lists of two and three. See Matera, *Kingship of Jesus*, 50–51.

75. To correspond to the four soldiers (John 19:23). See Richard Atwood, *Mary Magdalene in the New Testament Gospels and Early Tradition* (New York: Peter Lang, 1993), 60–61; P. Benoit, *The Passion and Resurrection of Jesus Christ* (New York: Herder and Herder, 1969), 189; Barrett, *John*, 551–52; Brown, *Death of the Messiah*, 2:1014–15; Barnabas Lindars, *The Gospel of John* (London: Oliphants, 1972), 579.

76. It is unwise to try to conflate the names. Nearly 50 percent of the women in Second Temple Palestine were named either Mary or Salome. In Josephus, 13 of 40 bear these names (32.5 percent) in funerary inscriptions, 80 out of 152 (52.6 percent); in epigraphic materials 15 out of 19 (78.9 percent); in the New Testament, 5 out of 16 (37.5 percent); in rabbinic literature 9 out

of 25 (36 percent). Johanna was also popular (occurring 8 times total); Susanna less so (found only one other place besides Luke 8:2). See Tal Ilan, "Notes on the Distribution of Jewish Women's Names in Palestine in the Second Temple and Mishnaic Periods." *Journal of Jewish Studies* 40 (1989): 186–200. On caution in regard to names besides Mary Magdalene's see Beasley-Murray, *John*, 349; Schnackenburg, *John*, 276–77. Mark may intend his readers to understand "Mary the mother of James and Joses" to be Jesus' mother. Her presence at the cross with Mary Magdalene would then be part of the Markan theme of failure, only in this case the failure of his family. See John Dominic Crossan, "Mark and the Relatives of Jesus," *Novum Testamentum* 15 (1973): 81–113, esp. 105–10.

77. Bultmann, *Synoptic Tradition*, 276; Matera, *Kingship of Jesus*, 51.

78. See above.

79. Munro, "Women Disciples?"

80. Positing a pre-Markan written source is difficult, in spite of the valiant attempts of many scholars to do so. Lack of agreement among scholars in this endeavor may be a sign of hopelessness of the task. For a review of scholarship, see Mack, *Myth of Innocence*, 249–68; William R. Telford, "The Pre-Markan Tradition in Recent Research," in *The Four Gospels: Festschrift for Frans Neirynck*, ed. F. van Segbroeck et al. (Leuven: Leuven University Press, 1992), 2:693–723. Most elements of the passion narrative can be accounted for on the basis of the "suffering *dikaios*" model, the "noble death" model, and references to lament psalms. See Mack, *Myth of Innocence*, 269–312, and the collection of articles in Werner H. Kelber, *Studies on Mark 14–16* (Philadelphia: Fortress Press, 1976). Crossan's thesis (*Cross That Spoke*) that the *Gospel of Peter* contains early elements is not convincing due to the late manuscript evidence, the novelistic developments in the story, and its lack of clear independence from the Markan account (see above).

81. So Crossan, "Empty Tomb," and *Cross That Spoke*, 281–90. See also discussion of the early nature and historical core of Mark 15:40-16:8 by Luise Schottroff, "Maria Magdalena und die Frauen am Grabe Jesu," *Evangelische Theologie* 42 (1982): 3–25.

82. Malbon, "Fallible Followers," passim; Munro, "Women Disciples," 230–31; Perkins, *Resurrection*, 122; Selvidge, "And Those Who Followed Feared," passim. See also David Catchpole, "The Fearful Silence of the Women at the Tomb: A Study in Markan Theology," *Journal for the Theology of South Africa* 18 (1977): 3–10; Corley, *Private Women, Public Meals*, 84–85; Kinukawa, *Women and Jesus*, 95–96.

83. Collins, "Genre of the Passion Narrative," 14. Again, this association is nowhere found in *Beginning of the Gospel*.

84. Malbon, "Fallible Followers," 43; Munro, "Women Disciples," 235; Kinukawa, *Women and Jesus*, 95.

85. Corley, *Private Women, Public Meals*, 85–86.

86. Some commentators juxtapose the women over against the men as positive role models of faith. See John Schmidt, "The Women in Mark's Gospel," *Bible Today* 19 (1981): 228–33.

87. Weeden, *Mark—Traditions in Conflict*. See also Ernst Best, *Following Jesus: Discipleship in the Gospel of Mark* (Sheffield: JSOT Press, 1981); Corley, *Private Women, Public Meals*, 84–85; Crossan, *Who Killed Jesus?* 182–84; Joanna Dewey, *Disciples on the Way: Mark on Discipleship* (Women's Division, Board of Global Ministries, UMC, 1976), 123–37; Kinukawa, *Women and Jesus*, 105–6; Malbon, "Fallible Followers,"passim.

88. Smith, "Good News Is No News," Passim.

89. It seems reasonable to conclude that Mark is the author of both crucifixion and empty tomb narratives (so Crossan), but that does not mean he has no oral traditions at his disposal (see below).

90. Eileen F. de Ward, "Mourning Customs in 1, 2 Samuel II," *Journal of Jewish Studies* 23 (1972): 159.

91. Emanuel Feldman, *Biblical and Post-Biblical Defilement and Mourning: Law as Theology* (New York: KTAV; Yeshiva University Press, 1977), 120–32.

92. Ibid., 127.

93. Ibid., 124.

94. *Barn.* 5–8. I would like to thank Dom Crossan for this observation.

95. For information on laments in Greece, see Margaret Alexiou, *Ritual Lament in Greek Tradition* (Cambridge: Cambridge University Press, 1974); Anna Caraveli-Chaves, "Bridge between Worlds: The Greek Women's Lament as Communicative Event," *Journal of American Folklore* 93 (1980); 129–57; idem, "The Bitter Wounding: The Lament as Social Protest in Rural Greece," in *Gender and Power in Rural Greece*, ed. Jill Dubisch (Princeton, N.J.: Princeton University Press, 1986), 169–84; Susan Auerbach, "From Singing to Lamenting: Women's Musical Role in a Greek Village," in *Women and Music in Cross-Cultural Perspective*, ed. Ellen Koskoff (New York: Greenwood, 1987), 25–43; Loring M. Danforth, *The Death Rituals of Rural Greece*. Princeton, N.J.: Princeton University Press, 1982), 71–152; Holst-Warhaft, *Dangerous Voices*, passim; C. Nadia Seremtakis, *The Last Word: Women, Death, and Divination in Inner Mani* (Chicago: University of Chicago Press, 1991), passim; for Ireland, see Angela Bourke, "More in Anger Than in Sorrow: Irish Women's Lament Poetry," in *Feminist Messages: Coding Women's Folk Culture*, ed. Joan Newlon Radner (Urbana: University of Illinois Press, 1993), 160–82; Christina Sinclair Brophy, "The Irish *Caoineadh*, Words of Rage and Protest from Wailing Women: A Religious Interpretation" (M.A. thesis, Claremont Graduate School, 1995); Heather Nicole Feldmeth, "In the Face of a Thousand Sorrows: The Seven Joys of the Virgin" (B.A. thesis, Harvard University, 1994); Peter Levi, *The Lamentation of the Dead with the Lament for Arthur O' Leary by Eileen O' Connell,* trans. Eilis Dillon (London: Annual Press Poetry, 1984); Angela Partridge, "Wild Men and Wailing Women," *Eigse* 18 (1976): 25–37; Lawrence J. Taylor, "BAS InEIRINN: Cultural Constructions of Death in Ireland," *Anthropological Quarterly* 62 (1989): 175–87; on Africa, see J. H. Nketia, *Funeral Dirges of the Akan People* (New York: Negro University Press, 1969); Emilie M. Townes, *In a Blaze of Glory: Womanist Spirituality as Social Witness* (Nashville: Abingdon, 1995), 21–22; on Black Carib women, see Virginia Kerns, *Women and*

the Ancestors: Black Carib Kinship and Ritual (Urbana: University of Illinois Press, 1983), 147–66; for China, see Elizabeth L. Johnson, "Grieving for the Dead, Grieving for the Living: Funeral Laments of Hakka Women," in *Death Ritual in Late Imperial and Modern China*, ed. James L. Watson and Evelyn S. Rawski (Berkeley, Calif.: University of California Press, 1988), 135–63; on Spain, see Holst-Warhaft, *Dangerous Voices*, 59–60; on Central America, see Virginia Kerns, "Garifuna Women and the Work of Mourning," in *Unspoken Worlds: Women's Religious Lives*, ed. Nancy Auer Falk and Rita M. Gross (Belmont, Calif.: Wadsworth, 1989), 93–101; for Yemenite Jews, see S. D. Goitein, "Women as Creators of Biblical Genres," *Prooftexts* 8, no. 1 (1988): 21–27.

96. See remarks by Alexiou, *Ritual Lament*, 92–93, on the popular folk laments concerning the destruction of cities.

97. Auerbach, "Women's Musical Role," 37; Bourke, "Irish Women's Lament Poetry," 169–70; Brophy, "The Irish *Caoineadh*," 47; Caraveli-Chavez, "Bitter Wounding," 183–84, 186; idem, "Bridge between Worlds," 150–51; Holst-Warhaft, *Dangerous Voices*, 59–60; Levi, *Lamentation*, 16, 25; Nketia, *Funeral Dirges*, 12; Seremetakis, *Last Word*, 128–29; 131; 145–47; Taylor, "BAS InEIRINN," 177.

98. Caraveli-Chavez, "Bridge between Worlds," 133–37; Holst-Warhaft, *Dangerous Voices*, 60–61; Levi, *Lamentation*, 30, 33; Nketia, *Funeral Dirges*, 39–42. See also lament quoted by Auerbach, "Women's Musical Roles," 41, where the deceased is narrated as walking down a dark mountain.

99. Holst-Warhaft, *Dangerous Voices*, 60–61; Kerns, *Women and the Ancestors*, 153; Nketia, *Funeral Dirges*, 19; Seremetakis, *Last Word*, 103–4; 145–47.

100. Bourke, "Irish Women's Lament Poetry," 170, 172; Holst-Warhaft, *Dangerous Voices*, 75–97: Levi, *Lamentation*, 27–28, 34; Seremetakis, *Last Word*, 128–29; Sometimes the deceased is blamed. See Alexiou, *Ritual Lament*, 182.

101. Holst-Warhaft, *Dangerous Voices*, 81; see also Seremetakis, *Last Word*, 135. The theme of Christ's passion is well known in Christian lament cultures such as those in Ireland and Greece. An entire lament tradition is devoted to the passion of Jesus, Jesus' mother, Mary, being the lamenter of his death. In Ireland, the Virgin Mary is considered the founder of women's lament traditions. See Margaret Alexiou, "The Lament of the Virgin in Byzantine Literature and Greek Folk Song," *Byzantine and Modern Greek Studies* 1 (1975): 111–40; idem, *Ritual Lament*, 62–78; Brophy, "The Irish *Caoineadh*," 20–21, 50–51; Feldmeth, "In the Face of a Thousand Sorrows"; Partridge, "Wild Men and Wailing Women."

102. Holst-Warhaft, *Dangerous Voices*, 67; Levi, *Lamentation*, 19.

103. For the timing of the Passover and the passion narrative, see Brown, *Death of the Messiah*, 2:1356–69.

104. Mack, *Myth of Innocence*, 296.

105. See Betz, *Sermon on the Mount*, 370.

106. Visions of departed loved ones in the first years following a death have been documented in modern times. Stacy Davids, M.D., "Appearances of the Resurrected Jesus and the Experience of Grief" (paper presented to the Jesus

Seminar, Spring 1995); idem, "What Is the Truth about the Resurrection of Jesus? The Testimony of Mary Magdalene," (unpublished paper); A. Grimby, "Bereavement among Elderly People: Grief Reactions, Post-Bereavement Hallucinations and Quality of Life," *Acta Psychiatrica Scandinavia* 87 (1993): 72–80; Luis Varga, Fred Loya, and Janet Hodde-Vargas, "Exploring the Multidimensional Aspects of Grief Reactions," *American Journal of Psychiatry* 146 (1989): 1484–88; See also Danforth, *Death Rituals*, 135.

107. E. R. Dodds, *The Greeks and the Irrational*, 108–11, 117, 118–19, 127n52.

108. Lüdemann, *Resurrection*, 99.

109. Sawicki, *Seeing the Lord*, 164–65.

110. Schüssler Fiorenza, "Wisdom Mythology," 35–37.

111. Fuller, *Formation*, 32–34; Lüdemann, *Resurrection*, 54–60; Riley, *Resurrection*, 68, 179.

112. If the desertion of a teacher by his followers is an aretalogical theme, there is no reason not to consider the possibility that a few men mingled with a crowd to watch the crucifixion.

113. Like the family of Yehohanan. One ossuary from Giv'at ha-Mivtar is inscribed "Simon, a builder of the temple." This confirms that a certain level of artisan, like temple builders, masons, or engineers, could afford large tombs and expensive ossuaries. See J. Naveh, "The Ossuary Inscriptions from Giv'at ha-Mivtar," *Israel Exploration Journal* 20 (1970): 33–37.

114. E. A. Judge, "The Early Christians as a Scholastic Community," *Journal of Religious History* (1960): 4–15, esp. 9–11.

115. Rohde, *Psyche*, 144n38.

BIBLIOGRAPHY

Ancient Authors

Achilles Tatius. Edited and translated by S. Gaselee. *Achilles Tatius*. LCL. London: William Heinemann; New York: G. P. Putnam's Sons, 1917.

Acts of John. Edited by Eric Junod and Jean-Daniel Kaestli. *Acta Iohannes. Praefatio-Textus*. Corpus Christianorum, Series Apocryphorum 1. Brepols: Turnhout, 1983. Translated by Knut Schäferdiek. In *New Testament Apocrypha*, vol. 2, 152–212. Edited by Wilhelm Schneemelcher. Louisville: Westminster John Knox, 1992.

Aeschylus. *The Persians*. Edited and translated by Herbert Weir Smythe. *Aeschylus*, vol. 1. LCL. Cambridge, Mass.: Harvard University Press; William Heinemann, 1956.

Apuleius. *Metamorphoses*. Edited and translated by W. Adlington, *Apuleius. The Golden Ass*. LCL. Cambridge, Mass.: Harvard University Press; London: William Heinemann, 1958.

Aristophanes. *The Lysistrata*. Edited and translated by Benjamin Bickley Rogers. *Aristophanes*, vol. 3. LCL. Cambridge, Mass.: Harvard University Press; London: William Heinemann, 1955.

Chariton. *Chaereas and Callirhoe*. Edited by G. Molinié. *Chariton. Le roman de Chairéas et Callirhoé*. Paris: Collection des universités de France, 1979. Translated by B. P. Reardon, "Chaereas and Callirhoe." In *Collected Ancient Novels*, 17–124. Edited by B. P. Reardon. Berkeley and Los Angeles: University of California Press, 1989.

Cicero. *Tusculan Disputations*. Edited and translated by J. E. King. *Cicero. Tusculan Disputations*. LCL. Cambridge, Mass.: Harvard University Press; London: William Heinemann, 1945.

First Letter of Clement. Edited and translated by Kirsopp Lake. *The Apostolic Fathers*, vol. 1. LCL. London: William Heinemann, 1962.

Gospel of Peter. Edited by H. B. Swete. *The Apocryphal Gospel of St. Peter: The Greek Text of the Newly Discovered Fragment*. London: Macmillan, 1893. Translated by Christian Maurer, "The Gospel of Peter." In *New Testament Apocrypha*, vol. 1, 223–27. Edited by Wilhelm Schneemelcher. Louisville: Westminster John Knox, 1991.

The Gospel of Thomas. Edited and translated by Bentley Layton, *Nag Hammadi Codex II, 2–7*, vol. 1, 38–128. Leiden: Brill, 1989. Edited and translated by Marvin Meyer. *The Gospel of Thomas: The Hidden Sayings of Jesus*. San Francisco: HarperSanFrancisco, 1992.

Lobel, Edgar, and Denys Page. *Poetarum Lesbiorum Fragmenta*. Oxford: Clarendon, 1955.

Lucian. *On Funerals*. Edited and translated by A. M. Harmon. *Lucian*, vol. 4. LCL. London: William Heinemann; Cambridge, Mass.: Harvard University Press, 1969.

————. *The Passing of Peregrinus*. Edited and translated by A. M. Harmon. *Lucian*, vol. 6. LCL. Cambridge, Mass.: Harvard University Press; London: William Heinemann, 1936.

Minucius Felix, *Octavius* 8.4–12.5. Translated by Jo-Ann Shelton. *As the Romans Did: A Sourcebook in Roman Social History*. Oxford: Oxford University Press; New Haven, Conn., and London: Yale University Press, 1984, 15–47.

The Mishnah. Translated by Herbert Danby. Oxford: Oxford University Press, 1992.

Munich Coptic Papyrus 5. Edited by W. Henstenberg, "Koptische Papyri." In *Beiträge zur Forschung: Studien und Mitteilungen aus dem Antiquariat Jacques Rosenthal, München*, vol. 1 (= "erste Folge"), 8–11, 95–100. Edited by Jacques Rosenthal. Munich: Verlag von Jacques Rosenthal, 1915. Translated by Marvin Meyer. In *Ancient Christian Magic: Coptic Texts of Ritual Power*, 188–90. Ed. Marvin Meyer and Richard Smith. San Francisco: HarperSanFrancisco, 1994.

Origen. *Contra Celsum*. Translated by Henry Chadwick. *Origen: Contra Celsum*. Cambridge: Cambridge University Press, 1953.

Papyrus Bremner-Rhind. Edited by Raymond O. Faulkner. *The Papyrus Bremner-Rhind*. Bruxelles: Édition de la fondation égyptologique reine Élisabeth, 1933. Translated by Raymond O. Faulkner. "The Bremner-Rhind Papyrus—I." *Journal of Egyptian Archaeology* 22 (1936): 121–40.

Philostratus. *Life of Apollonius of Tyana.* Edited and translated by F. C. Conybeare. *Philostratus: Life of Apollonius of Tyana.* LCL. Cambridge, Mass.: Harvard University Press; London: William Heinemann, 1960.

Plato. *Phaedo.* Edited and translated by Harold North Fowler. *Plato,* vol. 1. LCL. London: William Heinemann; Cambridge, Mass.: Harvard University Press, 1971.

Plutarch. *Lives.* Edited and translated by Bernadotte Perrin. *Plutarch's Lives.* LCL; Cambridge, Mass.: Harvard University Press; London: William Heinemann, 1914–22.

———. *Moralia.* Edited and translated by F. C. Babbitt et al. *Plutarch's Moralia.* LCL. Cambridge, Mass.: Harvard University Press; London: William Heinemann, 1927–69.

Porphyry. *Life of Pythagoras.* Edited by Édouard des Places. *Porphyre. Vie de Pythagore, Lettre a Marcella.* Paris: Collection des universités des France, 1982.

Pseudo-Philo. *Biblical Antiquities.* Edited by Daniel J. Harrington, *Pseudo-Philon,* vol. 1. Source chrétiennes 229. Paris: Editions du cerf, 1976. Translated by D. J. Harrington, *Old Testament Pseudepigrapha,* vol. 2, 297–377. Edited by James H. Charlesworth. Garden City, N.Y.: Doubleday, 1985.

Pseudo-Phocylides. *Sentences.* Edited and translated by P. W. Van der Horst. *The Sentences of Pseudo-Phocylides.* Leiden: Brill, 1978.

Seneca. *Hercules Oetaeus.* Edited and translated by Frank Justus Miller. *Seneca. Tragedies,* vol. 2. LCL. Cambridge, Mass.: Harvard University Press; London: William Heinemann, 1968.

Septuaginta. Stuttgart: Deutsche Bibelgesellschaft, 1979.

Zlotnick, Dov. *The Tractate "Mourning" (Semahot).* New Haven, Conn.: Yale University Press, 1966.

Modern Authors

Abrahams, I. "Publicans amd Sinners." In *Studies in Pharisaism and the Gospels,* 54–61. New York: KTAV, 1967.

Ackerman, Susan. "'And the Women Knead Dough': The Worship of the Queen of Heaven in Sixth-Century Judah." In *Gender and Difference in Ancient Israel,* 109–24. Edited by Peggy L. Day. Minneapolis: Fortress Press, 1989.

Achtemeier, Paul J. "The Disciples in Mark." In *Mark.* Proclamation Commentaries. Philadelphia: Fortress Press, 1986.

———. "Gospel Miracle Traditions and the Divine Man." *Interpretation* 26 (1972): 174–97.

———. "The Origin and Function of the Pre-Markan Miracle Catenae." *Journal of Biblical Literature* 91 (1972): 198–221.

————. "Toward the Isolation of Pre-Markan Miracle Catenae." *Journal of Biblical Literature* 89 (1970): 265–91.

Adams, Margaret. "The Hidden Disciples. Luke's Stories about Women in His Gospel." D. Min. dissertation, San Francisco Theological Seminary, 1980.

Ahlberg, Gudrun. *Prothesis and Ekphora in Greek Geometic Art.* Göteborg: Elanders Boktryckeri Aktiebolag, 1971.

Aiken, Ellen Bradshaw. *Jesus' Death in Early Christian Memory: The Poetics of the Passion.* Göttingen: Vandenhoeck and Ruprecht, 2004.

Albright, W. F. *Yahweh and the Gods of Canaan.* Winona Lake, Ind.: Eisenbrauns, 1968.

Alexander, Loveday. "Sisters in Adversity: Retelling Martha's Story." In *Women in Biblical Tradition*, 167–86. Edited by George Brooke. Lewiston; Queenston; Lampeter: Edwin Mellen, 1992.

Alexandre, Monique. "Early Christian Women." In *A History of Women I: From Ancient Goddesses to Christian Saints*, 409–44. Edited by Pauline Schmitt Pantel. Cambridge, Mass.: Harvard University Press, 1992.

Alexiou, Margaret. "The Lament of the Virgin in Byzantine Literature and Greek Folk Song." *Byzantine and Modern Greek Studies* 1 (1975): 111–40.

————. *Ritual Lament in Greek Tradition.* Cambridge: Cambridge University Press, 1974.

Alexiou, Margaret, and Peter Dronke. "The Lament of Jephtha's Daughter: Themes, Traditions, Originality." *Studi Medievali* 2 (1971): 819–63.

Allberry, C. R. C., ed. *A Manichaean Psalmbook*, II. Stuttgart: W. Kohammer, 1938.

Allen, Willoughby. *A Critical and Exegetical Commentary on the Gospel according to St. Matthew.* Edinburgh: T. and T. Clark, 1965.

Amaru, Betsy Halpern. "Portraits of Biblical Women in Josephus' Antiquities." *Journal of Jewish Studies* 39 (1988): 143–70.

Anderson, Bonnie S., and Judith P. Zinsser. *A History of Their Own: Women from Pre-history to the Present*, vol. 1. New York: Harper and Row, 1988.

Anderson, Gary A. *A Time to Mourn and an Time to Dance: The Expression of Grief and Joy in Israelite Tradition.* University Park: Pennsylvania State University Press, 1991.

Antonaccio, Carla. *An Archaeology of Ancestors: Tomb Cult and Hero Cult in Early Greece.* Lanham, Md: Rowman and Littlefield, 1995.

————. "The Archaeology of the Ancestors." In *Cultural Poetics in Archaic Greece: Cult Performance Politics*, 46–70. Edited by Carol Dougherty and Leslie Kurke. Cambridge: Cambridge University Press, 1993.

Archer, Léonie J. *Her Price Is beyond Rubies: The Jewish Woman in Greco-Roman Palestine.* Sheffield: JSOT Press, 1990.

Arnal, William E. "Gendered Couplets in Q and Legal Formulations: From Rhetoric to Social History." *Journal of Biblical Literature* 116 (1997): 75–94.

————. "Reconstruction of Q 7:29–30." Paper presented to the International Q Project. Claremont, Calif., May 1994.

Ascough, Richard S. "Greco-Roman Philosophic, Religious and Voluntary Associations." In *Community Formation in the Early Church and in the Church*

Today, 3–19. Edited by R. N. Longnecker. Peabody, Mass.: Hendrickson, 2002.

———. "Matthew Community Formation." In *The Gospel of Matthew in Current Study. Studies in Memory of William G. Thompson, S. J.*, 96–126. Edited by David Aune. Grand Rapids: Eerdmans, 2001.

———. "A Question of Death: Paul's Community Building Language in 1 Thessalonians 4:13-18." *Journal of Biblical Literature* 123 (2004): 509–30.

———. "The Thessalonian Christian Community as a Professional Voluntary Association." *Journal of Biblical Literature* 119 (2000): 311–28.

———. "Voluntary Associations and the Formation of Pauline Christian Communities: Overcoming Objections." In *Vereine Synagogen und Gemeinden im kaiserzeitlichen Kleinasien*, 149–83. Edited by A. Gutsfeld and D-A. Koch. Tübingen: Mohr Siebeck, 2006.

Asgeirsson, Jon Ma, and James M. Robinson. "The International Q Project: Work Sessions 12-14 July, 22 November 1991." *Journal of Biblical Literature* 111 (1992): 500–08.

Attridge, Harold W. "Greek Equivalents to Two Coptic Phrases: CG I, 1.65, 9–10 and CG II, 2.43.26." *Bulletin of the American Society of Papyrologists* 18 (1981): 27–32.

———. "Masculine Fellowship in the *Acts of Thomas*." In *The Future of Early Christianity: Essays in Honor of Helmust Koester*, 406–13. Edited by Birger Pearson. Minneapolis: Fortress Press, 1991.

Atwood, Richard. *Mary Magdalene in the New Testament and Early Tradition*. New York: Peter Lang, 1993.

Auerbach, Susan. "From Singing to Lamenting: Women's Musical Role in a Greek Village." In *Women and Music in Cross-Cultural Perspective*, 24–43. Edited by Ellen Koskoff. New York: Greenwood, 1987.

Aune, David E. "Heracles and Christ: Heracles Imagery in the Christology of Early Christianity." In *Greeks, Romans and Christians: Essays in Honor of Abraham Malherbe*. Minneapolis: Fortress Press, 1990.

Avigad, N. "Aramaic Inscriptions in the Tomb of Jason." *Israel Exploration Journal* 17 (1967): 101–11.

———. "The Epitaph of a Royal Steward from a Siloam Village." *Israel Exploration Journal* 3 (1953): 137–52.

———. "The Rock Carved Facades of the Jerusalem Necropolis." *Israel Exploration Journal* 1 (1950–51): 96–106.

———. "A Seal of a Slave-Wife (Amah)." *Palestine Exploration Quarterly* 78 (1946): 125–32.

Avisur, Y. "A Ghost-Expelling Incantation from Ugarit." *Ugarit-Forschungen* 13 (1981): 13–25.

Ayrout, Henry Habib. *The Egyptian Peasant*. Boston: Beacon, 1963.

Baarda, T. "2 Clement 12 and the Sayings of Jesus." In *Early Transmission of the Words of Jesus*, 261–88. Edited by J. Heldermann and S. J. Noorda. Amsterdam: VU Boekhandel/Uitgeverig, 1983.

Baer, Richard A. *Philo's Use of the Categories Male and Female*. Leiden: Brill, 1970.

Bailey, James L. "Experiencing the Kingdom as a Little Child: A Rereading of Mark 10:13-16." *Word and World* 15 (1995): 58–67.

Bailey, John Amedee. *The Traditions Common to the Gospels Luke and John.* Leiden: Brill, 1963.

Balch, David L. "1 Cor 7:32-35 and Stoic Debates about Marriage, Anxiety and Distraction." *Journal of Biblical Literature* 102 (1983): 429–39.

———. *Let Wives Be Submissive: The Domestic Code in 1 Peter.* Chico, Calif.: Scholars Press, 1981.

Baltzer, Klaus. "Liberation from Debt Slavery after the Exile in Second Isaiah and Nehemiah." In *Ancient Israelite Religion: Essays in Honor of Frank Moore Cross*, 477–84. Edited by Patrick D. Miller et al. Philadelphia: Fortress Press, 1987.

Barr, James. "'Abba, Father' and the Familiarity of Jesus' Speech." *Theology* 91 (1988): 173–79.

———. "Abba Isn't Daddy." *Journal of Theological Studies* 39 (1988): 28–47.

Barrett, C. K. *The Gospel according to St. John.* London: SPCK, 1978.

Barton, Stephen C. "Mark as Narrative: The Story of the Anointing Woman (Mk 14:3-9)." *Expository Times* 102 (1991): 230–34.

Basser, Herbert W. "Let the Dead Bury Their Dead: Rhetorical Features of Rabbinic and New Testament Literature. In *Approaches to Ancient Judaism*, vol. 5, 79–95. Edited by Herbert W. Basser and Simcha Fishbane. New Series. Atlanta: Scholars Press, 1993.

Batey, Richard A. *Jesus and the Forgotten City: New Light on Sepphoris and the Urban World of Jesus.* Grand Rapids: Baker, 1991.

Batten, Alicia. "More Queries for Q: Women and Christian Origins." *Biblical Theology Bulletin* 24 (1994): 44–51.

Bauckman, Richard. "Salome the Sister of Jesus, Salome the Disciple of Jesus and the Secret Gospel of Mark." *Novum Testamentum* 33 (1991): 245–75.

Baumgarten, Joseph M. "4Q502: Marriage or Golden Age Ritual?" *Journal of Jewish Studies* 34 (1983): 125–35.

———. "Hanging and Treason in Qumran and Roman Law." *Eretz-Israel* 16 (1982): 7–16.

———. "On the Testimony of Women in 1QSa." *Journal of Biblical Literature* 26 (1957): 108–22.

———. "The Qumran-Essene Restraints on Marriage." In *Archaeology and History in the Dead Sea Scrolls*, 13–24. Edited by Lawrence Schiffman. Sheffield: JSOT Press, 1990.

Bayliss, Miranda. "The Cult of Dead Kin in Assyria and Babylonia." *Iraq* 35 (1973): 115–25.

Beames, Michael. *Peasants and Power. The Whiteboy Movements and Their Control in Pre-Famine Ireland.* Sussex: Harvester; New York: St. Martin's, 1983.

Beasley-Murray, George. *John.* Waco, Tx: Word, 1987.

Beavis, Mary Ann. "Ancient Slavery as an Interpretive Context for the New Testament Servant Parables with Special Reference to the Unjust Steward." *Journal of Biblical Literature* 111 (1992): 37–54.

————. "Women as Models of Faith in Mark." *Biblical Theology Bulletin* 18 (1988): 3–9.

Benoit, P. *The Passion and Resurrection of Jesus Christ*. New York: Herder and Herder, 1969.

Bercé, Yves-Marie. *Revolt and Revolution in Early Modern Europe*. New York: St. Martin's, 1987.

Best, Ernst. *Disciples and Discipleship. Studies in the Gospel according to Mark*. Edinburgh: T. and T. Clark, 1986.

————. *Following Jesus: Discipleship in the Gospel of Mark*. Sheffield: JSOT Press, 1981.

————. "Mark 10:13-16: The Child as Model Recipient." In *Biblical Studies: Essays in Honor of William Barclay*, 119–34. Edited by Johnston R. McKay and James F. Miller. Philadelphia: Westminster, 1976.

————. "The Role of the Disciples in Mark." *New Testament Studies* 23 (1977): 377–401.

Betz, Hans Dieter. *The Greek Magical Papyri in Translation*. Chicago: University of Chicago Press, 2nd ed., 1992.

————. "Jesus as Divine Man." In *Jesus the Historian*, 114–31. Edited by F. T. Trotter. Philadelphia: Westminster, 1968.

————. *The Sermon on the Mount*. Minneapolis: Fortress Press, 1995.

Beuken, W. A. M. "1 Samuel 28: The Prophet as Hammer of Witches." *Journal for the Study of the Old Testament* 6 (1978): 3–17.

The Bible and Culture Collective. *The Postmodern Bible*. New Haven, Conn., and London: Yale University Press, 1995.

Bieler, L. *Theios Aner: das Bild des "göttlichen Menchen" im Späntike und Frühchristentum*. Darmstadt: Wissenschaftliche Buchgessellschaft, 1976.

Bird, Phyllis A. "The Harlot as Heroine: Narrative Art and Presupposition in Three Old Testament Texts." *Semeia* 46 (1989): 119–39.

Bjorndahl, Sterling. "Thomas 61–67: A Chreia Elaboration." Major Paper presented to the New Testament Seminar, Claremont Graduate School, February 2, 1988.

Blackburn, Barry. *Theios Aner and the Markan Miracle Traditions*. Tübingen: J. C. B. Mohr, 1991.

Blasi, Anthony J. *Early Christianity as a Social Movement*. Toronto Studies in Religion 5. New York: Peter Lang, 1988.

Bloch-Smith. *Judahite Burial Practice and Beliefs about the Dead*. Sheffield: Sheffield, 1992.

Bode, Edward Lynn. *The First Easter Morning: The Gospel Accounts of the Woman's Visit to the Tomb of Jesus*. Rome: Biblical Institute Press, 1970.

Booth, Alan, "The Age of Reclining and Its Attendant Perils." In *Dining in a Classical Context*, 105–20. Edited by William J. Slater. Ann Arbor: University of Michigan Press, 1991.

Borg, Marcus J. *Jesus, A New Vision: Spirit, Culture, and the Life of Discipleship*. San Francisco: HarperSanFrancisco, 1987.

————. *Jesus in Contemprary Scholarship*. Valley Forge, Pa.: Trinity Press International, 1994.

————. *Meeting Jesus Again for the First Time: The Historical Jesus and the Heart of Contemporary Faith.* San Francisco: HarperSanFrancisco, 1994.

Bourke, Angela. "More in Anger Than in Sorrow: Irish Women's Lament Poetry." In *Feminist Messages: Coding Women's Folk Culture*, 160–82. Edited by Joan Newlon Radner. Urbana; Chicago: University of Illinois Press, 1993.

Boyarin, Daniel. *Carnal Israel: Reading Sex in Talmudic Culture.* Berkeley: University of California Press, 1993.

Bradley, K. R. "The Roman Family at Dinner." In *Meals in a Social Context: Aspects of the Communal Meal in the Hellenistic and Roman World*, 36–55. Edited by I. Nielson and H. S. Nielson (Oxford: Aarhus University Press, 1998).

————. *Slaves and Masters in the Roman Empire: A Study in Social Control.* New York and Oxford: Oxford University Press, 1984.

Brenner, Athalya, and Fokkelien van Dijk-Hemmes. *On Gendering Texts: Female and Male Voices in the Hebrew Bible.* Leiden; New York; Köln: Brill, 1993.

Brichto, Herbert Chanan. "Kin, Cult, Land and Afterlife—A Biblical Complex." *Hebrew Union College Annual* 44 (1973): 1–54.

Broadhead, H. D. *The Persae of Aeschylus.* Cambridge: Cambridge University Press, 1960.

Brock, S. P. "Early Syrian Asceticism." *Numen* 20 (1973): 1–19.

Brock Sebastian, and Susan Harvey. *Holy Women of the Syrian Orient.* Berkeley: University of California Press, 1987.

Brodie, Thomas L. "Luke 7, 36–50 as an Internalization of 2 Kings 4, 1–77: A Study in Luke's Use of Rhetorical Imitation." *Biblica* 64 (1983): 457–85.

Broneer, Oscar. "Hero Cults in the Corinthian Agora." *Hesperia* 11 (1942): 128–61.

Bronner, Leila Leah. *From Eve to Esther: Rabbinic Reconstructions of Biblical Women.* Louisville: Westminster John Knox, 1994.

Brooke, George J. "Power to the Powerless: A Long-lost Song of Miriam." *Biblical Archaeology Review* 20 (May/June 1994): 62–65.

————, ed. *Women in the Biblical Tradition.* Lewiston; Queenston; Lampeter: Edwin Mellen Press, 1992.

Brooten, Bernadette. "Early Christian Women and Their Cultural Context: Issues in Method and Historical Reconstruction." In *Feminist Perspectives on Biblical Scholarship*, 65–91. Edited by Adela Yarbro Collins. Chico, Calif.: Scholars, 1985.

————. "Konnten Frauen im alten Judentum die Scheidung betreiben?" *Evangelische Theologie* 42 (1982): 66–80.

————. *Women Leaders in the Ancient Synagogue.* Chico, Calif.: Scholars Press, 1982.

Brophy, Christina Sinclair. "The Irish Caoineadh, Words of Rage and Protest from Wailing Women: A Religious Interpretation." M.A. thesis. The Claremont Graduate School, 1995.

Brown, Carol Anne. *No Longer Silent: First-Century Jewish Portraits of Biblical Women.* Louisville: Westminster John Knox, 1992.

Brown, Colin. "The Parable of the Rebellious Son(s)." Unpublished manuscript.

Brown, G. M. et al., Edited by *The Oxyrhynchus Papyri,* v. 41. London: Egypt Exploration Society, 1972.

Brown, Nathan J. *Peasant Politics in Modern Egypt: The Struggle against the State.* New Haven, Conn. and London: Yale University Press, 1990.

Brown, Peter. *The Cult of the Saints: Its Rise and Function in Latin Christianity.* Chicago: University of Chicago Press, 1981.

Brown, Raymond E. *The Death of the Messiah. A Commentary on the Passion Narratives in the Four Gospels.* 2 vols. New York: Doubleday, 1994.

————. "Roles of Women in the Fourth Gospel." *Theological Studies* 36 (1975): 688–99.

———— et al. *Mary in the New Testament.* New York; Mahwah, N.J.: Fortress Press, 1978.

Browne, G. M. *The Oxyrhynchus Papyri,* vol. 41. London: Egypt Exploration Society, 1972.

Buchanan, George Wesley. "Jesus and the Upper Class." *Novum Testamentum* 7 (1964–65): 195–209.

Bullough, Vern and Bonnie. *Prostitution: An Illustrated Social History.* New York: Crown, 1978.

Bultmann, Rudolf. *Gospel of John: A Commentary.* Philadelphia: Westminster, 1971.

————. *History of the Synoptic Tradition.* Translated by John Marsh. New York: HarperCollins, 1963.

Burkert, Walter. *Greek Religion.* Cambridge, Mass.: Harvard University Press, 1985.

————. *Structure and History in Greek Mythology and Ritual.* Berkeley: University of California Press, 1979.

Burkill, T. A. "The Historical Development of the Story of the Syro-Phoenician Woman (Mark 7:34–31)." *Novum Testamentum* 9 (1967): 161–77.

Burns, John Barclay. "Necromancy and the Spirits of the Dead in the Old Testament." *Transactions of the Glaskow University Historical Society* 26 (1976): 1–14.

Burrus, Virginia. *Chastity as Autonomy: Women in the Stories of the Apocryphal Acts.* Lewiston, New York: Edwin Mellen, 1987.

Burton, Joan B. "The Function of the Symposium Theme in Theocritus' *Idyll* 11." *Greek, Roman and Byzantine Studies* 33 (1992): 227–45.

————. "Women's Commensality in the Ancient Greek World." *Greece and Rome* 45 (1998): 143–65.

Cady, Susan et al. *Sophia: The Future of Feminist Spirituality.* San Francisco: Harper and Row, 1986.

Callan, Terrence. "The Sayings of Jesus in Gos. Thom. 22/ 2 Clem 12/ Gos. Eg. 5." *Journal of Religious Studies* 16 (1990): 46–64.

Cameron, Averil. "Neither Male Nor Female." *Greece and Rome* 27 (1980): 60–68.

————. "Redrawing the Map: Early Christian Territory after Foucault." *Journal of Roman Studies* 76 (1986): 266–71.

Cameron, Ron. "Gospel of Thomas." In *Anchor Bible Dictionary*, vol. 6, 535–40. Edited by David Noel Freedman. New York: Doubleday, 1992.

————. "The Gospel of Thomas and Christian Origins." *The Future of Early Christianity: Essays in Honor of Helmust Koester.* Edited by Birger Pearson. Minneapolis: Fortress Press, 1991.

————. "Parable and Interpretation in the Gospel of Thomas." *Forum* 2 (1986): 3–39.

————. "What Have You Come Out to See? Characterizations of John and Jesus in the Gospels." *Semeia* 49 (1990): 35–69.

Cannon, Aubrey. "The Historical Dimension in Mortuary Expressions of Status and Sentiment." *Current Anthropology* 30 (1989): 437–58.

Caraveli-Chavez, Anna. "The Bitter Wounding: The Lament as Social Protest in Rural Greece." In *Gender and Power in Rural Greece*, 169–84. Edited by Jill Dubisch. Princeton, N.J.: Princeton University Press, 1986.

————. "Bridge between Worlds: The Greek Women's Lament as Communicative Event." *Journal of American Folklore* 93 (1980): 129–57.

Carr, Anne E. *Transforming Grace: Christian Tradition and Women's Experience.* San Francisco: HarperSanFrancisco, 1988.

Casson, Lionel. *Travel in the Ancient World.* Baltimore and London: Johns Hopkins University Press, 1994.

Castelli, Elizabeth. "Rethinking the Feminist Myth of Christian Origins." Paper presented at Candler School of Theology, Emory University. February 15, 1994.

————. Review: Elisabeth Schüssler Fiorenza, *But She Said* and *Jesus: Miriam's Child and Sophia's Prophet. Religious Studies Review* 22 (1996): 296–300.

————. "Virginity and Its Meaning for Women's Sexuality in Early Christianity." *Journal of Feminist Studies in Religion* 2 (1986): 61–88.

————, and Hal Taussig, Edited by *Reimagining Christian Origins: A Colloquium Honoring Burton L. Mack.* Valley Forge, Pa.: Trinity Press International, 1996.

Castner, Catherine J. "Epicurean Hetairai as Dedicants to Healing Deities?" *Greek, Roman and Byzantine Studies* 23 (1982): 51–57.

Catchpole, David. "The Fearful Silence of the Women at the Tomb: A Study in Markan Theology." *Journal of Theology for Southern Africa* 18 (1977): 3–10.

Charlesworth, James H. "A Caveat on Textual Transmission and the Meaning of the Lord's Prayer." In *The Lord's Prayer and Other Prayer Texts from the Greco-Roman Era*, 1–14. Edited by James H. Charlesworth et al. Valley Forge, Pa.: Trinity Press International, 1994.

————. "The Foreground of Christian Origins and the Commencement of Jesus Research." In *Jesus' Jewishness: Exploring the Place of Jesus within Early Judaism*, 63–83. New York: Crossroad, 1991.

————. "Greek, Persian, Roman, Syrian and Egyptian Influences in Early Jewish Theology." In *Hellenica et Judaica: Hommage á Valentin Nikiprowetzky*, 219–43. Edited by A. Caquot et al. Leuven and Paris: Peeters, 1986.

————, ed. *Jesus' Jewishness: Exploring the Place of Jesus within Early Judaism*. New York: Crossroad, 1991.

Cheney, Emily. "Honor and Shame: From Whose Point of View?" Paper presented at the Social Science and New Testament Interpretation and Rhetoric and New Testament Sections, Annual Meeting of the Society of Biblical Literature. San Francisco, Calif., November 1992.

Chilton, Bruce. "Jesus within Judaism." In *Judaism and Late Antiquity*, vol. 2, 278–80. Edited by Jacob Neusner. Leiden: Brill, 1995.

————. *Pure Kingdom: Jesus' Vision of God*. Grand Rapids: Eerdmans, 1996.

Chilton, Bruce, and Jacob Neusner. *Judaism in the New Testament: Practices and Beliefs*. New York and London: Routledge, 1995.

Coakley, J. F. "The Anointing at Bethany and the Priority of John." *Journal of Biblical Literature* 107 (1988): 241–56.

Cohen, Shaye J. D., ed. *The Jewish Family in Antiquity*. Atlanta: Scholars Press, 1993.

————. "Menstruants and the Sacred in Judaism and Christianity." In *Women's History and Ancient History*, 273–99. Edited by S. B. Pomeroy, Chapel Hill and London: University of North Carolina Press, 1991.

Collins, Adela Yarbro. *The Beginning of the Gospel: Probings of Mark in Context*. Minneapolis: Fortress Press, 1992.

————. "The Composition of the Markan Passion Narrative." *Sewanee Theological Review* 36 (1992): 57–77.

————. "The Empty Tomb in the Gospel according to Mark." In *Hermes and Athena: Biblical Exegesis and Philosophical Theology*, 107–40. Edited by E. Stump and T. P. Flint. Notre Dame, Ind.: University of Notre Dame Press, 1993.

————. "From Noble Death to Crucified Messiah." *New Testament Studies* 40 (1994): 481–503.

————. "The Genre of the Passion Narrative." *Studia Theologica* 47 (1993): 3–28.

Collins, John J. "Marriage, Divorce and Family in Second Temple Judaism." In *Families in Ancient Israel*, 104–62. Edited by Leo Perdue et al. Louisville: Westminster John Knox, 1997.

Connolly, A. K. "*Kynarion*." In *New Documents Illustrating Early Christianity*, vol. 4, 157–59. Edited by G. R. H. Horsley. Macquarie University, Australia: The Ancient History Documentary Research Centre, 1987.

Conzelmann, Hans. "History and Theology in the Passion Narratives." *Interpretation* 2 (1979): 178–97.

Corley, Kathleen E. "The Anointing of Jesus in the Synoptic Tradition." Paper presented to the Jesus Seminar. Spring 1994.

————. "Feminist Myths of Christian Origins." In *Reimagining Christian Origins: A Colloquium Honoring Burton L. Mack*, 49–65. Edited by Elizabeth

A. Castelli and Hal Taussig. Valley Forge, Pa.: Trinity Press International, 1996.

———. "Jesus' Table Practice: Dining with 'Tax Collectors and Prostitutes,' Including Women." In *Society of Biblical Literature 1993 Seminar Papers*, 444–59. Edited by Eugene H. Lovering. Atlanta: Scholars Press, 1993.

———. *Private Women, Public Meals: Social Conflict in the Synoptic Tradition*. Peabody, Mass.: Hendrickson, 1993.

———. "Salome." *International Standard Bible Encyclopedia*, vol. 4, 286. Grand Rapids: Eerdmans, 1988.

———. "Were the Women around Jesus Really Prostitutes? Women in the Context of Greco-Roman Meals." *Society of Biblical Literature 1989 Seminar Papers*, 487–521. Edited by David J. Lull. Atlanta: Scholars Press, 1989.

———. *Women and the Historical Jesus: Feminist Myths of Christian Origins*. Santa Roas, Calif.: Polebridge, 2002.

Cornfeld, Gaalyah. *Archaeology of the Bible: Book by Book*. New York and San Francisco: Harper and Row, 1976.

Cotter, Wendy. "Parable of the Children in the Marketplace [Q [Lk]] 7:31-35]: An Examination of the Parable's Image and Significance." *Novum Testamentum* 29 (1987): 289–304.

Craig, W. L. "The Historicity of the Empty Tomb of Jesus." *New Testament Studies* 31 (1985): 39–67.

Crossan, John Dominic. *The Cross that Spoke: The Origins of the Passion Narrative*. San Francisco: HarperCollins, 1988.

———. "Empty Tomb and Absent Lord (Mark 16:1-8)." In *The Passion in Mark: Studies on Mark 14-16*, 135–52. Edited by W. H. Kelber. Philadelphia: Fortress Press, 1976.

———. *The Essential Jesus: Original Sayings and Earliest Images*. San Francisco: HarperSanFrancisco, 1994.

———. *Four Other Gospels*. Minneapolis; Chicago; New York: Winston Press, 1985.

———. *The Historical Jesus: The Life of a Mediterranean Jewish Peasant*. San Francisco: HarperCollins, 1991.

———. "Mark and the Relatives of Jesus." *Novum Testamentum* 15 (1973): 81–113.

———. *In Parables: The Challenge of the Historical Jesus*. Sonoma, Calif.: Polebridge, 1992.

———. "The Servant Parables of Jesus." *Semeia* 1 (1974): 17–62.

———. *Who Killed Jesus? Exposing the Roots of Anti-Semitism in the Gospel Story of the Death of Jesus*. San Francisco: HarperSanFrancisco, 1995.

Crown Alan D., and Lena Cansdale. "Qumran: Was It an Essene Settlement?" *Biblical Archaeology Review* (September–October 1994): 24–35.

Cullmann, Oscar. "Immortality of the Soul or Resurrection of the Dead?" In *Immortality and Resurrection*, 9–53. Edited by K. Stendahl. New York: Macmillan, 1965.

————. "Infancy Gospels: The Protevangelium of James." In *New Testament Apocrypha*, vol. 1, 421–69. Edited by E. Hennecke and W. Schneemelcher. Philadelphia: Westminster, 1991.

Cumont, Franz. *Afterlife in Roman Paganism*. New Haven, Conn.: Yale University Press, 1922.

Daly, Lloyd W. *Aesop without Morals*. New York and London: Thomas Yoseloff, 1961.

Danforth, Loring M. *The Death Rituals of Rural Greece*. Princeton, N.J.: Princeton University Press, 1982.

D'Angelo, Mary Rose. "'Abba' and 'Father': Imperial Theology and the Jesus Traditions." *Journal of Biblical Literature* 111 (1992): 611–30.

————. "Images of Jesus and the Christian Call in the Gospels of Luke and John." *Spirituality Today* 37 (1985): 196–212.

————. "Re-membering Jesus: Women, Prophecy and Resistance in the Memory of the Early Churches." *Horizon* 19 (1992): 199–218.

————. "Theology in Mark and Q: 'Abba' and 'Father' in Context." *Harvard Theological Review* 85 (1992): 149–74.

————. "Women Partners in the New Testament." *Journal of Feminist Studies in Religion* 6 (1990): 65–86.

D'Arms, John H. "Slaves at Roman Convivia." In *Dining in a Classical Context*, 171–83. Edited by William Slater. Ann Arbor: University of Michigan Press, 1991.

Daube, David. "The Anointing at Bethany and Jesus' Burial." *Anglican Theological Review* 32 (1950): 186–99.

————. "Rabbinic Methods of Interpretation and Hellenistic Rhetoric." *Hebrew Union College Annual* 22 (1949): 239–64.

————. *Roman Law: Linguistic, Social and Philosophical Aspects*. Edinburgh: Edinburgh University Press, 1969.

Dauer, Anton. *Die Passionsgeschichte im Johannesevangelium*. Munich: Kösel-Verlag, 1972.

Davids, Stacy. "Appearances of the Resurrected Jesus and the Experience of Grief." Paper presented to the Jesus Seminar. Spring 1995.

————. "What Is the Truth about the Resurrection of Jesus? The Testimony of Mary Magdalene." Unpublished paper.

Davies, Stephen T. "Was the Tomb Empty?" In *Hermes and Athena: Biblical Exegesis and Philosophical Theology*, 77–105. Edited by Eleonore Stump and Thomas Flint. Notre Dame, Ind.: University of Notre Dame Press, 1993.

D'Avino, Michele. *The Women of Pompeii*. Translated by Monica Hope Jones and Luigi Nusco. Napoli: Loffredo, 1967.

Dawson, Letha and Nancy Hardesty. *All We're Meant to Be: Biblical Feminism for Today*. Reprint; Nashville: Abingdon, 1986.

Day, Peggy L. "From the Child Is Born the Woman: The Story of Jephthah's Daughter." In *Gender and Difference in Ancient Israel*, 58–74. Edited by Peggy L. Day. Minneapolis: Fortress Press, 1989.

De Conick, April D., and Jarl Fossum. "Stripped before God: A New Interpretation of Logion 37 in the Gospel of Thomas." *Vigiliae christianae* 45 (1991): 123–50.

Deere, Carmen Diana. *Household and Class Relations: Peasants and Landlords in Northern Peru.* Berkeley; Los Angeles; Oxford: University of California Press, 1990.

Deissler, Alfons. "The Spirit of the Lord's Prayer in the Faith and Worship of the Old Testament." In *The Lord's Prayer and Jewish Liturgy*, 3–17. Edited by Jakob J. Petuchowski and Michael Brocke. New York: Seabury, 1978.

Deissmann, Adolf. *Light from the Ancient Near East.* Translated by L. R. M. Strachan. London: Hodder and Stoughton, 1927.

Delobel, Joël. "L'onction par la pécheresse: la composition littéraire de Lc VII, 36–50." *Ephemerides theologicae lovanienses* 42 (1966): 415–75.

―――. "Lk 7, 47 in Its Context: An Old Crux Revisited." In *The Four Gospels: Festschrift Frans Neirynck*, 1581–1590. Edited by R. van Segbroeck et al. Leuven: University Press; Peeters, 1992.

DeMaris, Richard E. "Corinthian Religion and the Baptism for the Dead (1 Corinthians 15:29): Insights from Archaeology and Anthropology." *Journal of Biblical Literature* 114 (1995): 661–82.

De Melo, C. M. "Mary of Bethany: The Silent Contemplative." *Review for Religious* 48 (1989): 690–97.

Dentzer, Jean Marie. *Le motif du banquet couché dans le proche-orient et le monde grec du VIIe and VIe siécle avant J.-C.* École Francaise de Rome: Palais Farnése, 1982.

De Romilly, Jacqueline. *Magic and Rhetoric in Ancient Greece.* Cambridge, Mass.: Harvard University Press, 1975.

Derrett, J. Duncan M. "The Anointing at Bethany and the Story of Zacchaeus." In *Law and the New Testament*, 266–85. London: Darton, Longman and Todd, 1970.

―――. "Law in the New Testament: The Syro-Phoenician Woman and the Centurion of Capernaum." *Novum Testamentum* (1973): 161–86.

―――. "Why Jesus Blessed the Children (Mark 10:13-16, Par.)." *Novum Testamentum* 15 (1983): 1–18.

Dessau, Hermannus. *Inscriptiones Latinae. Selectae.* Vol. 2, pt. 2. Chicago: Ares, 1979.

Detienne, Marcel. *The Gardens of Adonis: Spices in Greek Mythology.* Translated by Janet Lloyd. Sussex: Harvester Press, 1977.

De Vaux, Roland. *Ancient Israel: Its Life and Institutions.* London: Darton, Longman and Todd, 1961.

De Ward, Eileen F. "Mourning Customs in 1, 2 Samuel." *Journal of Jewish Studies* 23 (1972): 1–27.

―――. "Mourning Customs in 1, 2 Samuel II." *Journal of Jewish Studies* 23 (1972): 145–66.

Dewey, Arthur. "A Hymn in the Acts of John: Dance as Hermeneutic." *Semeia* 38 (1986): 67–80.

————. "A Prophetic Pronouncement: Q 12:42-46." *Forum* 5.2 (1989): 99–108.

Dewey, Joanna. *Disciples on the Way: Mark on Discipleship.* United Methodist Church: Women's Division, Board of Global Ministries, 1976.

————. "The Gospel of Mark." In *Searching the Scriptures,* vol. 2, 470–509. Edited by Elisabeth Schüssler Fiorenza. New York, Crossroad, 1994.

Dibelius, Martin. *From Tradition to Gospel.* Greenwood, S.C.: Attic, 1982.

Dinkler, Erich. "Comments on the History of the Symbol of the Cross." In *The Bultmann School of Biblical Interpretation: New Directions,* 124–46. Translated by Gerhard Krodel. Edited by James M. Robinson et al. Tübingen: J. C. B. Mohr; New York: Harper and Row, 1965.

Dobbs-Allsopp, F. W. *Weep, O Daughter of Zion: A Study of the City-Lament Genre in the Hebrew Bible.* Rome: Pontificio Istituto Biblico, 1993.

Dodd, C. H. *The Parables of the Kingdom.* New York: Scribner's, 1961.

Dodds, E. R. *The Greeks and the Irrational.* Berkeley: University of California Press, 1968.

Donahue, John F. "Toward a Typology of Roman Public Feasting." *American Journal of Philology* 124 (2003): 423–41.

Donahue, John R. "Tax Collectors and Sinners: An Attempt at Identification." *Catholic Biblical Quarterly* 33 (1971): 39–60.

Dothan, T. "A Female Mourner Figure from the Lachish Region." *Eretz-Israel* 9 (1966): 43–47.

Douglas, Mary. *Purity and Danger: An Analysis of the Concepts of Pollution and Taboo.* London: Routledge, 1966.

Downing, F. Gerald. "*A Bas Les Aristos*: The Relevance of Higher Literature for the Understanding of Earliest Christian Writings." *Novum Testamentum* 30 (1988): 212–30.

————. *Christ and the Cynics.* Sheffield: Sheffield Academic Press, 1988.

————. *Jesus and the Threat of Freedom.* London: SCM, 1987.

————. "The Woman from Syro-Phoenicia and Her Doggedness: Mark 7:24-31 [Matthew 15:21-28]." In *Women in the Biblical Tradition,* 129–49. Edited by George J. Brooke. Lewiston; Queenston; Lampeter: Edwin Mellen, 1992.

Draper, Jonathan. "Torah and Troublesome Apostles in the Didache Community." *Novum Testamentum* 33 (1991): 347–72.

————. "Recovering Oral Performance from Written Text in Q." In *Whoever Hears You Hears Me: Prophets, Performance and Tradition in Q,* 29–45. Edited by R. A. Horsley and J. A. Draper. Harrisburg, Pa., 1999.

————. "Wandering Charismatics and Scholarly Circularities." In *Whoever Hears You Hears Me: Prophets, Performance and Tradition in Q,* 175–94. Edited by R. A. Horsley and J. A. Draper. Harrisburg, Pa., 1999.

Droge, Arthur J., and James D. Tabor. *A Noble Death: Suicide and Martyrdom among Christians and Jews in Antiquity.* San Francisco: HarperCollins, 1992.

Dufton, Francis. "The Syro-Phoenician Woman and Her Dogs." *Expository Times* 100 (1989): 417.

Dunn, James D. G. "Pharisees, Sinners and Jesus." In *The Social World of Formative Christianity and Judaism: Essays in Tribute to Howard Clark Kee*, 264–89. Edited by Jacob Neusner et al. Philadelphia: Fortress Press, 1988.

Durber, Susan. "The Female Reader of the Parables of the Lost." *Journal for the Study of the New Testament* 45 (1992): 59–78.

Edwards, R. B. "Woman." *International Standard Bible Encyclopedia*, vol. 4, 1089–97. Grand Rapids: Eerdmans, 1988.

Edwards, Douglas. "The Socio-Economic and Cultural Ethos of the Lower Galilee in the First Century: Implications for the Nascent Jesus Movement." In *The Galilee in Late Antiquity*, 53–73. Edited by Lee I. Levine. New York and Jerusalem: Jewish Theological Seminary of America; Cambridge, Mass.: Harvard University Press, 1992.

Ehrenreich, Barbara. "A Term of Honor." *Time,* January 23, 1995, 64.

Eitrem, S. "The Necromancy in the Persai of Aischylos." *Symbolae Osloenses* 6 (1928): 1–6.

Elder, Linda Bennett. "The Woman Question and Female Ascetics among Essenes." *Biblical Archaeologist* 57:4 (1994): 220–34.

Elderkin, G. W. "Architechtural Detail in Antique Sepulchral Art." *American Journal of Archaeology* 39 (1935): 518–25.

Elliott, J. K. "The Anointing of Jesus." *Expository Times* 85 (1973-74): 105–07.

Ellis, E. Earle. *The Gospel of Luke*. London; Edinburgh: Thomas Nelson, 1966.

Ellis, Ieuan. "Jesus and the Subversive Family." *Scottish Journal of Theology* 38 (1985): 173–88.

Esterline, David. "Jesus and the Woman. Luke 7:26-50." *Pacific Journal of Theology* 7 (1992): 64–68.

Evans, C. F. *Resurrection and the New Testament*. London: SCM, 1970.

Farmer, William R. *The Last Twelve Verses of Mark*. Cambridge: Cambridge University Press, 1974.

———. "Who Are the 'Tax Collectors and Sinners' in the Synoptic Tradition?" In *From Faith to Faith. Essays in Honor of Donald G. Miller on His 70th Birthday*, 167–74. Edited by D. Y. Hadidan. Pittsburgh: Pickwick, 1979.

Faulkner, Raymond O. "The Bremner-Rhind Papyrus—I." *Journal of Egyptian Archaeology* 22 (1936): 121–40.

———. "The Lamentations of Isis and Nephthys." *Memoires publiées par l'Institut francais d'archéologie oriental du Caire* 66 = *Mélanges Maspero*, 1 (1934): 337–48.

———. *The Papyrus Bremner-Rhind*. Bruxelles: Édition de la fondation égyptologique reine Élisabeth, 1933.

Faxon, Alicia Craig. *Women and Jesus*. Philadelphia: United Church Press, 1973.

Feldman, Emanuel. *Biblical and Post-Biblical Defilement and Mourning: Law as Theology*. New York: Yeshiva University Press, KTAV, 1977.

Feldman, Louis H. "How Much Hellenism in Palestine?" *Hebrew Union College Annual* 57 (1986): 83–111.

Feldmeth, Heather Nicole. "In a Face of a Thousand Sorrows: The Seven Joys of the Virgin." B.A. thesis. Harvard University Press, 1994.

Filoramo, Giovanni. *A History of Gnosticism.* Translated by Anthony Alcock. Oxford: Basil Blackwell, 1991.

Finegan, Jack. *The Archaeology of the New Testament.* Princeton, N.J.: Princeton University Press, 1992.

Finkel, Irving L. "Necromancy in Ancient Mesopotamia." *Archiv für Orientforschung* 29–30 (1983-84): 1–17.

Fishwick, Duncan. "The Talpioth Ossuaries Again." *New Testament Studies* 10 (1963-64): 49–61.

Fitzmyer, Joseph A. "Crucifixion in Ancient Palestine, Qumran Literature, and the New Testament." *Catholic Biblical Quarterly* 40 (1978): 493–513.

———. "Did Jesus Speak Greek?" *Biblical Archaeology Review* 18, no. 5 (1992): 58–63, 76–77.

———. "Divorce Among First-Century Palestinian Jews." *Eretz-Israel* 14 (1978): 103–10.

———. *The Gospel according to Luke.* 2 vols. Garden City, N.Y.: Doubleday, 1981–85.

———. "The Matthean Divorce Texts and Some New Palestinian Evidence." *Theological Studies* 37 (1976): 197–226.

———. "The Story of the Dishonest Manager (Luke 16:1-3)." In *Essays on the Semitic Background of the New Testament,* 161–84. Missoula, Mont.: Scholars Press, 1974.

Flammer, Barnabas. "Die Syro-Phoenizerin: Mark 7:24-30." *Theologische Quartalschrift* 148 (1968): 463–78.

Flanagan, Neal M. "The Position of Women in the Writings of St. Luke." *Marianum* 40 (1978): 288–304.

Flesher, Paul Virgil McCracken. *Oxen, Women, or Citizens? Slaves in the System of the Mishnah.* Atlanta: Scholars Press, 1988.

Flusser, D. "Paganism in Palestine," In *The Jewish People of the First Century,* vol. 2, 1065-1100. Edited by S. Safrai et al. Assen/Maastricht: Van Gorcum; Philadelphia: Fortress Press, 1987.

Foley, Helene P. "The Politics of Tragic Lamentation." In *Tragedy, Comedy, and the Polis: Papers from the Greek Drama Conference, Nottingham 18–20 July 1990,* 101–43. Edited by A. M. Sommerstein et al. Bari: Levante, 1993.

Ford, J. Massyingbaerde, "The Crucifixion of Women in Antiquity." *Journal of Higher Criticism* 3 (1996): 291–309.

Fortna, Robert T. "Chistology in the Fourth Gospel: Redaction-Critical Perspectives." *New Testament Studies* (1975): 489–504.

———. *The Fourth Gospel and Its Predecessor.* Minneapolis: Fortress Press, 1988.

Fowl, Stephen. "Receiving the Kingdom of God as a Child: Children and Riches in Luke 18:15ff." *New Testament Studies* 39 (1993): 153–58.

Frader, Laura Levine. *Peasant Protest: Agricultural Workers, Politics and Unions in the Aude, 1850–1914.* Berkeley; Los Angeles; Oxford: University of California Press, 1991.

Fredriksen, Paula. "Did Jesus Oppose the Purity Laws?" *Bible Review* 11, no. 3 (June 1995): 18–25, 42–45.

————. *From Jesus to Christ: The Origins of the New Testament Images of Jesus.* New Haven, Conn., and London: Yale University Press, 1988.

Freyne, Seán. *Galilee, Jesus and the Gospels: Literary Approaches and Historical Investigations.* Philadelphia: Fortress Press, 1988.

————. "The Geography, Politics, and Economics of Galilee and the Quest for the Historical Jesus." In *Studying the Historical Jesus: Evaluations of the State of Current Research,* 75–121. Edited by Bruce Chilton and Craig Evans. Leiden and New York: Brill, 1994.

————. "Urban-Rural Relations in First-Century Galilee: Some Suggestions from the Literary Sources." In *The Galilee in Late Antiquity,* 75–91. Edited by Lee I. Levine. New York and Jerusalem: Jewish Theological Seminary of America; Cambridge, Mass.: Harvard University Press, 1992.

Fuller, Reginald H. *The Formation of the Resurrection Narratives.* Philadelphia: Fortress Press, 1980.

Funk, Robert. *Honest to Jesus: Jesus for a New Millennium.* San Francisco: HarperSanFrancisco, 1996.

————. *Parables and Presence: Forms of the New Testament Tradition.* Philadelphia: Fortress Press, 1982.

———— et al. *The Parables of Jesus: Red Letter Edition.* Sonoma, Calif.: Polebridge, 1988.

Funk, Robert, Roy Hoover, and the Jesus Seminar. *The Five Gospels: The Search for the Authentic Words of Jesus.* New York: Macmillan, 1993.

Gager, John G. *Moses in Greco-Roman Paganism.* New York: Abingdon, 1972.

Gallagher, Eugene V. *Divine Man or Magician? Celsus and Origen on Jesus.* Chico, Calif.: Scholars Press, 1982.

Garlan, Yvon. *Slavery in Ancient Greece.* Translated by Janet Lloyd. Ithaca and London: Cornell University Press, 1988.

Garland, Robert. *The Greek Way of Death.* Ithaca, N.Y.: Cornell University Press, 1985.

————. "The Well-Ordered Corpse: An Investigation into the Motives behind Greek Funerary Legislation." *Bulletin of the Institute for Classical Studies* 36 (1989): 1–15.

Garrow, Alan J. P. *The Gospel of Matthew's Dependence on the Didache.* London and New York: T. and T. Clark, 2004.

Gasparro, G. Sfameni. *Soteriology and Mystic Aspects in the Cult of Attis and Cybele.* Leiden: Brill, 1985.

Gedo, John E. *The Artist and the Emotional World.* New York: Columbia University Press, 1996.

————. *Portraits of the Artist: Psychoanalysis of Creativity and Its Vicissitudes.* New York and London: Guilford Press, 1983.

Gibbs, John G. and Louis H. Feldman, "Josephus' Vocabulary for Slavery." *Jewish Quarterly Review* 76 (1986): 281–310.

Gibson, J. "*Hoi Telōnai kai hai Pornai.*" *Journal of Theological Studies* 32 (1981): 429–33.

Gillian, J. F. "Invitations to the *Kline* of Sarapis." In *Collectanea Papyrologica. Texts Published in Honor of H. C. Young*, pt. 1, 315–24. Edited by Ann Ellis Hanson. Bonn: Rudolf Habelt, 1976.

Goitein, S. D. "Women as Creators of Biblical Genres." *Prooftexts* 8, no. 1 (1988): 1–33.

Golden, Mark. "Chasing Change in Roman Childhood." *Ancient History Bulletin* 4 (1990): 90–94.

———. "*Pais*, 'Child' and 'Slave.'" *L' antique classique* 54 (1985): 91–104.

Goldman, Bernard. *The Sacred Portal. A Primary Symbol in Ancient Judaic Art.* Detroit: Wayne State University Press, 1966.

Goodenough, Erwin R. "Contents of Jewish Tombs in Palestine." In *Jewish Symbols in the Greco-Roman Period*, vol. 1, 103–39. New York: Pantheon, 1953.

———. *Jewish Symbols in the Greco-Roman Period.* 13 vols. New York: Pantheon, 1953.

Goodman, Martin. "The First Jewish Revolt: Social Conflict and the Problem of Debt." *Journal of Jewish Studies* 33 (1982): 417–27.

———. *The Ruling Class of Judea: The Origins of the Jewish Revolt against Rome A.D. 66–70.* Cambridge: Cambridge University Press, 1987.

Grabar, André. *The Beginnings of Christian Art 200–395.* Translated by Stuart Gilbert and James Emmons. London: Thames and Hudson, 1967.

Grant, Jacquelyn. *White Woman's Christ, Black Woman's Jesus: Feminist Christology and Womanist Responses.* Atlanta: Scholars Press, 1989.

Grassi, Joseph A. *Hidden Heroes of the Gospels: Female Counterparts of Jesus.* Collegeville, Minn.: Liturgical, 1989.

———. "The Secret Heroine of Mark's Drama." *Biblical Theology Bulletin* 18 (1988): 10–15.

Greeley. Andrew M. "Domestic Violence: One Strike and You're Out." *The Press Democrat.* July 9, 1994, D4.

Green, Joel B. *The Death of Jesus: Tradition and Interpretation in the Passion Narrative.* Tübingen: J. C. B. Mohr, 1988.

———. "Good News to Whom? Jesus and the 'Poor' in the Gospel of Luke." In *Jesus of Nazareth: Lord and Christ*, 54–74. Edited by J. B. Green and M. Turner. Grand Rapids: Eerdmans, 1994.

Greenhut, Zvi. "Burial Cave of the Caiaphas Family." *Biblical Archaeology Review* 18, no. 5 (1992): 29–36.

Griffiths, Frederick T. "Home before Lunch: The Emancipated Woman in Theocritus." In *Reflections of Women in Antiquity*, 247–73. Edited by H. P. Foley. New York: Gordon and Breach, 1981.

Griffiths, J. Gwyn. *Plutarch's De Iside et Osiride.* Cardiff: University of Wales Press, 1970.

Grimby, "Bereavement among Elderly People: Grief Reactions, Post-bereavement Hallucinations and Quality of Life." *Acta Psychiatrica Scandinavia* 87 (1993): 72–80.

Grossman, Susan. "Women and the Jerusalem Temple." In *Daughters of the King: Women and the Synagogue*, 15–37. Edited by Susan Grossman and Rivka Hunt. Philadelphia; New York; Jerusalem: Jewish Publication Society, 1992.

Guelich, Robert A. *Mark 1–8:26*. Word Biblical Commentary 34. Dallas: Word, 1989.

Guenther, Heinz, O. "When 'Eagles' Draw Together." *Forum* 5 (1989): 140–50.

Gundry, Robert H. "The Language of First-Century Palestine: Its Bearing on the Authenticity of the Gospel Tradition." *Journal of Biblical Literature* 83 (1964): 404–8.

————. *Mark: A Commentary on His Apology for the Cross*. Grand Rapids: Eerdmans, 1993.

————. *Matthew: A Commentary on His Literary and Theological Art*. Grand Rapids: Eerdmans, 1982.

Gundry-Volf, Judy. "Spirit, Mercy and the Other." *Theology Today* 51 (1995): 508–23.

Gustafsson, Berndt. "The Oldest Graffiti in the History of the Church?" *New Testament Studies* 3 (1956–57): 65–69.

Haas, N. "Anthropological Observations of the Skeletal Remains from Giv'at ha-Mivtar." *Israel Exploration Journal* 20 (1970): 38–59.

Hachlili, R. "Ancient Burial Customs Preserved in the Jericho Hills." *Biblical Archaeology Review* 5, no. 4 (1979): 28–35.

————. *Ancient Jewish Art and Archaeology of Israel*. Leiden: Brill, 1988.

Hadas, Moses, and Morton Smith. *Heroes and Gods: Spiritual Biographies in Antiquity*. New York: Harper and Row, 1965.

Haenchen, Ernst. *John*. 2 vols. Philadelphia: Fortress Press, 1984.

Hagner, Donald. *The Jewish Reclamation of Jesus: An Analysis and Critique of the Modern Jewish Study of Jesus*. Grand Rapids: Zondervan, 1984.

Halliday, W. R. "Cenotaphs and Sacred Localities." *Annual of the British School at Athens* 17 (1910–11): 182–92.

Hamel, Gilda. *Poverty and Charity in Roman Palestine, First Three Centuries C.E.* Berkeley; Los Angeles; Oxford: University of California Press, 1990.

Hammerton-Kelly, Robert. "God the Father in the Bible and in the Experience of Jesus: The State of the Question." In *God as Father?* 95–102. Edited by Johannes-Baptist Metz and Edward Schillebeeckx. Edinburgh: T. and T. Clark; New York: Seabury, 1981.

————. *God the Father: Theology and Patriarchy in the Teaching of Jesus*. Philadelphia: Fortress Press, 1979.

Hanson, A. T. "Rahab the Harlot in Early Christian Tradition." *Journal for the Study of the New Testament* 1 (1978): 53–60.

Harland, Philip. *Associations, Synagogues and Congregations*. Minneapolis: Fortress Press, 2003.

Hartin, Patrick J. "First Response: Q 7:29-30." Paper presented to the International Q Project. Claremont, Calif., May 1994.

Harvey, Susan Ashbrook. "Women in Early Syrian Christianity." In *Images of Women in Antiquity*, 288–98. Edited by Averil Cameron and Amélie Kuhrt. Detroit: Wayne State University Press, 1983.

Haskins, Susan. *Mary Magdalene: Myth and Metaphor*. New York; San Diego; London: Harcourt Brace, 1993.

Hasler, J. Ireland. "The Incident of the Syro-Phoenician Woman (Matt 15:21-28; Mark 7:24-30)." *Expository Times* 45 (1933–34): 459–61.

Havelock, Christine Mitchell. "Mourners on Greek Vases: Remarks on the Social History of Women." In *The Greek Vase*, 102–65. Edited by Stephen L. Hyatt. Latham, N.Y.: Hudson-Mohawk Assocation of Colleges and Universities, 1981.

Havener, Ivan. *Q: The Sayings of Jesus*. Wilmington, Del.: Michael Glazier, 1987.

Headlam, W. "Ghost Raising Magic and the Underworld." *Classical Review* 16 (1902): 52–61.

Hedrick, Charles W. *Parables as Poetic Fictions: The Creative Voice of Jesus*. Peabody, Mass.: Hendrickson, 1994.

Heichelheim, F. M. *An Economic Survey of Ancient Rome: Roman Syria*. Baltimore: John Hopkins Press, 1938.

Heine, Susan. "Eine Person von Rang und Namen: Historische Konturen der Magdalenerin." In *Jesu Rede von Gott und ihre Nachgeschichte im frühen Christentum: Beiträge zur Verkündigung Jesu und zum Kerygma der Kirche. Festschrift für Willi Marxen zum 70. Geburtstag*, 179–94. Edited by D.-A. Koch et al. Gütersloh: Gütersloher Verlagshaus Gerd Mohn, 1989.

Heinemann, Joseph. "The Status of the Labourer in Jewish Law and Society in the Tannaitic Period." *Hebrew Union College Annual* 25 (1954): 263–325.

Hengel, Martin. *Crucifixion*. Philadelphia: Fortress Press, 1977.

———. *Judaism and Hellenism*. Philadelphia: Fortress Press, 1974.

Herrenbrück, F. "Wer waren die 'Zöllner'?" *Zeitschrift für die neutestamentliche Wissenschaft* 72 (1981): 178–94.

———. "Zum Vorwurf der Kollaboration des Zöllners mit Rom." *Zeitschrift für die neutestamentliche Wissenschaft* 78 (1987): 186–99.

Hertz, Robert. *Death and the Right Hand*. Glencoe, Ill.: Free Press, 1960.

Herzog, William R. *Parables as Subversive Speech: Jesus as Pedagogue of the Oppressed*. Louisville: Westminster John Knox 1994.

Heschel, Susannah. "Anti-Judaism in Christian Feminist Theology." *Tikkun* 5 (1990): 25–28, 95–97.

Heyob, Sharon Kelly. *The Cult of Isis among Women in the Greco-Roman World*. Leiden: Brill, 1975.

Himmelmann, N. *Typologische untersuchungen an römischen Sarkophagareliefs des 3. und 4. Jarhunderts n. Chr.* Mainz: Philipp von Zabern, 1973.

Hock, Ronald F. *The Infancy Gospels of James and Thomas*. Santa Rosa, Calif.: Polebridge, 1995.

———. "The Will of God and Sexual Morality: I Thess. 4:3-8 in Its Social and Intellectual Context." Paper presented at the Society of Biblical Literature Annual Meeting. New York, 1982.

Hoenig, Sidney B. "Oil and Pagan Defilement." *Jewish Quarterly Review* 61 (1970/71): 63–75.

Hoffman, Paul. "Q 7:29-30: Fourth Response." Paper presented to the International Q Project. Claremont, Calif., May 1994.

Holst, Robert. "The One Anointing of Jesus. Another Application of the Form-Critical Method." *Journal of Biblical Literature* 95 (1976): 435–46.

Holst-Warhaft, Gail. *Dangerous Voices: Women's Laments in Greek Literature.* London: Routledge, 1992.

Horsley, G. R. H. "The 'Early Christian' Ossuary Inscriptions from Jerusalem." In *New Documents Illustrating Early Christianity*, vol. 1, 112. Edited by G. R. H. Horsley. Macquarie University: Ancient History Documentary Research Centre, 1981.

———. "Funerary Practice in Hellenistic and Roman Rhodes." In *New Documents Illustrating Early Christianity*, vol. 2, 48–52. Edited by G. R. H. Horsley. Macquarie University: Ancient History Documentary Research Centre, 1982.

———. "Invitation to the *Kline* of Sarapis." In *New Documents Illustrating Early Christianity*, vol. 1, 5–9. Edited by G. R. H. Horsley. Macquarie University: Ancient History Documentary Research Centre, 1981.

———. "*Paidarion.*" In *New Documents Illustrating Early Christianity*, vol. 1, 87. Edited by G. R. H. Horsley. Macquarie University: Ancient History Documentary Research Centre, 1981.

Horsley, Richard A. *Galilee: History, Politics, People.* Valley Forge, Pa.: Trinity Press International, 1995.

———. "The Historical Jesus and Arhcaeology of the Galilee: Questions from Historical Research to Archaeologists." *Society of Biblical Literature 1994 Seminar Papers*, 91–135. Edited by E. H. Lovering. Atlanta: Scholars Press, 1994.

———. *Jesus and the Spiral of Violence: Popular Jewish Resistance in Roman Palestine.* Minneapolis: Fortress Press, 1987.

———. *Sociology and the Jesus Movement.* New York: Continuum, 1994.

———. "Wisdom Is Justified by All Her Children: Examining Allegedly Disparate Traditions in Q." In *Society of Biblical Literature 1994 Seminar Papers*, 733–51. Edited by E. H. Lovering. Atlanta: SBL, 1994.

Humphreys, S. C. "Family Tombs and Tomb-Cult in Ancient Athens: Tradition or Traditionalism? *Journal of Hellenic Studies* 100 (1980): 96–126.

———. *The Family, Women and Death: Comparative Studies.* London: Routledge and Kegan Paul, 1983.

Huntington, Richard, and Peter Metcalf. *Celebrations of Death: The Anthropology of Mortuary Ritual.* Cambridge: Cambridge University Press, 1979.

Ilan, Tal. *Jewish Women in Greco-Roman Palestine: An Inquiry into Image and Status.* Tübingen: J .C. B. Mohr, 1995; reprint, Peabody, Mass.: Hendrickson, 1996.

———. "'Man Born of Woman...' (Job 14:1): The Phenomenon of Men Bearing Metronymes at the Time of Jesus." *Novum Testamentum* 34 (1992): 23–45.

————. "Notes and Observations on a Newly Published Divorce Bill from the Judean Desert." *Harvard Theological Review* 89 (1996): 195–202.

————. "Notes on the Distribution of Jewish Women's Names in Palestine in the Second Temple and Mishnaic Periods." *Journal of Jewish Studies* 40 (1989): 186–200.

Ingram, John Kells. *A History of Slavery and Serfdom.* London: Adam and Charles Black, 1895.

Isaac, Benjamin. "The Babatha Archive: A Review Article." *Israel Exploration Journal* 42 (1992): 62–75.

Jackson, Howard M. "The Death of Jesus in Mark and the Miracle from the Cross." *New Testament Studies* 33 (1987): 16–37.

Jacobs-Malina, Diane. *Beyond Patriarchy: The Images of Family in Jesus.* New York/Mahwah, N.J.: Paulist, 1993.

Jacobsen, Arland. "Divided Families and Christian Origins." In *The Gospel behind the Gospel: Current Studies on Q*, 361–80. Edited by Ronald A. Piper. Leiden: Brill, 1995.

————. *The First Gospel: An Introduction to Q.* Sonoma, Calif.: Polebridge, 1992.

Jacobsen, Thorkild. *Toward the Image of Tammuz and Other Essays on Mesopotamian History and Culture.* Cambridge, Mass.: Harvard University Press, 1970.

————. *The Treasures of Darkness: A History of Mesopotamian Religion.* New Haven, Conn., and London: Yale University Press, 1976.

Jacobsen-Buckley, Jorunn. *Female Fault and Fulfillment in Gnosticism.* Chapel Hill; London: University of North Carolina Press, 1986.

————. "An Interpretation of Logion 114 in the Gospel of Thomas." *Novum Testamentum* 27 (1985): 243–72.

James, M. *The Apocryphal New Testament.* Oxford: Clarendon, 1963.

Japhet, Sara. "The Laws of Manumission of Slaves and the Question of the Relationship between Collections of Laws in the Pentateuch." In *Studies in Bible and the Ancient Near East. Presented to Samuel E. Loewenstamm*, vol. 1, 199–200. Edited by Yitschak Avishur and Joshua Blau. Jerusalem: E. Rubinstein's, 1978.

Jefford, Clayton N. "The Dangers of Lying in Bed: Luke 17:34-35 and Parallels." *Forum* 5 (1990): 106–10.

Jensen, Robin M. "Dining with the Dead: From the Mensa to the Altar in Christian Late Antiquity." In *Commemorating the Dead: Texts and Artifacts in Context*, 197–243. Edited by L. Brink and D. Green. Berlin and New York: Walter de Gruyter, 2008.

Jeremias, Joachim. *Abba. Studien zur neutestamentlischen Theologie und Zeitgeschichte.* Göttingen: Vandenhoeck and Ruprecht, 1966.

————. *The Eucharistic Words of Jesus.* London: SCM, 1966.

————. *Heilingengräber in Jesus Umwelt.* Göttingen: Vandenhoeck and Ruprecht, 1958.

————. *Jerusalem in the Time of Jesus.* Philadelphia: Fortress Press, 1975.

————. *New Testament Theology.* New York: Scribner's, 1971.

————. *The Parables of Jesus*. New York: Scribner's, 1972.

————. *The Prayers of Jesus*. Translated by John Bowden. Naperville, Ill.: Allec Allenson, 1967.

Jewett, Paul K. *Man as Male and Female*. Grand Rapids: Eerdmans, 1975.

Johnson, Benjamin A. "Empty Tomb Tradition in the Gospel of Peter." Ph.D. thesis. Cambridge, Mass.: Harvard University, 1965.

Johnson, Elizabeth A. *Consider Jesus: Waves of Renewal in Christology*. New York: Crossroad, 1995.

————. "Jesus the Wisdom of God: A Biblical Basis for Non-Androcentric Christology." *Ephemerides Theologicae Lovanienses* 61 (1985): 261–94.

————. "Redeeming the Name of Christ: Christology." In *Freeing Theology: The Essentials of Theology in Feminist Perspective*, 115–37. Edited by Catherine Mowry Lacugna. San Francisco: HarperSanFrancisco, 1993.

————. "Wisdom Was Made Flesh and Pitched Her Tent among Us." In *Reconstructing the Christ: Essays in Feminist Christology*, 95–117. Edited by Maryanne Stevens. New York; Mahwah, N.J.: Paulist, 1993.

Johnson, Elizabeth L. "Grieving for the Dead, Grieving for the Living: Funeral Laments of Hakka Women." In *Death Ritual in Late Imperial and Modern China*, 135–63. Edited by James L. Watson and Evelyn S. Rawski. Berkeley; Los Angeles; London: University of California Press, 1988.

Johnson, Luke T. *The Literary Function of Possessions in Luke-Acts*. Chico, Calif.: Scholars Press, 1977.

————. "The New Testament's Anti-Jewish Slander and the Conventions of Ancient Polemic." *Journal of Biblical Literature* 108 (1989): 419–41.

Johnson, Sherman E. "Greek and Jewish Heroes: Fourth Maccabees and the Gospel of Mark." In *Early Christian Literature and the Classical Intellectual Tradition*, 155–75. Edited by W. R. Schoedel and R. L. Wilken. Paris: Éditions Beauchesne, 1979.

Johnson, Steven R. "Second Response: Q 7:29-30." Paper presented to the International Q Project. Claremont, Calif., May 1994.

Jones, A. H. M. "Slavery in the Ancient World." In *Slavery in Classical Antiquity*. Edited by M. I. Finley. Cambridge: W. Heffer and Sons, 1960.

Judge, E. A. "The Early Christians as a Scholastic Community." *Journal of Religious History* 1 (1960): 4–15.

Jungmann, Josef A. *The Early Liturgy to the Time of Gregory the Great*. Translated by F. A. Brunner. Notre Dame, Ind.: Notre Dame University Press, 1959.

Just, Arthur A. *The Ongoing Feast: Table Fellowship and Eschatology at Emmaus*. Collegeville, Minn.: The Liturgical Press, 1993.

Kam, Rose Sallberg. *Their Stories, Our Stories: Women of the Bible*. New York: Continuum, 1995.

Kampen, Natalie. *Image and Status: Roman Working Women in Ostia*. Berlin: Gebr. Mann, 1981.

Kane, J. P. "By No Means the 'Earliest Records of Christianity' with an Emended Reading of the Talpioth Inscription *Iesous Oui*." *Palestine Exploration Quarterly* 103 (1971): 103–08.

Kearsley, R. A. "The Goliath Family at Jericho." *New Documents Illustrating Early Christianity*, vol. 6, 162–64. Edited by S. R. Llewelyn and R. A. Kearsley. Macquarie University: Ancient History Documentary Research Centre, 1992.

Kee, Howard Clark. "Aretalogy and Gospel." *Journal of Biblical Literature* 92 (1972): 402–22.

———. "The Changing Role of Women in the Early Christian World." *Theology Today* 49 (1992): 225–38.

———. *Community of the New Age: Studies in Mark's Gospel*. Philadelphia: Westminster Press, 1977.

———. *Miracle in the Early Christian World. A Study in Sociohistorical Method*. New Haven, Conn., and London: Yale University Press, 1983.

Kelber, Werner H. *The Passion in Mark: Studies on Mark 14-16*. Philadelphia: Fortress Press, 1976.

Kelsey, Neal. "A Barking Baptist? An Appraisal of the Cynic Hypothesis." Paper presented to the New Testament Seminar. Claremont, Calif., May 3, 1994.

Kennedy, Charles A. "Cult of the Dead." *Anchor Bible Dictionary*, vol. 2, 106. New York: Doubleday, 1992.

———. "The Cult of the Dead in Corinth." In *Love and Death in the Ancient Near East. Essays in Honor of Marvin H. Pope*, 227–36. Edited by John H. Marks and Robert M. Good. Guilford, Conn.: Four Quarters, 1987.

Kerns, Virginia. "Garifuna Women and the Work of Mourning." In *Unspoken Worlds: Women's Religious Lives*, 93–101. Edited by Nancy Auer Falk and Rita M. Gross. Belmont, Calif.: Wadsworth, 1989.

———. *Women and the Ancestors. Black Carib Kinship and Ritual*. Urbana; Chicago; London: University of Illinois Press, 1983.

Keuls, Eva C. *The Reign of the Phallus; Sexual Politics in Ancient Athens*. New York: Harper and Row, 1985.

Kilgallen, John J. "John the Baptist, the Sinful Woman and the Pharisee." *Journal of Biblical Literature* 104 (1985): 675–79.

King, Karen L. "The Gospel of Mary Magdalene." In *Searching the Scriptures*, vol. 2, 601–34. Edited by Elisabeth Schüssler Fiorenza. New York: Crossroad, 1994.

———. "The Kingdom of God in the Gospel of Thomas." *Forum* 3 (1987): 48–97.

Kingsbury, Jack D. *The Christology of Mark's Gospel*. Philadelphia: Fortress Press, 1983.

———. "The Title 'Son of David' in Matthew's Gospel." *Journal of Biblical Literature* 95 (1976): 591–602.

Kinukawa, Hisako. *Women and Jesus in Mark: A Japanese Feminist Perspective*. Maryknoll, N.Y.: Orbis, 1994.

Klassen, William. "Musonius Rufus, Jesus and Paul: Three First Century Feminists?" In *From Jesus to Paul. Studies in Honor of Francis Wright Beare*,

185–206. Edited by P. Richardson and J. Hurd. Ontario: Wilfred Laurier University Press, 1984.

Klijn, A. F. J. "The 'Single One' in the Gospel of Thomas." *Journal of Biblical Literature* 81 (1962): 271–78.

Kloppenborg, John S. "Alms, Debt and Divorce: Jesus' Ethics in Their Mediterranean Context." *Toronto Journal of Theology* 6 (1990): 182–200.

————. "The Dishonored Manager." *Biblica* 70 (1989): 474–95.

————. "*Exitus clari viri*: The Death of Jesus in Luke." *Toronto Journal of Theology* 8 (1992): 106–20.

————. *The Formation of Q: Trajectories in Ancient Wisdom Collections.* Philadelphia: Fortress Press, 1987.

————. "Literary Convention, Self-Evidence and the Social History of the Q People." *Semeia* 55 (1991): 77–102.

————. *Q Parallels.* Sonoma, Calif.: Polebridge, 1988.

———— et al. *A Q-Thomas Reader.* Sonoma, Calif.: Polebridge, 1990.

————. "The Sayings Gospel Q: Recent Opinion on the People behind the Document." *Currents in Research* 1 (1993): 9–34.

————. "Symbolic Eschatology and the Apocalypticism of Q." *Harvard Theological Review* 80 (1987): 287–306.

————. "Wisdom Christology in Q." *Laval théologique et philosophique* 34 (1978): 129–37.

————, and Stephen Wilson, Edited by *Voluntary Associationa in the Graeco-Roman World.* London and New York: Routledge, 1996.

Klosinski, Lee. "Meals in Mark." Ph.D. dissertation, Claremont Graduate School, 1988.

Knowles, Michael. *Jeremiah in Matthew's Gospel: The Rejected-Prophet Motif in Matthean Redaction.* Sheffield: JSOT Press, 1993.

Knox, W. L. "The 'Divine Hero' Christology in the New Testament." *Harvard Theological Review* 41 (1948): 229–49.

Koester, Helmut. *Ancient Christian Gospels.* Philadelphia: Trinity Press International; London: SCM, 1990.

————. "One Jesus and Four Primitive Gospels." *Harvard Theological Review* 61 (1968): 203–47.

Kopas, Jane. "Jesus and Women in Mark's Gospel." *Review for Religious* 44 (1985): 912–20.

Kraeling, Carl H. "Christian Burial Urns?" *Biblical Archaeologist* 9 (1946): 16–20.

Kraemer, Ross. "The Conversion of Women to Ascetic Forms of Christianity." *Signs* 6 (1980): 298–307.

————. *Her Share of the Blessings: Women's Religions among Pagans, Jews and Christians in the Greco-Roman World.* New York and Oxford: Oxford University Press, 1992.

————. "Jewish Mothers and Daughters in the Greco-Roman World." In *The Jewish Family in Antiquity,* 89–112. Edited by Shaye J. D. Cohen. Atlanta: Scholars Press, 1993.

————. "Monastic Jewish Women in Graeco-Roman Egypt: Philo Judaeus on the Therapeutrides." *Signs* 14 (1989): 342–70.

————. "Review: Elisabeth Schüssler Fiorenza, *In Memory of Her.*" *Religious Studies Review* 11 (1985): 1–9.

Kramer, Samuel Noah. "BM 98396: A Sumerian Prototype of the *Mater-Dolorosa.*" *Eretz-Israel* 16 (1982): 141–46.

————. "The Weeping Goddess: Sumerian Prototypes of the *Mater Dolorosa.*" *Biblical Archaeologist* 46 (Spring, 1983): 69–80.

Kugelmass, Jack. "Undser Shtik: The Meaning of Humor for American Jews." Paper presented to the Institute for Research in the Humanities Seminar. University of Wisconsin-Madison, Spring 1996.

Kurtz, Donna C. and John Boardman. *Greek Burial Customs.* Ithaca, N.Y.: Cornell University Press, 1971.

Lachs, Samuel Tobias. *A Rabbinic Commentary on the New Testament: The Gospels Matthew, Mark and Luke.* Hoboken, N.J.: KTAV; New York: Anti-defamation League of B'nai B'rith, 1987.

Laffey, Alice L. *An Introduction to the Old Testament: A Feminist Perspective.* Philadelphia: Fortress Press, 1988.

Lagrand, James. "How Was the Virgin Mary 'Like a Man'? A Note on Mt 1:18b and Related Syriac Christian Texts." *Novum Testamentum* 22 (1980): 97–107.

Larson, Jennifer. *Greek Heroine Cults.* Madison, Wisc.: University of Wisconsin Press, 1995.

LaSor, William Sanford. "Discovering What Jewish Miqva'ot Can Tell Us about Christian Baptism." *Biblical Archaeology Review* 13 (January/February 1987): 52–59.

Lassner, Jacob. *Demonizing the Queen of Sheba: Boundaries of Gender and Culture in Postbiblical Judaism and Medieval Islam.* Chicago: University of Chicago Press, 1993.

Lattimore, Richard. *Themes in Greek and Latin Epitaphs.* Urbana: University of Illinois Press, 1942.

Lawson, J. C. "The Evocation of Darius." *Classical Quarterly* 28 (1934): 79–89.

Layton, Bentley. *The Gnostic Scriptures.* Garden City, N.Y.: Doubleday, 1987.

Legault, André. "An Application of the Form-Critical Method to the Anointings in Galilee (Lk 7, 36–50), and Bethany (Mt 26, 6–13, Mk 14, 3–9; Jn 12, 1–8)." *Catholic Biblical Quarterly* 16 (1954): 131–45.

Lemche, N. P. "The 'Hebrew Slave.'" *Vetus Testamentum* 25 (1975): 129–44.

————. "The Manumission of Slaves—The Fallow Year—The Sabbatical Year—The Jobel Year." *Vetus Testamentum* 26 (1976): 38–59.

Lenski, Gerhard E. *Power and Privilege. A Theory of Social Stratification.* New York; St. Louis; San Francisco: McGraw-Hill, 1966.

Levi, Peter. *The Lamentation of the Dead with the Lament of Arthur O' Leary by Eileen O Connell.* Translated by Eilis Dillon. London. Annual Press Poetry, 1984.

Levin, Saul. "The Early History of Christianity in Light of the Secret Gospel of Mark." *Aufstieg und Niedergang der römischen Welt* II.25, 4270-92. Edited by W. Haase. Berlin and New York: Walter de Gruyter, 1988.

Levine, Amy-Jill. "Lilies of the Field and Wandering Jews: Biblical Scholarship, Women's Roles and Social Location." I. R. Kitzberger, ed. *Transformative Encounters: Jesus and Women Re-viewed*. Leiden: Brill, forthcoming.

————. "Matthew." In *The Woman's Bible Commentary*, 252–62. Edited by Carol A. Newsom and Sharon H. Ringe. Louisville: Westminster John Knox, 1992.

————. "Response by Levine to L. Swidler." *Journal of Ecumenical Studies* 26 (1989): 720–21.

————. "Review: L. Swidler, *Yeshua: A Modern for Moderns*." *Journal of Ecumenical Studies* 26 (1989): 535–36.

————. "Sacrifice and Salvation: Otherness and Dosmestication in the Book of Judith." In *"No One Spoke Ill of Her": Essays on Judith*, 17–30. Edited by James C. VanderKam. Atlanta: Scholars Press, 1992.

————. "Second Temple Judaism, Jesus and Women: Yeast of Eden." *Biblical Interpretation* 2 (1994): 8–33.

————. *The Social and Ethnic Dimensions of Matthean Salvation History*. Lewiston; Queenston; Lampeter: Edwin Mellen, 1988.

————. "Who's Catering the Q Affair? Feminist Observations on Q Parenesis." *Semeia* 50 (1990): 145–62.

————, ed. *"Women Like This": New Perspectives on Jewish Women in the Graeco-Roman World*. Atlanta: Scholars Press, 1991.

Lewis, Naphtali, and Meyer Reinhold. *Roman Civilization: Selected Readings with an Introduction and Notes*, vol. 2. New York: Columbia University Press, 1955.

Lewis, Theodore J. *Cults of the Dead in Ancient Israel and Ugarit*. Atlanta, Ga.: Scholars Press, 1989.

Licht, Hans. *Sexual Life in Ancient Greece*. New York: Barnes and Noble, 1953.

Liebermann, Saul. *Greek in Jewish Palestine: Studies in the Life and Manners of Jewish Palestine in the II–IV Centuries C.E.* New York: Jewish Theological Seminary of America, 1942.

Lifshitz, Baruch. "Notes d'épigraphie palestinienne." *Revue biblique* 73 (1966): 248–57.

Lindars, Barnabas. *The Gospel of John*. London: Oliphants, 1972.

Lindsay, Hugh. "Eating with the Dead: The Roman Funerary Banquet." In *Meals in a Social Context: Aspects of the Communal Meal in the Hellenistic and Roman World*, 67–80. Edited by I. Nielson and H. S. Nielson. Oxford: Arthus University Press, 1998.

Linnemann, Eta. *Parables of Jesus: Introduction and Exposition*. London: SPCK, 1982.

Linton, Olaf. "The Parable of the Children's Game." *New Testament Studies* 22 (1976): 159–79.

Lipinski, E. "The Wife's Right to Divorce in Light of An Ancient Near Eastern Tradition." *Jewish Law Annual* 4 (1981): 9–27.

Llewelyn, S. R. "The Sale of a Slave-Girl: The New Testament's Attitude to Slavery." In *New Documents Illustrating Early Christianity*, vol. 6, 48–55. Edited by S. R. Llewelyn. Macquarie University, Australia: Ancient Documentary Research Centre, 1992.

———. "A Petition Concerning a Runaway: Paul's Letter to Philemon." In *New Documents Illustrating Early Christianity*, vol. 6, 55–60. Edited by S. R. Llewelyn. Macquarie University, Australia: Ancient Documentary Research Centre, 1992.

Loraux, Nicole. *The Experience of Tiresias: The Feminine and the Greek Man.* Princeton, N.J.: Princeton University Press, 1995.

———. "Herakles: The Supermale and the Feminine." In *Before Sexuality: The Construction of Erotic Experience in the Ancient Greek World*, 21–52. Edited by D. M. Halperin et al. Princeton, N.J.: Princeton University Press, 1990.

———. *The Invention of Athens: The Funeral Oration in the Classical City.* Cambridge, Mass.: Harvard University Press, 1986.

———. *Tragic Ways of Killing a Woman.* Cambridge, Mass.: Harvard University Press, 1987.

Luck, Georg. *Arcana Mundi: Magic and the Occult in the Greek and Roman Worlds.* Baltimore and London: Johns Hopkins University Press, 1985.

Luck, William F. *Divorce and Remarriage: Recovering the Biblical View.* San Francisco: Harper and Row, 1987.

Lüdemann, Gerd. *The Resurrection of Jesus: History, Experience, Theology.* Minneapolis: Fortress Press, 1994.

MacHaffie, Barbara J. *Her Story: Women in Christian Tradition.* Philadelphia: Fortress Press, 1986.

Mack, Burton L. "The Anointing of Jesus: Elaboration within a Chreia." In *Patterns of Persuasion in the Gospels*, 85–106. Burton L. Mack and Vernon K. Robbins. Sonoma, Calif.: Polebridge, 1989.

———. "The Kingdom That Didn't Come: Social History of the Q Tradents." In *Society of Biblical Literature 1988 Seminar Papers*, 608–35. Edited by David Lull. Atlanta: Scholars Press, 1988.

———. *The Lost Gospel: The Book of Q and Christian Origins.* San Francisco: HarperSanFrancisco, 1993.

———. *A Myth of Innocence: Mark and Christian Origins.* Minneapolis: Fortress Press, 1988.

———. *Who Wrote the New Testament? The Making of the Christian Myth.* San Francisco: HarperSanFrancisco, 1995.

MacMullen, Ramsey. *The Second Church: Popular Christianity AD 200–400.* Atlanta: Scholars Press, 2009.

MacNamara, E. A. "The Syro-Phoenican Woman." *American Ecclesiastical Review* 127 (1952): 360–69.

Malbon, Elizabeth Struthers. "Fallible Followers: Women and Men in the Gospel of Mark." *Semeia* 28 (1983): 29–48.

———. *Narrative Space and Mythic Meaning in Mark.* San Francisco: Harper and Row, 1986.

Malcolm, Kari Torjesen. *Women at the Crossroads.* Downers Grove, Ill.: Inter-Varsity, 1982.

Malina, Bruce J., and Richard Rohrbaugh. *Social Science Commentary on the Synoptic Gospels.* Minneapolis: Fortress Press, 1992.

Maly, Eugene H. "Women in the Gospel of Luke." *Biblical Theology Bulletin* 10 (1980): 99–104.

Manning, C. E. "Stoicism and Slavery in the Roman Empire." *Aufstieg und Niedergang der römischen Welt.* II.36, 1518–43. Edited by W. Haase. Berlin and New York: Walter de Gruyter, 1989.

Matera, Frank J. *The Kingship of Jesus: Composition and Theology in Mark 15.* Chico, Calif.: Scholars Press, 1982.

Martin, Dale B. "Slavery and the Ancient Jewish Family in Antiquity." In *The Jewish Family in Antiquity,* 113–29. Edited by Shaye J. D. Cohen. Atlanta, Ga.: Scholars Press, 1993.

Martin, Hubert, Jr., and Jane E. Phillips. "*Consolatio ad Uxorem* (Moralia 608A–612B)." In *Plutarch's Ethical Writings and Early Christian Literature,* 394–441. Edited by Hans Dieter Betz. Leiden: Brill, 1978.

Massey, Lesly F. *Women and the New Testament.* Jefferson, N.C., and London: McFarland, 1989.

Masten, B. A. "Chalcolithic Ossuaries and 'Houses for the Dead.'" *Palestine Exploration Quarterly* 97 (1965): 153–60.

Matera, Frank J. *The Kingship of Jesus: Composition and Theology in Mark 15.* Chico, Calif.: Scholars Press, 1982.

Maunder, C. J. "A Sitz im Leben for Mark 14:9." *Expository Times* 99 (1987): 78–80.

Mayer, Günter. *Die jüdische Frau in der hellenistisch-römischen Antike.* Stuttgart; Berlin; Köln; Mainz: W. Kolhammer, 1987.

McArthur, Harvey. "On the Third Day." *New Testament Studies* 18 (1971–72): 81–86.

———. "Son of Mary." *Novum Testamentum* 15 (1973): 38–58.

McCane, Byron R. "Jews, Christians and Burial in Roman Palestine." Ph.D. dissertation. Duke University, 1992.

———. "Let the Dead Bury Their Own Dead: Secondary Burial and Matt 8:21-22." *Harvard Theological Review* 83 (1990): 31–43.

———. "Where No One Had Yet Been Laid: The Shame of Jesus' Burial." *Society of Biblical Literature 1993 Seminar Papers,* 473–84. Edited by by E. H. Lovering. Atlanta: Scholars Press, 1993.

McCasland, Vernon S. "Abba, Father." *Journal of Biblical Literature* 72 (1953): 79–91.

Meeks, Wayne. *The First Urban Christians: The Social World of the Apostle Paul.* New Haven, Conn.: Yale University Press, 1983.

———. "The Image of the Androgyne: Some Uses of a Symbol in Earliest Christianity." *History of Religions* 13 (1974): 165–208.

Meier, John P. *A Marginal Jew: Rethinking the Historical Jesus.* 2 vols. New York: Doubleday, 1991, 1994.

Meltzer, Milton. *Slavery from the Rise of Western Civilization to the Renaissance.* New York: Cowles, 1971-72.

Mendelsohn, Isaac. *Slavery in the Ancient Near East.* New York: Oxford University Press, 1949.

Metzger, Bruce M. "A Suggestion Concerning the Meaning of 1 Cor. 15:4b." *Journal of Theological Studies* 8 (1957): 118–23.

———. *A Textual Commentary on the Greek New Testament.* London; New York: United Bible Society, 1975.

Mernisi, Fatima, "Women, Saints and Sanctuaries," *Signs* 3 (1977): 101–12.

Meritt, Benjamin D. "A Decree of Oregeones." *Hesperia* 11 (1942): 282–87.

Metcalf, Peter. *Celebrations of Death: The Anthropology of Mortuary Ritual.* Cambridge: Cambridge University Press, 1979.

Meyer, Marvin. *The Ancient Mysteries: A Sourcebook.* San Francisco: Harper and Row, 1987.

———. *The Gospel of Thomas: The Hidden Sayings of Jesus.* San Francisco: HarperSanFrancisco, 1992.

———. "Making Mary Male in the Gospel of Thomas." *New Testament Studies* 31 (1985): 554–70.

———. "The Youth in Secret Mark and the Beloved Disciple in John." In *Gospel Origins and Christian Beginnings: In Honor of James M. Robinson*, 94–105. Edited by James E. Goehring et al. Sonoma, Calif.: Polebridge, 1990.

———. "The Youth in the Secret Gospel of Mark." *Semeia* 49 (1990): 129–53.

Meyer, Marvin, and Richard Smith, Edited by *Ancient Christian Magic: Coptic Texts of Ritual Power.* San Francisco: HarperSanFrancisco, 1994.

Meyers, Eric M. "The Cultural Setting of Galilee: The Case of Regionalism and Early Judaism." *Aufstieg und Niedergang der römischen Welt.* II. 19.1, 686–702. Edited by W. Haase. Berlin and New York: Walter de Gruyter, 1979.

———. *Jewish Ossuaries: Burial and Rebirth.* Rome: Biblical Institute Press, 1971.

Michaelis, W. "*Myron, ktl.*" *Theological Dictionary of the New Testament*, vol. 8, 800–01. Edited by G. Kittel and G. Friedrick. Translated by Geoffrey W. Bromiley. Grand Rapids: Eerdmans, 1972.

Milik, J. T. "Le travail d' éditions des manuscrits du Désert de Juda." *Volume du congres Strasbourg 1956. Supplements to Vetus Testamentum IV*, 17–26. Leiden: Brill, 1956.

Miller, Barbara Butler. "Women, Death and Mourning in the Ancient Mediterranean." Ph.D. dissertation, University of Michigan, 1994.

Miller, Robert J. "The Rejection of Prophets in Q." *Journal of Biblical Literature* 107 (1988): 225–40.

Moessner, *The Lord of the Banquet: The Literary and Theological Significance of the Lukan Travel Narrative.* Minneapolis: Fortress Press, 1989.

Mollenkott, Virginia Ramey. *Women, Men and the Bible.* Nashville: Abingdon, 1977.

Moltmann-Wendel, Elisabeth. *Liberty, Equality, Sisterhood: On the Emancipation of Women in Church and Society*. Philadelphia: Fortress Press, 1978.

―――. *The Women around Jesus*. New York: Crossroad, 1988.

Morris, Ian. *Death Ritual and Social Structure in Classical Antiquity*. Cambridge: Cambridge University Press, 1992.

Mott, Stephen Charles. "Jesus as a Social Critic and Anti-Semitism." *Christian Social Action* 3, no. 9 (1990): 37.

Motto, Anna Lydia. "Seneca on Women's Liberation." *Classical World* 65 (1972): 155–57.

Munro, Winsome. "The Anointing in Mark 14:3-9 and John 12:1-8." *Society of Biblical Literature 1979 Seminar Papers*, vol. 1, 127–30. Edited by Paul J. Achtemeier. Missoula, Mont.: Scholars Press, 1979.

―――. "The Honor of 'Shameless' Biblical Women." Unpublished manuscript.

―――. "Women Disciples in Mark?" *Catholic Biblical Quarterly* 44 (1982): 225–41.

―――. "Women Disciples: Light from Secret Mark." *Journal of Feminist Studies in Religion* 9 (1992): 47–64.

Murphy, Cullen. "Women and the Bible." *Atlantic Monthly* 272, no. 2 (August 1993): 39–64.

Murray, Oswyn. "Death at the Symposium." *Annali. Istituto Universitario Orientale* 10 (1988): 239–57.

―――. *Early Greece*. Atlantic Highlands, N.J.: Humanities, 1980.

Mussies, G. "Greek in Palestine and the Diaspora." In *The Jewish People of the First Century*, vol. 2, 1040-64. Edited by S. Safrai et al. Assen/Maastrict: Van Gorcum; Philadelphia: Fortress Press, 1987.

Nauck, Wolfgang. "Die Bedeutung des leeren Grabe für den Glauben an den Aufstandenen." *Zeitschrift für die neutestamentlische Wissenschaft und die Kunde der Alteren Kirche* 47 (1956): 243–67.

Navneh, J. "The Ossuary Inscriptions from Giv'at ha-Mivtar." *Israel Exploration Journal* 20 (1970): 33–37.

Neusner, Jacob. *From Politics to Piety: The Emergence of Pharasaic Judaism*. Englewood Cliffs, N.J.: Prentice-Hall, 1973.

―――. *The Pharisees: Rabbinic Perspectives*. Hoboken, N.J.: KTAV, 1985.

―――. *Rabbinic Literature and the New Testament: What We Cannot Show We Do Not Know*. Valley Forge, Pa.: Trinity Press International, 1994.

―――. "Two Pictures of the Pharisees: Philosophical Circle or Eating Club?" *Anglican Theological Review* 64 (1982): 525–38.

―――. *Wrong Ways and Right Ways in the Study of Formative Judaism*. Atlanta: Scholars Press, 1988.

Newsom, Carol A., and Sharon H. Ringe, Edited by *The Woman's Bible Commentary*. London: SPCK; Louisville: Westminster John Knox, 1992.

Neyrey, Jerome H. "Jesus' Address to the Women of Jerusalem (Lk 23:27-31)—A Prophetic Judgment Oracle." *New Testament Studies* 29 (1983): 74–86.

Nickelsburg, George W. E. "Genre and Function of the Markan Passion Narrative." *Harvard Theological Review* 73 (1980): 153–84.

———. *Resurrection, Immortality, and Eternal Life in Intertestamental Judaism.* Cambridge: Cambridge University Press, 1972.

Nielson, Hans Sigismund. "Roman Children at Mealtimes." In Meals in a Social Context: Aspects of the Communal Meal in the Hellenistic and Roman World, 56–66. Edited by I. Nielson and H. S. Nielson. Oxford: Aarhus University Press, 1998.

Nketia, J. H. *Funeral Dirges of the Akan People.* New York: Negro University Press, 1969.

Nkwoka, A. O. "Mark 10:13-16: Jesus' Attitude to Children and Its Modern Challenges." *Africa Theological Journal* 14 (1985): 100–110.

Nock, Arthur Darby. "Cremation and Burial in the Roman Empire." In *Arthur Darby Nock: Essays on Religion and the Ancient World*, 278–307. Edited by by Z. Stewart. Cambridge : Harvard University Press, 1972.

———. "The Cult of the Heroes." *Harvard Theological Review* 37 (1944): 141–74.

Noy, David. "The Sixth Hour Is Mealtime for Scholars: Jewish Meals in the Roman World." In *Meals in a Social Context: Aspects of the Communal Meal in the Hellenistic and Roman World*, 134–44. Edited by I. Nielson and H. S. Nielson. Oxford: Aarhus University Press, 1998.

Nunnally-Cox, Janet. *Foremothers: Women of the Bible.* New York: Seabury, 1981.

Oakman, Douglas E. "Jesus and Agrarian Palestine: The Factor of Debt." *Society of Biblical Literature 1985 Seminar Papers*, 57–73. Edited by Kent Richards. Atlanta: Scholars Press, 1985.

———. *Jesus and the Economic Questions of His Day.* Lewiston and Queenston: Edwin Mellen, 1986.

O'Collins, Gerald, and Daniel Kendall. "Did Joseph of Arimathea Exist?" *Biblica* 75 (1994): 235–41.

Oesterrecher, John M. "Abba, Father! On the Humanity of Jesus." In *The Lord's Prayer and Jewish Liturgy*, 119–36. Edited by Jacob J. Petuchowski and Michael Brocke. New York: Seabury, 1978.

Olrik, Axel. "Epic Laws of Fol-k Narrative." In *The Study of Folklore*, 129–41. Edited by Alan Dunde. Engelwood Cliffs, N.J.: Prentice-Hall, 1965.

O'Rahilly, A. "The Two Sisters." *Scripture* 4 (1949): 68–76.

Osborne, Delores. "Women: Sinners and Prostitutes." Paper presented at the Society of Biblical Literature Pacific Coast Region. Long Beach, Calif., April 1987.

Osborne, Grant R. "Women in Jesus' Ministry." *Westminster Theological Journal* 51 (1989): 259–91.

Osiek, Carolyn. "Slavery in the Second Testament World." *Biblical Theology Bulletin* 22 (1992): 174–79.

———. *What Are They Saying about the Social Setting of the New Testament?* New York/Mahwah, N.J.: Paulist, 1992.

————. "The Women at the Tomb: What Are They Doing There?" *Ex Auditu* 9 (1993): 97–107.

Partridge, Angela. "Wild Men and Wailing Women." *Eigse* 18 (1976): 25–37.

Paton, Lewis Bayles. *Spiritism and the Cult of the Dead in Antiquity.* New York: Macmillan, 1921.

Patte, Daniel, ed. *Kingdom and Children: Aphorism, Chreia, Structure. Semeia* 29 (1983).

Patterson, Orlando. *Slavery and Social Death: A Comparative Study.* Cambridge, Mass.: Harvard University Press, 1982.

Patterson, Stephen. *The Gospel of Thomas and Jesus.* Sonoma, Calif.: Polebridge, 1993.

Perrin, Norman. *Rediscovering the Teaching of Jesus.* New York and Evanston: Harper and Row, 1967.

Perkins, Pheme. *Gnosticism and the New Testament.* Minneapolis: Fortress Press, 1993.

————. "I Have Seen the Lord (John 20:18): Women Witnesses to the Resurrection." *Interpretation* 46 (1992): 31–41.

————. *Resurrection: New Testament Witness and Contemporary Reflection.* Garden City, N.Y.: Doubleday, 1984.

Perrin, Norman. *Rediscovering the Teaching of Jesus.* New York and Evanston: Harper and Row, 1967.

Pervo, Richard. *Profit with Delight: The Literary Genre of the Acts of the Apostles.* Philadelphia: Fortress Press, 1987.

————. "Wisdom and Power: Petronius' Satyricon and the Social World of Early Christianity." *Anglican Theological Review* 67 (1985): 307–25.

Peskowitz, Miriam. "Family/ies in Antiquity: Evidence from Tannaitic Literature and Roman Galilean Architecture." In *The Jewish Family in Antiquity,* 9–36. Edited by Shaye J. D. Cohen. Atlanta: Scholars Press, 1993.

Pesch, R. *Das Markusevangelium.* Freiburg: Herder, 1970.

Pfister, F. "Herakles und Christus." *Archiv für Religionswissenschaft* 34 (1937): 42–60.

Pilch, John J. "Death with Honor: The Mediterranean Style of the Death of Jesus in Mark." *Biblical Theological Bulletin* 25 (1995): 65–70.

Plaskow, Judith. "Anti-Judaism in Christian Feminist Interpretation." In *Searching the Scriptures,* vol. 1, 117–29. Edited by Elisabeth Schüssler Fiorenza. New York: Crossroad, 1993.

————. "Blaming the Jews for Inventing Patriarchy." *Lilith* 7 (1980): 11–12.

Platt, Elizabeth E. "The Ministry of Mary of Bethany." *Theology Today* 34 (1977): 29–39.

Plummer, Alfred. *The Gospel according to Luke.* New York: Scribner's, 1925.

————. "The Woman That Was a Sinner." *Expository Times* 27 (1915–19): 42–43.

Pomeroy, Sarah B. *Goddesses, Whores Wives and Slaves: Women in Classical Antiquity.* New York: Schocken, 1975.

Pope, Marvin. "The Cult of the Dead at Ugarit." In *Ugarit in Retrospect,* 159–79. Edited by Gordon Douglas Young. Winona Lake, Ind.: Eisenbrauns, 1981.

————. "Love and Death." in Song of Songs, 210–29. Garden City, N.Y.: Doubleday, 1977.

Porkorny, P. "From Puppy to the Child: Some Problems of Contemporary Biblical Exegesis Demonstrated from Mark 7:24–30/Matt 15:21-8." *New Testament Studies* (1995): 321–37.

Porter, Stanley E. "Jesus and the Use of Greek in Galilee." In *Studying the Historical Jesus: Evaluations of the State of Current Research*, 123–54. Edited by Bruce Chilton and Craig A. Evans. Leiden: Brill, 1994.

Porton, Gary G. "Diversity in Postbiblical Judaism." In *Early Judaism and Its Interpreters*, 57–80. Edited by Robert A. Kraft and George W. E. Nickelsburg. Philadelphia: Fortress Press; Atlanta: Scholars Press, 1986.

Qimron, Elisha. "Celibacy in the Dead Sea Scrolls and the Two Kinds of Sectarians." In *The Madrid Congress Proceedings of the International Congress on the Dead Sea Scrolls, Madrid. 18–21 March 1991*, vol. 1, 287–294. Edited by Julio Trebolle Barrea and Luis Vegas Montaner. Leiden; New York; Köln: Brill, 1992.

Rabello, Alfredo Mordechai. "Divorce of Jews in the Roman Empire." *Jewish Law Annual* 4 (1981): 79–102.

Raglan, Lord. "The Hero of Tradition." In *The Study of Folklore*, 140–57. Edited by Alan Dundes. Englewood Cliffs, N.J.: Prentice-Hall, 1965.

Rahmani, L. Y. "Ancient Jerusalem's Funerary Customs and Tombs," Parts 1–4. *Biblical Archaeologist* 44, no. 3 (1981): 171–77; 44, no. 4 (1981): 229–35 (Part 2); 45, no. 1 (1981): 43–53 (Part 3); 45, no. 2 (1982): 109–19 (Part 4).

————. "Jason's Tomb." *Israel Exploration Journal* 17 (1967): 61–100.

————. "Jerusalem's Tomb Monuments on Jewish Ossuaries." *Israel Exploration Journal* 18 (1968): 220–225.

Ravens, D. A. S. "The Setting of Luke's Account of the Anointing of Luke 7:2—8:3." *New Testament Studies* 34 (1988): 282–292.

Reardon, B. P. *Collected Greek Novels*. Berkeley, Calif.: University of California Press, 1989.

Reed, Jonathan L. "Population Numbers, Urbanization and Economics: Galilean Archaeology and the Historical Jesus." *Society of Biblical Literature 1994 Seminar Papers*, 203–19. Edited by Eugene H. Lovering. Atlanta: Scholars Press, 1984.

Reich, Ronny. "The Great Mikveh Debate." *Biblical Archaeology Reveiw* 19 (March/April 1993): 52–53.

————. "The Hot Bath-House (*balneum*), the Mikveh and the Jewish Community in the Second Temple Period." *Journal of Jewish Studies* 39 (1988): 102–07.

Rengstorf, H. "*Harmartolos, ktl.*" In *Theological Dictionary of the New Testament*, vol. 1, 317–35. Edited by G. Kittel. Grand Rapids: Eerdmans, 1964.

Ricci, Carla. *Mary Magdalene and Many Others: Women Who Followed Jesus*. Translated by Paul Burns. Minneapolis: Fortress Press, 1994.

Richardson, H. Neil. "Some Notes on 1QSa." *Journal of Biblical Literature* 76 (1957): 108–22.

Riddle, John M., et al. "Ever Since Eve. . . Birth Control in the Ancient World." *Archaeology* (March–April 1994): 29–35.

Riley, Gregory. *Resurrection Reconsidered: Thomas and John in Controversy.* Minneapolis: Fortress Press, 1995.

Ringe, Sharon H. "A Gentile Woman's Story." In *Feminist Interpretation of the Bible*, 65–72. Edited by Letty Russell. Phildelphia: Fortress Press, 1985.

Robbins, Vernon K. "Foxes, Birds, Burials and Furrows." In *Patterns of Persuasion in the Gospels*, 69–84. Burton L. Mack and Vernon K. Robbins. Sonoma, Calif.: Polebridge, 1989.

Robins, W. "Woman's Place: Jesus Reverses Traditional Understanding." *Church and Society* 82 (1992): 85–88.

Robinson, James M. "The Jesus of Q as Liberation Theologian." In *The Gospel behind the Gospels: Current Studies on Q*, 259–274. Edited by R. Piper. Leiden: Brill, 1995.

———. "Luke 7:29-30/Matt 21:31b-32." Paper presented to the International Q Project. Claremont, Calif., May 1994.

———. *The Problem of History in Mark and Other Markan Studies.* Philadelphia: Fortress Press, 1985.

———. "Q 7:29-30: Third Response." Paper presented to the International Q Project. Claremont, Calif., May 1994.

———. "The Q Trajectory: Between John and Matthew via Jesus." In *The Future of Early Christianity: Essays in Honor of Helmut Koester*, 173–94. Edited by Birger Pearson. Minneapolis: Fortress Press, 1991.

Rogers, Susan Carol. "Female Forms of Power and the Myth of Male Dominance: A Model of Female/Male Interaction in Peasant Society." *American Ethnologist* 2 (1975): 727–56.

———. "A Woman's Place: A Critical Review of Anthropological Theory." *Comparative Studies in Society and History* 20 (1978): 123–62.

Rohde, Erwin. *Psyche: The Cult of the Souls and Belief in Immortality among the Greeks.* New York: Harcourt, Brace; London: Kegan Paul, Trench, Trubner, 1925.

Roller, Matthew. *Dining Posture in Ancient Rome: Bodies, Values and Status.* Princeton, N.J.: Princeton University Press, 2006.

———. "Horizontal Women: Posture and Sex in the Roman Convivium." *American Journal of Philology* (2003): 377–422.

Rollin, Sue. "Women and Witchcraft in Ancient Assyria (900-600 B.C.)." In *Images of Women in Antiquity*, 34–45. Edited by Averil Cameron and Amélie Kuhrt. Detroit: Wayne State University Press, 1983.

Rollins, Rebecca. "The Singing of Women in the Early Church: Why It Occurred, Why It Disappeared." D. Mus. dissertation, Claremont Graduate School, 1988.

Rose, H. J. "Ghost Ritual in Aeschylus." *Harvard Theological Review* 43 (1950): 257–280.

———. "Heracles and the Gospels." *Harvard Theological Review* 31 (1938): 113–42.

Rostovtzeff, M. I., and C. Bradford Welles. "A Parchment Contract of Loan from Dura-Europas on the Euphrates." In *Yale Classical Studies*, vol. 2, 1–78. Edited by Austin M. Harmon. New Haven, Conn.: Yale University Press, 1931.

Ruether, Rosemary Radford. *Sexism and God-Talk: Toward a Feminist Theology.* Boston: Beacon, 1993.

Rush, Alfred C. *Death and Burial in Christian Antiquity.* Washington D.C.: Catholic University Press of America, 1941.

Ryan, Rosalie. "The Women of Galilee and Discipleship in Luke." *Biblical Theology Bulletin* 15 (1985): 56–59.

Safrai, Hannah. "Women and the Ancient Synagogue." In *Daughters of the King: Women and the Synagogue*, 39–49. Edited by Susan Grossman and Rivka Haut. Philadelphia; New York; Jerusalem: Jewish Publication Society, 1992.

Safrai, S. "Home and Family." In *The Jewish People in the First Century*, vol. 2, 728–92. Edited by S. Safrai et al. Philadelphia: Fortress Press; Assen/Maastricht: Van Gorcum, 1987.

———. "Pilgrimage to Jerusalem at the End of the Second Temple Period." In *Studies on the Jewish Background of the New Testament*, 12–21. Edited by O. Michel et al. Assen, The Netherlands: Van Gorcum, 1969.

Saldarini, Anthony. *Matthew's Christian-Jewish Community.* Chicago: University of Chicago Press, 1994.

———. *Pharisees, Scribes, and Sadducees in Palestinian Society: A Sociological Approach.* Wilmington, Del.: Michael Glazier, 1988.

———. "Political and Social Roles of the Pharisees and Scribes in Galilee." *Society of Biblical Literature 1988 Seminar Papers*, 200–209. Edited by David J. Lull. Atlanta: Scholars Press, 1988.

———. "The Social Class of the Pharisees in Mark." In *The Social World of Formative Christianity and Judaism. Essays in Tribute to Howard Clark Kee*, 69–77. Edited by Jacob Neusner et al. Philadelphia: Fortress Press, 1988.

Sanders, E. P. *The Historical Figure of Jesus.* London: Penquin, 1993.

———. *Jesus and Judaism.* Philadelphia: Fortress Press, 1990.

———. "Jesus and the Sinners." *Journal for the Study of the New Testament* 19 (1983): 5–36.

———. *Jewish Law from Jesus to the Mishnah.* Philadelphia: Fortress Press, 1990.

Sanders, E. P., and Margaret Davies. *Studying the Synoptic Gospels.* London: SCM; Philadelphia: Trinity Press International, 1989.

Sanders, Jack T. *Schismatics, Sectarians, Dissidents, Deviants: The First One Hundred Years of Jewish-Christian Relations.* Valley Forge, Pa.: Trinity Press International, 1993.

Sanders, J. N. "Those Whom Jesus Loved (John 11.5)." *New Testament Studies* 1 (1954): 29–41.

Sandifer, D. Wayne. "The Humor of the Absurd in the Parables of Jesus." In *Society of Biblical Literature 1991 Seminar Papers*, 287–97. Edited by Eugene Lovering. Atlanta: Scholars, 1991.

Satlow, Michael. "Reconsidering the Rabbinic *ketubah* Payment." In *The Jewish Family in Antiquity*, 133–51. Edited by Shaye J. D. Cohen. Atlanta, Ga.: Scholars Press, 1993.

Sawicki, Marianne. "Making the Best of Jesus." Social Science and New Testament Interpretation and Rhetoric and the New Testament Sections, Annual Meeting of the Society of Biblical Literature. San Francisco, Calif., November 1992.

———. *Seeing the Lord: Resurrection and Early Christian Practices*. Minneapolis: Fortress Press, 1994.

Schaberg, Jane. "(The): Feminist (Contribution to): Experience of Historical Jesus Scholarship." *Continuum* 3 (1994): 266–85.

———. *The Illegitimacy of Jesus. A Feminist Theological Interpretation of the Infancy Narratives*. San Francisco: Harper and Row, 1987.

———. "The Infancy of Mary of Nazareth." In *Searching the Scriptures*, vol. 2, 708–27. Edited by Elisabeth Schüssler Fiorenza. New York: Crossroad, 1994.

———. "Luke." In The *Woman's Bible Commentary*, 275–92. Edited by Carol A. Newsom and Sharon H. Ringe. Louisville: Westminster John Knox, 1992.

Schaps, David. "The Woman Least Mentioned: Etiquette and Women's Names." *Classical Quarterly* 27 (1977): 323–30.

Schierling, Marla J. "Women as Leaders in the Markan Community." *Listening* 15 (1980): 250–56.

Schiffman, Lawrence H. "The Impurity of the Dead in the Temple Scroll." In *Archaeology and History in the Dead Sea Scrolls*, 135–56. Edited by Lawrence H. Schiffman. Sheffield: JSOT, 1990.

———. "Laws Pertaining to Women in the Temple Scroll." In *The Dead Sea Scrolls: Forty Years of Research*, 210–28. Edited by Devorah Dimant and Uriel Rappaport. Leiden: Brill, 1992.

Schille, Gottfried. "Das Leden des Herrn: Die evangelisch Passionstradition und ihr 'Sitz im Leben.'" *Zeitschrift für Theologie und Kirche* 52 (1955): 161–205.

Schmidt, John. "The Women in Mark's Gospel." *Bible Today* 19 (1981): 228–33.

Schnackenburg, Rudolf. *The Gospel according to John*. 3 vols. New York: Crossroad, 1982.

———. *Jesus in the Gospels: A Biblical Christology*. Louisville: Westminster John Knox, 1995.

Schneiders, Sandra M. *Women and the Word: The Gender of God in the New Testament and the Spirituality of Women*. New York; Mahwah, N.J.: Paulist, 1986.

Scholer, David. "Women." *Dictionary of Jesus and the Gospels*, 880–87. Downers Grove, Ill.: InterVarsity, 1992.

Schottroff, Luise. "Itinerant Prophetesses: A Feminist Analysis of the Sayings Source Q." In *The Gospel behind the Gospels: Current Studies on Q*, 347-60. Edited by Ronald A. Piper. Leiden: Brill, 1995; Institute for Antiquity and Christianity Occasional Papers 21, August 1991.

————. *Let the Oppressed Go Free: Feminist Perspectives on the New Testament.* Louisville: Westminster John Knox, 1992.

————. *Lydia's Impatient Sisters: A Feminist Social History of Early Christianity.* Translated by Barbara and Martin Rumscheidt. Louisville: Westminster, 1995.

————. "Maria Magdalena und die Frauen am Grabe Jesus." *Evangelische Theologie* 42 (1982): 3–25.

————. "The Saying Source Q." In *Searching the Scriptures*, vol. 2, 510–34. Edited by Elisabeth Schüssler Fiorenza. New York: Crossroad, 1994.

————. "Women as Followers of Jesus in New Testament Times: Exercise in Social-Historical Exegesis of the Bible." In *The Bible and Liberation: Politics and Social Hermeneutics*, 418–27. Edited by N. K. Gottwald. Mary Knoll, N.Y.: Orbis, 1983.

Schuller, Eileen M. "4Q372 1: A Text about Joseph." *Revue de Qumran* 55 (1990): 349–76.

————. *Post-exilic Prophets.* Wilmington, Del.: Michael Glazier, 1988.

————. "The Psalm of 4Q372 1 Within the Context of Second Temple Prayer." *Catholic Biblical Quarterly* 54 (1992): 67–79.

————. "Women in the Dead Sea Scrolls." In *Methods of Investigation of the Dead Sea Scrolls and the Khirbet Qumran Site: Present Realities and Future Prospects*, 115–31. Edited by Michael O. Wise et al. New York: New York Academy of Sciences, 1994.

Schüssler Fiorenza, Elisabeth. *But She Said: Feminist Practices of Biblical Interpretation.* Boston: Beacon, 1992.

————. *In Memory of Her: A Feminist Theological Reconstruction of Christian Origins.* New York: Crossroad, 1983; 1994.

————. *Jesus, Miriam's Child, Sophia's Prophet: Critical Issues in Feminist Christology.* New York: Crossroad, 1994.

————. "The Practice of Biblical Interpretation: Luke 10:38-42." In *The Bible and Liberation: Political and Social Hermeneutics*, 172–97. Edited by Norman K. Gottwald and Richard A. Horsley. Maryknoll, N.Y.: Orbis, 1993.

————, ed. *Searching the Scriptures, vol. 2: A Feminist Commentary.* New York: Crossroad, 1994.

————. "Text and Reality—Reality as Text: The Problem of Feminist Historical and Social Reconstruction Based on Texts." *Studia Theologica* 43 (1989): 19–34.

————. "Theological Criteria and Historical Reconstruction: Martha and Mary, Luke 10:38-40." *Colloquy* 53. Berkeley Calif.: Center for Hermeneutical Studies in Hellenistic and Modern Culture, 1987.

————. "Wisdom Mythology and the Christological Hymns of the New Testament." In *Aspects of Wisdom in Judaism and Early Christianity*, 17–41. Edited by Robert L. Wilken. Notre Dame and London: University of Notre Dame Press, 1975.

Schwank, B. "Neue Funde in Nabatäerstädten und ihre Bedeutung für die neutestamentliche Exegese." *New Testament Studies* 29 (1983): 429–35.

Schweizer, Eduard. *The Good News according to Matthew.* Translated by David E. Green. Atlanta: John Knox, 1975.

Schwiebert, Jonathan. *Knowledge and the Coming Kingdom: The Didache's Meal Ritual and Its Place in Early Christianity.* New York: T. and T. Clark, 2008.

Scott, Bernard Brandon. "The Empty Jar." *Forum* 3 (1987): 77–81.

———. *Hear Then the Parable: A Commentary on the Parables of Jesus.* Minneapolis: Fortress Press, 1989.

Scott, Joan W. "Gender: A Useful Category of Historical Analysis." In *Coming to Terms: Feminism, Theory, Politics,* 81–100. Edited by Elizabeth Weed. New York and London: Routledge, 1989.

———. *Gender and the Politics of History.* New York: Columbia University Press, 1988.

———. "Women's History." In *New Perspectives on Historical Writing,* 42–66. Edited by Peter Burke. University Park, Pa.: Pennsylvania State University Press, 1992.

Scroggs, R. "Woman in the New Testament." *Interpreter's Dictionary of the Bible,* Suppl. vol., 966–68. Nashville: Abindgon, 1976.

Seeley, David. "Blessing and Boundaries: The Interpretation of Jesus'Death in Q." *Semeia* 55 (1991): 131–46.

———. *Deconstructing the New Testament.* Leiden: Brill, 1994.

———. "Jesus' Death in Q." *New Testament Studies* 38 (1992): 222–234.

———. *The Noble Death: Graeco-Roman Martyrology and Paul's Concept of Salvation.* Sheffield: JSOT, 1990.

———. "Rulership and Service in Mark 10:41-45." *Novum Testamentum* 35 (1993): 234–250.

Segal, Alan. *Life After Death: A History of the Afterlife in Western Religion.* New York: Doubleday, 1989.

Seim, Turid Karlsen. "Ascetic Autonomy? New Perspectives on Single Women in the Early Church." *Studia Theologica* 43 (1989): 125–40.

———. *The Double Message: Patterns of Gender in Luke-Acts.* Nashville: Abingdon, 1994.

———. "The Gospel of Luke." In *Searching the Scriptures,* vol. 2, 728–62. Edited by Elisabeth Schüssler Fiorenza. New York: Crossroad, 1994.

———. "Roles of Women in the Gospel of John." In *Aspects on the Johannine Literature,* 56–73. Edited by L. Hartman and B. Olsson. Uppsala: Almqvist and Wiksell, 1986.

Sellew, Philip. "Death, Body and the World in the Gospel of Thomas." *Studia Patristica,* vol. 31, 530–34. Edited by Elizabeth A. Livingstone. Leuven: Peeters, 1996.

Selvidge, Marla. "And Those Who Followed Feared." *Catholic Biblical Quarterly* 45 (1983): 396–400.

Sered, Susan Starr. Priestess, *Mother, Sacred Sister: Religions Dominated by Women.* New York and London: Oxford University Press, 1994.

———. *Women as Ritual Experts: the Religious Lives of Elderly Jewish Women in Jerusalem.* New York and Oxford: Oxford University Press, 1992.

Seremetakis, C. Nadia. *The Last Word: Death and Divination in Inner Mani.* Chicago; London: University of Chicago Press, 1991.

Sergio, Lisa. *Jesus and Women: An Exciting Discovery of What He Offered Her.* EPM Publications, 1975.

Sijepesteijn, P. J. *Custom Duties in Greco-Roman Egypt.* Zutphen: Terra, 1987.

Silberman, Lou. "The Queen of Sheba in Judaic Tradition." In *Solomon and Sheba*, 65–84. Edited by James B. Pritchard. London: Phaidon, 1974.

Silva, Moisés. "Bilingualism and the Character of Palestinian Greek." In *The Language of the New Testament: Classic Essays*, 205–26. Edited by Stanley A. Porter. Sheffield: Sheffield Academic Press, 1991.

Sim, David C. "What about the Wives and Children of the Disciples? The Cost of Discipleship from Another Perspective." *Heythrop Journal* 35 (1994): 373–90.

———. "Women Followers of Jesus: The Implications of Luke 8:1-3." *Heythrop Journal* 30 (1989): 51–62.

Simon, Marcel. *Heracle et le Christianisme.* Paris: University of Strasbourg, 1965.

Simpson, A. R. "Mary of Bethany, Mary of Magdala and Anonyma." The *Expositor* 8 (1909): 307–18.

Skupinska-Lovset, Llona. *Funerary Portraiture of Roman Palestine: An Analysis of the Production in Its Culture-Historical Context.* Gotab: Kungälv, 1983.

Slater, William, ed. *Dining in a Classical Context.* Ann Arbor: University of Michigan Press, 1991.

Slee, Nicola. "Parables and Women's Experience." *Modern Churchman* 26 (1984): 20–31.

Small, David B. "Late Hellenistic Baths in Palestine." *Bulletin of the American Schools of Oriental Research* 266 (1987): 59–74.

Smart James D. "Jesus, the Syro-Phoenician Woman and the Disciples." *Expository Times* 50 (1939): 469–72.

Smelik, K. A. D. "The Witch of Endor: 1 Samuel in Rabbinic and Christian Exegesis Till 800 A.D." *Vigiliae christianae* 33 (1977): 160–79.

Smith, Dennis E. "The Banquet of the King: Meal and Irony in Mark." Presidential Address to the Society of Biblical Literature Southwest Region, 1995.

———. *From Symposium to Eucharist: The Banquet in the Early Christian World.* Minneapolis: Fortress Press, 2003.

———. "The Historical Jesus at Table." In *Society of Biblical Literature Seminar Papers*, 466–86. Edited by David Lull. Atlanta Scholars Press, 1989.

———. "Social Obligation in the Context of Communal Meals: A Study of the Christian Meal in 1 Corinthians in Comparison with Graeco-Roman Meals." Th.D. dissertation, Harvard Divinity School, 1980.

———. "Table Fellowship and the Historical Jesus." In *Religious Propaganda and Missionary Competition in the New Testament World: Essays Honoring Dieter Georgi*, 135–62. Edited by Lukan Bormann et al. Leiden; New York; Köln: Brill, 1994.

―――. "Table Fellowship as a Literary Motif in the Gospel of Luke." *Journal of Biblical Literature* 106 (1987): 613–38.

Smith, Jonathan Z. *Drudgery Divine: On the Comparision of Early Christianities and the Religions of Late Antiquity.* Chicago: Chicago University Press, 1990.

―――. "Garments of Shame." *History of Religions* 5 (1965): 217–38.

―――. "Good News Is No News: Aretalogy and Gospel." In *Christianity, Judaism and Other Greco-Roman Cults: Studies for Morton Smith at Sixty*, vol. 1, 21–38. Edited by Jacob Neusner. Leiden: Brill, 1975.

―――. *Map Is Not Territory.* Chicago: Chicago University Press, 1978.

―――. *To Take Place. Toward Theory in Ritual.* Chicago: Chicago University Press, 1987.

Smith, Mark S. *The Early History of God: Yahweh and the Other Deities in Ancient Israel.* San Francisco: Harper and Row, 1990.

Smith, Morton. *Clement of Alexandria and a Secret Gospel of Mark.* Cambridge, Mass.: Harvard University Press, 1973.

―――. "Palestinian Judaism in the First Century." In *Israel: Its Role in Civilization*, 67–81. Edited by Moshe Davis. New York: Harper and Brothers, 1956.

―――. "Prolegomena to a Discussion of Aretalogies: Divine Men, the Gospels and Jesus." *Journal of Biblical Literature* 90 (1970): 174–99.

Smith, Robert Houston. "The Cross Mark on Jewish Ossuaries." *Palestine Exploration Quarterly* 106 (1974): 53–66.

Snyder, Graydon F. *Ante Pacem: Archaeological Evidence of Church Life before Constantine.* Macon, Ga.: Mercer University Press, 1985.

Soggin, J. Alberto. "Child Sacrifice and the Cult of the Dead in the Old Testament." In *Old Testament and Oriental Studies*, 84–87. Edited by Alberto Soggin. Rome: Biblical Institute Press, 1975.

Solodukho, Yu. A. "Slavery in the Hebrew Society of Iraq and Syria in the Second through the Fifth Centuries A.D." In *Soviet Views of Talmudic Judaism: Five Papers by Yu. A. Solodukho in English Translation*, 1–9. Edited by Jacob Neusner. Leiden: Brill, 1973.

Spencer, Scott F. "The Ethiopian Eunuch and His Bible: A Social Science Analysis." *Biblical Theology Bulletin* 22 (1992): 155–65.

Spicq, C. "Le vocabulaire de l'esclave dans le Noveau Testament." *Revue Biblique* 85 (1978): 201–26.

Stagg, Evelyn, and Frank Stagg. *Woman in the World of Jesus.* Philadelphia: Westminster, 1978.

Stählin, G. "*Xenos, ktl.*" *Theological Dictionary of the Bible*, vol. 5, 1–36. Edited by G. Friedrich. Translated by Geoffrey W. Bromiley. Grand Rapids: Eerdmans, 1967.

Starr, Chester G. "An Evening with the Flute-Girls." *La parola del passato* 33 (1978): 401–10.

Steck, Odil Hannes. *Israel und das gewaltsame Geschick der Propheten.* WMANT 23; Neukirchen-Vluyn: Neukirchner Verlag, 1967.

Stemberger, Günter. *Jewish Contemporaries of Jesus: Pharisees, Sadducees and Essenes.* Translated by Allan W. Mahnke. Minneapolis: Fortress Press, 1995.

Stephens, Shirley. *A New Testament View of Women.* Nashville: Broadman, 1980.

Stevenson, James. *The Catacombs: Life and Death in Early Christianity.* Nashville: Thomas Nelson, 1978.

Strack, H. L. and P. Billerbeck. *Kommentar zum neuen Testament.* 6 vols. Munich: C. H. Beck, 1922–56.

Strange, James F. "Late Hellenistic and Herodian Ossuary Tombs Found at French Hill Jerusalem." *Bulletin of the American Schools of Oriental Research* 219 (1975): 39–67.

Strubbe, J. H. M. "Cursed Be He That Moves My Bones." In *Magica Hiera: Ancient Greek Magic and Religion,* 33–59. Edited by Christopher A. Faraone and Dirk Obbink. New York and Oxford: Oxford University Press, 1991.

Sukenick, E. L. "Arrangements for the Cult of the Dead in Ugarit and Samaria." In *Mémorial Lagrange,* 59–64. Paris: Librairie Lecoffre, 1940.

———. "The Earliest Records of Christianity." *American Journal of Archaeology* 51 (1947): 351–65.

Swidler, Leonard. *Biblical Affirmations of Women.* Philadelphia: Westminster, 1979.

———. "Jesus Was a Feminist." *Catholic World* 212 (1971): 177–83.

———. "Leonard Swidler's Response to A.-J. Levine's Review." *Journal of Ecumenical Studies* 26 (1989): 717–19.

———. *Women in Judaism. The Status of Women in Formative Judaism.* Metuchen, N.J.: Scarecrow, 1976.

———. *Yeshua: A Modern for Moderns.* Kansas City: Sheed and Ward, 1988.

Talbert, Charles H. *Reading Luke: A Literary and Theological Commentary on the Third Gospel.* New York: Crossroad, 1982.

Tannehill, Robert C. "The Disciples in Mark: The Function of a Narrative Role." In *The Interpretation of Mark,* 134–57. Edited by W. Telford. Philadelphia: Fortress Press; London: SPCK, 1985.

Taussig, Hal. "Dealing under the Table: Ritual Negotiation of Women's Power in the Syro-Phoenician Woman Pericope." In *Reimagining Christian Origins: A Colloquium Honoring Burton L. Mack,* 264–79. Edited by Elizabeth Castelli and Hal Taussig. Valley Forge, Pa.: Trinity Press International, 1996.

———. *In the Beginning as the Meal: Social Experimentation and Early Christianity.* Minneapolis: Fortress Press, 2009.

Taylor, Lawrence J. "BAS InEIRINN: Cultural Constructions of Death in Ireland." *Anthopological Quarterly* 62 (1989): 175–87.

Telford, William R. "The Pre-Markan Tradition in Recent Research." In *The Four Gospels: Festschrift for Frans Neirynck,* vol. 2, 693–723. Edited by F. van Segbroeck et al. Leuven: University Press, 1992.

Tetlow, Elizabeth M. *Women and Ministry in the New Testament.* New York/Mahwah, N.J.: Paulist, 1980.

Theimann, Ronald E. "The Unnamed Woman of Bethany." *Theology Today* 44 (1987): 179–88.

Theissen, Gerd. "Itinerant Radicalism: The Tradition of Jesus Sayings from the Perspective of the Sociology of Literature." *Radical Religion* 2 (1975): 84–93.

————. "Lokol-und Soziolkolorit in der Geschichte von der syrophönikischen Frau (Mark 7:24-30)." *Zeitschrift für die neutestamentliche Wissenschaft* 75 (1984): 202–25.

————. *The Miracle Stories of the Early Christian Tradition.* Translated by Francis McDonagh. Philadelphia: Fortress Press, 1983.

————. "Review: Kathleen E. Corley, *Private Women, Public Meals.*" *Journal of Theological Studies* 46 (1995): 631–34.

————. *Social Reality and the Early Christians: Theology, Ethics and the World of the New Testament.* Translated by Margaret Kohl. Minneapolis: Fortress Press, 1992.

————. *The Sociology of Early Palestinian Christianity.* Philadelphia: Fortress Press, 1978.

Thibeaux, Evelyn R. "'Known to be a Sinner': The Narrative Rhetoric of Luke 7:36–50." *Biblical Theology Bulletin* 23 (1993): 151–60.

Thistlethwaite, Susan Brooks. *Sex, Race and God: Christian Feminism in Black and White.* New York: Crossroad, 1989.

Thompson, George and Walter G. Headlam. *The Oresteia of Aeschylus,* vol. 2. Cambridge: Cambridge University Press, 1938.

Tolbert, Mary Ann. "Mark." In *The Woman's Bible Commentary,* 263–74. Edited by Carol A. Newsom and Sharon H. Ringe. Louisville: Westminster John Knox, 1992.

Torjesen, Karen Jo. *When Women Were Priests: Women's Leadership in the Early Church and the Scandal of Their Subordination in the Rise of Christianity.* San Francisco: HarperCollins, 1993.

Townes, Emilie M. *In a Blaze of Glory: Womanist Spirituality as Social Witness.* Nashville: Abingdon, 1995.

Toynbee, J. M. C. *Death and Burial in the Roman World.* Ithaca, N.Y.: Cornell University Press, 1971.

————. *A Study of History,* vol. 4. London: Humphrey Milford; Oxford University Press, 1939.

Trautman, C. "Salomé l 'incrédule: récits d'une conversion." In *Ecritures et traditions dans la littérature copte,* 61–72. Cashiers de la bibliothéque copte 1; Louvain: Peeters, 1983.

Treat, Jay C. "The Two Manuscript Witnesses to the Gospel of Peter." In *Society of Biblical Literature 1990 Seminar Papers,* 191–99. Edited by David E. Lull. Atlanta: Scholars Press, 1990.

Trenchard, Warren C. *Ben Sira's View of Women: A Literary Analysis.* Chico, Calif.: Scholars Press, 1982.

Treu, K. "Die Bedeutung des Griechischen für die Juden im römischen Reich." *Kairos* 15 (1973): 123–44.

Trompf, G. W. "The First Resurrection Appearance and the Ending of Mark's Gospel." *New Testament Studies* 18 (1972): 308–30.

Trompf, Nicholas. *Primitive Conceptions of Death and the Netherworld in the Old Testament.* Rome: Pontifical Biblical Insitute, 1969.

Tuckett, Christopher. "Feminine Wisdom in Q?" In *Women in the Biblical Tradition*, 112–28. Edited by George J. Brooke. Lewiston: Edwin Mellen, 1992.

Tufarina, Emma. "Women in Cultural Life. Mark 7:24-30: Jesus and the Syro-Phoenician Woman." *Pacific Journal of Theology* (March 1990): 48–50.

Tulloch, Janet. "Women Leaders in Family Funerary Banquets." In *A Woman's Place: House Churches in Earliest Christianity*, 164–93, Carolyn Osiek and Margaret Y. MacDonald. Minneapolis: Fortress Press, 2006.

Tzaferis, V. "Crucifixion: The Archaeological Evidence." *Biblical Archaeology Review* 9, no. 1 (1985): 44–53.

———. "Jewish Tombs at and Near Giv'at ha-Mivtar." *Israel Exploration Journal* 20 (1970): 18–32.

Urbach, E. E. "Laws Regarding Slavery as a Source for Social History of the Period of the Second Temple, the Mishnah and Talmud." In *Papers of the Institute of Jewish Studies London*, vol. 1, 1–94. Edited by J. G. Weiss. Jerusalem: Magna, 1964.

Vaage, Leif E. *Galiean Upstarts: Jesus' First Followers according to Q.* Valley Forge, Pa.: Trinity Press International, 1994.

Van der Horst, Pieter W. *Ancient Jewish Epitaphs.* Kampen, The Netherlands: Kok Pharos, 1991.

———. "Jewish Funerary Inscriptions: Most are in Greek." *Biblical Archaeology Review* 18, no. 5 (1992): 46–57.

Van der Meer, F. "The Feasts of the Dead." In *Augustine the Bishop: The Life and Work of a Father of the Church*, 498–526. Translated by B. Battershaw and G. R. Lamb. London and New York: Sheed and Ward, 1961.

Van de Sandt, H., ed. *Matthew and the Didache: Two Documents from the Same Christian Mileu?* Assen: Royal van Gorcum; Minneapolis: Fortress Press, 2005.

Van der Toorn, Karel. *From Her Cradle to Her Grave: The Role of Religion in the Life of the Israelite and the Babylonian Woman.* Sheffield: JSOT, 1994.

Varga, Luis, Fred Loya, and Janet Hodde-Vargas." Exploring the Multidimentional Aspects of Grief Reactions." *American Journal of Psychiatry* 146 (1989): 1484-88.

Vermes, Geza. *Jesus the Jew. A Historian's Reading of the Gospels.* Philadelphia: Fortress Press, 1973.

———. "Sectarian Matrimonial Halakhah in the Damascus Rule." In *Post-Biblical Jewish Studies*, 50–56. Leiden: Brill, 1975.

Vermule, Emily. *Aspects of Death in Early Greek Art and Poetry.* Berkeley: University of California Press, 1979.

Vernant, Jean-Pierre. *Myth and Society in Ancient Greece.* Translated by Janet Lloyd. Sussex: Harvester Press; New Jersey: Humanities Press, 1980.

Veyne, Paul. "Slavery." In *A History of Private Life: From Pagan Rome to Byzantium*, 51–69. Edited by Paul Veyne. Translated by Arthur Goldhammer. Cambridge; London: Belknap Press of the Harvard University Press, 1987.

Von Kellenbach, Katharina. *Anti-Judaism in Feminist Writings*. Atlanta: Scholars Press, 1994.

Wainwright, Elaine Mary. *Towards a Feminist Reading of the Gospel According to Matthew*. Berlin; New York: Walter de Gruyter, 1991.

Walker, Wm O. "Jesus and the Tax Collectors." *Journal of Biblical Literature* 97 (1978): 221–38.

Wall, Robert W. "Martha and Mary (Luke 10:38-42): in the Context of a Christian Deuteronomy." *Journal for the Study of the New Testament* 35 (1989): 19–35.

Waller, Elizabeth. "The Parable of the Leaven: Sectarian Teaching and the Inclusion of Women." *Union Seminary Quarterly Review* 35 (1979–80): 99–109.

Watson, Paul E. "The Queen of Sheba in Christian Tradition." In *Solomon and Sheba*, 115–51. James B. Pritchard. London: Phaidon, 1974.

Weber, Hans Ruedi. *Jesus and the Children: Biblical Resources for Study and Preaching*. Geneva: World Council of Churches, 1979.

Webster, Jane S. *Ingesting Jesus: Eating and Drinking in the Gospel of John*. Atlanta: Society of Biblical Literature.

Weeden, Theodore J. *Mark—Traditions in Conflict*. Philadelphia: Fortress Press, 1971.

Wegner, Judith Romney. *Chattel or Person? The Status of Women in the Mishnah*. New York: Oxford University Press, 1988.

———. "Philo's Portrayal of Women—Hebraic or Hellenic? In *"Women Like This": New Perspectives on Jewish Women in the Graeco-Roman World*. Edited by Amy-Jill Levine. Atlanta: Scholars Press, 1991.

Westermann, William L. *The Slave Systems of Greek and Roman Antiquity*. Philadelphia: American Philosophical Society, 1955.

Whalen, Ribar John. "Death Cult Practices in Ancient Palestine." Ph. D. dissertation, University of Michigan, 1973.

White, Michael L. "Regulating Fellowship in the Communal Meal: Early Jewish and Christian Evidence." In *Meals in a Social Context: Aspects of the Communla Meal in the Hellenistic and Roman World*, 177–205. Edited by I. Nielson and H. S. Nielson. Oxford: Aarhus University Press, 1998.

Wicker, Kathleen O'Brian. "Mulierum Virtutes." In *Plutarch's Ethical Writings and Early Christianity*, 106–34. Edited by Hans Dieter Betz. Leiden: Brill, 1978.

Wiedemann, Thomas. *Adults and Children in the Roman Empire*. New Haven, Conn., and London: Yale University Press, 1989.

Williams, Clarence Russell. *The Appendices to the Gospel according to Mark*. New Haven, Conn.: Yale University Press, 1915.

Williams, Larry and Charles S. Finch. "The Great Queens of Ethiopia." In *Black Women in Antiquity*, 12–35. Edited by Ivan Van Sertima. New Brunswick and London: Transaction, 1988.

Wink, Walter. "And the Lord Appeared First to Mary: Sexual Politics in the Resurrection Witness." In *Social Themes of the Christian Year*, 177–82. Edited by Dieter T. Hessel. Philadelphia: Geneva, 1983.

————. *Engaging the Powers: Discernment and Resistance in a World of Domination*. Minneapolis: Fortress Press, 1992.

————. "Neither Passivity Nor Violence: Jesus' Third Way (Matt 5:38-41/ Luke 6:29-30)." *Forum* 7 (1991): 5–28.

Wire, Antoinette Clark. *The Corinthian Women Prophets: A Reconstruction through Paul's Rhetoric*. Minneapolis: Fortress Press, 1990.

————. "Gender Roles in a Scribal Community." In *A Social History of the Matthean Community: Cross-Cultural Disciplinary Approaches*, 87–121. Edited by David L. Balch. Minneapolis: Fortress Press, 1991.

Wisse, Frederik. "Flee Femininity: Anti-femininity in Gnostic Texts and the Question of Social Milieu." In *Images of the Feminine in Gnosticism*, 297–307. Edited by Karen L. King. Minneapolis: Fortress Press, 1988.

Witherington, Ben. "The Anti-Feminist Tendencies of the 'Western' Text of Acts." *Journal of Biblical Literature* 103 (1984): 82–84.

————. "On the Road with Mary Magdalene, Joanna and Other Disciples— Luke 8:1-3." *Zeitschrift für die neutestamentliche Wissenschaft* 70 (1979): 243–48.

————. "Rite and Rights for Women—Galatians 3:28." *New Testament Studies* 27 (1981): 593–604.

————. "Women (NT)." *Anchor Bible Dictionary*, vol. 6, 957–61. New York; London: Doubleday, 1992.

————. *Women in the Ministry of Jesus: A Study of Jesus' Attitudes to Women and Their Roles as Reflected in His Earthly Life*. Cambridge: Cambridge University Press, 1984.

Wolf, Eric R. *Peasants*. Englewood Cliffs, N.J. Prentice-Hall, 1966.

Wright, Benjamin G. "Jewish Ritual Baths—Interpreting the Digs and the Texts: Some Issues in the Social History of Second Temple Judaism." In *The Archaeology of Israel: Constructing the Past, Interpreting the Present*, 190–214. Edited by Neil Asher Silberman and David Small. Sheffield: JSOT Press, 1997.

Wright, N. T. *Jesus and the Victory of God*. Minneapolis: Fortress Press, 1996.

————. *The New Testament and the People of God*. Minneapolis: Fortress Press, 1992.

Yadin, Y. et al. "Babatha's *Ketuba*." *Israel Exploration Journal* 44 (1944): 75–99.

————. "Epigraphy and Crucifixion." *Israel Exploration Journal* 23 (1973): 18–22.

————. *Masada*. London: Weidenfeld and Nicolson, 1966.

Yamaguchi, Satoko. "Revisioning Martha and Mary. A Feminist Critical Reading of a Text in the Fourth Gospel." D.Min. thesis, Episcopal Divinity School, 1996.

Yardeni, Ada. *Nahal Se'elim Documents*. Jerusalem: Israel Exploration Society and the Ben Gurion University in the Negev Press, 1995.

————. and Greenfield, Jonas C. "A Receipt for a Ketubba." In *The Jews in the Hellenistic-Roman World: Studies in Memory of Menahem Stern*, 197–208. Edited by I. M. Gafni et al. Jerusalem: Zalman Shazar Center for Jewish History and the Historical Society of Israel, 1996.

Young, Brad H. *Jesus the Jewish Theologian*. Peabody, Mass.: Hendrickson, 1995.

Young, Serinity. *An Anthology of Sacred Texts by and about Women*. New York: Crossroad, 1993.

Zanker, Paul. *The Power of Images in the Age of Augustus*. Ann Arbor: University of Michigan Press, 1990.

Zaphiropoulou, Photini. "Banquets funéraires sur des reliefs de Paros." *Bulletin de correspondence hellenique* 115 (1991): 524–43.

Zeitlin, Solomon. "Slavery during the Second Commonwealth and the Tannaitic Period." In *Solomon Zeitlin's Studies in the Early History of Judaism: History of Early Talmudic Law*, vol. 4, 225–69. Edited by Solomon Zeitlin. New York: KTAV, 1978.

Zias, J. and E. Sekeles. "The Crucified Man from Giv'at ha-Mivtar: A Reappraisal." *Israel Exploration Journal* 35 (1985): 22–28.

Zeisler, J. A. "Luke and the Pharisees." *New Testament Studies* 25 (1978–79): 146–57.

Scriptures Index

OLD TESTAMENT

Ancient Sources Index

Subject/Names Index